Lecture Notes in Computer Science 8804

Commenced Publication in 1973
Founding and Former Series Editors:
Gerhard Goos, Juris Hartmanis, and Jan van Leeuʷ

Rajat Subhra Chakraborty   Vashek Matyas
Patrick Schaumont (Eds.)

Security, Privacy, and Applied Cryptography Engineering

4th International Conference, SPACE 2014
Pune, India, October 18-22, 2014
Proceedings

 Springer

Volume Editors

Rajat Subhra Chakraborty
Indian Institute of Technology
Department of Computer Science and Engineering
Kharagpur, India
E-mail: rschakraborty@cse.iitkgp.ernet.in

Vashek Matyas
Masaryk University
Department of Computer Systems and Communications
Brno, Czech Republic
E-mail: matyas@fi.muni.cz

Patrick Schaumont
Virginia Tech
The Bradley Department of Electrical and Computer Engineering
Blacksburg, VA, USA
E-mail: schaum@vt.edu

ISSN 0302-9743   e-ISSN 1611-3349
ISBN 978-3-319-12059-1   e-ISBN 978-3-319-12060-7
DOI 10.1007/978-3-319-12060-7
Springer Cham Heidelberg New York Dordrecht London

Library of Congress Control Number: 2014950894

LNCS Sublibrary: SL 4 – Security and Cryptology

Typesetting: Camera-ready by author, data conversion by Scientific Publishing Services, Chennai, India

Printed on acid-free paper

Springer is part of Springer Science+Business Media (www.springer.com)

Preface

It gives us immense pleasure to present the proceedings of the 4th International Conference on Security, Privacy, and Applied Cryptography Engineering 2014 (SPACE 2014), held during October 18–22, 2014, at the Defence Institute of Advanced Technology (DIAT), Pune, India. This annual event is devoted to various aspects of security, privacy, applied cryptography, and cryptographic engineering. This is indeed a very challenging field, requiring the expertise from diverse domains, ranging from mathematics to solid-state circuit design.

This year we received 66 submissions from seven different countries, out of which 18 papers were accepted for presentation at the conference after an extensive review process. The submissions were evaluated based on their significance, novelty, technical quality, and relevance to the SPACE conference. The submissions were reviewed in a "double-blind" mode by at least three members of the Program Committee. The Program Committee was aided by 29 sub-reviewers. The Program Committee meetings were held electronically, with intensive discussions over a period of almost two weeks.

The program also includes six invited talks and tutorials on several aspects of applied cryptology, delivered by world-renowned researchers: Virgil Gligor (Carnegie Mellon University), Adrian Perrig (ETH Zurich), Anand Raghunathan (Purdue University), Peter Schwabe (Radboud University Nijmegen), Vashek Matyas (Masaryk University), and Phuong Ha Nguyen (Nanyang Technical University and Indian Institute of Technology Kharagpur). We sincerely thank the invited speakers for accepting our invitations in spite of their busy schedules.

Over the last four years, the SPACE conference has seen a steady growth in the number of submitted papers of outstanding technical merit. SPACE 2014 was built upon the strong foundation led by dedicated academicians and industry professionals. In particular, we would like to thank the Program Chairs of the previous editions: Debdeep Mukhopadhyay, Benedikt Gierlichs, Sylvain Guilley, Andrey Bodganov, Somitra Sanadhya, Michael Tunstall, and Marc Joye. Because of their efforts, SPACE is already in the "must submit" list of many leading researchers of applied security around the world. It still has a long way to go, but it is moving in the right direction.

Like its previous editions, SPACE 2014 was organized in co-operation with the International Association for Cryptologic Research (IACR). We would like to extend our gratitude to Bimal Roy for his support through the aegis of the Cryptology Research Society of India (CRSI). We are also thankful to the Defence Institute of Advanced Technology (DIAT) for being the gracious hosts of SPACE 2014. The conference was sponsored by the Defence Research and Development Organisation (DRDO), under the auspices of the Ministry of Defence (Govt. of India), and the Cryptology Research Society of India (CRSI). We would like to thank these organizations for their generous financial support, which helped us to avoid steep hikes in the registration fees in comparison to previous editions, thus ensuring wider participation, particularly from the student community of India.

There is a long list of volunteers who invested their time and energy to put together the conference, and who deserve accolades for their efforts. We gratefully acknowledge all the members of the Program Committee and the sub-reviewers for all their hard work in the evaluation of the submitted papers. Our heartiest thanks to Cool Press Ltd., owners of the EasyChair conference management system, for allowing us to use it for SPACE 2014. EasyChair was largely instrumental in the timely and smooth operation needed for managing such an international event. We also sincerely thank our publisher, Springer, for agreeing to continue to publish the SPACE proceedings as a volume in the *Lecture Notes in Computer Science* (LNCS) series. We are further very grateful to all the members of the local Organizing Committee, for their assistance in ensuring a smooth organization of the conference, especially Arun Mishra who had the dual roles of organizing chair and finance chair, and the prime mover of managing the local affairs at DIAT. Special thanks to our general chairs, Veezhinathan Kamakoti and Sanjay Burman, for their constant support and encouragement. We would also like to thank Abhijit Das, Mahesh Jagtap, and Rajesh Pillai for managing the tutorials and the pre-conference workshop. We would like to thank Swarup Bhunia for taking on the extremely important role of publicity chair. No words can express our sincere gratitude to Debdeep Mukhopadhyay, for being constantly involved in SPACE since its very inception, and being the person most responsible for SPACE reaching its current status. We thank Durga Prasad for his commendable job in maintaining the website for SPACE 2014, and timely updates.

Last, but certainly not least, our sincere thanks go to all the authors who submitted papers to SPACE 2014, and to all the attendees. The conference is made possible by you, and it is dedicated to you. We sincerely hope you find the proceedings stimulating and inspiring.

October 2014   Rajat Subhra Chakraborty
                                                                    Vashek Matyas
                                                                  Patrick Schaumont

Message from the General Chairs

We were pleased to extend a warm welcome to all participants of the 4th International Conference on Security, Privacy, and Applied Cryptographic Engineering 2014 (SPACE 2014). Over the years, SPACE has progressed to become a major international forum for researchers to present and discuss ideas on challenging problems in the ever-expanding field of security and applied cryptography. SPACE 2014 was held at the Defence Institute of Advanced Technology (DIAT), Pune, Maharashtra, India, during October 18-22, 2014, in cooperation with the International Association for Cryptologic Research (IACR). The proceedings are being published by Springer as an LNCS volume.

The importance of SPACE, as a platform for the development and discussions on "engineering the system right" by the researchers working in the areas of security, privacy, and applied cryptography, needs to be seen in the light of the revelations of Edward Snowden. These revelations demonstrate the ease with which current deployed security in today's connected world can be subverted. Society's trust in the increasing use of information systems in critical applications has been severely eroded. This is a challenge that needs to be addressed by the research community, to ensure that the necessary assurance about the adequacy of the security technologies can be provided.

With emerging technologies and increasing complexity of hardware and software systems, security is not confined to a single layer and needs to be addressed across layers: hardware, microarchitecture, operating system, compiler and application software. We are happy to note that over the years there has been a steady increase in the diversity of topics in the submissions to SPACE.

The program chairs, Rajat Subhra Chakraborty, Vashek Matyas, and Patrick Schaumont, deserve a special mention for their efforts in selecting an outstanding Program Committee and conducting a rigorous review process. Our sincere thanks go to the Program Committee members and sub-reviewers for their time and efforts in reviewing the submissions and selecting high-quality papers. The main technical program was accompanied by several tutorials, invited talks, and a two-day workshop. We are extremely grateful to DRDO, CRSI, and all the other sponsors for their generous financial support. The conference would not have been possible without their support. Last but not the least, our special thanks to the local Organizing Committee at DIAT, especially Arun Mishra for ensuring the smooth operation of the conference.

October 2014

Sanjay Burman
Veezhinathan Kamakoti

Organization

The 4th International Conference on
Security, Privacy, and Applied Cryptography Engineering
Defence Institute of Advanced Technology, Pune, India
October 18–22, 2014.

In cooperation with the *International Association for Cryptologic Research.*

General Co-chairs

Sanjay Burman	CAIR, India
Veezhinathan Kamakoti	IIT Madras, India

Program Co-chairs

Rajat Subhra Chakraborty	IIT Kharagpur, India
Vashek Matyas	Masaryk University, Czech Republic
Patrick Schaumont	Virginia Tech, USA

Organizing Chair

Arun Mishra	DIAT, India

Tutorial Chair

Abhijit Das	IIT Kharagpur, India

Publicity Chair

Swarup Bhunia	Case Western Reserve University, USA

Finance Chair

Arun Mishra	DIAT, India

Workshop Co-chairs

Mahesh Jagtap	ANURAG, India
Rajesh Pillai	SAG, India

Program Committee

Toru Akishita	University of Tokyo, Japan
Elena Andreeva	KU Leuven, Belgium
Josep Balasch	KU Leuven, Belgium
Shivam Bhasin	Telecom ParisTech, France
Swarup Bhunia	CWRU, USA
Abhijit Das	IIT Kharagpur, India
Dieter Gollmann	TUHH, Germany
Aniket Kate	Saarland University, Germany
Mehran Karmani	RIT, USA
Yang Li	University of Electro-communications, Japan
Michail Maniatakos	NYU-Poly Abu Dhabi, UAE
Anish Mathuria	DAICT, India
Arun Mishra	DIAT, India
Debdeep Mukhopadhyay	IIT Kharagpur , India
Rajesh Pillai	SAG, India
David Naccache	ENS Paris, France
Chester Rebeiro	Columbia University, USA
Bimal Roy	ISI, India
Dipanwita Roychowdhury	IIT Kharagpur, India
Somitra Sanadhya	IIIT-Delhi, India
Indranil Sengupta	IIT Kharagpur, India
Michael Tunstall	Cryptography Research, USA

External Reviewers

Amit Kumar Chauhan	Annelie Heuser	Ruchira Naskar
Elke De Mulder	Kimmo Jarvinen	Xuan Thuy Ngo
Dipti Deodhare	Anastasis Keliris	Saibal Pal
Dhananjoy Dey	Abhishek Kumar	Roberta Piscitelli
Navneet Gaba	Prasanna Kumar	Thomas Poeppelmann
Mohona Ghosh	Yogesh Kumar	Wang Qingju
Santosh Ghosh	Jake Longo Galea	Francesco Regazzoni
Shamit Ghosh	Eduard Marin	Oscar Reparaz
Sylvain Guilley	Bodhisatwa Mazumdar	Abhrajit Sengupta
Nupur Gupta	Jelena Milosevic	Sujoy Sinha Roy
Jens Hermans	Sweta Mishra	Suphannee Sivakorn
Michael Herrmann	Dukjae Moon	Alan Szepieniec

Invited Talks

SCION: Scalability, Control, and Isolation on Next-Generation Networks

Adrian Perrig

Network Security Group D-INFK, ETH Zürich
CAB F 85.1, Universitätstrasse 6, 8092 Zürich, Switzerland
`adrian.perrig@inf.ethz.ch`

Abstract. We present an Internet architecture designed to provide route control, failure isolation, and explicit trust information for end-to-end communications. SCION separates ASes into groups of independent routing sub-planes, called isolation domains, which then interconnect to form complete routes. Isolation domains provide natural separation of routing failures and human misconfiguration, give endpoints strong control for both inbound and outbound traffic, provide meaningful and enforceable trust, and enable scalable routing updates with high path freshness. As a result, our architecture provides strong resilience and security properties as an intrinsic consequence of good design principles, avoiding piecemeal add-on protocols as security patches. Meanwhile, SCION only assumes that a few top-tier ISPs in the isolation domain are trusted for providing reliable end-to-end communications, thus achieving a small Trusted Computing Base. Both our security analysis and evaluation results show that SCION naturally prevents numerous attacks and provides a high level of resilience, scalability, control, and isolation.

Multiprecision Arithmetic

Peter Schwabe

Radboud University Nijmegen
Digital Security Group
PO Box 9010, 6500GL Nijmegen, The Netherlands
peter@cryptojedi.org

All modern microprocessors offer native support for arithmetic on certain fixed-size integers. Typical sizes range from 8-bit integers through 16-bit and 32-bit integers to 64-bit integers. Many processors additionally offer native support for arithmetic on single-precision, double-precision, or extended-precision floating-point values. Furthermore, many processors support arithmetic on fixed-length vectors of some of these data types. Arithmetic on data types, whose size exceeds those of natively supported data types, is called *multiprecision arithmetic*. Most important for cryptographic applications is multiprecision arithmetic on integers, for example, integers of sizes between 160 bits and 512 bits for various security levels of elliptic-curve cryptography and arithmetic on 1024-bit up to 4096-bit integers for RSA.

The performance of cryptographic schemes that require multiprecision arithmetic is typically largely determined by the efficiency of these arithmetic operations. Non-surprisingly, many papers describe efficient approaches to make best use of the specifics of various computer architectures and microarchitectures for multiprecision arithmetic. One might think that algorithms for addition, subtraction, multiplication, squaring, and modular reduction are well understood and that after a new microarchitecture is introduced the community quickly settles on the fastest approach to perform those operations on integers of various relevant sizes on the new microarchitecture. However, this is not the case as illustrated by recent papers that increase performance for multiprecision multiplication on simple RISC processors like the AVR ATmega, which exists for more than 15 years. Furthermore, on more complex processors, there are many subtle interactions between the representation of big integers, algorithms for arithmetic on these integers, efficient vectorization of these algorithms, and higher-level algorithmic choices, as, for example, representation of elliptic-curve points and related elliptic-curve arithmetic.

In my tutorial talk I will explain the basic ideas behind efficient multiprecision arithmetic and show that some of the algorithms we use today range back to the 12th and 13th century, when mathematicians like Bhāskara in India and Fibonacci in Italy considered efficient ways to perform arithmetic on *multi-digit* integers. I will illustrate these ideas on the example of the AVR ATmega 8-bit microcontroller and present recent results from joint work with Hutter, which improve the performance of multiprecision multiplication on that architecture.

In a second part of my talk I will explain why the algorithmic design space is much larger on processors that support arithmetic on larger integers and processors with floating-point and vector units. I will conclude the talk with results from recent join work with Bernstein, Chuengsatiansup, and Lange. In this work we use vectorized multiprecision arithmetic to set new speed records for scalar multiplication at the 128-bit security level on Intel Sandy Bridge and Ivy Bridge, and ARM Cortex-A8 processors.

Table of Contents

Cryptographic Building Blocks II

Attacks and Countermeasures

Tools and Methods

Secure Systems and Applications

Lightweight and Secure PUFs: A Survey (Invited Paper)

Phuong Ha Nguyen and Durga Prasad Sahoo

Secured Embedded Architecture Laboratory (SEAL),
Dept. of Computer Science and Engineering,
Indian Institute of Technology,
Kharagpur, West Bengal, INDIA–721302
phuongha.ntu@gmail.com, dpsahoo@cse.iitkgp.ernet.in

Abstract. In this paper, we study all existing designs for lightweight PUF. We discuss the implementation and security analysis of those designs.

1 Introduction

The modern secure systems are designed mostly based on the assumption of *black-box* security model where the sensitive secrets of the system, i.e., passwords, the secret keys, are securely stored in a non-volatile memory (NVM). In recent years, there is a large scale of physical attacks developed to directly retrieve the stored secret from secure memory in efficient ways such as *Side Channel Attacks* [16] and *cold-boot attacks* [8]. Thus, the black box model cannot provide the expected level of security anymore, and Physically Unclonable Function (PUF) [10,19] is a promising solution to mitigate the effect of physical attacks.

Physically Unclonable Functions are physical entities that generate output (response) based on the input (challenge) and intrinsic physical properties of embedding hardware. It exploits only those physical properties of embedding device that are random (but static) and uncontrollable to make the challenge-response mapping instance-specific, unpredictable and unclonable. In addition, PUF posses one-way property, i.e., computation of response R of a given challenge C is easy, but inverse computation is hard.

PUFs are used as the root-of-trust for cryptographic primitives. It is used to generate *secret* on-fly and need not to store in secure NVM [11]. In addition, any physical attempt to read out the PUF e.g., depackaging of PUF chip, destroy the challenge-response behavior of PUF due to its tamper-evident property. PUFs are also used in device identification and authentication [12], binding software to hardware platforms [9], IP-protection, design of underlying cryptographic primitive in security applications [1]. Since the modern devices become smaller and resource-constrained, lightweight cryptographic primitives come to the picture. In the recent days, RFID applications are employing PUF for security purpose.

R.S. Chakraborty et al. (Eds.): SPACE 2014, LNCS 8804, pp. 1–13, 2014.

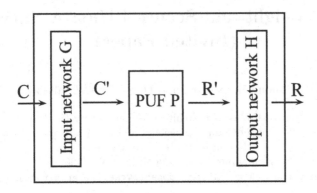

Fig. 1. Architectural overview of controlled PUF

So, lightweight PUF design and its use in the development of lightweight security primitives are most important areas of research in the context of PUF-based security for resource-constrained devices.

All PUF designs can be categorized as follows:

1. *Design from scratch.* This approach is used in the design of primitive PUFs. Objective is to design a process variation (PV) sensor that can sense the effect of existing variations in the silicon devices, and a circuit to convert the sensed signal to digital information. Ring Oscillator is one such traditional sensor to measure the effect of processor variation. Ring Oscillator PUF (ROPUF) [25], Arbiter PUF (APUF) [10], Bistable-ring PUF [2], Loop PUF [3], scan PUF [27] are designed based on this design style.
2. *Design by composition.* The *Controlled PUF* [7] (see Fig. 1) and *Composite PUF* (coPUF) [21, 22, 24] (see Fig. 2) are two PUF designs that exploit the multiple insecure PUF instances (e.g. Arbiter PUF) to improve the quality of PUFs (e.g., uniqueness, uniformity, and reliability) and robustness against machine learning based modeling attack, side-channel attack, and cryptanalysis. *Hash PUFs* (HPUFs) [7] and *Lightweight Secure PUFs* (LSPUFs) [15] are two controlled PUF designs.

However, a good PUF design is the one which is not only lightweight and qualitative but also secure. A PUF instance P is considered to be secured if it satisfies the unpredictability property: Let Q be a set of N challenge-response pairs (CRPs) and it is said to be secured if there is no algorithm to predict the response R of a given challenge $C \notin Q$ rather than brute-force search. In order to analyze the security of PUFs and PUF-based applications, we need to analyze the design with respect to: *cryptanalysis, machine-learning based modeling attacks* (MA) and *Side Channel Attacks based MA* (SCA-based MA) [4, 5, 10, 13, 18, 26].

In this article, we discuss the state-of-the-art lightweight PUF designs and their security analysis. The rest of the article is organized as follows: Section 2 introduces various PUF evaluation metrics that could be used to rank various PUF

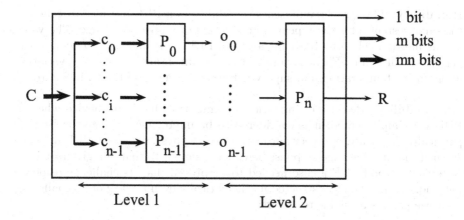

Fig. 2. Architectural overview of composite PUF

designs and the security threats on PUFs. In Section 3, we explain three design approaches for lightweight PUFs. Then we make a comprehensive study on all existing lightweight PUFs in Section 4. Finally, Section 5 concludes the paper.

2   Fundamental on PUF

2.1   Properties of PUF

Without loss of generality, we focus on intrinsic PUFs [12]. Intrinsic PUFs are those PUFs which are constructed based on intrinsic physical properties of the PUF hardware [10], for example the random delay in signal transmission. In general, a PUF instance P posses the following properties: *uniqueness, uniformity, reliability, unclonability, unpredictability, one-way function,* and *tamper-evident.*

We use notation (n, m)-bit P to represent a PUF instance P with n-bit challenge C and m-bit response R.

Uniqueness. Since the PUF instances are constructed based on the intrinsic random properties of the embedding hardware, the challenge-response behavior of a given PUF instance P is random and unique. In other words, for any given pair of instances P_1 and P_2 of PUF (n, m)-bit P on two different chips, the event $\forall C : P_1(C) = P_2(C)$ happens with probability $\frac{1}{2^m}$, i.e., $Pr(P_1(C) = P_2(C)) = \frac{1}{2^m}, \forall C.$

Uniformity. Let us consider a PUF (n, m)-bit P. Since R is a m-bit value, there are 2^m different values of R, i.e., $R = 0, \ldots, 2^m - 1$. The uniformity property is formalized as follows: for each value of R, there are 2^{n-m} different C such that $P(C) = R$. Typically, the output distribution of a good quality PUF is close to uniform distribution.

Reliability. This property presents the ability of a PUF instance to generate the same response for the repeated application of a given challenge. The value of this metric is close to 100% for an ideal PUF. It is difficulty to achieve the perfect stability in PUF's behavior due to environmental noises namely, variation in operating temperature and supply voltages, and aging of the CMOS gates.

Unclonability. Because of intrinsic randomness of hardware device where a PUF P is implemented, it is considered to be impossible to clone the PUF P physically. Typically, it is very hard to construct physically a new PUF instance P' such that its challenge-response behavior is similar to that of a given PUF P. Note that a good PUF is also needed to be proved that its challenge-response behavior can not be reconstructed mathematically even a set Q of its challenge-response pairs is available to adversary.

Unpredictability. The unpredictability property presents the fact that the generation of a response R for a given challenge C is random or unpredictable. Indeed, from the view of point of security, the unpredictability of a given PUF P is very important. A PUF (n,m)-bit P is regarded as secure if only if there is no attack predicting the value of the corresponding m-bit response R for any challenge C with success probability larger than $\frac{1}{2^m}$ even the set Q is available to the adversary.

One-Way Function. Specifically, this property refers not only the computation ability but also the security property of a PUF P. Without loss of generality, a (n,n)-bit PUF P is considered and the challenge-response of this PUF is one-to-one mapping. The generation of R for a given challenge C is easy but it is very hard to compute the C for a given response R. This property is similar to the one-way property of a cryptographic hash function and this is why PUF is also regarded as physical one-way function.

Tamper-Evident. The tamper-evident property is very important and it helps to detect the physical attacks on system where PUFs are used as the underlying primitives. The tamper-evident makes sure that any external temptation to make a very small change on PUF instance destroys its original challenge-response behavior.

2.2   Security Threats

The security analysis of PUFs and PUF-based applications mainly focuses on following attacks: *cryptanalysis, Machine Learning based modeling attacks* (MA) and *Side Channel Attacks based MA* (SCA-based MA) [4, 5, 10, 13, 18, 26].

Cryptanalysis. The cryptanalysis attacks exploit a certain flaw in the design of PUFs or PUF-based applications [23] and the set Q of CRPs to predict the m-bit response R of a given n-bit challenge C or to reduce the search space of response R that is less than 2^m. A cryptanalysis attack is considered as successful when $|Q| < 2^n$ and time complexity is less than 2^n. Note that the cryptanalysis can not be applied to the true primitive PUFs such as APUFs, RO-PUFs because they are considered as *true random resources*. The cryptanalysis is only applicable to controlled PUFs and composite PUFs where many true primitive PUFs combined together to build a PUF instance [23].

Machine Learning Based Modeling Attack. Regarding machine-learning based modeling attacks [26] (MA), the attack can be applied to primitive PUFs such as APUFs, ROPUFs [26], composable PUFs (e.g., XOR-PUF) and controlled PUFs (e.g, LSPUF) [13] based on given set Q of CRPs. The attack does not exploit the architectural flaw in the design. Typically, the attack uses machine-learning techniques to build a model by using set Q of CRPs. After that, the constructed model of PUF instance is used to predict the response R of an unknown challenge C. Compared to cryptanalysis, this method is more powerful because it can be applied to true PUF primitive as well as controlled and composite PUF. Indeed, we can develop an attack which is called MA-based cryptanalysis where the cryptanalytic technique is used to weaken the considered PUF instance and the MA is used to model that PUF instance. We can employ MA-based cryptanalysis to attack coPUFs and LSPUFs as discussed in [23].

Side Channel Based Modeling Attack. Side channel attack (SCA) exploits the information leaked from the physical implementation of security primitives. It does not rely on theoretical weakness of security primitives. Leaked information can be in the form of computing time, power consumption, electromagnetic emission [16]. Some SCA needs the details of the physical implementation so that it can relate the processing of secret information and leaked information.

In the context of PUF, side-channel information is used when raw CRPs of PUF are inaccessible e.g., in case of XOR-PUF and LSPUF response of individual PUFs are not accessible and subsequently it prevents the modeling of individual APUFs. In [13], authors discuss about the power analysis in XOR-PUF (XPUF) and LSPUF. Both of these designs use multiple APUFs, and arbiters (or latches) of APUFs are the main source of information leakage and it relates to the response of APUFs. It is difficult to determine what is the exact latched value of arbiters of XPUF (or LSPUF), but we can observe the two specific patterns of outputs that are either all 0's (minimum power consumption) or all 1's (maximum power consumption). In CMOS technology, dynamic power is linearly proportional to the number of switching. So, power consumption is minimum (maximum) when all arbiters produce 0's (1's), assuming that all arbiters are initialized by 0's. Authors also mention that this information is not useful for XOR-PUFs because it result same set of CRPs for all component APUFs of XPUF and yield similar models for all APUFs though they are different. But this power side-channel information is useful in case of LSPUF because inputs of APUFs in LSPUF are different when they all generate either 0's or 1's. Thus, it helps us to build model for each APUF by using machine learning and the accuracy of modeling depends on how many CRPs adversary can collect relying on the power traces of event: *all APUFs generate either 0's or 1's*. In the same paper, authors suggest a countermeasure to balance the power consumption by introducing two arbiters that generate complementary responses for each APUF. Though this concept of power side-channel is validated by HSPICE simulation, we have observed that it difficult to separate the power traces corresponding to all 0's and all 1's from other cases for FPGA implementation of LSPUF. So, LSPUF is vulnerable to SCA-based MA. In general, it can be conclude that SCA-based MA is the most powerful tool to analyze the security of PUFs and the PUF-based applications.

3 Design Paradigm for Lightweight PUFs

In this section, we discuss three main design approaches for lightweight PUF.

3.1 First Approach: Lightweight Primitive PUF

Indeed, design a PUF primitive is a starting point in PUF topic. There are many PUF primitives introduced already, for example optical PUFs [19], Arbiter PUFs (APUFs) [10], or Ring Oscillator PUFs (ROPUFs) [20], etc. Regarding the lightweight PUF, the Arbiter PUFs is a good PUF primitive because its hardware overhead is linearly proportional to the number of challenge bits. However, the major concern to the lightweight PUF primitive is the security, for example APUFs is not secure [10].

3.2 Second Approach: Controlled PUF

Since developing a new lightweight PUF primitive is challenging, an alternative is combining cryptographic primitives (hash functions, stream cipher, block cipher) and true PUF primitives (e.g. APUFs) to design a lightweight secure PUF. This approach is known as Controlled PUF [7,14]. The generic framework of controlled PUF is shown in Fig. 1.

Typically, a controlled PUF consists of three layers, the first and the last layers are implemented by using cryptographic primitives (e.g., hash functions). The second layer is a combination of multiple primitive PUF instances which are lightweight and insecure PUF primitives (e.g, APUFs). Lighweight Secure PUF (LSPUF) (see Fig. 4) is one lightweight controlled PUF design that exploits simple XOR-networks in first and last layers instead of resource hungry cryptographic primitives.

3.3 Third Approach: Composable PUF

The third approach is completely different from the second one. Specifically, it combines many true PUF primitives to make a secure PUF instance without using traditional cryptographic primitives. The constructed PUFs of the third design are called composite PUFs (coPUFs) [21, 22, 24] (see Fig. 2) and

XPUFs [10] (see Fig. 5). Advantage of this design approach is that we can improve the quality and security of PUF at the cost of resources. In the design of good composite PUF, designer has to find the good set of primitive PUFs and a topology to connect the primitive PUFs. So, there are many parameters to tune the PUF performance. This design style is useful for designing an *Application-specific* PUF.

4 Case Study: Lightweight PUF Designs

4.1 Arbiter PUF as Primitive PUF

The Arbiter PUF (APUF) is a silicon PUF that extracts random noise in silicon in terms of the delay difference of two symmetrically laid out parallel delay lines. Ideally, delay difference between these path pairs should be 0, but it does not happen due to uncontrollable and random variation in manufacturing process that introduces random offset between the two delays. Fig. 3 depicts the classical APUF design that comprises of n switches connected serially to build two distinct, but symmetrical paths. The arbiter at the end of two paths decides which path is faster. The challenge bits are used as the control input of path-swapping switches that eventually results two paths and input trigger signal runs through these paths; the arbiter, at the end, declares which path wins the race in the form of response.

Let, two paths p_1^C and p_2^C are emerged due to challenge C, and d_1 and d_2 are propagation delays of trigger pulse through paths p_1^C and p_2^C, respectively. The response of APUF is defined by (1).

$$r = \begin{cases} 1, & \text{if } d_1 < d_2 \\ 0, & \text{otherwise.} \end{cases} \tag{1}$$

If the delay offset between the two paths is too small, the *setup time constraint* or *hold time constraint* of the flip-flop arbiter will be violated, and its output will not depend on the outcome of the race any more, but be determined by random noise (as the flip-flop will go to a *metastable* state). The effect of such metastability would be manifested as statistical noise in the PUF responses.

The most significant feature of this design is its small hardware overhead. More specifically, the hardware overhead of n-bit APUF is linearly proportional

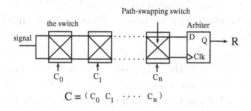

Fig. 3. Arbiter PUF

to the number of challenge bits n. Although APUF is lightweight, it is not recommended to use bare APUF as security primitive because it is not secure against modeling attacks. Adversary can build a model by exploiting the set Q of CRPs and machine learning techniques like Support Vector Machine (SVM) [10], Logistic Regression (LR), and Evolutionary Strategy (ES) [26].

4.2   Controlled PUF

In order to make APUF robust against modeling attacks, we have to prevent the adversary from accessing the CRPs of APUF. Controlled PUF is introduced based on this design philosophy. It consists of three layers: *input layer, PUF layer*, and *output layer*. Objective of *input* and *output* layers are used to hide CRPs of bare PUFs (e.g., APUFs) which are used as component in PUF layers. In practice, these two layers are implemented by using cryptographic primitives e.g., hash function, block cipher, and stream cipher. We discuss two following controlled PUFs:

– **Hash PUF** [7]. Input and output networks are built by using cryptographic hash functions.
– **LSPUF** [14,15]. XOR networks are used as input and output networks.

Hash PUF - Based on Cryptographic Primitives. Hash PUF (HPUF) [7] is a representative design of controlled PUF where input and output layers are implemented by using cryptographic hash functions to prevent *chosen challenge attack* on component APUFs in *PUF layer*. PUF layer consists of multiple independent APUF instances.

Input and output hash functions are used to hide the value of the actual CRPs of APUFs in PUF layers from model-building adversary. So, if adversary attempts to build the model for HPUF in terms of the modeling of component APUFs, then it is not applicable anymore. Note that the design of HPUFs is very important because this design is proved to be resistant not only cryptanalysis but also MA. Presence of hash functions at very beginning and at the end, prevents adversary to apply the cryptanalysis.

Let P be a HPUF instance with n-bit challenge and m-bit response. The structure of HPUF P consists of m APUFs e.g., $A_0, \ldots, A_{m-1}$. We denote r_i as the output of A_i, then $r_i = A_i(C')$ and $R' = (r_0, \ldots, r_{m-1})$. In practice, designer uses a m-bit register $\mathbf{r}$ to latch the output R' of the *PUF layer* before applying it to output layer to produce final response. Power side-channel information due the latching activities of $\mathbf{r}$ can be used for SCA-based MA [13]. Fortunately, HPUF is resistant against SCA-based MA because of its structure. Without loss of generality, assume that the adversary can vary C and observe the power consumption $(Pcon)$ due to the storing of R' in $\mathbf{r}$ to build a CRP set Q. Since all the APUFs are being challenged by the same hashed challenge, the CRP set Q of all APUFs are identical and it subsequently results identical model for all APUFs though they are different.Therefore, SCA-based MA is not applicable

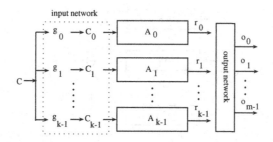

Fig. 4. Lightweight Secure PUF

to HPUFs. Here we mention that HPUFs is resistant against power SCA-based MA as in [13].

Moreover, the important drawback of this design is the significant increase in PUF evaluation time and hardware overhead [17] due to the input and output hash functions. So, HPUF is a good design in terms of security, but it is not lightweight in terms of hardware overhead, execution time and energy consumption. Note that there is one important thing with respect to unreliable property is that using many APUFs might make the HPUF unreliable.

Lightweight Secure PUF - Based on Simple XOR-Networks. Since the cryptographic hash functions in HPUF introduce a significant overhead in terms of hardware, power and execution time, the LSPUF [14] is developed. In this design, the input and output networks are implemented by using XOR networks. LSPUFs was designed to ensure that it is secure against reverse engineering and modeling attacks [14,15].

As shown in Fig. 4, a (n, m)-bit LSPUF instance consists of three layers like controlled PUF: (a) input network $G = (g_0, \ldots, g_{k-1})$, (b) PUF layer consisting of multiple APUFs $(A_0, \ldots, A_{k-1})$, and (c) output network $H = (o_0, \ldots, o_m)$. The input network G produces k n-bit inputs $C_0, \ldots, C_{k-1}$ based on n-bit input C (e.g, $C_i = g_i(C)$, where $i = 0, \ldots, k-1$). The output network produces m 1-bit outputs $o_0, \ldots, o_{m-1}$ based on k 1-bit outputs $r_0, \ldots, r_{k-1}$.

Input Network. The input network G produces intermediate challenges $C_0, \ldots, C_{k-1}$ for APUFs in PUF layer using the external input C. These intermediate challenges are generated as follows.

1. $D_i = C >>> i$, where $C >>> i$ denotes the right rotation of challenge vector C by i positions and $D_i = (d_0^i, \ldots, d_{n-1}^i)$ and $C = (c_0, \ldots, c_{n-1})$.
2. Let us denote $C_i = (c_0^i, \ldots, c_{n-1}^i)$ for $i = 0, \ldots, k-1$, then

$$c_{\frac{n+u+1}{2}}^i = d_u^i, u = 0$$

$$c_{\frac{u+1}{2}}^i = d_u^i \oplus d_{u+1}^i, u = 2, 4, \ldots, n-2$$

$$c_{\frac{N+u+2}{2}}^i = d_u^i \oplus d_{u+1}^i, u = 1, 3, 5, \ldots, n-1.$$

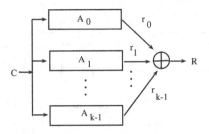

Fig. 5. k-XOR PUFs

PUF Layer. The inputs of PUF layer are $C_0, \ldots, C_{k-1}$ and it produces $(r_0, \ldots, r_{k-1})$, where $r_i = A_i(C_i)$ and A_i is a n-bit APUF instance.

Output Network. This layer is responsible for generating final response bits of LSPUF. It generates response bits $(o_0, \ldots, o_{m-1})$ using intermediate responses $(r_0, \ldots, r_{k-1})$ as defined in (2)

$$o_i = \bigoplus_{j=0}^{x-1} r_{((i+s+j) \mod k)}, \tag{2}$$

$i = 0, \ldots, m-1$, and $x(< k)$ and s are security parameters chosen by the designer.

However, the security claim of this design is challenged by Mahmoud et al. [13]. They show that this design is vulnerable to SCA-based MA as discussed in Section 2.2. In [23], authors develop a more powerful attack to analyze the LSPUFs and show that LSPUFs are insecure by exploiting a design flaw of output network. Authors called this attack as *MA-based Cryptanalysis*.

4.3 Composable PUF

Unlike controlled PUF, composable PUF design consists of multiple layers of PUFs. We discuss two PUF designs namely, XPUF [10] and composite PUFs [21, 22] (coPUF), under this category. CoPUF design consists of multiple small PUF primitives of different types and they are connected with a topology so that resultant PUF quality is improved. Whereas XPUF design exploits only lightweight primitives like APUF as component.

XOR-PUF - Based on Lightweight PUF Primitives. In this design, several insecure lightweight PUF instances having similar length of challenges are combined together to make a lightweight and secure resultant PUF. A typical instance of XOR-PUF (XPUFs) [10] is shown in Fig. 5. Let P be a XPUF instance and it is defined by k different APUF instances $\{A_0, \ldots, A_{k-1}\}$. Then response R for a given challenge C is defined as:

$$R = P(C) = \bigoplus_{i=0}^{k-1} A_i(C).$$

Following three factors motivate to design XPUF:

1. a single APUF is not secure,
2. combining many APUFs results a secure PUF instance, and
3. the lightweight PUFs are used as components to achieve a lightweight resultant PUF instance.

It is shown that when $k > 6$, machine learning based MA attack is computationally expensive. Since all component APUFs are challenged by same challenge, SCA-based MA [13] is not applicable for XPUF. It is worth to mention that combining many APUFs makes the XPUF unreliable.

Composite PUF - Based on Smaller PUF Primitives. It is observed from the reported PUF designs on FPGA and ASIC that lightweight PUF primitives are not always good in the extraction of device intrinsic randomness. For instance, APUF is lightweight, but both the uniformity and uniqueness are poor, whereas the ROPUF can produce good uniformity and uniqueness at the cost additional hardware resources. In addition, it is shown that APUF is vulnerable to MA, but ROPUF is secure against MA attack though it is vulnerable to different type of SCA [6]. In [24], authors propose composite PUF as a design paradigm that exploits smaller PUFs of different types. Aim of this design approach is to exploit the advantages of different type of PUF designs like APUF and ROPUF together. Authors provide few examples to show the effectiveness of this design paradigm and how quality of the resultant composite PUF significantly depends on both the selected set of component PUFs and topology employed to connect the component PUFs. Authors also report that reliability of composite PUF is a function of both reliability of component PUFs and topology.

In general composite PUF consists of multiple layers. Figure 2 shows a composite PUF structure that consists of two layers of PUFs. First layer contains n PUF instances $P_0, \ldots, P_{n-1}$. Instead of applying challenge C to all first layer PUFs, challenge is partitioned into n segments (e.g., $C = (c_0, \ldots, c_{n-1})$) and challenge segment c_i is apply to P_i, $i = 0, \ldots, n-1$. Responses of all PUFs at first layer are applied as challenge to the second layer PUF P_n which is a PUF with n-bit challenge. The response of P_n is that of composite PUF. One instance of this design, reported in [24], consists of ROPUFs in first layer and one APUF in the second layer.

Table 1. Summary of Lightweight PUFs

PUFs	Threats			Lightweight
	Cryptanlaysis	MA	SCA-based MA	
APUF	No	Yes	Yes	Yes
HPUF	No	No	unknown	No
LSPUF	Yes	Yes	Yes	Yes
XPUF	No	Yes	No	Yes
coPUF	Yes	Yes	Yes	Yes

However, all the example designs reported in [24] are not secure against *MA-based Cryptanalysis* as reported in [23]. In [23], authors develop an attack based on the mutual independence among all challenge segment c_i. This is a most crucial flaw in the design of composite PUFs.

5   Conclusion

In this work, we study few well-known lightweight PUF designs. As discussed above, all existing lightweight PUFs are not secure and all secure PUFs are not lightweight. Table 1 shows the trade-off between the security and the hardware overhead of all existing lightweight PUFs. Hence, designing a lightweight PUFs which is secure and qualitative is still a challenging topic to explore.

References

1. Armknecht, F., Maes, R., Sadeghi, A.-R., Sunar, B., Tuyls, P.: Memory Leakage-Resilient Encryption Based on Physically Unclonable Functions. In: Matsui, M. (ed.) ASIACRYPT 2009. LNCS, vol. 5912, pp. 685–702. Springer, Heidelberg (2009)
2. Chen, Q., Csaba, G., Lugli, P., Schlichtmann, U., Rührmair, U.: The Bistable Ring PUF: A new architecture for strong Physical Unclonable Functions. In: Proc. of IEEE International Symposium on Hardware-Oriented Security and Trust (HOST), pp. 134–141 (June 2011)
3. Cherif, Z., Danger, J.-L., Guilley, S., Bossuet, L.: An Easy-to-Design PUF Based on a Single Oscillator: The Loop PUF. In: Proc. of 15th Euromicro Conference on Digital System Design (DSD), pp. 156–162 (2012)
4. Dai, J., Wang, L.: A study of side-channel effects in reliability-enhancing techniques. In: 2012 IEEE International Symposium on Defect and Fault Tolerance in VLSI and Nanotechnology Systems (DFT), pp. 236–244 (2009)
5. Delvaux, J., Verbauwhede, I.: Side Channel Modeling Attacks on 65nm Arbiter PUFs Exploiting CMOS Device Noise. In: IEEE 6th Int. Symposium on Hardware-Oriented Security and Trust (2013)
6. Delvaux, J., Verbauwhede, I.: Key-recovery Attacks on Various RO PUF Constructions via Helper Data Manipulation. In: Design, Automation and Test in Europe (DATE) (2014)
7. Gassend, B., Clarke, D., van Dijk, M., Devadas, S.: Controlled Physical Random Functions. In: Proc. of 18th Annual Computer Security Applications Conference(ACSAC), p. 149. IEEE Computer Society, Washington, DC (2002)
8. Halderman, J.A., Schoen, S.D., Heninger, N., Clarkson, W., Paul, W., Cal, J.A., Feldman, A.J., Felten, E.W.: Least we remember: Cold boot attacks on encryption keys. In: USENIX Security Symposium (2008)
9. Kumar, S.S., Guajardo, J., Maes, R., Schrijen, G.-J., Tuyls, P.: Extended abstract: The butterfly PUF protecting IP on every FPGA. In: Proc. of IEEE Int. Symposium on HOST, pp. 67–70 (June 2008)
10. Lim, D.: Extracting Secret Keys from Integrated Circuits. Master's thesis. MIT, USA (2004)
11. Lim, D., Lee, J.W., Gassend, B., Edward Suh, G., van Dijk, M., Devadas, S.: Extracting secret keys from integrated circuits. IEEE Transactions on Very Large Scale Integration (VLSI) Systems 13(10), 1200–1205 (2005)

12. Maes, R., Verbauwhede, I.: Physically Unclonable Functions: A Study on the State of the Art and Future Research Directions. In: Towards Hardware-Intrinsic Security. Information Security and Cryptography, pp. 3–37. Springer, Heidelberg (2010)
13. Mahmoud, A., Rührmair, U., Majzoobi, M., Koushanfar, F.: Combined Modeling and Side Channel Attacks on Strong PUFs. IACR Cryptology ePrint Archive, 2013:632 (2013)
14. Majzoobi, M., Koushanfar, F., Potkonjak, M.: Lightweight secure PUFs. In: Proc. of the, IEEE/ACM International Conference on Computer-Aided Design(ICCAD), pp. 670–673. IEEE Press, Piscataway (2008)
15. Majzoobi, M., Koushanfar, F., Potkonjak, M.: Techniques for Design and Implementation of Secure Reconfigurable PUFs. ACM Trans. Reconfigurable Technol. Syst. 2(1), 1–33 (2009)
16. Mangard, S., Oswald, E., Popp, T.: Power analysis attacks - revealing the secrets of smart cards. Springer (2007)
17. Menezes, A., Oorschot, P.V., Vanstone, S.: Handbook of Applied Cryptography. CRC Press, Inc. (1996)
18. Merli, D., Schuster, D., Stumpf, F., Sigl, G.: Side-channel analysis of PUFs and Fuzzy extractors. In: McCune, J.M., Balacheff, B., Perrig, A., Sadeghi, A.-R., Sasse, A., Beres, Y. (eds.) Trust 2011. LNCS, vol. 6740, pp. 33–47. Springer, Heidelberg (2011)
19. Pappu, R.S.: Physical one-way functions. PhD thesis, Massachusetts Institute of Technology (March 2001)
20. Paral, Z., Devadas, S.: Reliable and efficient PUF-based key generation using pattern matching. In: Proc. of IEEE International Symposium on Hardware-Oriented Security and Trust (HOST), pp. 128–133 (June 2011)
21. Sahoo, D.P., Mukhopadhyay, D., Chakraborty, R.S.: Design of Low Area-overhead Ring Oscillator PUF with Large Challenge Space. In: International Conference on Reconfigurable Computing and FPGAs (ReConFig) (2013)
22. Sahoo, D.P., Mukhopadhyay, D., Chakraborty, R.S.: Formal Design of Composite Physically Unclonable Function. In: Workshop on Security Proofs for Embedded Systems (PROOFS) (2013)
23. Sahoo, D.P., Nguyen, P.H., Mukhopadhyay, D., Chakraborty, R.S.: A Case of Lighweight PUF Constructions: Cryptanalysis and Machine Learning Attacks (under submission, 2014)
24. Sahoo, D.P., Saha, S., Mukhopadhyay, D., Chakraborty, R.S., Kapoor, H.: Composite PUF: A New Design Paradigm for Physically Unclonable Functions on FPGA. In: IEEE International Symposium on Hardware-Oriented Security and Trust, HOST (2014)
25. Edward Suh, G., Devadas, S.: Physical unclonable functions for device authentication and secret key generation. In: Design Automation Conference, pp. 9–14. ACM Press, New York (2007)
26. Rührmair, U., Sehnke, F., Sölter, J., Dror, G., Devadas, S., Schmidhuber, J.: Modeling attacks on physical unclonable functions. In: Proc. of 17th ACM Conference on Computer and Communications Security(CCS), pp. 237–249. ACM, New York (2010)
27. Zheng, Y., Krishna, A.R., Bhunia, S.: ScanPUF: Robust Ultralow Overhead PUF Using Scan Chain. In: Proc of IEEE/ACM Asia and South Pacific Design Automation Conference, ASP-DAC (2013)

Fibonacci LFSR vs. Galois LFSR: Which is More Vulnerable to Power Attacks?

Abhishek Chakraborty, Bodhisatwa Mazumdar, and Debdeep Mukhopadhyay

Department of Computer Science and Engineering
Indian Institute of Technology Kharagpur, India
{abhishek.chakraborty,bodhisatwa,debdeep}@cse.iitkgp.ernet.in

Abstract. Linear Feedback Shift Registers (LFSRs) with primitive connection polynomials as feedback functions are used as primary components of many stream ciphers and other cryptosystems. The motivation
of our work is to demonstrate that though hardware implementation
of Galois LFSR offers higher throughput than its Fibonacci counterpart, the former could be more susceptible to power analysis attacks.
This gains more importance with the fact that both the LFSR configurations are theoretically equivalent. We propose a new attack strategy
that deduces the initial state of a Galois LFSR by determining the LFSR
output stream from the difference of power dissipation values in consecutive clock cycles. In addition, experimental results on power traces
of both configurations implemented on SASEBO-GII board show that
LFSR output stream retrieval from power dissipation values in Galois
LFSR involve much less error in bit sequences compared to its Fibonacci
counterpart.

Keywords: Fibonacci LFSR, Galois LFSR, Side Channel Attacks,
Hamming distance, Grain stream cipher, SASEBO-GII development
board, Dynamic Power Dissipation, Berlekamp-Massey algorithm.

1 Introduction

Encryption and decryption algorithms are used in embedded devices for secured
and authorized data communication between a transmitter and a receiver over
an insecure channel. These algorithms are embed secret key based cryptographic
primitives. Traditionally the robustness of the cryptographic primitives has been
determined using mathematical models and statistical analysis. However, the *real
life implementations* of these cryptographic ciphers can be studied and analyzed
to launch Side Channel Attacks (SCA). The potential threat of SCA based on
information leakage from power consumption [9], timing variations [8] and electromagnetic radiations [5] from physical implementation of the cipher system
has been well established in the recent past where system breakdown can be
achieved with relatively less computational cost compared to the conventional
mathematical cryptanalysis. In SCA the adversary exploits the unintentional
leakage of information into the environment from the system implementing the

R.S. Chakraborty et al. (Eds.): SPACE 2014, LNCS 8804, pp. 14–27, 2014.
© Springer International Publishing Switzerland 2014

block ciphers or stream ciphers to attack the cryptographic device in order to reveal the secret key. These attacks are possible even on cryptosystems whose theoretical robustness has been well established under various standard mathematical models.

The vulnerability of a device implementation to differential power analysis (DPA) attack was first proposed by Kocher et.al. in [9]. In subsequent literature, research based on exploitation and countermeasure designs against information leakage through power side channel has progressed immensely. Power attack can be easily launched on a hardware implementation using widely available standard test and measurement instruments.

LFSRs are used as building blocks for many stream ciphers and other cryptographic primitives. They are widely used to generate pseudo-random numbers, in fast digital counters, whitening sequences etc. The Galois LFSR is an alternative of conventional Fibonacci LFSR. Both these LFSR configurations can generate the same output sequence if the tap positions are reversed and the initial states are cautiously selected [3]. In Galois configuration, the XOR operation is performed within the LFSR and the propagation delay is reduced to that of one XOR gate. This speeds up execution by computing the tap positions in parallel. Even in software implementations, Galois form is more preferable as the XOR operations can be performed in a word aligned format.

The vulnerability of stream ciphers based on Galois LFSRs is investigated in [7] and those based on Fibonacci LFSRs is analyzed in [1]. In [7], information leakage from XOR gates is exploited to execute simple side-channel attack. Literature shows that information leakage of linear operations like XOR operations in power traces is much lesser compared to the register load operations [11]. Also if leakage of the XOR gates is dominated by other operations in the ciphers, the attack in [7] will fail. Moreover, the attack in [7] has been demonstrated on simulated data. In this paper, our attack technique exploits the correlation between the absolute difference of Hamming distances (HDs) of consecutive LFSR states and the absolute difference of power dissipation values in the corresponding clock cycles. The novelties of our proposed attack strategy on Galois LFSR are as follows:

1. The initial seed of the shift register can be determined using quite a small number of power traces.
2. Our attack technique is feasible on actual hardware implementations.

The LFSR in our case has been considered for Grain v1 stream cipher [6] and is implemented on Xilinx Virtex 5 FPGA device on SASEBO-GII development board [4]. For CMOS logic based circuits, our attack scheme based on HD of consecutive LFSR states is stronger. We demonstrate that retrieval of absolute difference of HD values from the absolute difference of the corresponding power dissipation levels has reduced bit errors in case of Galois LFSRs (and hence increased vulnerability to power attacks) compared to Fibonacci LFSRs. We have also analyzed the power traces in order to validate our proposed theoretical model. The consecutive absolute differences of HD values are used to compute the output keystream of the Galois LFSR in our attack technique. This output keystream can be further used to derive the secret initial state of LFSR by applying Berlekamp-Massey (BM) algorithm [10].

The organization of the paper is as follows: In section 2 we provide a brief description of a LFSR and assumption regarding its power consumption. An overview of Fibonacci LFSR and its power attack scheme (as proposed in [1]) is presented in section 2.2. In Section 3, we present a detailed description of an n-stage Galois LFSR and its power attack algorithm using power measurements of consecutive clock cycles. Section 4 consists of descriptions of our practical implementation results and analysis. The final section has the conclusion of the paper.

2   Preliminaries

In this paper, we follow the conventions used in [1]. So for convenience, we restate these conventions and some introductory concepts in the subsections 2.1, 2.2 and appendix A.

2.1   Linear Feedback Shift Register

LFSRs with primitive connection polynomials as feedbacks are used as fundamental components of many binary stream ciphers because of their large periodicity and ease of hardware implementation. An n-stage binary LFSR is constructed using an array of n flipflops and XOR gates in its feedback path. The state of the LFSR at time t is denoted by ST_t.

The linear complexity $L(s)$ of a finite binary sequence s is defined to be the length of the shortest LFSR that generates s. If x is a subsequence of s of length at least $2L(s)$, then the Berlekamp-Massey algorithm on input x can determine the length $L(s)$ of the LFSR along with its connection polynomial.

In the proposed SCA strategy presented in this paper, we make the following assumption.

Assumption 1. If the number of toggles in the state of an LFSR in cycle t is different than that in cycle $t + 1$ (in other words $HD_t \neq HD_{t+1}$), then the power consumed by the LFSR in the two cycles are also different, else they are the same.

2.2   Fibonacci LFSR

A general Fibonacci LFSR structure is shown in figure 1. The state at time $t+1$ is computed by right shifting the LFSR by one bit. The value shifted into the first (leftmost) stage, denoted by $S(n)$, is a linear combination of the contents of the n-stages as defined by the feedback polynomial used to realize the LFSR. Therefore, if $ST_t = (S(n-1), \cdots, S(0))$ then,
$ST_{t+1} = (S(n), S(n-1), S(n-2), \cdots, S(1))$
where, $S(n) = c(1)S(n-1) \oplus c(2)S(n-2) \oplus \cdots \oplus c(n)S(0)$, $c(i) \in \{0, 1\}$, $\forall i$, $1 \leq i \leq n$.

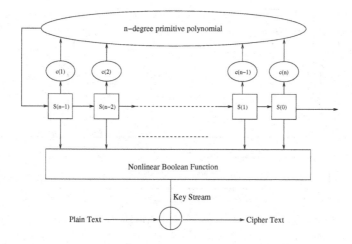

Fig. 1. An n-stage LFSR with a nonlinear filter [1]

Theorem 1. *Let HD_t be the* Hamming distance *between the n-bit vectors, ST_t and ST_{t-1}. Let $PD_t = (HD_{t+1} - HD_t)$. Then, $PD_t \in \{-1, 0, 1\}$.*

The proof of the above theorem and the side channel attack launched on Fibonacci LFSR using $O(n)$ power measurements in presented in [1]. The proposed attack utilizes Berlekamp-Massey algorithm which determines the initial state of a LFSR by only using twice the linear complexity number of consecutive output bits.

In the attack strategy proposed in this paper, we extend the approach as proposed in [1] to retrieve the initial seed of a Galois LFSR. Though both Fibonacci and Galois configurations of LFSR are theoretically equivalent, we show that the Galois LFSR is more vulnerable to power attacks than its Fibonacci counterpart. The *only* assumption of the proposed SCA strategy is that the adversary can compute the values of PD_t by measuring the power consumed by the LFSR in consecutive clock cycles.

3   Computing PD_t for Galois LFSR

A general Galois LFSR structure is shown in figure 2. The state of the LFSR after next clock cycle is computed by right shifting the LFSR, along with XOR operation with the output bit in the necessary tap positions as defined by the feedback polynomial. The value shifted into the first (leftmost) stage, denoted by $S(n)$, is the output of the previous state. As a result of this configuration, when the output of a state is 0, then all the bits of the LFSR shift to the right and $S(n)$ becomes 0. On the other hand, when the output of a state is 1, then all the bit values in the tap positions flip and then the entire register is shifted to the right with $S(n)$ being set to 1.

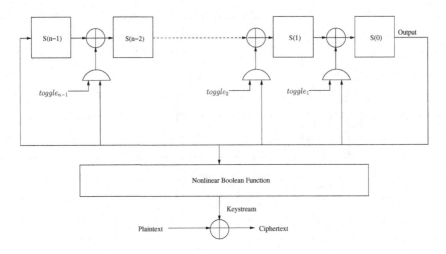

Fig. 2. An n-stage Galois LFSR with a nonlinear filter

Let us define a variable $toggle_j \in \{0,1\}$, $\forall j$, $1 \leq j \leq n-1$, which denotes the presence (*by value* 1) or absence (*by value* 0) of tap positions of an n-stage Galois LFSR depending upon the connection polynomial chosen.

Let us denote the state of the LFSR at time $t-1$ as follows:

$$ST_{t-1} = (S(n-1), S(n-2), \cdots, S(0)) \tag{1}$$

If the output at time $t-1$ (OP_{t-1}) is 0, then the state of the LFSR at time t is denoted as follows:

$$ST_t = (0, S(n-1), S(n-2), \cdots, S(1)) \tag{2}$$

Using equations 1 and 2, the corresponding Hamming distance at time t (HD_t) is obtained as follows:

$$
\begin{aligned}
HD_t &= HW(ST_t \oplus ST_{t-1}) \\
&= HW((S(n-1) \oplus 0), (S(n-1) \oplus S(n-2)), \cdots, (S(1) \oplus S(0)))
\end{aligned} \tag{3}
$$

On the other hand, if OP_{t-1} is 1, then its state at time t is as follows:

$$ST_t = (1, S(n-1) \oplus toggle_{n-1}, S(n-2) \oplus toggle_{n-2}, \cdots, S(1) \oplus toggle_1) \tag{4}$$

Using equations 1 and 4, the corresponding HD_t is obtained as follows:

$$
\begin{aligned}
HD_t &= HW(ST_t \oplus ST_{t-1}) \\
&= HW((S(n-1) \oplus 1), (S(n-1) \oplus S(n-2) \oplus toggle_{n-1}), \\
&\quad \cdots (S(1) \oplus S(0) \oplus toggle_1)))
\end{aligned} \tag{5}
$$

If OP_t is 0 and OP_{t-1} was also 0, then its state at time $t+1$ is given by:

$$ST_{t+1} = (0, 0, S(n-1), \cdots, S(2)) \tag{6}$$

Using equations 2 and 6, the corresponding HD_{t+1} is obtained as follows:

$$
\begin{aligned}
HD_{t+1} &= HW(ST_{t+1} \oplus ST_t) \\
&= HW(0, (S(n-1) \oplus 0), (S(n-1) \oplus S(n-2)), \\
&\quad \cdots, (S(2) \oplus S(1))) \tag{7}
\end{aligned}
$$

Similarly, if OP_t is 0 and OP_{t-1} was 1, then the state of the LFSR at time $t+1$ is as follows:

$$
ST_{t+1} = (0, 1, (S(n-1) \oplus toggle_{n-1}), \cdots, (S(2) \oplus toggle_2)) \tag{8}
$$

Using equations 4 and 8, the corresponding HD_{t+1} is obtained as follows:

$$
\begin{aligned}
HD_{t+1} &= HW(ST_{t+1} \oplus ST_t) \\
&= HW(1, (S(n-1) \oplus toggle_{n-1} \oplus 1), (S(n-1) \oplus toggle_{n-1} \\
&\quad \oplus S(n-2) \oplus toggle_{n-2}), \cdots, (S(2) \oplus toggle_2 \oplus S(1) \oplus toggle_1)) \tag{9}
\end{aligned}
$$

Again, if OP_t is 1 and OP_{t-1} was 0, then the state at time $t+1$ is as follows:

$$
ST_{t+1} = (1, toggle_{n-1}, (S(n-1) \oplus toggle_{n-2}), \cdots, (S(2) \oplus toggle_1)) \tag{10}
$$

Using equations 2 and 10, the corresponding HD_{t+1} is obtained as follows:

$$
\begin{aligned}
HD_{t+1} &= HW(ST_{t+1} \oplus ST_t) \\
&= HW(1, (S(n-1) \oplus toggle_{n-1}), (S(n-1) \oplus S(n-2) \oplus toggle_{n-2}), \\
&\quad \cdots, (S(2) \oplus S(1) \oplus toggle_1)) \tag{11}
\end{aligned}
$$

Similarly, if OP_t is 1 and OP_{t-1} was also 1 then the state at time $t+1$ is as follows:

$$
\begin{aligned}
ST_{t+1} &= (1, (toggle_{n-1} \oplus 1), (S(n-1) \oplus toggle_{n-1} \oplus toggle_{n-2}), \\
&\quad \cdots, (S(2) \oplus toggle_2 \oplus toggle_1)) \tag{12}
\end{aligned}
$$

Using equations 4 and 12, the corresponding HD_{t+1} is obtained as follows:

$$
\begin{aligned}
HD_{t+1} &= HW(ST_{t+1} \oplus ST_t) \\
&= HW(0, (S(n-1) \oplus toggle_{n-1} \oplus toggle_{n-1} \oplus 1), \\
&\quad \cdots, (S(2)) \oplus toggle_2 \oplus toggle_1 \oplus S(1) \oplus toggle_1)) \tag{13}
\end{aligned}
$$

Considering OP_t as 0 and OP_{t-1} also as 0, we get $S(1) = 0$ and $S(0) = 0$. Using equations (3) and (7) we get the following expression for difference of power consumptions at time t (PD_t):

$$
\begin{aligned}
PD_t &= HD_{t+1} - HD_t = HW(0) - HW(S(1) \oplus S(0)) \\
&= 0 \tag{14}
\end{aligned}
$$

Considering OP_t as 1 and OP_{t-1} as 0, we get $S(1) = 1$ and $S(0) = 0$. Using equations (3) and (11) we get the following expression for PD_t:

$$
\begin{aligned}
PD_t &= HD_{t+1} - HD_t \\
&= HW(1) - HW(S(1) \oplus S(0)) \\
&+ HW(S(n-1) \oplus toggle_{n-1}) - HW(S(n-1)) \\
&+ HW(S(n-1) \oplus S(n-2) \oplus toggle_{n-2}) - HW(S(n-1) \oplus S(n-2)) \\
&\vdots \\
&+ HW(S(2) \oplus S(1) \oplus toggle_1) - HW(S(2) \oplus S(1)) \\
&= 1 - 1 + \sum_{num\_taps-1} \{1, -1\} \\
&= \sum_{num\_taps-1} \{1, -1\}
\end{aligned}
\tag{15}
$$

Considering OP_t as 1 and OP_{t-1} as 1, we get $S(1) \oplus toggle_1 = 1$ and $S(0) = 1$. Using equations (5) and (13) we get the following PD_t expression:

$$
\begin{aligned}
PD_t &= HD_{t+1} - HD_t \\
&= HW(0) - HW(S(0) \oplus S(1) \oplus toggle_1) \\
&+ HW(S(n-1) \oplus toggle_{n-1} \oplus S(n-2) \oplus toggle_{n-2} \oplus toggle_{n-2}) \\
&- HW(S(n-1) \oplus S(n-2) \oplus toggle_{n-1}) \\
&\vdots \\
&+ HW(S(2) \oplus toggle_2 \oplus S(1) \oplus toggle_1 \oplus toggle_1) \\
&- HW(S(2) \oplus S(1) \oplus toggle_2) \\
&= 0 - HW(1 \oplus 1) \\
&= 0
\end{aligned}
\tag{16}
$$

Considering OP_t as 0 and OP_{t-1} as 1, we get $S(1) \oplus toggle_1 = 0$ and $S(0) = 1$. Using equations (5) and (9) we get the following PD_t equation:

$$
\begin{aligned}
PD_t &= HD_{t+1} - HD_t \\
&= HW(1) - HW(S(0) \oplus S(1) \oplus toggle_1) \\
&+ HW(S(n-1) \oplus toggle_{n-1} \oplus 1) - HW(S(n-1) \oplus 1) \\
&+ HW(S(n-2) \oplus toggle_{n-2} \oplus S(n-1) \oplus toggle_{n-1}) \\
&- HW(S(n-1) \oplus S(n-2) \oplus toggle_{n-1}) \\
&\vdots \\
&+ HW(S(2) \oplus toggle_2 \oplus S(1) \oplus toggle_1) \\
&- HW(S(2) \oplus S(1) \oplus toggle_2) \\
&= 1 - HW(1 \oplus 0) + \sum_{num\_taps-1} \{1, -1\} \\
&= \sum_{num\_taps-1} \{1, -1\}
\end{aligned}
\tag{17}
$$

In case of a Galois LFSR with primitive connection polynomial, the number of taps is always even. Therefore, if the magnitudes of successive outputs are same then the corresponding value of PD_t is zero, while for complementary such outputs it is a nonzero odd value. The maximum possible magnitude that such a nonzero odd value can attain is one less than the number of taps.

3.1   Proposed Attack Strategy on Galois LFSR

Let PD'_t be defined as follows: $PD'_t = 0$ when, $HD_t{=}HD_{t+1}$, else it is a non-zero value from the set $\{1, 3, 5, \cdots, num\_taps - 1\}$. Let $POW(k)$ and $outbit_k$ denote the dynamic power consumed by the nonlinear filter generator and the output bit of the Galois LFSR respectively at time instant k.

1. Measure $POW(0)$ and $POW(1)$
   - $PD'_0{=}$ $POW(1){-}POW(0)$
   (a) if($PD'_0{=}0$)
       $outbit_1{=}0$ [**Assumption**: $outbit_0{=}0$.]
   (b) else
       $outbit_1{=}1$
2. for each time instant $k, k \geq 2$
   - Measure $POW(k)$
   - $PD'_{k-1}{=}$ $POW(k){-}POW(k-1)$
   (a) if($PD'_{k-1}{=}0$)
       $outbit_k{=}$ $outbit_{k-1}$
   (b) else
       $outbit_k{=}$ $\overline{outbit_{k-1}}$
3. Input $outbit_k$ into the Berlekamp-Massey (BM) Algorithm. If BM terminates then exit *for loop* in *step2* else repeat *step2* .
4. Result
   (a) BM algorithm outputs the length n of the Galois LFSR and the connection polynomial of the register.
   (b) Now that the length of the LFSR and its connection polynomial are known, an attack can be launched to determine the initial register polynomial using the following equation:

$$I(x) = C(x).O(x) \tag{18}$$

   where $I(x)$ is the initial register polynomial, $C(x)$ is the connection polynomial realized by the Galois LFSR and $O(x)$ is the output sequence polynomial.

The attack will be easier in cases where the feedback polynomial of the shift register is known as the adversary can construct a set of linear equations which must be simultaneously satisfied. But our attack strategy works even if the feedback polynomial is unknown.

4   Experimental Evaluation

4.1   Experimental Results

The detailed descriptions of our evaluation environment and the technique of retrieval of difference of consecutive Hamming distances from real power traces are presented in appendices B and C respectively. We selected the primitive connection polynomial of the LFSR of Grain v1 stream cipher [6] as the feedback polynomial for both the Fibonacci and Galois LFSR implementations. The connection polynomial $f(x)$ of degree 80 is as follows:

$$f(x) = 1 + x^{18} + x^{29} + x^{42} + x^{57} + x^{67} + x^{80}$$

It is to be noted that the number of taps for Galois LFSR with $f(x)$ as feedback polynomial is 6. We collected power traces with a known initial state for both Fibonacci and Galois LFSR configurations. In figures 3 and 4 we present a comparison of the absolute difference of power dissipation values (obtained from SASEBO-GII board) in consecutive clock cycles with the theoretical absolute difference of corresponding Hamming distance values (HDs) of Fibonacci and Galois LFSR states respectively. This was repeated for different, fixed length windows of successive clock cycles and after each such iteration, the size of the window was varied. The number of samples of successive absolute differences is one less than the window length of consecutive clock cycles. Henceforth we will refer to the number of samples of consecutive absolute differences as *sample window length*. Figures 3 and 4 show such plots for different magnitudes of *sample window length*, corresponding to Fibonacci and Galois configurations respectively.

4.2   Analysis and Discussions

The interesting point to be noted from the figures 3 and 4 is that for a Galois LFSR configuration, with feedback polynomial $f(x)$, the theoretical absolute difference of HDs can take a value from the set $\{0, 1, 3, 5\}$ compared to a value from the set $\{0, 1\}$ for corresponding Fibonacci LFSR counterpart. This can be easily established from equations 14, 15, 16, 17 in section 3 and theorem 1 in section 2.2. In both the LFSR configurations, the 0 value of absolute difference of consecutive HDs signify that the absolute difference of consecutive power dissipation values is ideally zero or less than a certain threshold power value. On the other hand, a non zero value corresponds to a high absolute difference. Therefore, a proper threshold value must be chosen to distinguish between two such power difference levels (PDLs).

The differences of consecutive power traces do not always correctly correlate to corresponding difference of Hamming distance, especially when the variation is small. This is due to the fact that the sample points with low Signal-to-noise-ratio (SNR) degrades the overall power signature in a clock cycle [11]. The lesser the difference between PDLs, more is the influence of the noisy sample points. In other words, a higher difference between PDLs means an implementation is

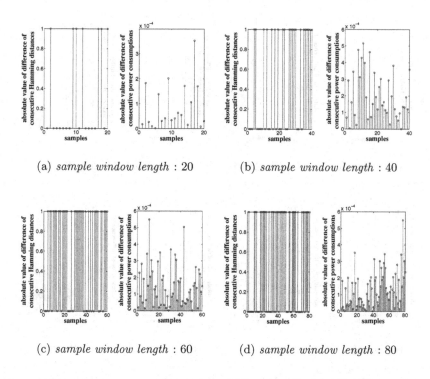

(a) *sample window length* : 20   (b) *sample window length* : 40

(c) *sample window length* : 60   (d) *sample window length* : 80

Fig. 3. Comparison of theoretical absolute difference of consecutive Hamming distances with absolute difference of successive power consumption values for Fibonacci LFSR

more susceptible to power analysis attack as it easier to obtain a suitable threshold value. For a Fibonacci LFSR with primitive feedback polynomial $f(x)$, as the nonzero absolute difference of consecutive HDs can only attain value 1, the corresponding power difference values will be considerably lesser than its Galois counterpart in certain cases. This is because in a Galois LFSR with the same feedback polynomial $f(x)$, the nonzero absolute difference of successive HDs can be also 3 and 5 apart from 1. This means the PDLs for a Galois LFSR can be significantly higher in certain cases than that for the corresponding Fibonacci LFSR. This can be seen for Fibonacci and Galois LFSRs from the the values of PDL in figures 3 and 4 respectively. It can also be observed from those two figures that the maximum value of PDL for Fibonacci LFSR is significantly below the value 6×10^{-4}, while for its Galois counterpart there are a large number of PDL values above that magnitude. So for a predetermined noise margin, thresholding operation on consecutive absolute power differences to obtain corresponding absolute difference of HDs will involve less error for a Galois LFSR compared to its Fibonacci counterpart. This makes the Galois LFSR based design more vulnerable to power analysis.

To reduce the effect of noise, we considered the mean of power traces with a constant initial state for both the LFSR configurations. As the Fibonacci LFSR

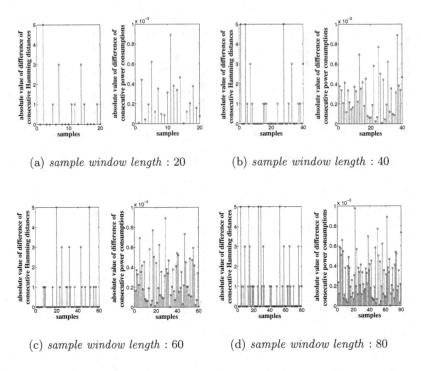

(a) *sample window length* : 20   (b) *sample window length* : 40

(c) *sample window length* : 60   (d) *sample window length* : 80

Fig. 4. Comparison of theoretical absolute difference of consecutive Hamming distances with absolute difference of successive power consumption values for Galois LFSR

implementation is more prone to be affected by noise due to lower range of PDL values compared to a Galois LFSR design, we took an average over repeated 5, 550 power traces for the Fibonacci configuration whereas for its Galois counterpart we took an average over 2, 400 power traces. Then we observed thresholding results for different window sizes and for both the implementations of the LFSRs. For every *sample window length*, we considered the best case results of thresholding operation which produced maximum correct output bits. Those bits were declared correct for which there was a match between theoretically derived absolute differences of consecutive HDs and the corresponding absolute differences of power dissipation values obtained from the experimental setup. The comparison of correctness of thresholding results for Fibonacci and Galois configurations of the LFSRs for different sizes of *sample window length* is shown in figure 5. It is evident from the figure that Galois LFSR implementation shows higher percentages of correctness post thresholding than its Fibonacci counterpart for every *sample window length*. Therefore, even though an average over significantly more number of power traces was considered for the Fibonacci LFSR compared to its Galois counterpart, lower values of PDLs in the former case lead to the lower percentages of correct determinations of HDs. Again, correct determination of consecutive absolute differences of HDs leads us to successfully recover the initial secret seed of a LFSR using Berlekamp-Massey algorithm as discussed earlier.

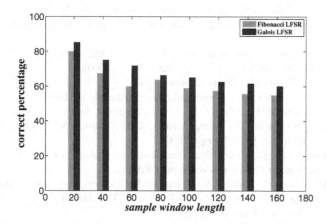

Fig. 5. Comparison of best case thresholding results between Fibonacci and Galois LFSRs for different values of *sample window length*

The results obtained are based on an assumption that all equal values of differences among HDs correspond to same differences of power dissipations in consecutive clock cycles. However, in practice this may not hold true [11]. Therefore, the adversary may need to construct power trace templates for all possible HD classes in order to classify an unknown power trace with the aid of the preconstructed templates [2]. This kind of a template attack may lead to high success rates of correct power trace classification. In [12], the authors have outlined several novel techniques to increase the rate of successful classifications of differences among consecutive HDs.

5   Conclusion

In this paper, we present a theoretical formulation based on differences of Hamming distances of three consecutive states of a Galois LFSR and use them to approximate the differences in power dissipation values in corresponding clock cycles. We compare this formulation with that of a Fibonacci LFSR as proposed in [1]. We observe that Galois LFSRs are more vulnerable to power attacks compared to its Fibonacci counterpart. We conclude this based on the thresholding results over various *sample window length* values in case of both the LFSR configurations. Our proposed formulation can be used as an efficient tool to mount a power analysis attack in order to determine the initial state (secret key) of a Galois LFSR implementation. The presented attack strategy may also expose the vulnerability of stream ciphers (realized using Galois LFSRs) to power attacks.

References

1. Burman, S., Mukhopadhyay, D., Veezhinathan, K.: LFSR based stream ciphers are vulnerable to power attacks. In: Srinathan, K., Rangan, C.P., Yung, M. (eds.) INDOCRYPT 2007. LNCS, vol. 4859, pp. 384–392. Springer, Heidelberg (2007)

2. Chari, S., Rao, J.R., Rohatgi, P.: Template Attacks. In: Kaliski Jr., B.S., Koç, Ç.K., Paar, C. (eds.) CHES 2002. LNCS, vol. 2523, pp. 13–28. Springer, Heidelberg (2003)
3. Dubrova, E.: A transformation from the fibonacci to the galois nlfsrs. IEEE Transactions on Information Theory 55(11), 5263–5271 (2009)
4. Standard Side Channel Evaluation Board G-II, http://www.rcis.aist.go.jp/special/sasebo/index-en.html
5. Gandolfi, K., Mourtel, C., Olivier, F.: Electromagnetic Analysis: Concrete Results. In: Koç, Ç.K., Naccache, D., Paar, C. (eds.) CHES 2001. LNCS, vol. 2162, pp. 251–261. Springer, Heidelberg (2001)
6. Hell, M., Johansson, T., Meier, W.: Grain-a stream cipher for constrained environments. ecrypt stream cipher project report (2005)
7. Joux, A., Delaunay, P.: Galois LFSR, Embedded Devices and Side Channel Weaknesses. In: Barua, R., Lange, T. (eds.) INDOCRYPT 2006. LNCS, vol. 4329, pp. 436–451. Springer, Heidelberg (2006)
8. Kocher, P.C.: Timing Attacks on Implementations of Diffie-Hellman, RSA, DSS, and Other Systems. In: Koblitz, N. (ed.) CRYPTO 1996. LNCS, vol. 1109, pp. 104–113. Springer, Heidelberg (1996)
9. Kocher, P.C., Jaffe, J., Jun, B.: Differential power analysis. In: Wiener, M. (ed.) CRYPTO 1999. LNCS, vol. 1666, pp. 388–397. Springer, Heidelberg (1999)
10. Massey, J.L.: Shift-register synthesis and bch decoding. IEEE Transactions on Information Theory 15(1), 122–127 (1969)
11. Mangard, T.P.S., Oswald, E.: Power Analysis Attacks revealing the secrets of Smart Cards. Springer (2007)
12. Zadeh, A.A., Heys, H.M.: Simple power analysis applied to nonlinear feedback shift registers. IET Information Security 8(3), 188–198 (2014)

A   Dynamic Power Consumption of an LFSR

The dynamic power consumed by a digital circuit is directly proportional to the switching activity (number of components in the circuit that has a state-transition from 0 to 1 or vice-versa). In the case of LFSRs the dynamic power consumed during the transition in cycle $t+1$, that is, from time period t to time period $t+1$, is proportional to HD_{t+1}, as the computed Hamming distance is a measure of the total number of toggles in the state of the LFSR during the time interval t to $t+1$.

B   Experimental Evaluation Environment

We implemented both Fibonacci and Galois configurations of a 80-bit length LFSR on SASEBO-GII Side-Channel Attack Standard Evaluation Board and evaluated the feasibility of our proposed attack technique on the LFSR based designs. SASEBO-GII consists of two Xilinx FPGAs – Spartan-3A and Virtex-5. The control circuit and the targeted LFSR were implemented in Spartan-3A XC3S400A and Virtex-5 xc5vlx50 (driven by a 2 MHz clock) respectively. The power consumptions of the LFSR circuit were captured using a Tektronix digital oscilloscope DPO 4034B at a sampling rate of 2.5 GSa/s.

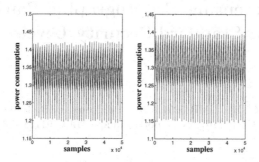

Fig. 6. Samples of power traces collected for Fibonacci (left) and Galois (right) configurations of LFSR using SASEBO-GII board

C   Retrieval of Differences of Hamming Distances from LFSR Power Dissipation Profile

In our proposed attack strategy, we considered the absolute difference of power consumptions over consecutive clock cycles to determine the absolute difference of corresponding Hamming distances (HDs) of LFSR states. Let us suppose that the power dissipation values of the LFSR during $t0$, $t1$ and $t2$ are P_{t0}, P_{t1} and P_{t2} respectively. The HD of the LFSR states between times $t0$ and $t1$ is denoted by HD_{t1}, while the HD between times $t1$ and $t2$ is denoted by HD_{t2} as shown in figure 7.

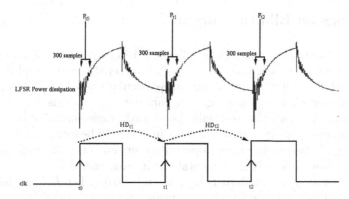

Fig. 7. Relationship between LFSR power dissipation profile and corresponding Hamming distance values

In order to determine the absolute difference of successive HDs, we first took the mean of about 300 sample points after the positive clock edge of each clock cycle for which there was a significant value of power consumption (as shown in figure 7) and then computed the absolute difference of the mean values of two consecutive clock cycles. Finally we performed thresholding on such absolute differences of power dissipation values to retrieve the discrete values of absolute differences of corresponding HDs.

Implementing Cryptographic Pairings
at Standard Security Levels

Andreas Enge[*] and Jérôme Milan

[1] INRIA, LFANT, CNRS, UMR 5251, Univ. Bordeaux, IMB, 33400 Talence, France
[2] INRIA, CNRS, UMR 7161, École polytechnique, LIX, 91128 Palaiseau, France

Abstract. This study reports on an implementation of cryptographic pairings in a general purpose computer algebra system. For security levels equivalent to the different AES flavours, we exhibit suitable curves in parametric families and show that optimal ate and twisted ate pairings exist and can be efficiently evaluated. We provide a correct description of Miller's algorithm for signed binary expansions such as the NAF and extend a recent variant due to Boxall *et al.* to addition-subtraction chains. We analyse and compare several algorithms proposed in the literature for the final exponentiation. Finally, we give recommendations on which curve and pairing to choose at each security level.

Keywords: elliptic curve cryptology, pairings, implementation.

1   Pairings on Elliptic Curves

In this article, we treat cryptographic bilinear pairings $G_1 \times G_2 \to G_T$ on elliptic curves E defined over some finite field $\mathbb{F}_q$ of characteristic p. We emphasise that our aim is not to set new speed records for particular curves, cf. [2,20,1], but to compare different choices of pairings and parameters at various security levels, using a general purpose, but reasonably optimised, implementation in a general purpose computer algebra system. Such an analysis will be meaningful assuming that the ratios between the various operations remain constant when switching to hand-optimised assembly implementations in each instance.

We fix the following standard notations and setting. Let $E(\mathbb{F}_q)$ denote the $\mathbb{F}_q$-rational points on E, and let r be a prime divisor of $\#E(\mathbb{F}_q) = q + 1 - t$ that does not divide $q - 1$, where t is the trace of Frobenius. Let the embedding degree k be the smallest integer such that r divides $q^k - 1$, and denote by π the Frobenius map $E(\mathbb{F}_{q^k}) \to E(\mathbb{F}_{q^k})$, $(x, y) \mapsto (x^q, y^q)$. The r-torsion subgroup $E[r]$ is defined over $\mathbb{F}_{q^k}$, and it contains the non-trivial subgroup $E(\mathbb{F}_q)[r]$ of $\mathbb{F}_q$-rational r-torsion points. Denote by μ_r the subgroup of r-th roots of unity in $\mathbb{F}_{q^k}^*$.

Typically, $G_T = \mu_r$, $G_1 = E(\mathbb{F}_q)[r]$, and G_2 is a subgroup of order r of either $E[r]$ or of $E(\mathbb{F}_{q^k})/rE(\mathbb{F}_{q^k})$.

---

[*] This research was partially funded by ERC Starting Grant ANTICS 278537.

1.1 Functions with Prescribed Divisors

Let E be given over $\mathbb{F}_q$ by an equation in the variables x and y. For a rational function $f \in \overline{\mathbb{F}}_q(E) := \overline{\mathbb{F}}_q(x)[y]/(E)$ and a point $P \in E$, denote by $\mathrm{ord}_P(f)$ the positive multiplicity of the zero P of f, the negative multiplicity of the pole P of f, or 0 if P is neither a zero nor a pole of f. Denote by $\mathrm{div}(f) = \sum_P \mathrm{ord}_P(f)[P]$ the divisor of f, an element of the free abelian group generated by the symbols $[P]$, where P is a point on E.

The definition and computation of pairings involve certain rational functions with given divisors, in particular, $f_{n,P}$ with

$$\mathrm{div}(f_{n,P}) = n[P] - [nP] - (n-1)[\mathcal{O}],$$

the lines $\ell_{P,Q}$ through two (not necessarily distinct) points P and Q with

$$\mathrm{div}(\ell_{P,Q}) = [P] + [Q] + [-(P+Q)] - 3[\mathcal{O}]$$

and the vertical lines v_P through a point P with

$$\mathrm{div}(v_P) = [P] + [-P] - 2[\mathcal{O}].$$

All these functions are defined up to a multiplicative constant, and they are normalised at infinity by the condition $\left(f \left(\frac{Y}{X} \right)^{\mathrm{ord}_{\mathcal{O}}(f)} \right)(\mathcal{O}) = 1$.

In particular, we have $\ell_{P,-P} = v_P$, $f_{1,P} = 1$ and $f_{-1,P} = 1/v_P$.

The function $f_{n,P}$ is of degree $O(n)$ and may be evaluated in $O(\log n)$ steps by the algorithms of §3.

1.2 Cryptographic Pairings

We quickly recall the main cryptographic pairings. In applications, they are usually restricted to $E(\mathbb{F}_q)[r]$ in one argument and to a subgroup of order r in the other argument.

Weil Pairing

$$e_{\mathrm{W}} : E(r) \times E(r) \to \mu_r, \quad (P,Q) \mapsto (-1)^r \frac{f_{r,P}(Q)}{f_{r,Q}(P)}$$

Computing the pairing requires the evaluation of two functions; moreover, with $P \in E(\mathbb{F}_q)$ and $Q \in E(\mathbb{F}_{q^k})$, the function $f_{r,Q}$ is much costlier to evaluate by the algorithms of §3.

Tate Pairing

$$e_{\mathrm{T}} : E(\mathbb{F}_q)[r] \times E(\mathbb{F}_{q^k})/rE(\mathbb{F}_{q^k}) \to \mathbb{F}_{q^k}^*/(\mathbb{F}_{q^k}^*)^r \simeq \mu_r,$$
$$(P,Q) \mapsto f_{r,P}(Q) \leftrightarrow f_{r,P}(Q)^{(q^k-1)/r}.$$

The pairing requires only one evaluation of a rational function, but the original definition with a quotient group as domain is unwieldy since there is no easy way of defining unique representatives. The final exponentiation step of raising to the power $\frac{q^k-1}{r}$ realises an isomorphism with μ_r, and the resulting pairing is usually called the reduced Tate pairing.

Ate Pairing. By restricting its arguments to the two eigenspaces of $E[r]$ under the Frobenius with eigenvalues 1 and q, respectively, the ate pairing introduced in [14] replaces $f_{r,P}(Q)$ with $r \in O(q)$ by $f_{T,Q}(P)$, where $T = t-1 \in O(\sqrt{q})$. This saving may be offset by the swap of arguments P and Q, so that the function is defined over $\mathbb{F}_{q^k}$ instead of $\mathbb{F}_q$.

$$e_A : E(\mathbb{F}_q)[r] \times E[r] \cap \ker(\pi - q) \to \mu_r, \quad (P,Q) \mapsto f_{T,Q}(P)^{(q^k-1)/r}.$$

Twisted Ate Pairing. The curve E admits a twist of degree $d = \gcd(k, \# \operatorname{Aut}(E))$; let $e = k/d$. The twisted ate pairing of [14] works again with a function over $\mathbb{F}_q$, at the expense of a factor of $O(e)$ in its evaluation:

$$e_{A'} : E(\mathbb{F}_q)[r] \times E[r] \cap \ker(\pi - q) \to \mu_r, \quad (P,Q) \mapsto f_{T^e,P}(Q)^{(q^k-1)/r}.$$

Optimal Pairing Generalisations of the ate and twisted ate pairings requiring several functions for their evaluation have been given in [13,23]. All of them take $G_1 = E(\mathbb{F}_q)$ and $G_2 = E[r] \cap \ker(\pi - q)$. They are evaluated with low degree functions, typically requiring $O(\log r/\varphi(k))$ operations (not counting the final exponentiation), where φ is Euler's function.

Let $\lambda = mr = \sum_{i=0}^n \lambda_i q^i$ be a suitably chosen multiple of r with $r \nmid m$ such that the λ_i are small; more precisely, one requires a short addition-subtraction sequence passing through all λ_i. An optimal ate pairing is obtained by

$$e_O : G_1 \times G_2 \to \mu_r, \quad (P,Q) \mapsto \left(\prod_{i=0}^n f_{\lambda_i,Q}^{q^i}(P) \prod_{i=0}^{n-1} \frac{\ell_{s_{i+1}Q,\lambda_i q^i Q}(P)}{v_{s_i Q}(P)} \right)^{(q^k-1)/r},$$

where $s_i = \sum_{j=i}^n \lambda_j q^j$. Since $\lambda = \varphi_k(q)$ yields a degenerate pairing, one may assume $n < \varphi(k)$; a precise condition for non-degeneracy is given in [23, Th. 4]. Finding such a multiple of r with small coefficients in base q is a common integer relation problem. It may be solved, for example, by using the LLL algorithm to find a short vector $(\lambda_0, \ldots, \lambda_{\varphi(k)-1})$ in the lattice generated by $(r, 0, \ldots, 0)$ and the $(-q^{i-1}, 0, \ldots, 0, 1, 0, \ldots, 0)$ with 1 at position i for $i = 2, \ldots, \varphi(k)$.

Optimal Twisted Pairing. In the presence of a twist of degree d such that $k = de$, a pairing can be obtained in a similar fashion from $\lambda = mr = \sum_{i=0}^n \lambda_i T^{ei}$ with $n < \varphi(d)$. The only interesting cases are $d \in \{3, 4, 6\}$ with $\varphi(d) = 2$ (otherwise, we obtain again the twisted ate pairing). Then

$$e_{O'} : G_1 \times G_2 \to \mu_r, \quad (P,Q) \mapsto \left(f_{\lambda_0,P}(Q) f_{\lambda_1,P}^{q^e}(Q) v_{\lambda_0 P}(Q) \right)^{(q^k-1)/r}$$

defines a pairing, where (λ_0, λ_1) is a short vector in the lattice generated by $(r, 0)$ and $(-T^e, 1)$.

2   Curves and Associated Optimal Pairings

2.1   Curve Selection

Pairing-based cryptographic settings should be designed so that the discrete logarithm problem is intractable in each group involved. Current best attacks on a subgroup of prime order r of an elliptic curve require on the order of $\sqrt{r}$ operations. For the sake of efficiency of the implementation and to save bandwidth in transmitting points on the curve, it would be desirable that $\#E(\mathbb{F}_q) = r \approx q$ by Hasse's theorem. This condition, however, is not easily met for arbitrary embedding degree k, and the parameter $\rho = \frac{\log q}{\log r}$ measures to which extent it is violated: Values close to 1 would be optimal. Discrete logarithms in finite fields $\mathbb{F}_{q^k}$ of large characteristic, which we deal with in this article, may be computed by algorithms with subexponential complexity $L_{q^k}(1/3)$ (as opposed to quasi-polynomial complexity in small characteristic [5]). One is thus looking for parameter values such that $\sqrt{r} \approx L_{q^k}(1/3) = L_{r^{\rho k}}(1/3)$. Taking logarithms on both sides shows that for bounded ρ, the embedding degree k grows asymptotically as $\log^2 q$.

Several studies have refined this argument. Table 1 summarises security levels equivalent to the AES secret key sizes, all given in bits, according to the Ecrypt2 recommendations [22], validated by a large community of cryptologists.

Table 1. Recommended curve sizes

Security	$\log_2 r$	$\log_2 q^k$	Target $k\rho$
128	256	3248	12.7
192	384	7936	20.7
256	512	15424	30.1

For each security level, we have selected from [9] several curve families approximately fulfilling the requirements on the parameter sizes, trying to stay as close as possible to the ideal $k\rho$ values.

These curves, together with their main parameters, are given in Table 2; for more details, see Appendix A. The entries in column "construction" refer to the algorithms of [9]. Supersingular curves are ruled out at these security levels by their too small embedding degree $k \leq 6$, so we restricted the search to ordinary curves. Since non-prime base fields $\mathbb{F}_q$ are virtually impossible to reach, all curves are defined over prime fields $\mathbb{F}_p$. We favoured a small Hamming weight of r and field extensions $\mathbb{F}_{p^k}$ which may be defined by a binomial $X^k - a$ with a small $a \in \mathbb{F}_p$. For comparison purposes, we also included the Barreto-Naehrig curves $E_{12,2}$ and $E_{12,3}$, widely considered the best choice for 128 bit security due to their optimal value of $\rho = 1$, for security levels of 192 and 256 bits by artificially increasing p. Some curve families are very sparse, which forced us to relax the constraints, for instance for E_{25}.

Table 2. Main curve parameters

Security	k	ρ	$k\rho$	Curve	Construction	$\deg q$	$\deg r$	$\deg t$	$\varphi(k)$
128	9	4/3	12.0	E_9	6.6	8	6	4	6
	11	6/5	13.2	E_{11}	6.6	24	20	12	10
	12	1	12	$E_{12,1}$	6.8	4	4	2	4
192	12	1	12	$E_{12,2}$	6.8	4	4	2	4
	15	3/2	22.5	E_{15}	6.6	12	8	6	8
	16	5/4	20	E_{16}	6.11	10	8	5	8
	17	19/16	20.2	E_{17}	6.2	38	32	2	16
	18	4/3	24	E_{18}	6.12	8	6	4	6
	19	10/9	21.1	E_{19}	6.6	40	36	20	18
256	12	1	12	$E_{12,3}$	6.8	4	4	2	4
	24	5/4	30	E_{24}	6.6	10	8	1	8
	25	13/10	32.5	E_{25}	6.6	52	40	26	20
	26	7/6	30.34	E_{26}	6.6	28	24	14	12
	27	10/9	30	E_{27}	6.6	20	18	10	18

2.2 Optimal Pairings

Each curve family gives rise to different optimal pairings, which are obtained via short vectors in certain lattices as explained in §1.2. For each curve family in Table 2, such short vectors are given in Table 11. Notice that for E_{17} and E_{24}, the ate pairings are already optimal, and that for $d \notin \{3,4,6\}$ and moreover for E_{24}, the twisted optimal pairings are exactly the twisted ate pairings.

3 The Miller Loop

The procedure to evaluate the function $f_{n,P}$ is given by Miller in [17] and relies on the recursive relations $f_{1,P} = 1$ and

$$f_{n+m,P} = f_{n,P} f_{m,P} \frac{\ell_{nP,mP}}{v_{(n+m)P}}, \tag{1}$$

which can be easily checked by taking divisors on both sides of the equality, see §1.1. This allows to compute $f_{x,P}$ alongside xP in a standard double-and-add fashion, resulting in the special case of Algorithm 1 in which all digits x_i are 0 or 1. To avoid field inversions, the numerator and the denominator of the function are kept separate; the correctness of the algorithm may be derived from the loop invariant $f_{x',P}(Q) = f/g$, where $x' = \sum_{j=0}^{n-i-1} x_{i+j+1} 2^j$.

Techniques for speeding up scalar products on elliptic curves may be adapted. For instance, allowing addition-subtraction chains for computing xP, preferably by writing x in non-adjacent form (NAF), in which no two consecutive digits are non-zero, results in Algorithm 1. Notice the additional multiplication by v_P in the case of a digit -1, due to $f_{-1,P} = 1/v_P$, which is often incorrectly left out in the literature; in particular, [17, Algorithm 1] is only correct for addition chains. The common omission may be explained by the use of denominator elimination: If k is even and $G_2 = E(\mathbb{F}_{q^k}) \cap \ker(\pi - q)$, then the x-coordinates of P and Q and thus all values $v_R(Q)$ lie in the subfield $\mathbb{F}_{q^{k/2}}$ and disappear for reduced pairings involving a final exponentiation. In particular, g may be dropped completely.

Algorithm 1. Miller's algorithm using a NAF

Input: $P \neq \mathcal{O}, Q \neq \lambda P$, two points on an elliptic curve E over a field
$\quad\quad x = \sum_{i=0}^{n} x_i 2^i$ with $x_i \in \{-1, 0, 1\}$
Output: $f_{x,P}(Q)$
$R \leftarrow P$
$f \leftarrow 1, g \leftarrow 1$
for $i \leftarrow n - 1$ **downto** 0 **do**
$\quad\quad f \leftarrow f^2 \ell_{R,R}(Q)$
$\quad\quad R \leftarrow 2R$
$\quad\quad g \leftarrow g^2 v_R(Q)$
$\quad\quad$**if** $x_i = 1$ **then**
$\quad\quad\quad\quad f \leftarrow f \ell_{R,P}(Q)$
$\quad\quad\quad\quad R \leftarrow R + P$
$\quad\quad\quad\quad g \leftarrow g v_R(Q)$
$\quad\quad$**if** $x_i = -1$ **then**
$\quad\quad\quad\quad f \leftarrow f \ell_{R,-P}(Q)$
$\quad\quad\quad\quad R \leftarrow R - P$
$\quad\quad\quad\quad g \leftarrow g v_R(Q) v_P(Q)$
return f/g

An observation made in [7] allows to simplify the expression in the case $x_i = -1$ also for odd k. Denote by λ the slope of the line between R and $-P$. Then

$$\ell_{R,-P}(Q) = y(Q) + y(P) - \lambda\big(x(Q) - x(P)\big),$$

which is computed with one multiplication, and f and g are updated with four multiplications altogether, or with two multiplications if denominator elimination applies. Then

$$\ell'_{R,-P}(Q) := \frac{\ell_{R,-P}(Q)}{v_P(Q)} = \frac{y(Q) + y(P)}{x(Q) - x(P)} - \lambda \tag{2}$$

is obtained without any multiplication since the first term may be precomputed once and for all. So replacing the block in the case of $x_i = -1$ by

$$f \leftarrow f \ell'_{R,-P}(Q), \quad R \leftarrow R - P, \quad g \leftarrow g v_R(Q)$$

reduces the number of multiplications to 2, the same as in the presence of denominator elimination.

In the same article [7], Boxall *et al.* introduce a variant of the algorithm based on

$$f_{n+m,P} = (f_{-n,P} f_{-m,P} \ell_{-nP,-mP})^{-1},$$

which contains only three factors instead of the four in (1), but requires a swap of the numerator and the denominator for each doubling or adding on the elliptic curve. The algorithm of [7] is given only for addition chains, but can be generalised to addition-subtraction chains, yielding Algorithm 2. The correctness of

---

Algorithm 2. Boxall *et al.*'s algorithm using a NAF

Input: $P \neq \mathcal{O}, Q \neq \lambda P$, two points on an elliptic curve E over a field
$\quad\quad x = \sum_{i=0}^{n} x_i 2^i$ with $x_i \in \{-1, 0, 1\}$
Output: $f_{x,P}(Q)$
$h \leftarrow n + \#\{x_i | x_i \neq 0\}_{0 \leq i \leq n} - 1$
$\delta \leftarrow (-1)^h$
$g \leftarrow f_{\delta,P}(Q)$, where $f_{1,P} = 1$ and $f_{-1,P} = 1/v_P$
$f \leftarrow 1, R \leftarrow P$
for $i \leftarrow n-1$ **downto** 0 **do**
$\quad$ **if** $\delta = 1$ **then**
$\quad\quad f \leftarrow f^2 \ell_{R,R}(Q)$ $\qquad\qquad\qquad$ // $f_{-2n,P} = (f_{n,P}^2 \ell_{[n]P,[n]P})^{-1}$
$\quad\quad g \leftarrow g^2$
$\quad\quad R \leftarrow 2R, \ \delta \leftarrow -\delta$
$\quad\quad$ **if** $x_i = 1$ **then** $\qquad\qquad\qquad$ // $f_{n+1,P} = (f_{-n,P} f_{-1,P} \ell_{[-n]P,-P})^{-1}$
$\quad\quad\quad g \leftarrow g \ell'_{-R,-P}(Q)$
$\quad\quad\quad R \leftarrow R + P, \ \delta \leftarrow -\delta$
$\quad\quad$ **if** $x_i = -1$ **then** $\qquad\qquad$ // $f_{n-1,P} = (f_{n,P} \ell_{[-n]P,P})^{-1}$
$\quad\quad\quad g \leftarrow g \ell_{-R,P}(Q)$
$\quad\quad\quad R \leftarrow R - P, \ \delta \leftarrow -\delta$
$\quad$ **else**
$\quad\quad g \leftarrow g^2 \ell_{-R,-R}(Q)$ $\qquad\qquad$ // $f_{2n,P} = (f_{-n,P}^2 \ell_{[-n]P,[-n]P})^{-1}$
$\quad\quad f \leftarrow f^2$
$\quad\quad R \leftarrow 2R, \ \delta \leftarrow -\delta$
$\quad\quad$ **if** $x_i = 1$ **then** $\qquad\qquad\qquad$ // $f_{-(n+1),P} = (f_{n,P} \ell_{[n]P,P})^{-1}$
$\quad\quad\quad f \leftarrow f \ell_{R,P}(Q)$
$\quad\quad\quad R \leftarrow R + P, \ \delta \leftarrow -\delta$
$\quad\quad$ **if** $x_i = -1$ **then** $\qquad\qquad$ // $f_{-(n-1),P} = (f_{n,P} f_{-1,P} \ell_{[n]P,-P})^{-1}$
$\quad\quad\quad f \leftarrow f \ell'_{R,-P}(Q)$
$\quad\quad\quad R \leftarrow R - P, \ \delta \leftarrow -\delta$

$\quad$ **return** f/g

---

the algorithm stems from the equations given in commentary and (2), and the loop invariant $f_{\delta x',P}(Q)^{\delta} = f/g$, where $x' = \sum_{j=0}^{n-i-1} x_{i+j+1} 2^j$. The value of h is the total number of curve doublings, additions and subtractions carried out during the algorithm; δ is $+1$ or -1, respectively, depending on whether the number of curve operations still to be carried out is odd or even. In the end, $\delta = 1$, and f/g is the desired result.

4 Final Exponentiation

After the evaluation of a rational function, most pairings require a final powering to obtain a uniquely defined result. It has been suggested that at high levels of security the final exponentiation would become so computationally expensive that the Weil pairing should be preferred to the Tate pairing [16], but this conclusion was quickly contradicted by a finer analysis of the exponentiation step [11]. The rather special form of the exponent $(q^k - 1)/r$ makes the final powering less daunting than it may first appear. This exponent can be decomposed into three parts as follows. Let i be the smallest prime divisor of k.

$$\frac{q^k - 1}{r} = \underbrace{(q^{k/i} - 1) \cdot \frac{q^k - 1}{(q^{k/i} - 1)\Phi_k(q)}}_{\text{easy}} \cdot \underbrace{\frac{\Phi_k(q)}{r}}_{\text{hard}}$$

where Φ_k is the k-th cyclotomic polynomial. The first two factors are sums of powers of q and are easily computed using only a few applications of the Frobenius map $x \mapsto x^q$ and multiplications in G_T, together with an extra division in G_T for the first part. Consequently, the powering by $N = \Phi_k(q)/r$, dubbed the "hard part", is the only truly expensive step of the final exponentiation. It is usually carried out with multi-exponentiation techniques.

Generic Exponentiation. An algorithm proposed by Avanzi and Mihăilescu in [3] makes particularly intensive use of the Frobenius map, which is very efficient for finite field extensions given by binomials, see Table 4. To compute b^N, it first decomposes N in base q, then each coefficient in base 2^ℓ for a suitably chosen small ℓ, such that $N = \sum_{i=0}^{\lceil \log_q N \rceil} \sum_{j=0}^{\lceil \log_{2^\ell}(q-1) \rceil} n_{ij} q^i 2^{j\ell}$, and $b^N = \prod_j \left(\prod_i b^{n_{ij} q^i} \right)^{2^{j\ell}}$. After precomputing all possible values of $b^{n_{ij}}$ with about 2^ℓ multiplications, for each j the inner product is evaluated in a Horner scheme; altogether, this requires $O((\log N)/\ell)$ Frobenius maps and as many multiplications. The outer product is then computed by a square-and-multiply approach with $O(\log q) = O((\log N)/k)$ multiplications, most of which are squarings. Notice that for $2^\ell \in O(\log N/ \log \log N)$ and k growing sufficiently fast with respect to N (which is the case due to the security equivalence of §2), the total complexity becomes $O(\log N/ \log \log N)$ operations, which is sublinear in the bit size of N.

As can be seen in Table 4, the Frobenius is not completely negligible when the field extension is realised by a trinomial, so we investigated an alternative approach due to Nogami *et al.* [18], which purportedly requires fewer applications of the Frobenius map. Let ℓ be an integer and $c = \lceil (\log_q N)/\ell \rceil$, and let $t = \lceil \log_2 q \rceil$. The algorithm of [18] creates a binary matrix with ℓ rows and ct columns by first writing N in basis q^c. Each coefficient corresponds to one row and is decomposed into c coefficients in base q, each of which is in turn written with t coefficients in base 2. These form the columns of the matrix, organised into c blocks of t columns each. To compute b^N, first the powers b^{2^i} are precomputed with $t - 1$ multiplications. If the same column occurs $d \geq 2$ times in $e \leq c$ column blocks, its occurrences can be combined with $d - 1$ multiplications and $e - 1$ applications of the Frobenius map. Taking into account that there are at most $2^\ell - 1$ different non-zero columns, this step can thus be carried out with at most $ct - 1$ multiplications and $(c-1)(2^\ell - 1)$ Frobenius maps. Heuristically, a fraction of $1/2^\ell$ of the columns are zero, for which there is nothing to do;

so one expects a number of multiplications closer to $ct(1 - 1/2^\ell)$, a noticeable difference for small values of ℓ. For each row, the combined columns which have a 1 in this row need to be multiplied, with at most $\ell(2^{\ell-1} - 1)$ multiplications. Finally, the rows are combined with $\ell - 1$ multiplications and $\ell - 1$ Frobenius maps. We arrive at a complexity of $(c - 1)(2^\ell - 1) + \ell - 1$ Frobenius maps and $ct + \ell(2^{\ell-1} - 1) + \ell + t - 3$ multiplications. The latter can be tightened heuristically by multiplying the first term with $1 - 1/2^\ell$, which turns out to be close to the experimentally observed values. Asymptotically, the number of multiplications is equivalent to $(\log_2 N)/\ell + \ell 2^\ell$. Recall from the security equivalence of §2 that k is of the order of $\log^2 q$, so that $c \in O\left((\log N)^{2/3}/\ell\right)$ and the number of Frobenius maps is in $O\left(2^\ell (\log N)^{2/3}/\ell\right)$. Letting $2^\ell = (\log N)^{1/3}$ yields a sublinear total complexity of $O(\log N/\log\log N)$. The analysis also shows that by preferring smaller values of ℓ, one may reduce the number of Frobenius maps compared to Avanzi and Mihăilescu's algorithm, at the price of more multiplications. Notice that ℓ fixes c, and that the exponentiality in ℓ implies that an optimal value is found easily in practice.

Family-Dependant Exponentiation. Scott *et al.* proposed in [21] an exponentiation technique for polynomial families of parameters $q(x)$ and $r(x)$. The exponent is written first in base $q(x)$, then each coefficient in base x as

$$N(x) = \Phi_k(q(x))/r(x) = \sum_{i=0}^{\lfloor \deg N(x)/\deg q(x)\rfloor} \sum_{j=0}^{\deg q(x)-1} \lambda_{i,j} x^j q(x)^i.$$

To obtain $b^{N(x_0)}$, the values $b^{x_0^j q^i}$ are precomputed with first $\deg q(x)$ exponentiations by x_0, which can be done with $O(\log q)$ multiplications, then about $\deg N(x)$ applications of the Frobenius map. The final result is then obtained by multi-exponentiation with the exponents $\lambda_{i,j}$. The exact complexity of this step depends on the length of an addition sequence passing through all of the $\lambda_{i,j}$. If $\Lambda = \max|\lambda_{i,j}|$, then the best rigorous bound currently available is $\log_2 \Lambda + \deg N(x) O(\log \Lambda/\log\log \Lambda)$, where $\deg N(x)$ is the number of potentially different values of $\lambda_{i,j}$, realised, for instance, by [24]. In practice, the coefficients are small, and there are addition sequences with only few additional terms, see Table 12, leading to a heuristic complexity of $O(\deg N(x))$ multiplications. The total complexity then becomes $O(\log q + \deg N(x))$ multiplications and $O(\deg N(x))$ Frobenius maps, where $\deg N(x) \approx \log N/\log x_0$.

5   Implementation

We have implemented the various pairings for the different curves of §2 in the PARI library and linked them into the free number theoretic computer algebra system GP [15]. Our aim was not to provide an optimal *ad hoc* implementation for any one of the curves or pairings, but rather to keep a sufficient level of genericity appropriate for a general purpose system, while still implementing algorithmic optimisations that apply in a broader context. All benchmarks were performed on a Macbook Pro with a 2.5 GHz Core 2 Duo processor, and timings are given in milliseconds (rounded to two significant digits).

5.1   Finite Field Arithmetic

Arithmetic in $\mathbb{F}_p$ is already available in PARI. The field extensions $\mathbb{F}_{p^k}$ are defined by binomials $X^k - a$ for all curves but E_{11}, E_{19} and E_{25}, for which only trinomials of the form $X^k + X + a$ exist. A defining binomial can be found if and only if all prime factors of k divide $p-1$, and, additionally for $4 \mid k$, if $p \equiv 1$ (mod 4) [19, Theorem 2], which happens quite often in our context where k has only few prime factors and there is a certain freedom in the choice of p. Fast reduction modulo binomials and trinomials had to be added to PARI. Definition by a binomial is crucial for an efficient pairing implementation, see Table 3, which shows the effect for the ate pairing on E_{18} when artificially switching to a trinomial.

Table 3. Timings for ate pairing depending on the finite field defining polynomial

Defining polynomial	unreduced ate	unreduced optimal
$x^{18} + x + 6$	490 ms	120 ms
$x^{18} + 19$	150 ms	35 ms

In several places in the literature, it is suggested to build $\mathbb{F}_{p^k}$ by successive extensions of degree dividing k, in particular of degree 2 or 3. It is unclear where the benefits of this strategy lie for multiplication: Virtually the same effect may be reached by using Karatsuba (degree 2) and Toom-Cook (degree 3) for polynomial arithmetic, which moreover speeds up the computations also when k is not a power product of 2 and 3. By keeping a single extension, it is also easier to reach the thresholds for asymptotically fast algorithms. In particular, PARI uses Kronecker substitution to replace the product of polynomials by that of large integers which is outsourced to the GMP library [12]; in experiments, this turned out to be faster than Karatsuba multiplication.

Note that using a binomial to define the field extensions also indirectly speeds up the arithmetic when field elements lie in subfields of $\mathbb{F}_{q^k}$, which happens systematically for the group $G_2 = E[r] \cap \ker(\pi - q)$ in the presence of twists. As an example consider again the curve E_{18}. Let $D \in \mathbb{F}_{p^3}$ be a quadratic and a cubic non-residue in $\mathbb{F}_{p^3}$, which implies that $\mathbb{F}_{p^{18}} = \mathbb{F}_{p^3}[D^{1/6}]$. Then E_{18}: $y^2 = x^3 + b$ admits a sextic twist E' : $y^2 = x^3 + b/D$, explicitly given by ϕ_6 : $E'(\mathbb{F}_3) \rightarrow E(\mathbb{F}_{18})$: $(x, y) \mapsto \left(\sqrt[3]{D}x, \sqrt{D}y \right)$, which yields an isomorphism of $E'(\mathbb{F}_{p^3})[r]$ with G_2. If $\mathbb{F}_{18}$ is defined by a binomial $X^{18} + A$, then $D = A^{1/3} = X^6$, the elements of $\mathbb{F}_{p^3}$ are written as $a_{12}X^{12} + a_6X^6 + a_0$, and an element Q of G_2 is given as $\phi_6(Q') = (a_{14}X^{14} + a_8X^8 + a_2X^2, a_{15}X^{15} + a_9X^9 + a_3X^3)$ with all $a_i \in \mathbb{F}_p$. These sparse polynomials lead to a faster arithmetic, and part of the speed gains for binomial field extensions as shown in Table 3 may be attributed to this implicit handling of subfields.

Explicit towers of finite fields could be useful for realising the Frobenius automorphism of $\mathbb{F}_{p^k}/\mathbb{F}_p$, since the non-trivial automorphism of a quadratic extension is a simple sign flip; while those of cubic extensions require a multiplication in the smaller field anyway. We chose instead to implement the Frobenius, as well as its powers, as linear maps by multiplying with precomputed $k \times k$ matrices. We originally intended to study the use of optimal normal bases of $\mathbb{F}_{p^k}/\mathbb{F}_p$, in which the Frobenius π is realised as a simple permutation of the coordinates. It turns out, however, that again binomial field extensions yield an efficient arithmetic: In their presence, the matrix of π is the product of a diagonal matrix and a permutation, so π and its powers can be computed with k multiplications in $\mathbb{F}_p$ [4, Theorem 3]. In the trinomial case, the Frobenius is computed with close to k^2 multiplications in $\mathbb{F}_p$.

Table 4 summarises the relative costs of the Frobenius π, the multiplication M_2 and the inversion I_2 in $\mathbb{F}_{p^k}$ and the multiplication M_1 and the inversion I_1 in $\mathbb{F}_p$. The effect of a defining trinomial on the cost of π is clearly visible.

Table 4. Costs of arithmetic in finite prime and extension fields

	E_9	E_{11}	$E_{12,1}$	$E_{12,2}$	E_{15}	E_{16}	E_{17}	E_{18}	E_{19}	$E_{12,3}$	E_{24}	E_{25}	E_{26}	E_{27}
$M_1/\mu s$	0.41	0.36	0.27	0.82	0.64	0.57	0.66	0.64	0.49	2.2	0.74	0.83	0.73	0.64
I_1/M_1	11	11	15	12	13	14	12	12	13	10	13	12	12	13
M_2/M_1	55	90	110	80	120	130	130	140	170	70	250	210	250	240
I_2/M_2	8.0	7.9	8.6	8.1	8.1	8.7	9.2	8.8	8.7	8.1	9.2	9.5	10	10
π/M_2	0.19	0.63	0.19	0.17	0.15	0.15	0.15	0.16	0.95	0.18	0.14	1.2	0.16	0.15

5.2 Miller Loop

Given the cost of inversion in Table 4, we implemented the elliptic curve arithmetic using affine coordinates. Timings for the Miller loop are summarised in Table 5. While mathematically not necessary, the Tate and Weil pairings have also been restricted to the subgroups G_1 and G_2 of eigenvalue 1 and p, respectively, which assures a fairer comparison and incidentally a type 3 pairing in the notation of [10], see also [8]. For even embedding degree, we applied denominator elimination. The first row uses a double-and-add approach, the second one a signed NAF with Algorithm 1. The variant of Algorithm 2 is only of interest when k is odd; we give its timings with a double-and-add chain and a NAF in the third and fourth rows, respectively. It makes an impressive difference.

Generically, one expects a NAF to save about 11% of the number of operations. For our curves, the effect is often much less. This can be explained by the sparsity of the integer r derived from a curve family, which is thus closer to non-adjacent form than a random integer. For instance, the binary decomposition of r for $E_{12,1}$ has only 87 entries 1 out of 256, a density that would be expected in a NAF of a random number. The NAF has 37 entries 1 and -1 each. Also counting the squarings, the gain in the number of operations is less than 4%. One could reduce the number of multiplications even further by combining with a sliding window technique; since the number of squarings is unchanged, the effect will be more and more marginal with an increasing window size.

Table 5. Timings of the function evaluation in milliseconds

Curve	e_T	$e_{A'}$	$e_{O'}$	e_A	e_O	e_W	$\deg q$	$\deg r$	$\deg t$	$\varphi(k)$
E_9	31	64	15	50	14	100	8	6	4	6
	29	59	15	45	14	97				
	21	46	11	46	12	85				
	20	42	11	42	12	80				
E_{11}	43	–	–	110	20	230	24	20	12	10
	39	–	–	100	20	200	24	20	12	10
	31	–	–	100	20	200				
	28	–	–	96	19	180				
$E_{12,1}$	14	13	7	18	9	70	4	4	2	4
	14	13	7	18	9	67				
$E_{12,2}$	93	91	53	110	54	420	4	4	2	4
	91	91	52	110	54	410				
E_{15}	130	520	73	270	44	460	12	8	6	8
	130	480	71	240	41	440				
	90	360	53	240	41	370				
	88	330	50	220	37	360				
E_{16}	64	170	35	150	230	360	10	8	5	8
	62	160	34	140	220	340				
E_{17}	160	–	–	54	54	930	38	32	2	16
	140	–	–	50	50	820				
	110	–	–	51	51	830				
	100	–	–	47	47	740				
E_{18}	78	160	39	160	35	400	8	6	4	6
	75	150	36	150	35	380				
E_{19}	130	–	–	350	40	760	40	36	20	18
	120	–	–	320	35	680				
	93	–	–	340	40	670				
	88	–	–	300	34	610				
$E_{12,3}$	410	400	240	450	220	1800	4	4	2	4
	400	400	240	450	230	1700				
E_{24}	190	88	88	55	55	960	10	8	1	8
	180	85	85	56	56	900				
E_{25}	450	–	–	1400	120	2700	52	40	26	20
	410	–	–	1300	130	2400				
	310	–	–	1400	130	2400				
	300	–	–	1200	120	2200				
E_{26}	210	–	–	660	99	1600	28	24	14	12
	190	–	–	610	90	1400				
E_{27}	370	1900	190	570	54	1300	20	18	10	18
	350	1800	180	510	53	1300				
	260	1300	130	530	52	1100				
	250	1200	130	450	47	1100				

At these high security levels and consequently big values of k, the ate pairing e_A is clearly in general slower than the Tate pairing; the smaller multiplier is more than offset by the need to work over the extension field. The only exception is E_{24} with a particularly small trace ($t(x)$ of degree 1 for $r(x)$ of degree 8). In fact, the ate pairing for this curve is already optimal. As can be expected, the twisted ate pairing $e_{A'}$ is even less efficient except for small values of k combined with a high degree twist: The power of the trace $T^e = T^{k/d}$ quickly exceeds r itself (in the table, we computed with T^e; one could reduce modulo r and arrive at the same timings as the Tate pairing, but may then as well stick with the original). The optimal versions indeed keep their promises. Due to the overhead of computing several functions, the total running time is not reduced by a factor of $\varphi(k)$, but the optimal ate pairing is generally faster than the Tate pairing. Twisted pairings are asymptotically slower, but interesting for the medium values of $k = 9$, 12 or 16 which admit a twist of (relatively) high degree 3, 6 or 4.

The Weil pairing with its two function evaluations could be expected to behave like a Tate followed by an ate pairing; due to the different loop lengths, the part $f_{r,Q}(P)$, however, has a complexity closer to $\deg r(x)/\deg t(x)$ times that of ate, as can be roughly verified in the table. As already stated in the literature, the enormous overhead of the Weil pairing is not offset by saving the final exponentiation, see §5.3.

At higher security levels, odd values of k lead to a bigger $\varphi(k)$ and thus a higher gain in the optimal pairing; together with the Miller loop improvement of [7], odd and in particular prime values of k become attractive. Notice that E_{11}, E_{19} and E_{25} are heavily penalised by the trinomial field extension. Indeed, odd or, worse, prime values of k make the divisibility conditions for the existence of a binomial extension harder to satisfy. Moreover, the degree of $p(x)$ also grows with $\varphi(k)$, so that the polynomial represents fewer numbers in the desired range and leaves less choice for p or a value of x_0 with low Hamming weight. Even if a binomial field extension exists, odd values of k that are not divisible by 3 (in particular, prime k again) suffer from a lack of twists and thus a less efficient field arithmetic as discussed in §5.1.

5.3   Final Exponentiation

Timings for the final exponentiation are compiled in Table 6.

The first column corresponds to a direct exponentiation by $(q^k - 1)/r$ via the sliding window algorithm built into PARI. The second column does so for the hard part, while computing the easy one using Frobenius maps. The next two columns relate the implementation of the hard parts following [3] and [18]. At low security level, the differences between these two algorithms are minimal. For the medium and high security range, our implementation confirms the claim of [18]: Their algorithm becomes faster when Frobenius maps are more expensive, as for the three curves E_{11}, E_{19} and E_{25}. The $k = 12$ curves stand out: The low value of $\varphi(k)$ makes the final exponentiation much easier with these two algorithms that rely on an expansion in base q.

Table 6. Final exponentiation times in milliseconds

Curve	$\varphi(k)$	Naive	Hard naive	AM04	NMKM08	SBCPK09
E_9	6	56	36	15	15	8
E_{11}	10	80	78	28	24	21
$E_{12,1}$	4	58	17	8	8	4
$E_{12,2}$	4	380	100	41	37	26
E_{15}	8	490	250	85	110	50
E_{16}	8	420	200	66	80	44
E_{17}	16	580	550	180	200	110
E_{18}	6	680	210	78	83	49
E_{19}	18	460	460	150	110	83
$E_{12,3}$	4	1800	470	170	170	120
E_{24}	8	2000	640	150	200	97
E_{25}	20	2600	2100	700	470	320
E_{26}	12	2300	1000	240	270	170
E_{27}	18	2100	1400	290	310	130

While the theoretical analysis of §4 is not conclusive, the experiments are unequivocal: The algorithm of [21] (which we used, as explained in the article, to potentially compute a small power of the true pairing if the coefficients of the polynomial contain denominators) is clearly the fastest one for curves obtained from polynomial families.

6   Overall Timings and Conclusion

For each of our reference curves, Table 7 summarises the timings obtained for the fastest pairing.

Optimal pairings are indeed optimal for higher security levels. Their unreduced version benefits from high values of $\varphi(k)$, as can be seen by comparing E_{24} and E_{27}. However, part of this advantage is offset by the lack of denominator elimination for odd k, although Boxall et al.'s variant almost closes the gap again. Moreover, the higher cost for the final exponentiation more than compensates the gain in the Miller loop. The decision which pairing to take then also depends on the concrete cryptographic protocol: Not all of them require reduced pairings throughout their execution. For instance, verification protocols such as [6] make do with testing equality of products of several pairings. All of these may then be computed unreduced, and only a final quotient of products needs to be raised to the power, which makes this exponentiation negligible.

For a reduced pairing at lower security levels, Barreto–Naehrig curves with $k = 12$ remain unbeaten, profiting from an exceptionally fast final exponentiation.

At 192 bit security, Barreto–Naehrig curves need to work with a larger than optimal size of the underlying elliptic curve, but still provide the fastest pairings. An equivalent performance, however, may be reached for $k = 16$ with curve E_{16}. The suboptimal $\rho = 5/4$ notwithstanding, this curve is of size 501 bits instead of

Table 7. Timings of the fastest reduced pairing variants

Security	Curve	$\varphi(k)$	Pairing	Unreduced	Final exp	Reduced
128 bit	E_9	6	$e_{O'}$	11	8	19
	E_{11}	10	e_O	19	21	40
	$E_{12,1}$	4	$e_{O'}$	7	4	11
192 bit	$E_{12,2}$	4	$e_{O'}$	52	26	78
	E_{15}	8	e_O	37	50	87
	E_{16}	8	$e_{O'}$	34	44	78
	E_{17}	16	$e_A = e_O$	47	110	157
	E_{18}	6	e_O	35	49	84
	E_{19}	18	e_O	34	83	120
256 bit	$E_{12,3}$	4	e_O	220	120	340
	E_{24}	8	$e_A = e_O$	55	97	150
	E_{25}	20	e_O	120	320	440
	E_{26}	12	e_O	90	170	260
	E_{27}	18	e_O	47	130	180

663 bits for the Barreto–Naehrig curve, resulting in less bandwidth for exchanging curve points. Thus our study shows that E_{16} is preferable at medium security level.

At the highest AES equivalent of 256 bit, Barreto–Naehrig curves are no longer competitive speed-wise. Here the curve E_{24} stands out. Although gaining only a factor of 8 in the Miller loop length, it profits from a very fast final exponentiation, while even the unreduced variant remains comparable to the closest competitor E_{27}.

As becomes clear from this study, extension fields $\mathbb{F}_{p^k}$ that do not allow a binomial as a defining polynomial are to be banned, see E_{11}, E_{19} and E_{25}.

Whether odd or even embedding degrees are preferable remains undecided. Our results seem to indicate that odd degrees are slightly slower. This can be explained by their higher probability of requiring a trinomial field extension, sparser families and the lack of twists as explained at the end of §5.2. Often, the gain odd and, in particular, prime embedding degrees provide through larger values of $\varphi(k)$ for the optimal pairings is more than offset by an expensive final exponentiation, as is well illustrated by E_{17}. In protocols that work with mostly unreduced pairings, however, Boxall et al.'s variant of the Miller loop makes odd embedding degrees competitive, see E_{15} and E_{27}.

A definite conclusion is made difficult by the lack of choice for any given security level: Some families are so sparse that they contain no curves of prime cardinality in the desired range or, if they do, no curves allowing to work with extension fields defined by binomials. Even if suitable curves exist, the sparsity of a family may have a big impact on the efficiency of the Miller loop. Notice that the loop for E_{27} is more than twice shorter than that of E_{24}. Nevertheless, the unreduced pairing is computed in almost the same time. This can be explained by the Hamming weight of the multiplier: The family of E_{27} is instantiated with x_0 of weight 13, that of E_{24} with x_0 of weight 7. So the search for new curve families remains a research topic of interest, not only for families with optimal ρ, as witnessed by the good performance of E_{15} despite its very bad $\rho = 3/2$.

References

1. Aranha, D.F., Fuentes-Castañeda, L., Knapp, E., Menezes, A., Rodríguez-Henríquez, F.: Implementing pairings at the 192-bit security level. In: Abdalla, M., Lange, T. (eds.) Pairing 2012. LNCS, vol. 7708, pp. 177–195. Springer, Heidelberg (2013)
2. Aranha, D.F., Karabina, K., Longa, P., Gebotys, C.H., López, J.: Faster explicit formulas for computing pairings over ordinary curves. In: Paterson, K.G. (ed.) EUROCRYPT 2011. LNCS, vol. 6632, pp. 48–68. Springer, Heidelberg (2011)
3. Avanzi, R.M., Mihăilescu, P.: Generic efficient arithmetic algorithms for PAFFs (processor adequate finite fields) and related algebraic structures (extended abstract). In: Matsui, M., Zuccherato, R.J. (eds.) SAC 2003. LNCS, vol. 3006, pp. 320–334. Springer, Heidelberg (2004)
4. Bailey, D.V., Paar, C.: Efficient arithmetic in finite field extensions with applications in elliptic curve cryptography. Journal of Cryptology 14(3), 153–176 (2001)
5. Barbulescu, R., Gaudry, P., Joux, A., Thomé, E.: A heuristic quasi-polynomial algorithm for discrete logarithm in finite fields of small characteristic. In: Nguyen, P.Q., Oswald, E. (eds.) EUROCRYPT 2014. LNCS, vol. 8441, pp. 1–16. Springer, Heidelberg (2014)
6. Blazy, O., Fuchsbauer, G., Izabachène, M., Jambert, A., Sibert, H., Vergnaud, D.: Batch Groth-Sahai. In: Zhou, J., Yung, M. (eds.) ACNS 2010. LNCS, vol. 6123, pp. 218–235. Springer, Heidelberg (2010)
7. Boxall, J., El Mrabet, N., Laguillaumie, F., Le, D.-P.: A variant of Miller's formula and algorithm. In: Joye, M., Miyaji, A., Otsuka, A. (eds.) Pairing 2010. LNCS, vol. 6487, pp. 417–434. Springer, Heidelberg (2010)
8. Chatterjee, S., Menezes, A.: On cryptographic protocols employing asymmetric pairings – the role of ψ revisited. Discrete Applied Mathematics 159, 1311–1322 (2011)
9. Freemann, D., Scott, M., Teske, E.: A taxonomy of pairing-friendly elliptic curves. Journal of Cryptology 23(2), 224–280 (2010)
10. Galbraith, S.D., Paterson, K.G., Smart, N.P.: Pairings for cryptographers. Discrete Applied Mathematics 156(16), 3113–3121 (2008)
11. Granger, R., Page, D., Smart, N.P.: High security pairing-based cryptography revisited. In: Hess, F., Pauli, S., Pohst, M. (eds.) ANTS 2006. LNCS, vol. 4076, pp. 480–494. Springer, Heidelberg (2006)
12. Granlund, T., et al.: gmp — GNU multiprecision library. Version 5.0.3, http://gmplib.org/
13. Hess, F.: Pairing lattices. In: Galbraith, S.D., Paterson, K.G. (eds.) Pairing 2008. LNCS, vol. 5209, pp. 18–38. Springer, Heidelberg (2008)
14. Hess, F., Smart, N.P., Vercauteren, F.: The eta pairing revisited. IEEE Transactions on Information Theory 52(10), 4595–4602 (2006)
15. Karim Belabas and the PARI Group, Bordeaux. PARI/GP. Version 2.5.0, http://pari.math.u-bordeaux.fr/
16. Koblitz, N., Menezes, A.: Pairing-based cryptography at high security levels. In: Smart, N.P. (ed.) Cryptography and Coding 2005. LNCS, vol. 3796, pp. 13–36. Springer, Heidelberg (2005)
17. Miller, V.S.: The Weil pairing, and its efficient calculation. Journal of Cryptology 17, 235–261 (2004)
18. Nogami, Y., Kato, H., Nekado, K., Morikawa, Y.: Efficient exponentiation in extensions of finite fields without fast Frobenius mappings. ETRI Journal 30(6), 818–825 (2008)

19. Panario, D., Thomson, D.: Efficient pth root computations in finite fields of characteristic p. Designs, Codes and Cryptography 50(3), 351–358 (2009)
20. Pereira, G.C.C.F., Simplcio Jr., M.A., Naehrig, M., Barreto, P.S.L.M.: A family of implementation-friendly BN elliptic curves. Journal of Systems and Software 84(8), 1319–1326 (2011)
21. Scott, M., Benger, N., Charlemagne, M., Dominguez Perez, L.J., Kachisa, E.J.: On the final exponentiation for calculating pairings on ordinary elliptic curves. In: Shacham, H., Waters, B. (eds.) Pairing 2009. LNCS, vol. 5671, pp. 78–88. Springer, Heidelberg (2009)
22. Smart, N., et al.: ECRYPT II yearly report on algorithms and keysizes (2009-2010). Technical Report D.SPA.13, European Network of Excellence in Cryptology II (March 2010), http://www.ecrypt.eu.org/documents/D.SPA.13.pdf
23. Vercauteren, F.: Optimal pairings. IEEE Transactions on Information Theory 56(1), 455–461 (2010)
24. Yao, A.C.-C.: On the evaluation of powers. SIAM Journal on Computing 5(1), 100–103 (1976)

A   Curve Parameters

Tables 8 to 10 give the exact parameters for the curves we studied for different security levels. The following notations are used: $p(x)$, $r(x)$ and $t(x)$ are the polynomials representing the cardinality of the finite prime field $\mathbb{F}_q$, a (large) prime factor of the curve cardinality and the trace of Frobenius, respectively; x_0 is the numeric value of the variable x; (a, b) gives the equation of the curve $y^2 = x^3 + ax + b$; F is the irreducible polynomial defining $\mathbb{F}_{p^k}$. For $k = 16$ or 17, no prime values $r(x_0)$ exist in the desired range. We thus admit a small cofactor and let r_0 denote the actual large prime factor of $r(x_0)$.

Table 11 provides the short lattice vectors yielding our optimal ate pairings e_O and optimal twisted ate pairings $e_{O'}$, see §2.2.

Table 12 records the addition sequences used in the final exponentiation of [21]. To remove denominators, the power s of the original pairing is computed; n is the number of (not necessarily distinct) non-zero coefficients λ_{ij}, see §4. The underlined terms are those that are added to the sequence. As can be seen, there is in general a very small number of very small distinct coefficients, and only a tiny number of terms, if any, needs to be added.

Table 8. Curves for security level 128 bit

E_9	$p(x) = (x^8 - x^7 + x^6 - x^5 - 2x^4 - x^3 + x^2 + 2x + 1)/3$
	$r(x) = (x^6 - x^3 + 1)/3$
	$t(x) = -x^4 + x + 1$
	$(a, b) = (0, 7)$ $F(X) = X^9 + 3$ $x_0 = 43980465324080$
E_{11}	$p(x) = (x^{24} - x^{23} + x^{22} - x^{13} + 4x^{12} - x^{11} + x^2 - x + 1)/3$
	$r(x) = x^{20} + x^{19} - x^{17} - x^{16} + x^{14} + x^{13} - x^{11} - x^{10} - x^9 + x^7 + x^6 - x^4 - x^3 + x + 1$
	$t(x) = x^{12} + 1$
	$(a, b) = (0, 4)$ $F(X) = X^{11} + X + 11$ $x_0 = 11210$
$E_{12,1}$	$p(x) = 36x^4 + 36x^3 + 24x^2 + 6x + 1$
	$r(x) = 36x^4 + 36x^3 + 18x^2 + 6x + 1$
	$t(x) = 6x^2 + 1$
	$(a, b) = (0, 5)$ $F(X) = X^{12} + 5$ $x_0 = 6917529027641094616$

Table 9. Curves for security level 192 bit

E_{15}	$p(x) = (x^{12} - x^{11} + x^{10} - x^7 - 2x^6 - x^5 + x^2 + 2x + 1)/3$
	$r(x) = x^8 + x^7 - x^5 - x^4 - x^3 + x + 1$
	$t(x) = -x^6 + x + 1$
	$(a, b) = (0, 13)$ $F(X) = X^{15} + 13$ $x_0 = 271533021386417$
E_{16}	$p(x) = (x^{10} + 2x^9 + 5x^8 + 48x^6 + 152x^5 + 240x^4 + 625x^2 + 2398x + 3125)/980$
	$r(x) = (x^8 + 48x^4 + 625)$ $r_0 = r(x_0)/20641250$
	$t(x) = (2x^5 + 41x + 35)/35$
	$(a, b) = (1, 0)$ $F(X) = X^{16} + 2$ $x_0 = 2251799888961585$
E_{17}	$p(x) = (x^{38} + 2x^{36} + x^{34} + x^4 - 2x^2 + 1)/4$
	$r(x) = x^{32} - x^{30} + x^{28} - x^{26} + x^{24} - x^{22} + x^{20} - x^{18} + x^{16} - x^{14} + x^{12} - x^{10}$
	$\quad + x^8 - x^6 + x^4 - x^2 + 1$ $r_0 = r(x_0)/12071636373225929$
	$t(x) = -x^2 + 1$
	$(a, b) = (13, 0)$ $F(X) = X^{17} + 2$ $x_0 = 12681$
E_{18}	$p(x) = (x^8 + 5x^7 + 7x^6 + 37x^5 + 188x^4 + 259x^3 + 343x^2 + 1763x + 2401)/21$
	$r(x) = (x^6 + 37x^3 + 343)/343$
	$t(x) = (x^4 + 16x + 7)/7$
	$(a, b) = (0, 19)$ $F(X) = X^{18} + 19$ $x_0 = 48422703193491756920$
E_{19}	$p(x) = (x^{40} - x^{39} + x^{38} - x^{21} - 2x^{20} - x^{19} + x^2 + 2x + 1)/3$
	$r(x) = x^{36} + x^{35} - x^{33} - x^{32} + x^{30} + x^{29} - x^{27} - x^{26} + x^{24} + x^{23} - x^{21} - x^{20} + x^{18}$
	$\quad - x^{16} - x^{15} + x^{13} + x^{12} - x^{10} - x^9 + x^7 + x^6 - x^4 - x^3 + x + 1$
	$t(x) = -x^{20} + x + 1$
	$(a, b) = (0, 9)$ $F(X) = X^{19} + X + 23$ $x_0 = 1274$
$E_{12,2}$	$p(x) = 36x^4 + 36x^3 + 24x^2 + 6x + 1$
	$r(x) = 36x^4 + 36x^3 + 18x^2 + 6x + 1$
	$t(x) = 6x^2 + 1$
	$(a, b) = (0, 13)$ $F(X) = X^{12} + 5$
	$x_0 = 2923003274661805836407369665432566039311865086996$

Table 10. Curves for security level 256 bit

E_{24}	$p(x) = (x^{10} - 2x^9 + x^8 - x^6 + 2x^5 - x^4 + x^2 + x + 1)/3$
	$r(x) = x^8 - x^4 + 1$
	$t(x) = x + 1$
	$(a, b) = (0, 1)$ $F(X) = X^{24} + 19$ $x_0 = 18446744073709602433$
E_{25}	$p(x) = (x^{52} - x^{51} + x^{50} - x^{27} - 2x^{26} - x^{25} + x^2 + 2x + 1)/3$
	$r(x) = x^{40} + x^{35} - x^{25} - x^{20} - x^{15} + x^5 + 1$
	$t(x) = -x^{26} + x + 1$
	$(a, b) = (0, 31)$ $F(X) = X^{25} + X + 19$ $x_0 = 6995$
E_{26}	$p(x) = (x^{28} + x^{27} + x^{26} - x^{15} + 2x^{14} - x^{13} + x^2 - 2x + 1)/3$
	$r(x) = x^{24} + x^{23} - x^{21} - x^{20} + x^{18} + x^{17} - x^{15} - x^{14} + x^{12} - x^{10} - x^9 + x^7 + x^6 - x^4 - x^3 + x + 1$
	$t(x) = x^{14} - x + 1$
	$(a, b) = (0, 12)$ $F(X) = X^{26} + 4$ $x_0 = 2685463$
E_{27}	$p(x) = (x^{20} - x^{19} + x^{18} - x^{11} - 2x^{10} - x^9 + x^2 + 2x + 1)/3$
	$r(x) = (x^{18} - x^9 + 1)/3$
	$t(x) = -x^{10} + x + 1$
	$(a, b) = (0, 9)$ $F(X) = X^{27} + 3$ $x_0 = 374298113$
$E_{12,3}$	$p(x) = 36x^4 + 36x^3 + 24x^2 + 6x + 1$
	$r(x) = 36x^4 + 36x^3 + 18x^2 + 6x + 1$
	$t(x) = 6x^2 + 1$
	$(a, b) = (0, 7)$ $F(X) = X^{12} + 2$
	$x_0 = 93449432821539816104782199644917905013868322853103558685183070342222113029\backslash$
	$\quad 03024063504591307 9014$

Table 11. Optimal pairings

Curve	Pairing	Vector
E_9	e_O	$\left(\frac{1}{3}(x-2), \frac{1}{3}(x+1), \frac{1}{3}(x+1), -\frac{1}{3}(x+1), -\frac{1}{3}(x-2), -\frac{1}{3}(x-2)\right)$
	$e_{O'}$	$\left(\frac{1}{3}(x^3+1), \frac{1}{3}(2-x^3)\right)$
E_{11}	e_O	$(x^2, -x, 1, 0, 0, 0, 0, 0, 0, 0)$
$E_{12,i}$	e_O	$(6x+2, 1, -1, 1)$
	$e_{O'}$	$(2x+1, 6x^2+2x)$
E_{15}	e_O	$(1, 0, 0, 0, x, 0, 0, 0)$
	$e_{O'}$	(x^3+x^2-1, x^4+x^3-x-1)
E_{16}	e_O	$((2x-15)/35, -(11x-30)/35, -(2x-1)/7, (x+10)/35,$
		$(2x+5)/5, (8x+10)/35, (2x+6)/7, (17x+30)/35)), x = 25 \bmod 70$
	$e_{O'}$	$(49x^4/625, 7+168x^4/625)$
E_{17}	e_O	$(x^2, 1, 0, 0, 0, 0, 0, 0, 0, 0, 0, 0, 0, 0, 0, 0, 0)$
E_{18}	e_O	$(1, 3x/7, 3x/7+1, 0, -2x/7, -2x/7-1)$
	$e_{O'}$	$(18(x/7)^3+1, -(x/7)^3)$
E_{19}	e_O	$(x^2, -x, 1, 0, 0, 0, 0, 0, 0, 0, 0, 0, 0, 0, 0, 0, 0, 0, 0, 0)$
E_{25}	e_O	$(x^2, -x, 1, 0, 0, 0, 0, 0, 0, 0, 0, 0, 0, 0, 0, 0, 0, 0, 0, 0)$
E_{26}	e_O	$(x^2, x, 1, 0, 0, 0, 0, 0, 0, 0, 0, 0, 0)$
E_{27}	e_O	$(x, 0, 0, 0, 0, 0, 0, 0, 0, 0, 0, 1, 0, 0, 0, 0, 0, 0, 0, 0)$
	$e_{O'}$	$(x^9, 1)$

Table 12. Addition sequences

Curve	s	n	Addition sequence
E_9	1	6	[1, 2, 3]
E_{11}	3	10	[1, 2, 3, 4, 5, 6]
$E_{12,i}$	1	4	[1, 2, 3, 6, 12, 18, 30, 36]
E_{15}	3	8	[1, 2, 3, 4, 5, 6]
E_{16}	857500	8	[1, 2, 4, 6, 10, 11, 15, 20, 22, 25, 29, 30, 40, 50, 54, 55, 75, 100, 125, 145, 220, 250, 272, 278, 300, 440, 585, 625, 875, 900, 950, 1025, 1100, 1172, 1226, 1280, 1372, 1390, 1750, 1779, 2290, 2780, 2925, 3000, 3300, 4250, 4375, 4704, 4750, 4850, 5125, 9700, 13000, 13250, 15000]
E_{17}	4	16	[1, 2, 3, 5]
E_{18}	1029	6	[1, 2, 3, 4, 5, 7, 14, 15, 21, 25, 35, 49, 54, 61, 62, 70, 87, 98, 112, 131, 224, 245, 249, 273, 319, 343, 350, 364, 434, 450, 504, 581, 609, 784, 931, 1057, 1407, 1715, 1911, 2842, 4753, 4802, 6517]
E_{19}	3	18	[1, 2, 3, 4]
E_{24}	3	8	[1, 2, 3]
E_{25}	3	20	[1, 2, 3]
E_{26}	3	12	[1, 2, 3, 4]
E_{27}	3	18	[1, 2, 3]

An Efficient Robust Secret Sharing Scheme with Optimal Cheater Resiliency

Partha Sarathi Roy[1,*], Avishek Adhikari[1,*,**], Rui Xu[2,***], Kirill Morozov[3†], and Kouichi Sakurai[4,**]

[1] Department of Pure Mathematics, University of Calcutta, India
{royparthasarathi0,avishek.adh}@gmail.com
[2] Graduate School of Mathematics, Kyushu University, Japan
r-xu@math.kyushu-u.ac.jp
[3] Institute of Mathematics for Industry, Kyushu University, Japan
morozov@imi.kyushu-u.ac.jp
[4] Graduate School of Information Science and Electrical Engineering, Kyushu University, Japan
sakurai@csce.kyushu-u.ac.jp

Abstract. In this paper, we consider the problem of (t, δ) robust secret sharing secure against rushing adversary. We design a simple t-out-of-n secret sharing scheme, which can reconstruct the secret in presence of t cheating participants except with probability at most δ, provided $t < n/2$. The later condition on cheater resilience is optimal for the case of public reconstruction of the secret, on which we focus in this work.

Our construction improves the share size of Cevallos et al. (EUROCRYPT-2012) robust secret sharing scheme by applying the "authentication tag compression" technique devised by Carpentieri in 1995. Our improvement is by a constant factor that does not contradict the asymptotic near-optimality of the former scheme. To the best of our knowledge, the proposed scheme has the smallest share size, among other efficient rushing (t, δ) robust secret sharing schemes with optimal cheater resilience.

Keywords: Robust secret sharing, optimal cheater resiliency, rushing adversary.

[*] Research supported in part by National Board for Higher Mathematics, Department of Atomic Energy, Government of India (No 2/48(10)/2013/NBHM(R.P.)/R&D II/695).

[**] The authors are thankful to DST, Govt. of India and JSPS, Govt. of Japan for providing partial support for this collaborative research work under India Japan Cooperative Science Programme (vide Memo no. DST/INT/JSPS/P-191/2014 dated May 27, 2014).

[***] The author is supported by The China Scholarship Council, No. 201206340057.

[†] The author is supported by a *kakenhi* Grant-in-Aid for Young Scientists (B) 24700013 from Japan Society for the Promotion of Science.

R.S. Chakraborty et al. (Eds.): SPACE 2014, LNCS 8804, pp. 47–58, 2014.

1   Introduction

Secret sharing scheme is one of the key components in various cryptographic protocols and in particular distributed systems. Shamir [26] and Blakley [4] independently addressed this problem in 1979 when they introduced the concept of the threshold secret sharing. A (t, n) *threshold scheme* is a method where n pieces of the secret, called *shares* are distributed to n participants so that the secret can be reconstructed from the knowledge of any $t + 1$ or more shares, while it cannot be reconstructed from the knowledge of fewer than $t + 1$ shares, where $t + 1 \leq n$. More formally, in a secret sharing scheme, there exist a set of n parties, denoted by $\mathcal{P} = \{P_1, \ldots, P_n\}$ and a special party called the dealer, denoted by $\mathcal{D}$. A (t, n) threshold secret sharing scheme consists of two phases:

1. **Sharing Phase:** During this phase, the dealer $\mathcal{D}$ shares the secret among the n participants. In this phase the dealer sends some information, known as *share*, to each participant.
2. **Reconstruction Phase:** In this phase, a set of parties (of size at least $t+1$) pool their shares to reconstruct the secret.

In the sharing phase, the dealer wants to share the secret in such a way that satisfies the following two conditions:

1. **Correctness:** Any set of $t+1$ or more parties can reconstruct the secret by pooling their shares.
2. **Secrecy:** Any set of t or less participants can not reconstruct the secret. Moreover, for *perfect secrecy*, any set of t or less participants will have no information regarding the secret.

In the basic form of secret sharing schemes, it was assumed that everyone involved with the protocol is semi-honest. But for the real life scenario, this assumption may not hold good due to the presence of adversary. This idea leads to the development of secret sharing under various adversarial models. It may happen that some participants behave maliciously during the execution of the protocol. Malicious participants may submit incorrect shares resulting in incorrect secret reconstruction. Secret sharing schemes that either detect or identify participants who submit incorrect shares during the recovery of secret have been extensively studied. Tompa and Woll [28] first presented a cheater-detecting secret sharing scheme and this work is followed by several other works (for example, [1], [2], [11], [6], [23], [24]). McEliece and Sarwate [21] were the first to point out cheater identification in secret sharing schemes and this work is followed by several other works (for example, [17], [22], [8], [31]). Verifiable secret sharing schemes [12] have been proposed for environments where the shares given to participants by the dealer may not be correct i.e., the dealer of these shares may be corrupted. These typically involve protocols that can be performed by various subsets of participants in order to check that the shares they possess are consistent in some sense. While such schemes make it apparent that cheating has occurred, they do not necessarily permit honest participants to recover the correct secret. This observation led to *robust secret sharing schemes* [25]. Informally, robust secret sharing schemes allow the correct secret to be recovered even when some of the shares presented during an attempted reconstruction are incorrect. In this paper, we deal with robust secret sharing schemes. More specifically, we show that the share size in Cevallos et al. scheme [5] can be further reduced.

1.1 State of the Art and Our Contribution

In case of up to t cheaters among n ($\geq 3t + 1$) participants, it was observed by McEliece and Sarwate [21] that Shamir secret sharing scheme [26] is robust via its connection to Reed-Solomon codes. However, for the case when $n = 2t + 1$, the above observation does not work. One solution to this problem, considered e.g., by Rabin and Ben-Or [25] is for the dealer to authenticate shares using some message authentication code [30].

In perfectly secure (even not robust) secret sharing schemes, the size of a share is at least that of the secret. Therefore, the main point in optimization of robust secret sharing is to reduce the *overhead* needed for ensuring robustness while efficiently reconstructing the secret. If efficient reconstruction is not required and $n \geq 2t + 2$ then one may use the ideal (i.e. without any overhead) scheme by Jhanwar and Safavi-Naini [15]. The case $n \geq 2t + 1$ can also be handled by the scheme of Cramer et al. [9] which features a constant overhead. Finally, a (quasi-)linear overhead in the number of players and the security parameter with efficient reconstruction was achieved by Cevallos et al. [5].

In this paper, we show that the overhead in Cevallos et al. scheme [5] can be further reduced by applying an authentication tag compression technique by Carpentieri [7]. The later technique was in fact proposed for improving the share size of the Rabin and Ben-Or scheme [25], which was a basis of Cevallos et al. construction. Since the scheme [5] is nearly-optimal, we achieve a constant factor improvement in the overhead. For example, for $t \leq 2$ we improve the overhead of Cevallos et al. by the factor of about $2/3$.

Table 1. Comparison of Our Proposal to Existing Efficient Robust Secret Sharing Schemes

Scheme	Overhead (bits)
Rabin and Ben-Or [25]	$3nk$
Cevallos et al. [5]	$3nq$
Proposed	$(2n + t - 2)q$

Here, k is the security parameter and q, which depends on k, is the parameter associated with the overhead (more specifically, the elements used to authenticate shares are chosen from the field of size 2^q).

1.2 Applications of Robust Secret Sharing Schemes

In the information-theoretically secure setting, the most natural application of robust secret sharing is related to the distributed information storage, such as for instance, secure cloud storage. User's data can be stored with several storage providers in a shared form. Clearly, an ordinary Shamir secret sharing provides protection against *passive* attacks where unqualified coalitions of storage providers may try to recover the secret. Also, reliability is ensured such that an information loss at several (few enough) providers does not hinder the reconstruction. However, in case of *active* attacks, when provider(s) deliberately submit incorrect shares, the recovery of a correct secret becomes crucial – and this is exactly the scenario [29,18], where robust secret sharing manifests its importance.

Moreover, robust secret sharing is also related to Secure Message Transmission (SMT) protocols [13,20]. Here, the sender is connected with the receiver by n distinct channels, t of which are controlled by an adversary. SMT realizes a private and reliable transmission in this setting. Finally, the techniques used in robust secret sharing schemes may also be applied to realizing verifiable secret sharing and secure multi party computation [25].

1.3 Roadmap

In section 2, the necessary prerequisites for the proposed construction are provided. In section 3, we discuss the related definition, the adversarial model and authentication techniques. In section 4, our construction along with its security proof is provided and finally we conclude in section 5.

2 Preliminaries

2.1 Message Authentication Codes

Carter and Wegman [30] invented unconditionally secure message authentication code which is a tool that enables to verify the integrity of a message without assuming any computational hardness.

Definition 1. *A message authentication code (or MAC) for a finite message space $\mathcal{M}$ consists of a function $MAC : \mathcal{M} \times \mathcal{K} \to \mathcal{T}$ for finite sets $\mathcal{K}$ and $\mathcal{T}$. It is called ϵ-secure if for all $m, m' \in \mathcal{M}$ with $m \neq m'$ and for all $\tau, \tau' \in \mathcal{T}$:*

$$P[MAC(m', K) = \tau' | MAC(m, K) = \tau] \leq \epsilon,$$

where the random variable K is uniformly distributed over $\mathcal{K}$.

Example: $MAC : \mathbb{F} \times \mathbb{F}^2 \to \mathbb{F}$ with $(m, (\alpha, \beta)) \to \alpha.m + \beta$ is a ϵ-secure MAC with $\epsilon = 1/|\mathbb{F}|$, where $\mathcal{M}$ is a finite field $\mathbb{F}$.
More generally, as first shown in [10], [16], [27]

$$MAC : \mathbb{F}^l \times \mathbb{F}^2 \to \mathbb{F}, ((m_1, \ldots, m_l), (\alpha, \beta)) \to \Sigma_{k=1}^l \alpha^i.m_i + \beta \tag{1}$$

is a ϵ-secure MAC with $\epsilon = l/|\mathbb{F}|$.

2.2   The Reed-Solomon Code

Let $(a_0, \ldots, a_t) \in \mathbb{F}^{t+1}$ and $f(x) = a_0 + a_1 x + \ldots + a_t x^t \in \mathbb{F}[X]$ be a polynomial of degree at most t. Let $x_1, x_2, \ldots, x_n \in \mathbb{F} \backslash \{0\}$, for $n > t$, be distinct elements. Then $C = (f(x_1), f(x_2), \ldots, f(x_n))$ is a codeword of Reed-Solomon error correcting code [19] of the message $(a_0, \ldots, a_t)$. Reed-Solomon code can correct up to e erroneous symbols, i.e. when e out of n evaluation points $f(x_i)$ $(1 \leq i \leq n)$ are manipulated, the polynomial (i.e., the message) can be uniquely determined if and only if $n \geq t + 1 + 2e$. Note that there exist efficient algorithms implementing Reed-Solomon decoding, such as Berlekamp-Welch algorithm [3].

3 (t, δ) Robust Secret Sharing Scheme

In a (t, δ) *robust secret sharing scheme*, there exists a set of n participants, denoted by $\mathcal{P} = \{P_1, \ldots, P_n\}$ and two special participants called the dealer and the reconstructor, denoted by $\mathcal{D}$ and $\mathcal{R}$ respectively. A (t, δ) robust secret sharing scheme consists of two phases:

1. **Sharing Phase:** During this phase, the dealer $\mathcal{D}$ shares the secret among the n participants. In this phase the dealer sends some information, which is known as *share*, to each participant.
2. **Reconstruction Phase:** In this phase, all the participants communicate their shares to the reconstructor.

In the sharing phase the dealer, in presence of an adversary $\mathcal{A}$ who can corrupt at most t participants, wants to share the secret s ($\in$ *secret space*) in such a way that satisfies the following two conditions:

1. **Privacy:** Before reconstruction phase is started, the adversary has no more information on the shared secret s than he had before the execution of sharing phase. This is called *perfect* privacy.
2. **Reconstructibility:** At the end of reconstruction phase, the reconstructor $\mathcal{R}$ outputs $s = s'$ except with probability at most δ.

3.1   Adversarial Model

The dealer $\mathcal{D}$ and the reconstructor $\mathcal{R}$ are assumed to be honest. The dealer delivers the shares to respective participants over point-to-point private channels.

We assume that $\mathcal{A}$ is computationally unbounded, active, adaptive, rushing adversary who can corrupt up to $t < n/2$ participants (but neither $\mathcal{D}$ nor $\mathcal{R}$). Once a participant P_i is corrupted, the adversary learns her share and internal state. Moreover from that point onwards, $\mathcal{A}$ has full control over P_i. By being *active*, we mean that $\mathcal{A}$ can deviate from the protocol in an arbitrary manner. By being *adaptive*, we mean that after each corruption, $\mathcal{A}$ can decide on whom to corrupt next, depending on the information she has obtained so far. During the reconstruction phase, the adversary gets to see the communication between all participants P_i and the reconstructor $\mathcal{R}$. By assumption, the adversary controls the information that the corrupted participants send to $\mathcal{R}$. By being *rushing* we mean that in every communication round, $\mathcal{A}$ can decide the messages of corrupted participants after seeing the messages of honest participants.

Note that assuming $\mathcal{R}$ to be honest is equivalent to assuming a broadcast channel available to each participant. In the later case, each participant simply broadcasts her share, executes the reconstruction algorithm and output the result.

3.2 Share Authentication

Suppose the dealer $\mathcal{D}$ wants to share the secret s with the help of a polynomial $f(x)$ of degree at most t over a finite field $\mathbb{F}$ as in Shamir scheme [26]. Then the share of a player P_i is just $f(\alpha_i)$, where α_i is a publicly known non-zero field element. Now, if there are some malicious participants, who can alter the original share at the time of reconstruction, the correctness may not hold good.

Let s_i be the Shamir share for the player P_i. For every pair of players P_i and P_j, P_i's Shamir share s_i is authenticated to the player P_j with an authentication tag $\tau_{i,j}$ obtained by message authentication code, where the corresponding authentication key $k_{j,i}$ is held by player P_j. Specifically, this step may be done by choosing $k_{j,i} = (g_{j,i}, b_{j,i})$ uniformly at random from $\mathbb{F} \times \mathbb{F}$ and then computing $\tau_{j,i} = s_i g_{j,i} + b_{j,i}$.

This similar method was used by Rabin and Ben-Or [25], but Carpentieri [7] observed that the authentication tags can be compressed as follows. Instead of first choosing the authentication key and then calculating the authentication tag, one may first fix the authentication tag and then may find the authentication key.

In Rabin and Ben-Or setting, for pairwise authentication, each player will get $n - 1$ keys and $n - 1$ tags. By using the above trick, one may, instead of sending $n - 1$ tags to each player, send a *seed* c_i to player P_i. Then, the necessary authentication tags will be generated from the *seed* c_i together with some public information. In fact, the *seed* for P_i is $c_i = (d_{i,1}, \ldots, d_{i,t})$, where $d_{i,j}$ for $j \in \{1, \ldots, t\}$ is randomly chosen from $\mathbb{F}$ and the authentication tag of P_i against P_j's key is $\tau_{i,j} = \alpha_i d_{j,1} + \alpha_i^2 d_{j,2} + \cdots + \alpha_i^t d_{j,t}$. Compared to the setting of Rabin and Ben-Or, each player now gets a *seed* of t field elements from which the $n - 1$ authentication tags are generated. Thus, the share size of each player is reduced by $n - t - 1$ field elements.

4 Optimal Cheater Resilient Robust Secret Sharing with Improved Share Size

The paper [5] can be considered as an adaptation of the Rabin and Ben-Or [25] scheme with modified reconstruction technique (against rushing adversary). In our proposal, we use the share authentication method derived from that of [7] (as described in the previous section) and adapt it to the reconstruction technique of [5].

4.1 Proposed Scheme

- **Initialization:** For $i = 1, \ldots, n$, let the distinct elements $\alpha_i \in \mathbb{F}_{2^m} \setminus \{0\}$ be fixed and public. Moreover, let α_i be also non-zero and distinct in $\mathbb{F}_{2^q}$, where m, q are two positive integers and the cardinalities of both fields are larger than n.

- **Sharing Phase:**
  - The dealer $\mathcal{D}$ chooses randomly a polynomial $f(x) \in \mathbb{F}_{2^m}[X]$ of degree at most t, where $f(0) = s$ is the secret to be shared, and computes $f(\alpha_i) = s_i$ in $\mathbb{F}_{2^m}$, where $i = 1, \ldots, n$.
  - If $q < m$, we let $l = m/q$ (for simplicity, assuming that l is an integer) and $s_j = s_{j,1} \| \ldots \| s_{j,l}$.

    $\mathcal{D}$ chooses randomly $d_{i,1}, \ldots, d_{i,t}$ and $g_{i,j}$ from $\mathbb{F}_{2^q}$, and computes
    $$b_{i,j} = \begin{cases} g_{i,j} s_j + \Sigma_{k=1}^{t} \alpha_i^k d_{j,k} & \text{for } q \geq m \\ \Sigma_{k=1}^{l} g_{i,j}^k s_{j,k} + \Sigma_{k=1}^{t} \alpha_i^k d_{j,k} & \text{for } q < m \end{cases}$$
    where $j = 1, \ldots, i-1, i+1, \ldots, n$ and $i = 1, \ldots, n$.

  - $\mathcal{D}$ privately sends to each P_i the share
    $$S_i = (s_i, d_{i,1}, \ldots, d_{i,t}, g_{i,1}, \ldots, g_{i,i-1}, g_{i,i+1}, \ldots, g_{i,n},$$
    $$b_{i,1}, \ldots, b_{i,i-1}, b_{i,i+1}, \ldots, b_{i,n}).$$

- **Reconstruction Phase:**
  - **Round 1:** Each P_i sends $(s_i', d_{i,1}', \ldots, d_{i,t}')$ to the reconstructor $\mathcal{R}$.
  - **Round 2:** Each P_i sends
    $$(g_{i,1}', \ldots, g_{i,i-1}', g_{i,i+1}', \ldots, g_{i,n}', b_{i,1}', \ldots, b_{i,i-1}', b_{i,i+1}', \ldots, b_{i,n}')$$
    to the reconstructor $\mathcal{R}$.
  - **Computation by $\mathcal{R}$:**
    1. $\mathcal{R}$ sets v_{ij}, $i, j \in \{1, 2, \ldots, n\}$, to be 1 if P_i's authentication tag is accepted by P_j, i.e., if $b_{i,j}' = \begin{cases} g_{i,j}' s_j' + \Sigma_{k=1}^{t} \alpha_i^k d_{j,k}' & \text{for } q \geq m \\ \Sigma_{k=1}^{l} g_{i,j}'^k s_{j,k}' + \Sigma_{k=1}^{t} \alpha_i^k d_{j,k}' & \text{for } q < m \end{cases}$,
    otherwise she sets v_{ij} to 0.
    2. $\mathcal{R}$ computes the largest set $\mathcal{I} \subseteq \{1, 2, \ldots, n\}$ with the property that
    $$\forall i \in \mathcal{I} : |\{j \in \mathcal{I} | v_{ij} = 1\}| = \Sigma_{j \in \mathcal{I}} v_{ij} \geq t + 1.$$

    Clearly, $\mathcal{I}$ contains all honest participants. Let $e = |\mathcal{I}| - (t+1)$ be the maximum number of corrupted participants in $\mathcal{I}$.
    3. Using the error correction algorithm for Reed-Solomon code, $\mathcal{R}$ computes a polynomial $f(x) \in \mathbb{F}_{2^m}[X]$ of degree at most t such that $f(\alpha_i) = s_i'$ for at least $(t+1) + \frac{e}{2}$ participants i in $\mathcal{I}$.
    If no such polynomial exists then output $\perp$,
    otherwise, output $s = f(0)$.

Remark 1. In the proposed scheme, a tradeoff between cheating probability and share size can be arranged. So, within the natural restrictions, the parameters can be set flexibly. Hence, q can be smaller or larger than m.

4.2 Security Proof

Lemma 1. *The above scheme provides perfect secrecy, i.e. the adversary $\mathcal{A}$ controlling any t participants during the sharing phase will get no information about the secret s.*

Proof: The dealer $\mathcal{D}$ shares the secret s through a polynomial $f(x)$, where the degree of the polynomial is at most t in x, and the share of each P_i is

$$S_i = (s_i, d_{i,1}, \ldots, d_{i,t}, g_{i,1}, \ldots, g_{i,i-1}, g_{i,i+1}, \ldots, g_{i,n},$$
$$b_{i,1}, \ldots, b_{i,i-1}, b_{i,i+1}, \ldots, b_{i,n}).$$

Without loss of generality, we may assume that the first t participants $P_1, \ldots, P_t$ are under $\mathcal{A}$'s control. Now, according to *Lagrange's interpolation*, $t+1$ such values s_i fully define a degree-t polynomial. Thus, we need to choose one more s_i, where $i \in \{1, 2, \ldots, n\} \setminus L$ and $L = \{1, 2, \ldots, t\}$. Without loss of generality, we may assume that $i = t+1$. Let us now estimate the information regarding s_{t+1} which is available to each P_i, $i \in L$, via $(g_{i,t+1}, b_{i,t+1})$.

Case 1 $(q \geq m)$:

For all $i \in L$,

$$b_{i,t+1} = g_{i,t+1}s_{t+1} + \alpha_i d_{t+1,1} + \alpha_i^2 d_{t+1,2} + \cdots + \alpha_i^t d_{t+1,t}.$$

So, for all $i \in L$,

$$b_{i,t+1} - g_{i,t+1}s_{t+1} = \alpha_i d_{t+1,1} + \alpha_i^2 d_{t+1,2} + \cdots + \alpha_i^t d_{t+1,t}.$$

Note that the above system of linear equations is associated with the following matrix, which is non-singular in $\mathbb{F}_{2^q}$:

$$\begin{bmatrix} \alpha_1 & \alpha_1^2 & \ldots & \alpha_1^t \\ \alpha_2 & \alpha_2^2 & \ldots & \alpha_2^t \\ \ldots & \ldots & \ldots & \ldots \\ \alpha_t & \alpha_t^2 & \ldots & \alpha_t^t \end{bmatrix}.$$

It is trivial to see that the linear system is consistent for all possible values of s_{t+1}. Now, we conclude that $\mathcal{A}$ can guess the correct s_{t+1} with probability at most $\frac{1}{2^m}$ as $s_{t+1} \in \mathbb{F}_{2^m}$.

Case 2 $(q < m)$:
For all $i \in L$,

$$b_{i,t+1} = \Sigma_{k=1}^{l} g_{i,t+1}^k s_{t+1,k} + \Sigma_{k=1}^{t} \alpha_i^k d_{t+1,k}.$$

Here $q < m$, $l = m/q$ (for simplicity, l is assumed to be an integer) and $s_j = s_{j,1} || \ldots || s_{j,l}$. So, for all $i \in L$,

$$b_{i,t+1} - \Sigma_{k=1}^{l} g_{i,t+1}^k s_{t+1,k} = \Sigma_{k=1}^{t} \alpha_i^k d_{t+1,k}.$$

Now, for any fixed value of $s_{t+1} = s_{t+1,1}||\ldots||s_{t+1,l}$, we can use the same argument as in Case 1 in order to show that the probability for $\mathcal{A}$ to guess s_{t+1} correctly is at most $(1/2^q)^l = 1/2^m$.

Lemma 2. *Any corrupted participant P_i who submits $s_i' \neq s_i$ in Round 1 of the reconstruction phase will be accepted by an honest participant with probability at most $\epsilon = \begin{cases} \frac{1}{2^q} \text{ for } q \geq m \\ \frac{l}{2^q} \text{ for } q < m \end{cases}$.*

Proof: Without loss of generality, we assume that the corrupted participant is P_1 who submits $s_i' \neq s_i$ in Round 1 of the reconstruction phase.

Case 1 $(q \geq m)$:
P_1 will be accepted by honest P_j if $b_{j,1} = g_{j,1}s_1' + \alpha_j d_{1,1}' + \alpha_j^2 d_{1,2}' + \cdots + \alpha_j^t d_{1,t}'$. Thus P_1 has to guess $g_{j,1}$ correctly. Now, let

$$g_{j,1}s_i' + \Sigma_{k=1}^t \alpha_j^k d_{1,k}' = g_{j,1}s_i + \Sigma_{k=1}^t \alpha_j^k d_{1,k}.$$

Then,

$$g_{j,1} = (s_1' - s_1)^{-1} \Sigma_{k=1}^t \alpha_j^k (d_{1,k} - d_{1,k}').$$

Note that $g_{j,1}$ is independent of all information that the adversary $\mathcal{A}$ has obtained and $g_{j,1} \in \mathbb{F}_{2^q}$. Thus, P_1 will be accepted by P_j with probability at most $\frac{1}{2^q} \geq Pr(v_{1j} = 1)$. Therefore, any dishonest participant P_i submitting $s_i' \neq s_i$ in Round 1 of the reconstruction phase will be accepted by a honest participant P_j with probability $Pr(v_{ij} = 1) \leq 1/2^q$.

Case 2 $(q < m)$:
P_1 will be accepted by honest P_j if $b_{j,1} = \Sigma_{k=1}^l g_{j,1}'^k s_{1,k}' + \Sigma_{k=1}^t \alpha_j^k d_{1,k}'$. As $s_1 \neq s_1'$, at least one of $s_{1,k} \neq s_{1,k}'$. Assume that only one $s_{1,k} \neq s_{1,k}'$. So, as in Case 1, P_1 will be accepted by P_j with probability at most $\frac{1}{2^q} \geq Pr(v_{1j} = 1)$. Taking into account the union bound, P_1 will be accepted by P_j with probability at most $\frac{l}{2^q} \geq Pr(v_{1j} = 1)$. Therefore, any dishonest participant P_i submitting $s_i' \neq s_i$ in Round 1 of the reconstruction phase will be accepted by a honest participant P_j with probability $Pr(v_{ij} = 1) \leq l/2^q$.

Theorem 1. *For any positive integer t such that $n = 2t + 1$, the proposed construction forms (t, δ)-robust secret sharing scheme for n participants with the space of secrets $\mathbb{F}_{2^m}$ and*

$$\delta \leq e.((t+1)\epsilon)^{(t+1)/2}$$

where $e = exp(1)$ and $\epsilon = \begin{cases} \frac{1}{2^q} \text{ for } q \geq m \\ \frac{l}{2^q} \text{ for } q < m \end{cases}$.

Proof:
Privacy: Follows from Lemma 1.
Reconstructability: From Lemma 2, we have found that $Pr(v_{ij} = 1) \leq \epsilon$. The rest of the proof is the same as in [5, Theorem 3.1].

4.3 Discussion

Let us compute the share size. During the sharing phase, each party gets one element from $\mathbb{F}_{2^m}$ and $2n + t - 2$ elements from $\mathbb{F}_{2^q}$. Therefore, the share size of each participant is $m + (2n + t - 2)q$ bits.

Consider the following instantiation. By Theorem 1, the resulting secret sharing scheme is δ-robust for $\delta \leq e.((t + 1)\epsilon)^{(t+1)/2}$. Therefore, for a given security parameter k, setting $q = \begin{cases} \lceil \log(t+1) + \frac{2}{t+1}(k + \log(e)) \rceil & \text{for } q \geq m \\ \lceil \log(t+1) + \log(l) + \frac{2}{t+1}(k + \log(e)) \rceil & \text{for } q < m \end{cases}$,
we obtain $\delta \leq 2^{-k}$.

Every perfectly secure secret sharing scheme must have the share size at least that of the secret. The first term in the sum is responsible for this, while the second term characterizes an overhead required for the share authentication. In Table 1, we compare the overhead of our scheme with those of the schemes by Rabin and Ben-Or [25], and Cevallos et al [5]. We can see that when $t \leq 2$, our scheme reduces the overhead by the factor about $2/3$ as compared to that of Cevallos et al.

5   Conclusion

We have shown and analyzed a new robust secret sharing scheme, which combines the techniques of [7] and [5] with an improvement of share size over the robust secret sharing scheme of [5]. The scheme of [5] has nearly-optimal share size, so that our improvement is by a constant factor. To the best of our knowledge, the proposed scheme has the smallest share size, among other efficient (t, δ) robust secret sharing schemes with optimal cheater resilience, secure against rushing adversary.

References

1. Araki, T., Obana, S.: Flaws in some secret sharing schemes against cheating. In: Pieprzyk, J., Ghodosi, H., Dawson, E. (eds.) ACISP 2007. LNCS, vol. 4586, pp. 122–132. Springer, Heidelberg (2007)
2. Araki, T.: Efficient (k,n) threshold secret sharing schemes secure against cheating from $n - 1$ cheaters. In: Pieprzyk, J., Ghodosi, H., Dawson, E. (eds.) ACISP 2007. LNCS, vol. 4586, pp. 133–142. Springer, Heidelberg (2007)
3. Berlekamp, E.R., Welch, L.R.: Error correction of algebraic block codes. U.S. Patent Number 4, 633.470 (1986)
4. Blakley, G.R.: Safeguarding cryptographic keys. In: AFIPS 1979, pp. 313–317 (1979)
5. Cevallos, A., Fehr, S., Ostrovsky, R., Rabani, Y.: Unconditionally-secure robust secret sharing with compact shares. In: Pointcheval, D., Johansson, T. (eds.) EUROCRYPT 2012. LNCS, vol. 7237, pp. 195–208. Springer, Heidelberg (2012)
6. Cabello, S., Padro, C., Saez, G.: Secret sharing schemes with detection of cheaters for a general access structure. Design Codes Cryptography 25(2), 175–188 (2002)
7. Carpentieri, M.: A perfect threshold secret sharing scheme to identify cheaters. Design Codes Cryptography 5(3), 183–187 (1995)

8. Choudhury, A.: Brief announcement: optimal amortized secret sharing with cheater identification. In: PODC 2012, pp. 101–102 (2012)

9. Cramer, R., Damgård, I.B., Fehr, S.: On the cost of reconstructing a secret, or VSS with optimal reconstruction phase. In: Kilian, J. (ed.) CRYPTO 2001. LNCS, vol. 2139, pp. 503–523. Springer, Heidelberg (2001)

10. Den Boer, B.: A simple and key-economical unconditional authentication scheme. Journal of Computer Security 2, 65–72 (1993)

11. Cramer, R., Dodis, Y., Fehr, S., Padró, C., Wichs, D.: Detection of algebraic manipulation with applications to robust secret sharing and fuzzy extractors. In: Smart, N.P. (ed.) EUROCRYPT 2008. LNCS, vol. 4965, pp. 471–488. Springer, Heidelberg (2008)

12. Chor, B., Goldwasser, S., Micali, S., Awerbuch, B.: Verifiable Secret Sharing and Achieving Simultaneity in the Presence of Faults (Extended Abstract). In: FOCS 1985, pp. 383–395 (1985)

13. Dolev, D., Dwork, C., Waarts, O., Yung, M.: Perfectly secure message transmission. In: FOCS 1990, pp. 36–45 (1990), Journal version in J. ACM 40(1), 17–47 (1993)

14. Ishai, Y., Ostrovsky, R., Seyalioglu, H.: Identifying cheaters without an honest majority. In: Cramer, R. (ed.) TCC 2012. LNCS, vol. 7194, pp. 21–38. Springer, Heidelberg (2012)

15. Jhanwar, M.P., Safavi-Naini, R.: Unconditionally-secure ideal robust secret sharing schemes for threshold and multilevel access structure. Mathematical Cryptology 7(4), 279–296 (2013)

16. Johansson, T., Kabatianskii, G., Smeets, B.: On the relation between A-codes and codes correcting independent errors. In: Helleseth, T. (ed.) EUROCRYPT 1993. LNCS, vol. 765, pp. 1–11. Springer, Heidelberg (1994)

17. Kurosawa, K., Obana, S., Ogata, W.: t-cheater identifiable (k, n) threshold secret sharing schemes. In: Coppersmith, D. (ed.) CRYPTO 1995. LNCS, vol. 963, pp. 410–423. Springer, Heidelberg (1995)

18. Lakshmanan, S., Ahamad, M., Venkateswaran, H.: Responsive security for stored data. IEEE Trans. Parallel Distrib. Syst. 14(9), 818–828 (2003)

19. MacWilliams, F.J., Sloane, N.J.A.: The theory of error-correcting codes, vol. 16. Elsevier (1977)

20. Martin, K.M., Paterson, M.B., Stinson, D.R.: Error decodable secret sharing and one-round perfectly secure message transmission for general adversary structures. Cryptography and Communications 3(2), 65–86 (2011)

21. McEliece, R., Sarwate, D.: On sharing secrets and reed-solomon codes. Commun. ACM 24(9), 583–584 (1981)

22. Obana, S.: Almost optimum t-cheater identifiable secret sharing schemes. In: Paterson, K.G. (ed.) EUROCRYPT 2011. LNCS, vol. 6632, pp. 284–302. Springer, Heidelberg (2011)

23. Obana, S., Araki, T.: Almost optimum secret sharing schemes secure against cheating for arbitrary secret distribution. In: Lai, X., Chen, K. (eds.) ASIACRYPT 2006. LNCS, vol. 4284, pp. 364–379. Springer, Heidelberg (2006)

24. Ogata, W., Kurosawa, K., Stinson, D.R.: Optimum secret sharing scheme secure against cheating. SIAM J. Discrete Math. 20(1), 79–95 (2006)

25. Rabin, T., Ben-Or, M.: Verifiable secret sharing and multiparty protocols with honest majority (extended abstract). In: STOC 1989, pp. 73–85 (1989)

26. Shamir, A.: How to share a secret. Comm. ACM 22(11), 612–613 (1979)

27. Taylor, R.: An Integrity Check Value Algorithm for Stream Ciphers. In: Stinson, D.R. (ed.) CRYPTO 1993. LNCS, vol. 773, pp. 40–48. Springer, Heidelberg (1994)

28. Tompa, M., Woll, H.: How to share a secret with cheaters. J. Cryptology 1(2), 133–138 (1988)
29. Waldman, M., Rubin, A.D., Cranor, L.F.: The architecture of robust publishing systems. ACM Trans. Internet Techn. 1(2), 199–230 (2001)
30. Wegman, M.N., Lawrence Carter, J.: New classes and applications of hash functions. In: FOCS 1979, pp. 175–182 (1979)
31. Xu, R., Morozov, K., Takagi, T.: On Cheater Identifiable Secret Sharing Schemes Secure Against Rushing Adversary. In: Sakiyama, K., Terada, M. (eds.) IWSEC 2013. LNCS, vol. 8231, pp. 258–271. Springer, Heidelberg (2013)

CASH: Cellular Automata Based Parameterized Hash

Sukhendu Kuila[1], Dhiman Saha[2], Madhumangal Pal[1],
and Dipanwita Roy Chowdhury[2]

[1] Department of Mathematics, Vidyasagar University, India
{babu.sukhendu,mmpalvu}@gmail.com
[2] Department of Computer Science and Engineering, IIT Kharagpur, India
{dhimans,drc}@cse.iitkgp.ernet.in

Abstract. In this paper, we propose a new Cellular Automata (CA) based scalable parameterized hash function family named CASH. The construction of CASH is inspired by sponge function and the internal round transformation employs linear CA. For the first time, we have managed to merge the classical add-round-constant and subsequent diffusion layers. The primitive function of CASH family is proved to be secure against the state-of-the-art attacks. All the designs are implemented on Xilinx Virtex-6 FPGAs and compared with the best reported results in literature. The results show that CASH outperforms the SHA-3 finalists with respect to throughput and throughput/area.

Keywords: cellular automata, hash function, sponge function, FPGA.

1 Introduction

Cryptographic hash function is a one-way function that maps an arbitrary message input to a fixed length output. One-way Hash functions play a major role in secured communication. In todays world of mobile devices, where the operating environment is increasingly becoming resource constraint, it is imperative to design systems that are resource efficient and at the same time have low computational overhead. Even in the recently completed SHA-3 competition, NIST had stressed on the hardware efficiency of hash designs. It is evident from literature that designs that are provably secure are essentially inefficient from the implementation perspective. This brings researchers to the classical trade-off scenario where one tries to construct near optimal designs while compromising on some of the provable criterion. In this work we try to follow a similar path. In our research we have tried to exploit the properties of the Cellular Automata(CA) construction to design a hash function. In doing so we leverage on the simple, regular, modular and cascadable structure of CA with local interconnection structure that ideally suits VLSI technology. This directly gives us a construction that is by definition efficient due to the simplicity of operations involved making it suited for both software and dedicated hardware implementations. Because of its parallel execution and bit-wise operations, the regular structure of Cellular

R.S. Chakraborty et al. (Eds.): SPACE 2014, LNCS 8804, pp. 59–75, 2014.
© Springer International Publishing Switzerland 2014

Automata is well suited for hardware implementations [1], [2]. Our main aim is to construct parameterized as well as efficiently computable internal function. In addition, we provide sound theoretical proofs to affirm that our design remains secure in the light of current state-of-the-art attacks.

The idea of using CA for hash design was first proposed in CRYPTO'89 by Damgard [3]. CA was one of the three ideas to design hash function given by him. However, diffusion deficiency was reported in [1] which consequently broke the system. In the same paper, the authors promoted another hash function based on CA– CellHash [1]. It was Chang [4] who found the theoretical weakness of CellHash and he calculated that second preimage attack on it requires about $2^{128.5}$ -calls ($< 2^{256}$) of the compression function. In recent literature a few fast, lightweight hash proposals SPONGENT [5], GLUON [6], QUARK [7], PHOTON [8], [2] have taken place. Meanwhile, NIST has standardized Keccak [9] as SHA-3 hash algorithm. This standardization is for general purpose as far as usability is concerned. There are several usages of hash functions where better flexibility as well as better performance is required without deteriorating security.

In this paper, we propose a secured, parameterized, flexible hash family. The hash primitive is based on Cellular Automata. We are able to merge the classical *AddRoundConstants* layer and *Diffusion* layer into a single linear layer retaining all the advantages of those specific layers. Instead of employing same diffusive function to all rounds, our internal transformation applies round dependent distinct linear functions for different rounds. Moreover, diffusion can also be controlled by tuning an external parameter. Security analysis of the whole function has been made to show its resistance against other known attacks. The performance of the hash is compared with the top *five* hash designs of SHA-3 competition.

Our Contributions :

- CASH–a new hash function is proposed which is designed based on the simple and elegant CA structure and employs only bitwise operations making it hardware friendly.
- The construction and eventual security evaluation of CASH incorporates lessons learned during the past few years of extensive research triggered by the SHA-3 competition. This in turn implies that CASH is less likely to be susceptible to more recent attacks. The resistance against most attacks has already been theoretically proven in this work.
- The diffusion scheme adopted in CASH is innovative and introduces a new strategy to achieve round dependent diffusion that reduces hardware footprint and may motivate further mathematical analysis of this construction.
- CASH can encourage designers to look in CA based designs as an alternative design technique.

The rest of the paper is organized as follows. Section 2 describes the design in detail including design rationale of CASH. Hardware implementation results are given in Section 3. Security analysis is carried out in Section 4 and we conclude in Section 5.

2   CASH Design

The underlying primitive of CASH is Cellular Automata. So, before introducing the design, we briefly outline the concept of CA. Cellular Automata are discrete lattice of cells with a particular geometry. Each cell consists of a memory element *(Flip-Flop)* and a combinatorial logic. Cells can assume values from a finite set Q. At each clock pulse, the cells are updated simultaneously. A function $f : Q^k \to Q$ is said to be local transition rule depending on which the cell values are updated. The transition function f totally depends on local neighborhoods of cell and here the number of neighbors is denoted by k. e.g. for 3-neighborhood CA i^{th} cell at t^{th} clock cycle evolves as follows:

$$S_i^{t+1} = f(S_{i-1}^t, S_i^t, S_{i+1}^t) \tag{1}$$

If the CA is capable to generate all non-null states, starting from any non-null state, the CA is termed as maximum length CA. It has also been proved that the characteristic polynomial of an $n-$bit maximal length CA becomes a primitive polynomial of degree n. As for an example, the primitive polynomial $x^4 + x + 1$ over $GF(2)$ corresponds to the maximal length CA $[1, 0, 1, 0]$ where rule-90 is represented by $'0'$ while rule-150 is represented by $'1'$.

2.1   The Domain Extension Algorithm

In our design we have adopted a domain extension algorithm that is inspired from the sponge-construction. Though most hash algorithms use the Merkle-Damgard(MD) [10,3] mode of operation but it has been shown to be prone to several generic attacks [11] like length-extension attack, multi-collision attack [12], herding attack [13] etc. Moreover, the feed-forward nature of MD limits efficient hardware implementation thereby degrading performance. Sponge, which was introduced by Bertoni [14] gained immediate popularity in the research community. It is worth mentioning that Keccak [9], the SHA-3 winner, also has a Sponge-based mode of operation. Sponge function has several advantages over MD construction. It provides a security measure which depends on its tunable parameter. Unlike MD construction, it does not require feed-forward type state transition and hence require less hardware. Getting *variable* number of output bits is its another advantage. The proposed hash function follows Sponge function (Fig.1) as the mode of operation and thus provides simplicity, security and tuning flexibility.

For clear understanding, here we briefly sketch the sponge function. It uses a fixed internal transformation to be iterated to produce hash value. The internal state is divided into two parts : *c-bit* capacity and *r-bit* bit-rate. Initially the state is fed with some fixed value. A suitable padding rule is applied so that the length of the padded message becomes a multiple of r and with the sole constraint that the last message block be never all zero. It is then partitioned into *r-bit* blocks. These blocks go into the state sequentially by XORing with the bit-rate part. Then a fixed internal transformation *(h)* is executed over $b = (c+r)$

bit state. The convention to assign bit position number 0 to left-most bit and $b-1$ to right-most bit in the b bit state is adopted here.

The function Sponge is proved to be *indifferentiable* [15] from random oracle when the internal function is assumed to be random transformation. The security bound for an n-bit hash value, assuming h to be random transformation, is $min\{2^{\frac{n}{2}}, 2^{\frac{c}{2}}\}$ for collision resistance, $min\{2^n, 2^c, max\{2^{n-r}, 2^{\frac{c}{2}}\}\}$ for preimage security and $min\{2^n, 2^{\frac{c}{2}}\}$ for second-preimage resistance. So for optimal collision security it is enough to take $c = n$. To get optimal preimage security c should be at least $(n + r)$ and that for second-preimage security it should be at least $2n$. Hence, for general purpose hash, one needs to set $c \geq 2n$ to get optimal security for collision, preimage as well as second-preimage. Depending on the various requirements, one can make security-memory trade-offs tuning the parameter c. Padding is an important step in the preprocessing phase and must be properly dealt with to avoid attacks like the length-extension attack. In the next subsection we illustrate the padding scheme of CASH.

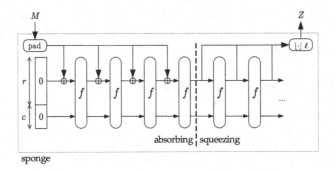

Fig. 1. Sponge Hash Construction[14]

2.2   State Preprocessing and Padding

The message M to be hashed is first padded with '1' followed by minimum number of '0's which makes padded message a multiple of r and such that the last r bits are never *all-zero*. The padded message is then partitioned into j number of chunks $\{m_1, m_2, \ldots, m_j\}$, each of length r bits, where $j = (\frac{|Pad(M)|}{r})$. Before executing absorbing phase, state is initialized with b number of 0s. In absorbing phase, right most r bits are XORed with incoming message chunk and then the internal transformation is applied. When the absorbing phase is over, r right most state bits are outputted and the same internal transformation is applied. This process is continued till n bits comes out. If n is not a multiple of r, the squeezing phase is executed $\lceil \frac{n}{r} \rceil$ times and then the output is truncated to $n-$bits. We now illustrate the round transformation function which encompasses the main novelty of this work.

2.3   Internal Transformation

The security as well as efficiency of sponge-like hash function directly depends on the security and efficiency of the underlying transformation. As mentioned earlier, our internal function is based on Cellular Automata. It acts on whole $(c + r)$ bit state and consists of n_r rounds, each of which (denoted by h) is composed of three different layers :

   Permutation layer, Non-linear layer, Linear layer.

-   **Permutation Layer:** A bitwise permutation[1] (P_b) is defined over the state to reorder the bit positions. The intention here is to distribute the input message bits into the state uniformly, setting the parameter α_i as follows:

$$\alpha_i \equiv i \times 11 \quad mod \quad (c-1) \tag{2}$$

    where i varies from 1 to r; any two consecutive entering message bits are placed 11-bit distance apart. As each permutation can be written as *composition of disjoint cycles*[2], the permutation P_b is represented as follows

$$P_b = (c, \alpha_1) \circ (c+1, \alpha_2) \cdots \circ (c+r-1, \alpha_r).$$

-   **Non-linear Layer:** CASH uses the Sbox given in Table 6 of LHASH hash function [16] The ANF of the Sbox is as follows:

$$\left.\begin{array}{l} y_0 = 1 \oplus x_0 \oplus x_2 x_3 \oplus x_1 x_3 \oplus x_0 x_2 \oplus x_0 x_1 x_3 \\ y_1 = 1 \oplus x_0 \oplus x_3 \oplus x_1 x_2 \oplus x_1 x_3 \oplus x_0 x_1 \oplus x_0 x_3 \oplus x_0 x_1 x_2 \oplus x_0 x_1 x_3 \\ y_2 = 1 \oplus x_0 \oplus x_1 \oplus x_3 \oplus x_1 x_2 \oplus x_1 x_3 \\ y_3 = x_0 \oplus x_1 \oplus x_2 \oplus x_3 \oplus x_0 x_1 \end{array}\right\} \tag{3}$$

-   **Linear Layer:** Linear 3-neighborhood Cellular Automata whose rules are determined from a set of primitive polynomials are employed at the linear layer. For each round of the linear layer a different CA-rule has to be generated. The ith rule is denoted by η^i, $i \in \{1, 2, \cdots, n_r\}$. The primary rule, denoted by $\mathcal{K}$, corresponding to each CASH variant is given in Table 5. Once $\mathcal{K}$ is selected, the CA rule for the ith round is derived from a CA of length $|\mathcal{K}|$ with rule $\mathcal{K}$ and seed η^{i-1} where $i \neq 1$. For i = 1, rule = seed = $\mathcal{K}$. This helps us to avoid storing an extra seed for the primary CA. η^i is then expanded to get the rule for the entire state. The expansion strategy to compute the rule for full state of CA from η^i is discussed in *Section 2.4*.

Selection of different parameters related to the hash algorithm is vital for making claims and ensuring and measuring the resulting security. The parameters selected in design of CASH are given in the following subsection.

---

[1] The permutation

$$\begin{pmatrix} 1 & 2 & 3 \\ 1 & 3 & 2 \end{pmatrix}$$

is equivalently represented by the cycle (2,3).

[2] The cycle (c, α_1) states that c^{th} bit goes to α_1^{th} position and vise versa after the application of P_b.

2.4   Selection of Parameters

- *Choice of Round Dependent Parameters* : In order to construct round dependent linear function, first we have to compute LHCA[3] corresponding to a polynomial. The method [17] based on Euclidean algorithm serves this purpose well. For the sake of efficiency, we choose primitive polynomials of degree $L \leftarrow (\frac{b}{2^\ell})$ such that 2^ℓ divides b and $(2^L - 1) \geq n_r$. List of primitive polynomials corresponding to different hash digests are given in Table 5. We generate b bit round dependent parameters from primitive polynomials of degree L in the following procedure. First $\mathcal{K}$, the LHCA corresponding to a primitive polynomial of degree L is generated using the technique given in [18]. From $\mathcal{K}$ compute $\eta^1 = [d_1, d_2, \cdots d_{L-1}, d_L]$ as given in *Section 2.3* and let us assume η^1 corresponds to the polynomial $[Q(x)]$. Then the expanded form of LHCA $[d_1, d_2, \cdots \bar{d}_L, \bar{d}_L, \cdots, d_2, d_1]$ corresponds to Q^2 and the LHCA $[d_1, d_2, \cdots \bar{d}_L, \bar{d}_L, \cdots, d_2, \bar{d}_1, \bar{d}_1, d_2 \cdots, \bar{d}_L, \bar{d}_L, \cdots, d_2, d_1]$ corresponds to Q^{2^2} and so on [19]. Now Q being a primitive polynomial, (except the all zero state) minimum number of cycle length that can appear in the state transition diagram of the expanded LHCA corresponding to Q^{2^ℓ} is $2^L - 1$. If 2^L is large enough, it is sufficient to choose primitive polynomials of degree L instead of b.
- *Value of 'c'* : We impose two constraints on the selection of the parameter c. First it must satisfy the inequality $c \geq n$ for n-bit hash digest. Secondly it is to be remembered that[4] $(c - 1)$ must be a prime number.
- *Value of 'r'* : The parameter r has a direct relation with the efficiency rather than security. So, depending on the application r can be any number with the constraints
  - $b = (c + r)$ is a multiple of size of the Sbox
  - L /b and be such that $\frac{b}{L}$ becomes 2^ℓ for some non-negative integer ℓ
- *Value of 'q'* : The parameter q is the number of clock cycles given in LHCA for each round function. As LHCA is composed of 3-neighborhood one dimensional CA, a single bit affects $2q+1$ consecutive bits after q clock cycles. So it provides high diffusion and as can be seen in *Theorem 1* that minimum number of diffusion occurs at rounds 2^i. We argue that the minimum value of q is 3 and q should not be a power of 2.

The specific values of the parameters c, r, n and security parameters are given in the Table 1.

Next subsection provides underlying reasons for the choice of various operations and parameters in the design of CASH hash function.

---

[3] A Cellular Automaton is called linear if it consists of linear functions only. Again a linear CA is called Linear Hybrid CA (LHCA) if all cells do not use the same rule.

[4] From *Equation*(2), we learn that to have a permutation, c should be chosen in such a way that $(c - 1)$ will become a prime.

Table 1. Specification of CASH Family

Hash Family	Hash length (n)	n_r	Capacity (c)	Bit-rate (r)	Preimage Security	2^{nd}Preimage Security	Collision Security
CASH-80	80	11	80	16	2^{64}	2^{40}	2^{40}
CASH-128	128	13	132	92	2^{66}	2^{66}	2^{64}
CASH-160	160	15	164	92	2^{82}	2^{82}	2^{80}
CASH-256A	256	15	264	248	2^{132}	2^{132}	2^{128}
CASH-256B	256	15	444	68	2^{222}	2^{222}	2^{128}

2.5 Design Rationale

The choice of operations in CASH design have sound theoretical background and are not heuristic. The following points will provide a better understanding of the theoretical framework behind the design of CASH.

- The fixed permutation provides dispersion. The permutation P_b distributes the r message bits to the entire state uniformly. Hence nearby entering bits get remote positions.
- In this nonlinear layer, each bit of the state gets updated by nonlinear functions. This being the only nonlinear part in the function, strength of security lies upon this section heavily. The smallest non-linear component is the 4×4 Sbox whose algebraic degree as well as inverse degree is 3. It can be formed from the Linear Approximation table given in *Table 7* that the *nonlinearity* of the Sbox is 4.
- The contribution of linear layer is many-fold. LHCA is given q iterations to produce much needed diffusion[5]. So each input bit propagates to a span of $(2q+1)$ output bits and each output bit depends on $(2q+1)$ input bits. Here user is allowed to get desired diffusion by fixing the *tweakable* parameter q. Note that SHA-3 algorithm *Keccak* achieves maximum diffusion when a single input bit is flipped and it propagates to *fixed* 11 output bits and each output bit depends on 11 input bits. CASH achieves as much diffusion as Keccak if one runs linear CA for $5(= q)$ cycles only and thus the diffusion of CASH can very easily be increased by increasing the number of cycles in LHCA. The name *tweakable Diffusion* is well justified as the diffusion can be controlled by the parameter q. Unlike other state-of-the-art primitives, the parameter q makes a trade-off between security and efficiency.

In the next section, the hardware implementations of CASH are outlined.

---

[5] Diffusion is measured by branch number. A measure is given in *Section 4.1.*

3   CASH Hardware

The hardware implementation of the CASH family has been carried out on Xilinx Virtex-6 FPGA and the results are presented in Table 2. The architectural details are given in Fig. 2.

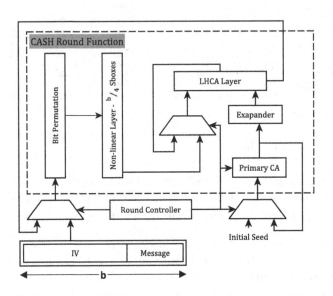

Fig. 2. The hardware architecture of CASH family

Table 2. Device Utilization of CASH Family on Virtex-6

Hash Function	Hash Length	Slices	Slice LUTs	Slice Registers
CASH-80	80	113	345	215
CASH-128	128	214	776	471
CASH-160	160	224	870	535
CASH-256A	256	483	1773	1047
CASH-256B	256	417	1589	1047

The hardware design of CASH has been made with the aim of achieving high efficiency in terms of throughput per unit area. We have compared CASH with work by Kerckhof *et. el.* [20] where they report compact hardware implementations of the SHA-3 finalists. We choose [20] since it is the nearest to our design strategy and as the implementation platform is also identical. This translates into a fair comparison which is summarized in Table 3. It can be seen that CASH is able reach throughputs as high as 1.675 Gbps which is almost double of the nearest competitor Groestl. Though the number of occupied slices is higher than others but the throughput to area ratio - 3.46 is significantly better than the rest of the hash functions. Only Groestl with an efficiency of 3.13 is closest to CASH. It is worth noting that CASH performs considerably better than the SHA-3 winner *Keccak*, which reasserts one of the motivations of this work.

Table 3. Comparative Study with *compact* 256-bit digest implementations of SHA-3 finalists [20] on Xilinix Virtex-6 platform

	Blake	Groestl	JH	Keccak	Skein	CASH-256A	CASH-256B
Input block message size	512	512	512	1088	256	248	68
Clock cycles per block	1182	176	688	2137	230	45	45
Number of LUTs	417	912	789	519	770	1773	1589
Number of Registers	211	556	411	429	158	1047	1047
Number of Slices	117	260	240	144	240	483	417
Frequency (MHz)	274	280	288	250	160	**304**	**304**
Throughput (Mbps)	105	815	214	128	179	**1675**	**459**
Efficiency (Mbps/slice)	0.9	3.13	0.89	0.89	0.75	**3.46**	**1.1**

The following section deals with the security evaluation of CASH in the light of classical and current state-of-the-art attacks.

4   Security Analysis

The domain extension algorithm being a Sponge function, the security of the hash directly depends upon the underlying function. In this section we analyze the security of the underlying internal function to satisfy the Hermetic Sponge[14] strategy.

4.1   Differential and Linear Cryptanalysis

Differential cryptanalysis (DC) is an important method to measure the cryptographic strength of a function. A differential of a function $g : A \rightarrow B$ is denoted by (a, b) with input difference a and output difference b. The cardinality of differential (a, b) is the cardinality of the set

$$\{(x, y) \in A \times A : (x \oplus y = a) \& (g(x) \oplus g(y) = b)\}$$

and the differential probability is the above cardinality divided by the cardinality of $\{(x, y) \in A \times A : x \oplus y = a\}$. Truncated differential attack is proved to be more efficient than classical differential attack. Here instead of fully specifying input-output difference patterns, active *group of bits*[6] are only concerned. The applicability of truncated differential cryptanalysis mostly depends on number of active Sboxes [7]. The following theorem measures a lower bound on the number of active Sboxes for CASH internal function.

Theorem 1. *A strict lower bound on the number of active Sboxes in a 2^x ($x \in N$, the set of Natural numbers) rounds differential trail is given by the sequence $U_{2^x} = \{U_{2^{x-1}}, 2U'_{2^{x-1}}, 2\}$ where $U'_{2^{x-1}}$ is the sequence of number of active Sboxes after $(2^{x-1} - 1)$ rounds; initially $U_{2^1} = \{2, 2\}$.*

Proof of the theorem is given in *Appendix A*.

Table 4. Strict Lower bound on Active Sboxes

#Round	2	4	8	16	32
#Active Sbox	5	11	29	83	245

Table 4 shows a lower bound on the number of active Sboxes for some specific rounds. The internal permutation of *CASH* is composed of parallel applications of Sbox. The input-output values of this Sbox are given in hexadecimal in Table 6. From the Difference Distribution Table we see that maximum differential probability is 2^{-2}. So, any n_r round differential trail consists of at least r_1 (determined by the recursive relation given in above theorem) active Sboxes and hence the maximum differential probability of any trail cannot be more than 2^{-2r_1}. Similarly from the Linear Approximation Table, we see that the maximum linear approximation probability is 2^{-2}. Because of the duality nature between differential and linear trails similar bounds can be made for linear cryptanalysis as obtained in differential probabilities.

4.2 Algebraic Attack

Algebraic attacks are used to get an insight to the internal function through equations in inputs and outputs. As can be seen in Section 2.3 the algebraic degree of the employed Sbox is 3 and hence any n_r forward round CASH must have degree at most 3^{n_r}. The algebraic degree of inverse of the Sbox is seen to be also 3 and hence similar bounds can be found for backward direction. An attacker tries to represent the Sbox in terms of equations in minimum number of input-output variables with minimum number of degree. It is a well known fact that any 4-bit Sbox can be expressed through at least 21 quadratic equations in 8 variables in $GF(2)$. So the internal function consisting of n_r rounds can be represented by $21(\frac{b}{4})n_r$ quadratic equations with $2bn_r$ variables over $GF(2)$ which is simply out of reach even for powerful attacker.

---

[6] The bits in a group is the size of the employed Sbox.

[7] The security against DC increases proportionally with the number of active Sboxes.

4.3   Zero-Sum Distinguisher

It is expected that a randomly chosen function does not have many zero-sums [21] because the existence of several such subsets of inputs can be seen as a distinguishing property of the internal permutation (h). This attack is a threat for any cryptographic primitive all of whose operations are bit oriented. $CASH$ being a primitive composed of several bit oriented operations, it has to provide a good security margin against this attack. In this regard it is to be noted that full rounds of SHA-3 standard $Keccak$ got distinguished by this attack [22].

Here, distinguisher collects some subsets ($\{S_j\}$) of input vectors (x_i) which sum to $zero$, and for which their corresponding $h - images$ also sum to $zero$.

$$\sum_{S_j} x_i = 0; \sum_{S_j} h(x_i) = 0 \quad \forall S_j \qquad (4)$$

Here degree of the round function is exploited. The main concept applies here is: if the round function h is of degree u, then the $(u + 1)^{th}$ or higher order derivative[8] of h must be zero. Hence as u gets smaller, the cardinality of the required set $\{S_j\}$ also gets smaller. Moreover one can reach more rounds by starting from intermediate round in such a way that the degree of forward and backward rounds be approximately same. So the attack is suitable for a function whose degree of forward as well as inverse round is small. Though zero-sum for any internal function does exist but the attack is practically applicable once u becomes reasonably small. The efficiency of the distinguisher directly depends on the set $\{S_j\}$: as the cardinality of the set decreases, the strength of the attack increases. In this regard, it is to be noted that the upper bound of degree of p forward round function of $Keccak$ is only 2^p and that for $CASH$ is 3^p while the degree of backward round function of both are same. The complexity of finding [9] zero-sum partition for $(2p + 1)$ round CASH is computed to be 3^p. Hence $CASH$ shows better resistance against this attack over $Keccak$. This attack also provides a measure on the number of rounds and that for $CASH$ is $n_r = 2p + 3$ where p is determined by the relation $3^p > min\{n, c\}$. The number of rounds for different variant of the hash family is shown in Table 1.

4.4   Super Sbox in Rebound Attack

Rebound attack [24] is a threat for any permutation based or block cipher based hash function. The core of the attack is based on well chosen (truncated) differential path that contains minimum number of active Sboxes. Rebound attack consists of two main phases –inbound and outbound. In inbound phase, most expensive part of the path i.e., the part of the path where more active bytes are present is covered by match-in-the middle technique. Outbound phase fulfills the differential path probabilistically and hence outbound part should have

---

[8] The derivative in GF(2) of a function h over the set $\{S\}$ is defined by $\bigoplus_{t \in S} h(x \oplus t)$ where S contains all linearly independent vectors.

[9] using the technique given in [23].

low complexity. So, a trail with most of its complexity at the middle is suitable for this attack. Basically, this sort of differential trails are found in *AES* based hash functions which have been successfully attacked. Unlike other hash constructions each round of *CASH* employs different diffusion layers and hence it is difficult to get a number of suitable truncated differential trails over a full internal permutation. Moreover, super Sbox in rebound attack tries to merge two Sbox layers into one in the inbound phase by the application of Super Sbox technique. This method is possible due to the fact that few linear operations commute with Sbox layer in AES based permutation and hence two Sbox layers in two rounds become close enough to form a Super Sbox layer. However in CASH internal permutation, linear transformation does not commute with Sbox layer and hence two Sbox layers cannot be made close enough to form Super Sbox.

4.5 Rotational Cryptanalysis

As there is no 'Add round constant' layer used in CASH, a natural choice for an attacker is to try with rotational cryptanalysis. In this regard, it is to be noted that reduced version of *K*eccak has been attacked through rotational cryptanalysis [25,26]. The very low Hamming weight of employed round constants on Keccak has been utilized to mount the attack. The basic philosophy of this attack is to exploit the rotational symmetries of the operations. Here we recall that if all the CA cells obey the same rule then the CA is called uniform CA and on the other hand when different cell uses different linear rule, the CA is called linear hybrid CA (LHCA). So in LHCA, updating rule depends on the position of the cell and it has been shown in *Section 2.4* that the rules in different rounds are different. So rotational relations get 'refreshed' in linear layer of every round. Moreover, the non-linear Sbox layer also contributes in randomizing the relations and thereby removing any such symmetry.

5 Conclusion

This paper presents a new hash function based on Cellular Automata named CASH. Here, linear CA are employed to construct the internal function along with a permutation layer. Round constant addition is merged with linear component to form round dependent linear function which provides high diffusion. CASH family is designed and implemented with different hash length and security parameters. All the designs are implemented on FPGA and the results conclude that CASH offers better throughputs and efficiency when compared with the best reported results of the top 5, SHA-3 candidates.

References

1. Daemen, J., Govaerts, R., Vandewalle, J.: A framework for the design of one-way hash functions including cryptanalysis of damgård's one-way function based on a cellular automaton. In: Matsumoto, T., Imai, H., Rivest, R.L. (eds.) ASIACRYPT 1991. LNCS, vol. 739, pp. 82–96. Springer, Heidelberg (1993)
2. Mihaljević, M.J., Zheng, Y., Imai, H.: A cellular automaton based fast one-way hash function suitable for hardware implementation. In: Imai, H., Zheng, Y. (eds.) PKC 1998. LNCS, vol. 1431, pp. 217–233. Springer, Heidelberg (1998)
3. Damgård, I.B.: A Design Principle for Hash Functions. In: Brassard, G. (ed.) CRYPTO 1989. LNCS, vol. 435, pp. 416–427. Springer, Heidelberg (1990)
4. Chang, D.: Preimage attack on cellhash, subhash and strengthen variations of cellhash and subhash. Cryptology ePrint Archieve: Report 2006/412 (2006)
5. Bogdanov, A., Knežević, M., Leander, G., Toz, D., Varıcı, K., Verbauwhede, I.: SPONGENT: A lightweight hash function. In: Preneel, B., Takagi, T. (eds.) CHES 2011. LNCS, vol. 6917, pp. 312–325. Springer, Heidelberg (2011)
6. Berger, T.P., D'Hayer, J., Marquet, K., Minier, M., Thomas, G.: The GLUON family: A lightweight hash function family based on fCSRs. In: Mitrokotsa, A., Vaudenay, S. (eds.) AFRICACRYPT 2012. LNCS, vol. 7374, pp. 306–323. Springer, Heidelberg (2012)
7. Aumasson, J.-P., Henzen, L., Meier, W., Naya-Plasencia, M.: Quark: A lightweight hash. Journal of Cryptology, 1–27 (2012)
8. Guo, J., Peyrin, T., Poschmann, A.: The photon family of lightweight hash functions. In: Rogaway, P. (ed.) CRYPTO 2011. LNCS, vol. 6841, pp. 222–239. Springer, Heidelberg (2011)
9. Bertoni, M.P.G., Daemen, J., Van Assche, G.: Keccak specifications. Submission to NIST (2009)
10. Merkle, R.C.: One way hash functions and DES. In: Brassard, G. (ed.) CRYPTO 1989. LNCS, vol. 435, pp. 428–446. Springer, Heidelberg (1990)
11. Coron, J.-S., Dodis, Y., Malinaud, C., Puniya, P.: Merkle-damgård revisited: How to construct a hash function. In: Shoup, V. (ed.) CRYPTO 2005. LNCS, vol. 3621, pp. 430–448. Springer, Heidelberg (2005)
12. Chabaud, F., Joux, A.: Differential collisions in SHA-0. In: Krawczyk, H. (ed.) CRYPTO 1998. LNCS, vol. 1462, pp. 56–71. Springer, Heidelberg (1998)
13. Kelsey, J., Kohno, T.: Herding hash functions and the nostradamus attack. In: Vaudenay, S. (ed.) EUROCRYPT 2006. LNCS, vol. 4004, pp. 183–200. Springer, Heidelberg (2006)
14. Bertoni, M.P.G., Daemen, J., Van Assche, G.: Sponge functions. In: Ecrytp Hash Workshop (2007)
15. Bertoni, G., Daemen, J., Peeters, M., Van Assche, G.: On the indifferentiability of the sponge construction. In: Smart, N.P. (ed.) EUROCRYPT 2008. LNCS, vol. 4965, pp. 181–197. Springer, Heidelberg (2008)
16. Wu, W., Wu, S., Zhang, L., Zou, J., Dong, L.: Lhash: A lightweight hash function (full version). IACR Cryptology ePrint Archive, 2013:867 (2013)
17. Cattell, K., Muzio, J.C.: Synthesis of one-dimensional linear hybrid cellular automata. IEEE Trans. on CAD of Integrated Circuits and Systems 15(3), 325–335 (1996)
18. Serra, M., Cattell, K., Zhang, S., Muzio, J., Miller, D.: One-dimensional linear hybrid cellular automata: Their synthesis, properties and applications to digital circuits testing (2009)

19. Fster-Sabater, A., Caballero-Gil, P.: Synthesis of cryptographic interleaved sequences by means of linear cellular automata. Appl. Math. Lett. 22(10), 1518–1524 (2009)

20. Kerckhof, S., Durvaux, F., Veyrat-Charvillon, N., Regazzoni, F., de Dormale, G.M., Standaert, F.-X.: Compact fpga implementations of the five sha-3 finalists. In: CARDIS, pp. 217–233 (2011)

21. Aumasson, J.-P., Meier, W.: Zero-sum distinguishers for reduced keccak-f and for the core functions of luffa and hamsi. rump session of Cryptographic Hardware and Embedded Systems-CHES, 2009:67 (2009)

22. Duan, M., Lai, X.: Improved zero-sum distinguisher for full round keccak-f permutation. Chinese Science Bulletin 57(6), 694–697 (2012)

23. Boura, C., Canteaut, A.: Zero-sum distinguishers for iterated permutations and application to KECCAK-f and hamsi-256. In: Biryukov, A., Gong, G., Stinson, D.R. (eds.) SAC 2010. LNCS, vol. 6544, pp. 1–17. Springer, Heidelberg (2011)

24. Mendel, F., Rechberger, C., Schläffer, M., Thomsen, S.S.: The rebound attack: Cryptanalysis of reduced whirlpool and grøstl. In: Dunkelman, O. (ed.) FSE 2009. LNCS, vol. 5665, pp. 260–276. Springer, Heidelberg (2009)

25. Kuila, S., Saha, D., Pal, M., Roy Chowdhury, D.: Practical distinguishers against 6-round keccak-f exploiting self-symmetry. In: Pointcheval, D., Vergnaud, D. (eds.) AFRICACRYPT. LNCS, vol. 8469, pp. 88–108. Springer, Heidelberg (2014)

26. Morawiecki, P., Pieprzyk, J., Srebrny, M.: Rotational cryptanalysis of round-reduced keccak. Technical report, Cryptology ePrint Archive, Report 2012/546 (2012), http://eprint.iacr.org

Appendix

A   Proof of Theorem Given in Section 4.1

Theorem 2. *A strict lower bound on the number of active Sboxes in a 2^x ($x \in N$) rounds differential trail is given by the sequence $U_{2^x} = \{U_{2^{x-1}}, 2U'_{2^{x-1}}, 2\}$ where $U'_{2^{x-1}}$ is the sequence of number of active Sboxes after $(2^{x-1} - 1)$ rounds; initially $U_{2^1} = \{2, 2\}$.*

Proof. The linear layer is constructed with linear CA (LHCA) which are defined by predetermined rules. If the infected bit corresponds to rule-150, infection spreads to *three* bits after 1 clock pulse while infected bit corresponding to rule-90 spreads into *two* bits. So, minimum diffusion will occur only when the local transition CA rules (in LHCA layer) corresponding to infected bits be rule-90 and at the same time they remain $2q$ bit distance apart (*Fig. 3*).

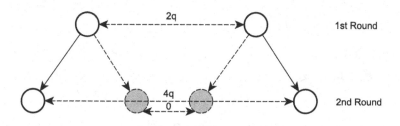

Fig. 3. Structure after round 2

Any configuration different from *Fig. 3* must produce more active Sboxes. As our intention is to find out minimum number of active Sboxes, throughout our analysis we will consider this structure as minimum diffusive structure.

If a single bit is infected at the initial state, after first round it will affect at least 2 bits with $2q$ bits apart thereby effecting 2 Sboxes i.e., if we denote U_{2^x} ($x \in N$) by the sequence of number of active Sboxes, then $U_{2^0} = 2$. Second round will infect only 2 Sboxes as internal 4 active bits will disinfect each other (*Fig. 4*). So after second round, the sequence of least active Sboxes becomes $U_{2^1} = \{2, 2\}$. The maximum internal disinfection of the active bits will happen in each of 2^x rounds only when infected bits be $2q$ distance apart. After each 2^x round, there will be only two active nodes. The active nodes maintain the stated distance for round r_i iff $2qr_i \leq b$. Going further, we see that the minimum bit distance between two infected nodes will become $2q$ at round 3. At round 2^2, the whole structure up to round $(2^1 - 1)$ repeats at each of its (after 2nd round) last two nodes.

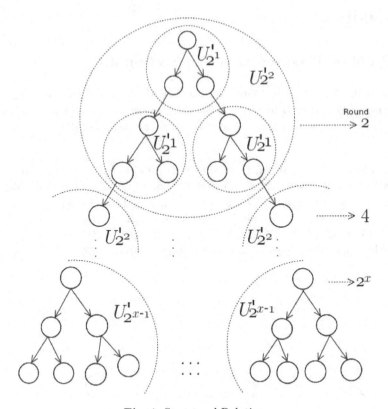

Fig. 4. Structural Relation

So after 4th round the sequence of active Sboxes become $U_{2^2} = \{U_{2^1}, 2U'_{2^1}, 2\}$ where U'_{2^1} is the sequence after $(2^1 - 1)$ rounds. If we are to maintain the minimum diffusive structure, the sequence of active Sboxes after 2^x rounds become $U_{2^x} = \{U_{2^{x-1}}, 2U'_{2^{x-1}}, 2\}$ as long as $2qr_{2^x} \leq b$.

$$U'_{2^1} = 2,$$
$$U_{2^2} = \{2,2,4,2\} \Rightarrow U'_{2^2} = \{2,2,4\}$$
$$U_{2^3} = \{2,2,4,2,4,4,8,2\} \Rightarrow U'_{2^3} = \{2,2,4,2,4,4,8\}$$
$$U_{2^4} = \{2,2,4,2,4,4,8,2,4,4,8,4,8,8,16,2\}$$
$$\text{and so on}$$

For ease of analysis we have ignored the effect of permutation P_b. But we assert that including the effect of P_b would led to more number of active Sboxes as it would violate the minimum diffusive structure. So in practice, the exact number of active Sboxes must be more than what we calculated. □

B Linear Approximation Table for LHASH[16] Sbox

Table 5. Primitive Polynomials corresponding to CASH variant

Hash Family	b	Polynomial $(Q(x))$	$\mathcal{K}$
CASH-80	96	$x^6 + x + 1$	011000
CASH-128	224	$x^7 + x + 1$	1011001
CASH-160	256	$x^8 + x^4 + x^3 + x^2 + 1$	00000110
CASH-256A	512	$x^8 + x^4 + x^3 + x^2 + 1$	00000110
CASH-256B	512	$x^8 + x^4 + x^3 + x^2 + 1$	00000110

Table 6. Sbox [16] used for the non-linear layer in CASH

x	0	1	2	3	4	5	6	7	8	9	A	B	C	D	E	F
$S[x]$	E	9	F	0	D	4	A	B	1	2	8	3	7	6	B	5

Table 7. Linear Approximation Table

in \ out	0	1	2	3	4	5	6	7	8	9	A	B	C	D	E	F
0	8	0	0	0	0	0	0	0	0	0	0	0	0	0	0	0
1	0	0	0	0	-2	2	2	-2	-4	-4	0	0	2	-2	2	-2
2	0	0	0	-4	-2	-2	2	-2	2	2	-2	2	0	0	0	-4
3	0	-4	0	0	0	0	0	4	2	-2	2	2	2	2	2	-2
4	0	0	0	0	4	0	4	0	0	0	0	0	4	0	-4	0
5	0	0	0	0	-2	-2	2	2	0	0	4	-4	-2	-2	-2	-2
6	0	0	0	-4	2	-2	-2	-2	-2	-2	2	-2	0	4	0	0
7	0	4	0	0	0	-4	0	0	2	-2	2	2	2	-2	2	2
8	0	0	0	0	0	0	0	0	-4	4	4	4	0	0	0	0
9	0	0	-4	-4	-2	2	-2	2	0	0	0	0	2	-2	-2	2
A	0	0	4	0	-2	-2	-2	2	-2	-2	-2	2	0	0	-4	0
B	0	4	0	0	0	0	0	4	-2	2	-2	-2	2	2	2	-2
C	0	0	0	0	-4	0	4	0	0	0	0	0	0	4	0	4
D	0	0	-4	4	-2	-2	-2	-2	0	0	0	0	2	2	-2	-2
E	0	0	-4	0	2	-2	2	2	-2	-2	-2	2	-4	0	0	0
F	0	4	0	0	0	4	0	0	2	-2	2	2	-2	2	-2	-2

Lattice Based Identity Based Unidirectional Proxy Re-Encryption Scheme

Kunwar Singh, C. Pandu Rangan, and A.K. Banerjee

[1] Computer Science and Engineering Department
NIT Trichy, Tiruchirappalli, India
kunwar@nitt.edu
[2] Computer Science and Engineering Department
IIT Madras, India
rangan@cse.iitm.ac.in
[3] Mathematics Department
NIT Trichy, Tiruchirappalli, India
banerjee@nitt.edu

Abstract. At Eurocrypt 1998, Blaze, Bleumer and Strauss [8] presented a new primitive called Proxy Re-Encryption (*PRE*). *PRE* is a public key encryption which allows a semi trusted proxy to alter a ciphertext for Alice (delegator) into a ciphertext for Bob (delegatee) without knowing the message. To the best of our knowledge there does not exist any lattice based identity based unidirection *PRE* scheme. In this paper, we have costructed lattice based identity based unidirection *PRE* scheme. Our scheme is noninteractive. In this scheme, we have used Micciancio and Peikert's strong trapdoor [16] for lattices which is simple, efficient and easy to implement than [3].

Keywords: Lattice, Proxy Re-encryption (PRE), Learning With Error (LWE).

1 Introduction

The concept of identity-based cryptosystem was introduced by Adi Shamir in 1984 [19]. In this new paradigm a user's public key can be a publicly known string which uniquely identifies the user. For example an email or phone number can be a public key. The corresponding private key can only be computed by a Private-Key Generator (PKG) who knows the master secret key. As a result, it significantly reduces system complexity and cost of establishing public key infrastructure. Although Shamir constructed an identity-based signature scheme using RSA function but he could not construct an identity-based encryption and this became a long-lasting open problem. Only in 2001, Shamir's open problem was independently solved by Boneh and Franklin [9] and Cocks [10].

Lattice based cryptography is a public key cryptography which is based on lattice hard problem. Seminal result of Ajtai [2] on the average case / worst case equivalence sparked great interest in lattice based cryptography. Informally,

R.S. Chakraborty et al. (Eds.): SPACE 2014, LNCS 8804, pp. 76–91, 2014.

it means breaking the lattice based cryptosystem in the average case is as hard as solving some lattice based hard problems in the worst case. So we can construct strong provable secure cryptosystem whose security depends on the hardness of lattice problem in the worst case. In addition to this, lattice based schemes enjoy following other advantages:

- Peter Shor [20] showed that once quantum computer becomes a reality all of the widely used and known public-key algorithms such as the RSA or Diffie-Hellman cryptosystems used to protect the Internet will be broken easily. Lattice based schemes are conjectured to be secure against quantum computers and holds a great promise for post-quantum cryptography.
- Lattice based schemes involve matrix vector multiplication and matrix addition with relatively small modular prime integer q. Typically q is small integer, so that basic operations involving mod q can be efficiently implemented without "big-num" library. These operations can be made more efficient using parallel algorithms.
- Fully homomorphic encryption pioneered by Gentry [12] is a powerful cryptographic primitives which makes possible the secure computation on encrypted data. Almost all fully homomorphic encryption schemes are based on lattices.

Recently Regev [18] defined the Learning With Error (LWE) problem and proved that it also enjoys similar average case / worst case equivalence hardness properties under a quantum reduction.

At Eurocrypt 1998, Blaze, Bleumer and Strauss [8] presented a new primitive called Proxy Re-Encryption (*PRE*). *PRE* is a public key encryption which allows a semi trusted proxy to alter a ciphertext for Alice (delegator) into a ciphertext for Bob (delegatee) without knowing the message. This primitive can be used in email forwarding, law enforcement monitoring, secure file system etc. Blaze et al. gave first *PRE* scheme which was bidirectional and multi-use. Bidirectional means proxy can alter a ciphertext for Alice to a ciphertext for Bob and vice-versa without knowing the message. In multi use, proxy can alter a ciphertext from Alice to Bob, then from Bob to Charlie and so on. Ateniese et al. [6] presented a first unidirectional *PRE* scheme. In unidirectional, proxy can alter a ciphertext for Alice to a ciphertext for Bob but does not allow vice-versa.

It will be interesting to combine three cryptographic primitives: lattice, identity based and *PRE* and construct lattice based identity based unidirectional proxy re-encryption scheme.

Related Work: Combining these two concepts: lattice and *PRE*, Xagawa [23] presented lattice based proxy bidirectional re-encryption scheme under LWE assumption. Singh et al. [21] gave lattice based identity based bidirectional proxy re-encryption scheme. Recently Aono et al. [4] presented first unidirectional lattice based proxy re-encryption scheme. Singh et al. [22] have shown that Aono et al.'s scheme [4] is not secure under *master secret security* model and presented unidirectional *PRE* which is also secure under *master secret security* model.

Our Contribution: To the best of our knowledge there does not exist any lattice based identity based unidirection proxy reencryption scheme. In this paper, we have costructed lattice based identity based unidirection PRE which is also secure under *master secret security* model. Our scheme is noninteractive. In this scheme, we have used Micciancio and Peikert'strong trapdoor [16] for lattices which is simple, efficient and easy to implement than [3].

Paper Outline: Our paper is organized as follows. In section 2, we describe basic definitions, security models, results and hard problems required to understand rest of the paper. In section 3, we briefly describe Micciancio and Peikert's strong trapdoor [16] for lattices. In section 4, we describe our scheme. In section 5 we give conclusion and related open problems.

2   Preliminaries

2.1   Notation

We denote $[j] = \{0, 1, ..., j\}$, set of real numbers by R and the set of integers by Z. We assume vectors to be in column form and are written using small letters, e.g. x. Matrices are written as capital letters, e.g. X. $\|S\|$ denotes the length of the longest vector in S, i.e. $\|S\| := max_i|s_i|$ for $1 \le i \le k$.

   We say that *negl(n)* is a negligible function in n if it is smaller than the inverse of any polynomial function in n for sufficiently large n.

Gram Schmidt Orthogonalization: $\widetilde{S} := \{\widetilde{s_1}, ..., \widetilde{s_k}\} \subset R^m$ denotes the Gram-Schmidt orthogonalization of the set of linearly independently vectors $S = \{s_1, ..., s_k\} \subset R^m$. It is defined as follows: $\widetilde{s_1} = s_1$ and $\widetilde{s_i}$ is the component of s_i orthogonal to span$(s_1, ..., s_i)$ where $2 \le i \le k$. Since $\widetilde{s_i}$ is the component of s_i so $\|\widetilde{s_i}\| \le \|s_i\|$ for all i. For more details please see [14].

2.2   Identity Based Unidirectional Proxy Re-Encryption Scheme(IB-UPRE)

IB-UPRE consists of six algorithms.

Setup(n): On input a security parameter n, this algorithm outputs the master public key mpk and the master secret key msk.

Extract(mpk, msk, id): On input master public key mpk, a master secret key msk, and an identity id, this algorithm outputs private key SK_{id} corresponding to an identity id.

Encrypt(mpk, id, m): On input master public key mpk, an identity id, and a message m, this algorithm outputs ciphertext C_{id}.

RKGen(mpk, sk_{id_i}, id_j): On input a secret key SK_{id_i} and a identity id_j, this algorithm outputs a re-encryption key rk_{id_i, id_j}.

Re-encryption($PP, rk_{id_i, id_j}, C_{id_i}$): On input a ciphertext C_{id_i} under identity id_i and re-encryption key rk_{id_i, id_j}, this algorithm outputs a re-encrypted ciphertext C_{id_j} for an identity id_j.

Decrypt(PP, sk_{id}, C_{id}): On input master public key mpk, a private key $SK_{id} = e_{id}$ and a ciphertext C_{id}, this algorithm outputs message m.

Correctness: Identity Based Unidirectional Proxy Re-encryption is correct if suppose $C_{id_i} \leftarrow Encrypt(mpk, id_i, m)$, $rk_{id_i, id_j} \leftarrow RKGen(PP, SK_{id_i}, skid_j)$ and $C_{id_j} \leftarrow$ Re-encryption($mpk, rk_{id_i, id_j}, C_{id_i}$), then the following equation holds.

- Decrypt $(mpk, SK_{id_i}, C_{id_i}) = m$.
- Decrypt $(mpk, SK_{id_j}, C_{id_j}) = m$.

2.3   Adaptive-ID Security Model for IB-UPRE Scheme

Here security model is adapted from [6]. Security of PRE is defined using two properties: semantic security (IND-p-CPA) and master secret security.

2.3.1 Semantic Security (IND-p-CPA)
Following security model captures the idea that when a group of polynomially bounded adversarial users and proxy collude against target delegator B, they can not get any bit of information with the condition that target delegator B never gives delegation rights to any adversarial users (including delegatee). We define security model using a following game that is played between the challenger and an adversary. This property implies both semantic security and recipient anonymity.

Setup: The challenger runs Setup (1^n) and gives the master public key (mpk) to the adversary and keeps master secret key msk to itself. Here CU denotes set of users for which adversary has made private key query (corrupted users) and HU denotes set of users for which adversary has not made private key query (honest users).

Phase 1: The adversary can make following queries.

- The adversary can issue a private key query on the identity id, challenger runs the *extract* algorithm and returns private key query d_{id} to the adversary $\mathcal{A}$. Adversary can repeat this polynomial number of times for different pair of identities adaptively.
- The adversary can issue re-encryption key query $rk_{i,j}$ corresponding to identities id_i and id_j such that either $id_i, id_j \in HU$ or $id_i, id_j \in CU$. Adversary can repeat this polynomial number of times for different pair of identities adaptivly.
- The adversary can issue re-encryption key query $rk_{i,j}$ corresponding to identities id_i and id_j such that $id_i \in CU$ and $id_j \in HU$. Adversary can repeat this polynomial times for different pair of identities adaptivly. Although it is not required since adversary knows the secret key so he can compute the re-encryption key.

- The adversary can issue re-encryption query corresponding to the identities id_i and id_j such that either $id_i, id_j \in HU$ or $id_i, id_j \in CU$. Challenger runs $RKGen$ algorithm to obtain $rk_{i,j}$ corresponding to identities id_i and id_j then challenger generates ciphertext C_{id_j} by running $Re-encryption$ algorithm.
- The adversary can issue re-encryption query corresponding to the identities id_i and id_j such that either $id_i \in CU$ or $id_j \in HU$. Challenger runs $RKGen$ algorithm to obtain $rk_{i,j}$ corresponding to the identities id_i and id_j then challenger generates ciphertext C_{id_j} by running $Re-encryption$ algorithm.

Challenge: The adversary submits identity id^* and message m. Identity id^* should belong to set HU. Challenger picks a random bit $r \in \{0, 1\}$ and a random ciphertext C. If $r = 0$ it sets the challenge ciphertext to $C^* :=$ Encrypt(PP, id^*, m). If $r = 1$ it sets the challenge ciphertext to $C^* := C$. It sends C^* as challenge to the adversary.

Phase 2: Phase 1 is repeated except that for private key query on the identity $id \neq id^*$ should not be part of re-encryption key query and re-encryption query of phase 1.

Guess: Finally, the adversary outputs a guess $r' \in \{0, 1\}$ and wins if $r = r'$.

We refer an adversary $\mathcal{A}$ as an IND-pID-CPA adversary. We define the advantage of the adversary $\mathcal{A}$ in attacking an IB-PRE scheme ξ as

$$Adv_{\xi,A}(n) = |Pr[r = r'] - 1/2|$$

Definition 1. We say that an IB-UPRE scheme is IND-pID-CPA if for all probabilistic polynomial time algorithm A and negligible function ϵ, $Adv_{\xi,A}(n) \leq \epsilon$.

2.3.2 Master Secret Security

Ateniese et al. [6] introduced *master secret security* as another security requirement for unidirectional *PRE*. Security model captures the idea that no coalition of dishonest proxy and malicious delegatees can compute the master secret key (private key) of the delegator. Ateniese et al. [6] gave following motivation for *master secret security*.

1. Some *PRE* may define two or more types of encryption schemes. In one encryption scheme ciphertext may be decrypted by only master secret key (private key) of the delegator and re-encrypted ciphertext can not be decrypted by the private key of the delegatee. Other encryption scheme re-encrypted ciphertext may be decrypted by the private key of the delegatee.
2. Delegator may want to delegate just decryption rights to delegatee but may not want to delegate signing rights to the delegatee.

We define security model using the following game played between the challenger and an active adversary.

Setup: The challenger C runs Setup(1^k) and gives the master public key mpk to an adversary and keeps master secret key msk to itself.

Challenge: The adversary submits target delegator's identity id^*.

Query Phase:

1. The adversary can issue private key query SK_{id_i} corresponding to any identities $id_i \neq id^*$ adaptively.
2. The adversary can issue re-encryption key query $rk_{i,j}$ corresponding to any identities id_i and id_j.
3. The adversary can issue re-encryption query $rk_{i,j}$ corresponding to any identities id_i and id_j.

Guess: Finally, the adversary outputs a guess x for private key SK_{id^*} of target delegator's identity id^* and wins the game if $x = SK_B$.
We define the adversary's advantage in winning this game as $AdvMSS_{\xi,A}(n) = |Pr[x = SK_B]|$

Definition 1. *We say that a PRE scheme is secure if for all probabilistic polynomial time algorithm A and negligible function ϵ, $Adv_{\xi,A}(n) \leq \epsilon$ and $AdvMSS_{\xi,A}(n) \leq \epsilon$.*

2.4 Integer Lattices ([11])

A lattice is defined as the set of all integer combinations

$$L(b_1, \ldots, b_n) = \left\{ \sum_{i=1}^{n} x_i b_i : x_i \in Z \text{ for } 1 \leq i \leq n \right\}$$

of n linearly independent vectors $\{b_1, \ldots, b_n\} \in R^n$. The set of vectors $\{b_1, \ldots, b_n\}$ is called a basis for the lattice. A basis can be represented by the matrix $B = [b_1, \ldots, b_n] \in R^{n \times n}$ having the basis vectors as columns. Using matrix notation, the lattice generated by a matrix $B \in R^{n \times n}$ can be defined as $L(B) = \{Bx : x \in Z^n\}$, where Bx is the usual matrix-vector multiplication. The determinant of a lattice is the absolute value of the determinant of the basis matrix $det(L(B)) = |det(B)|$.

q-ary Lattices. Most of the cryptogrsaphic constructions based on lattices use q-ary lattices as a basis. q-ary lattices are lattice L which satisfy the condition $qZ^n \subseteq L \subseteq Z^n$ for some prime q. In other words, any vector $x \in L'$ if and only if $x \bmod q \in L'$, where L' is a q-ary lattices.
For prime q, $A \in Z_q^{n \times m}$ and $u \in Z_q^n$, three m-dimensional q-ary lattices are defined as follows:

$$\Lambda_q(A) := \{e \in Z^m \text{ s.t. } \exists s \in Z_q^n \text{ where } A^T s = e \ (mod \ q)\}$$

$$\Lambda_q^\perp(A) := \{e \in Z^m \text{ s.t. } Ae = 0 \ (mod \ q)\}$$

$$\Lambda_q^u(A) := \{e \in Z^m \text{ s.t. } Ae = u \ (mod \ q)\}$$

2.5   Discrete Gaussians

Let L be a subset of Z^n. For any vector $c \in R^n$ and any positive parameter s, let Gaussian function centered in c be $\rho_{c,s}(x) = exp(-\pi \frac{\|x-c\|}{\sigma^2})$. Total $\rho_{c,s}(L) = \sum_{x \in L} \rho_{c,s}(x)$ over L,
So n-dimensional probability function $D_{L,c,s}$ is given as

$$\forall x \in L \ , \ D_{L,c}(x) = \frac{\rho_{c,s}(x)}{\rho_{c,s}(L)}$$

Theorem 1. *([2,3]) Let $q \geq 3$ be odd and $m := \lceil 6n \lg q \rceil$.*
There is probabilistic polynomial-time algorithm TrapGen(q,n) that outputs a pair $(A \in Z_q^{n \times m}, T \in Z^{n \times m})$ such that A is statistically close to a uniform matrix in $Z_q^{n \times m}$ and T is a basis for $\Lambda_q^\perp(A)$ satisfying

$$\|\widetilde{T}\| \leq O(\sqrt{n \log q}) \ \ and \ \ \|T\| \leq O(n \log q)$$

with all but negligible probability in n.

2.6   The LWE Hardness Assumption ([18,1])

The LWE (learning with error) hardness assumption is defined by Regev [18].

Definition 2. **LWE:** *Consider a prime q, a positive integer n, and a Gaussian distribution χ^m over Z_q^m. Given $(A, As+x)$ where matrix $A \in Z_q^{m \times n}$ is uniformly random and $x \in \chi^m$.*
LWE hard problem is to find s with non-negligible probability.

Definition 3. **Decision LWE:** *Consider a prime q, a positive integer n, and a Gaussian distribution χ^m over Z_q^m. The input is a pair (A, v) from an unspecified challenge oracle O, where $A \in Z_q^{m \times n}$ is chosen uniformly. An unspecified challenge oracle O is either a noisy pseudo-random sampler O_s or a truly random sampler $O_\$$. It is based on how v is chosen.*

1. *When v is chosen to be $As + e$ for a uniformly chosen $s \in Z_q^n$ and a vector $e \in \chi^m$, an unspecified challenge oracle O is a noisy pseudo-random sampler O_s.*
2. *When v is chosen uniformly from Z_q^m, an unspecified challenge oracle O is a truly random sampler $O_\$$.*

Goal of the adversary is to distinguish between the above two cases with non-negligible probability.
Or we say that an algorithm A decides the (Z_q, n, χ)-LWE problem if $|Pr[A^{O_s} = 1] - Pr[A^{O_\$} = 1]|$ is non-negligible for a random $s \in Z_q^n$.

Above decision LWE is also hard even if s is chosen from the Gaussian distribution rather than the uniform distribution [5,15].

2.7   Small Integer Solution (SIS) Assumption ([2])

SIS and ISIS hard problems were proposed by Ajtai [2] in 1996.

Definition 4. *Given an integer q, a matrix $A \in Z_q^{n \times m}$ and real β, find a short nonzero integer vector $x \in Z_q^m$ such that $Ax = 0 \mod q$ and $\|x\| \leq \beta$.*
OR find a nonzero integer vector $x \in Z_2^m$ such that $Ax = 0 \mod q$.

2.8   Inhomogeneous Small Integer Solution (ISIS) Assumption

Definition 5. *Given an integer q, a matrix $A \in Z_q^{n \times m}$, a syndrome $u \in Z_q^n$ and real β, find a short nonzero integer vector $x \in Z_q^m$ such that $Ax = u \mod q$ and $\|x\| \leq \beta$.*
OR find a nonzero integer vector $x \in Z_2^m$ such that $Ax = u \mod q$.

3   Strong Trapdoors for Lattices

Ajtai [2] has given a PPT algorithm that outputs a pair $(A \in Z_q^{n \times m}, S \in Z_q^{m \times m})$ such that A is statistically close to uniform and trapdoor S is a short basis for $\Lambda_q^\perp(A)$. Later on it was improved by [3]. These trapdoor generation algorithms are complex and involves costly computations of Hermite normal forms and matrix inverses.

Micciancio and Peikert [16] has given a new algorithm for generating and using strong trapdoor for lattices which are simple, efficient and easy to implement. Here we briefly describe Micciancio and Peikert's strong trapdoor for lattices [16] which is shown to be very efficient [7].

In this method, there is a gadget matrix G for which inversion (f_G^{-1} and g_G^{-1}) is easy. We know that f_A^{-1} and g_A^{-1} are hard without trapdoor as short basis. In this method strong trapdoor is matrix R not the short basis. So to invert using strong trapdoor matrix R first f_A^{-1} and g_A^{-1} are converted to f_G^{-1} and g_G^{-1} for gadget matrix G and then we know that f_G^{-1} and g_G^{-1} are easy. Detail description is as follows.

3.1   Gadget G and Inversion(f_G^{-1} and g_G^{-1}) Algorithms

Let $q \geq 2$ be an integer modulus and $k \geq 1$ be an integer dimension. Vector $g = (g_1, ..., g_k) \in Z_q^k$ is called primitive vector if $gcd(g_1, ..., g_k, q) = 1$. Let matrix $S_k \in Z_q^{k \times k}$ is a basis of lattice $\Lambda^\perp(g^t)$, i.e, $g^t.S_k = 0 \in Z_k^{1 \times k}$. A matrix G is a primitive matrix if its columns generate all of Z_q^n i.e. $G.Z^m = Z_q^n$. Matrix $G = I_n \otimes g^t \in Z_q^{n \times nk}$ and basis of $\Lambda^\perp(G)$, $S = I_n \otimes S_k \in Z^{nk \times nk}$. Matrix G, basis of $\Lambda^\perp(G)$ i.e. S are the direct sums of n copies of g^t and S_k respectively. Let $g_G(s, \epsilon) = s^t G + e^t$ and $f_G(x) = Gx \mod q$. g_G and f_G can be inverted in polynomial time. These inversions are parallelizable and offline. Inverting the functions g_G and f_G are summarized in the following theorem.

Theorem 2. *(Theorem 4.1 of [16]) For any integers $q \leq 2$, $n \leq 1$, $k = \lceil log_2 q \rceil$ and $m = nk$, there is a primitive matrix $G \in Z_q^{n \times m}$ such that*

- *The lattice $\Lambda^{\perp}(G)$ has a known basis $S \in Z^{m \times m}$ with $\|\widetilde{S}\| \leq \sqrt{5}$ and $\|\widetilde{S}\| \leq max\{\sqrt{5}, \sqrt{k}\}$. Moreover, when $q = 2^k$, we have $\widetilde{S} = 2I$ (so $\|\widetilde{S}\| = 2$) and $\|S\| = \sqrt{5}$.*
- *Both G and S require little storage. In particular, they are sparse (with only $O(m)$ nonzero entries) and highly structured.*
- *Inverting $g_G(s, \epsilon) = s^t G + e^t$ can be performed in quasilinear $O(n.log^c\ n)$ time for any $s \in Z_q^n$ and any $e \in P_{1/2}(q.B-t)$, where B can denote either S or $\widetilde{S}$. Moreover, the algorithm is perfectly parallelizable, running in polylog-arithmic $O(log^c\ n)$ time in n processors. When $q = 2^k$, the polylogarithmic term $O(log^c\ n)$ is essentially just the cost of k additions and shifts on k-bit integers.*
- *Preimage sampling for $f_G(x) = Gx$ mod q with Gaussian parameter $s \geq \|\widetilde{S}\|.w\sqrt{(log\ n)}$ can be performed in quasilinear $O(n log^c\ n)$ time, or parallel polylogarithmic $O(log^c n)$ time using n processors. When $q = 2^k$, the polylog-arithmic term is essentially just the cost of k additions and shifts on k-bit integers, plus the (offline) generation of about m random integers drawn from $D_{Z,s}$.*

3.2 $G \leftrightarrow A$

First matrix G is converted into semirandom matrix $A' = [\overline{A}|HG]$, where $\overline{A} \in Z_q^{n \times \overline{m}}$ is chosen at random and $H \in Z_q^{n \times n}$ is the desired tag. Now this semi random matrix A' is converted into random matrix A by applying random uni-modular transformation $T = \begin{pmatrix} I & -R \\ O & I \end{pmatrix}$ where matrix $R \in Z^{\overline{m} \times w}$ is "short" trapdoor matrix which is chosen from Gaussian distribution D.

$$A = [\overline{A}|HG]\begin{pmatrix} I & -R \\ O & I \end{pmatrix} = [\overline{A}|HG - \overline{A}R]$$

Definition 6. *Let $A \in Z_q^{n \times m}$ and $G \in Z_q^{n \times w}$ be matrices $m \geq w \geq n$. A G-trapdoor for A is a matrix $R \in Z^{(m-w) \times w}$ such that $A\begin{pmatrix} R \\ I \end{pmatrix} = HG$ for some invertible matrix $H \in Z_q^{n \times n}$. Matrix H is referred as the tag of the trapdoor.*

3.3 f_A^{-1}, g_A^{-1} to f_{HG}^{-1}, g_{HG}^{-1}:

g_A^{-1} to g_{HG}^{-1}: Given a trapdoor of R for $A \in Z_q^{n \times m}$ and an LWE instance $b^t = s^t A + e^t$ mod q for some short error vector $e \in Z^m$. We compute $\widehat{b}^t = b^t\begin{pmatrix} R \\ I \end{pmatrix} = s^t A\begin{pmatrix} R \\ I \end{pmatrix} + e^t\begin{pmatrix} R \\ I \end{pmatrix} = s^t(HG) + e^t\begin{pmatrix} R \\ I \end{pmatrix}$.

If $e^t \begin{pmatrix} R \\ I \end{pmatrix}$ is in $[-q/4, q/4)$ then g_A^{-1} is reduced to g_{HG}^{-1}.

f_A^{-1} **to** f_{HG}^{-1}: Given a trapdoor R for $A \in Z_q^{n \times m}$, syndrome $u \in Z_q^n$ and f_{HG}^{-1}, we have to compute f_A^{-1} which does not leak any information about trapdoor R. Inverting function f is finding short vector x such that $Ax = u$.

We sample a Gaussian z with parameter s from $\Lambda_u^{\perp}(G)$ such that $Gz = u$. Since $G = A \begin{pmatrix} R \\ I \end{pmatrix}$ so $A \begin{pmatrix} R \\ I \end{pmatrix} z = u$ and $y = \begin{pmatrix} R \\ I \end{pmatrix} z$ lie in $\Lambda_u^{\perp}(A)$. However the distribution of y is non-spherical. This leaks information about the trapdoor R. This is corrected using convolution technique from Peikert [17]. Specifically, a perturbation $p \in Z^m$ is sampled from Gaussian distribution having covariance $s^2 - \begin{pmatrix} R \\ I \end{pmatrix} \sum_G [R^t I]$. Syndrome u is changed to syndrome $v = u - Ap$. For this syndrome v, Gaussian z is sampled from $\Lambda_u^{\perp}(G)$ such that $Gz = v$. Now $A \begin{pmatrix} R \\ I \end{pmatrix} z = v$, $y = \begin{pmatrix} R \\ I \end{pmatrix} z \in \Lambda_u^{\perp}(A)$ and $Ay = v$. This implies $Ay = u - Ap \Rightarrow A(y + p) = u$ or $Ax = u$ where $x = y + p$. Since the distribution of y is non-spherical and the covariances of p and y are additive, the overall distribution of $x = y + p$ is spherical and does not leak any information about the trapdoor R.

4   Lattice Based Identity Based Unidirectional Proxy Re-Encryption Scheme

Before describing our scheme, first we describe functions **Bits()** and **Power2()** used in [4]. These functions are also used in our scheme.

Let $v = (v_1, \ldots, v_m) \in Z_q^m$, $k = \lceil lg\, q \rceil$ and $(b_{i,1}, \ldots, b_{i,k})$ be the bit representation of v_i such that $v_i = \sum_{j=1}^k 2^j b_{i,j}$. Then **Bits()** is defined as

$$Bits(v) = [b_{1,1} \ldots b_{m,1} | b_{1,2} \ldots b_{m,2} | \ldots | b_{1,k} \ldots b_{m,k}] \in \{0,1\}^{1 \times mk}$$

(First m bits are first bit of $v_1, \ldots, v_m$ and next m bits are second bit of $v_1, \ldots, v_m$ and so on).

Let $X = [X_1 | \ldots | X_l] \in Z_q^{m \times l}$ where X_i are columns. Then

$$Power2(X) = \begin{bmatrix} X_1 \ldots X_l \\ 2X_1 \ldots 2X_l \\ \vdots \quad \vdots \\ 2^{k-1}X_1 \ldots 2^{k-1}X_l \end{bmatrix} \in Z_q^{mk \times l}$$

It can be shown that

$$Bits(v)Power2(X) = vX \in Z_q^{1 \times l}$$

Now we describe our scheme which is based on [13,4].

Setup(n): On input a security parameter n, we set the parameter modulus $q = poly(n)$, a parameter $m = O(nlog\ q) = O(nlog\ n)$ and $k = \lceil lg\ q \rceil$. We choose two hash functions K_1, K_2 such that $K_1 : \{0,1\}^* \to Z_q^{n \times l}$ and $K_2 : \{0,1\}^* \to Z_q^{nk \times l}$ where l is the length of the message. We choose two Gadget matrices $G_1 \in Z_q^{n \times nk}$ and $G_2 \in Z_q^{nk \times nkk}$. Gadget matrix G_1 is converted into random matrix $A \in Z_q^{n \times m}$ by $A = [\overline{A}|G_1 - \overline{A}R]$, where $\overline{A} \in Z_q^{n \times (m-nk)}$ is chosen at random and $R_1 \in Z_q^{(m-nk) \times nk}$ is "short" trapdoor matrix.

Similarly Gadget matrix G_2 is converted into random matrix $X \in Z_q^{nk \times mk}$ by $X = [\overline{X}|G_2 - \overline{X}R_2]$, where $\overline{X} \in Z_q^{nk \times (mk-nkk)}$ is chosen at random and $R_2 \in Z_q^{(mk-nkk) \times nkk}$ is "short" trapdoor matrix chosen from Gaussian distribution D chosen from Gaussian distribution D. For more detail please see section 3. So master public key mpk is (A, X) and master secret key is $msk = R = (R_1, R_2)$.

Extract($mpk, R = (R_1, R_2), id$): Let $U_1 = (u_{1,1}, \ldots, u_{1,l}) = K_1(id) \in Z_q^{n \times l}$ and $U_2 = (u_{2,1}, \ldots, u_{2,l}) = K_2(id) \in Z_q^{nk \times l}$. Secret key SK_{id,U_1} corresponding to the identity id and U_1 is collection of l short column vector $x_{1,i}$'s such that $Ax_{1,i} = u_{1,i}\ mod\ q$ for all $1 \le i \le l$ (or $x_{1,i} \leftarrow f_A^{-1}(u_{1,i})$). So $SK_{id,U_1} = x_{1,1}, \ldots, x_{1,l} \in Z_q^{m \times l}$. Secret key SK_{id,U_2} corresponding to the identity id and U_2 is collection of l short column vector $x_{2,i}$'s such that $Ax_{2,i} = u_{2,i}\ mod\ q$ for all $1 \le i \le l$ (or $x_{2,i} \leftarrow f_A^{-1}(u_{2,i})$). So $SK_{id,U_2} = x_{2,1}, \ldots, x_{2,l} \in Z_q^{mk \times l}$. Return $SK_{id} = (SK_{id,U_1}, SK_{id,U_2}) \in Z_q^{m \times l} \times Z_q^{mk \times l}$.

Encrypt(PP, m, P_1, P_2): To encrypt a message $m \in \{0,1\}^l$, we do the following.

- We choose $s \leftarrow Z_q^n$ uniformly.
- Compute $c_1 = A^T s + e$, where $e \leftarrow \chi^m$. Here χ^m is error (Gaussian) distribution.
- Compute $c_2 = U_1^T s + m\lfloor \frac{q}{2} \rfloor + \overline{e}$, where $\overline{e} \leftarrow \chi^l$. Here χ^l is error (Gaussian) distribution.
- Output the ciphertext $C = (c_1, c_2) \in Z_q^{1 \times (m+l)}$.

RKGen($PP, id, SK_{id} = (SK_{id,U_1}, SK_{id,U_2})$): On input of Alice's private key SK_{id_A} and Bob's public key id_B, we do the following.

1. We choose noise vectors $e_1 \in \psi_s^{mk \times nk}$ and $e_2 \in \psi_s^{mk \times l}$ where ψ_s is a Gaussian distribution.
2. We compute proxy re-encryption key $rk_{id_A, id_B} = Q$ where

$$Q = \begin{bmatrix} e_1 X & e_1 U_2 + e_2 + Power2(SK_{id_A}) \\ 0_{l \times mk} & I_{l \times l} \end{bmatrix} \in Z_q^{(mk+l) \times (mk+l)}$$

Re-Encrypt($mpk, rk_{id_A, id_B}, C_{id_A}$): On input of re-encryption key rk_{id_A, id_B}, proxy alters Alice'ciphertext C_{id_A} to Bob's ciphertext C_{id_B} by the following equation.

$$C_{id_B} = (c_{1B}, c_{2B}) = [Bits(c_1)|c_2].rk_{A,B} \in Z_q^{1 \times (mk+l)}$$

Decrypt(PP, SK_{id}, C): To decrypt $C = (c_1, c_2)$, we do the following.

1. If size of the ciphertext $\|C\| = m + l$ (ciphertext is normal ciphertext) then
   - We compute $b = c_2 - SK_{id,U_1}^T c_1 \in Z_q^{1 \times l}$. We parse b as $b_1, \ldots, b_l$.
   - If b_i is closer to 0 than $\lfloor \frac{q}{2} \rfloor$ mod q then $b_i = 0$ else $b_i = 1$.
   - Output $b = b_1, \ldots, b_l$.
2. Else if the size of the ciphertext $\|C\| = mk + l$ (ciphertext is re-encrypted ciphertext) then
   - We compute $b = c_2 - SK_{id,U_2}^T c_1 \in Z_q^{1 \times l}$. We parse b as $b_1, \ldots, b_l$.
   - If b_i is closer to 0 than $\lfloor \frac{q}{2} \rfloor$ mod q then $b_i = 0$ else $b_i = 1$.
   - Output $b = b_1, \ldots, b_l$.

Correctness: First we decrypt the normal ciphertext

$$c_2 - SK_{id,U_1}^T c_1 = \bar{e} - SK_{id,U_1}^T e + m \lfloor \frac{q}{2} \rfloor,$$

which will yield m if $\bar{e} - SK_{id,U_1}^T e$ is less than $\lfloor \frac{q}{4} \rfloor$. Since these terms $e, \bar{e}$, and SK_{id_A, U_1} are drawn from Gaussian distribution ψ_s so with some $s = \alpha_q$ it is possible that $\bar{e} - SK_{id,U_1}^T e$ is less than $\lfloor \frac{q}{4} \rfloor$. Now we decrypt the re-encrypted ciphertext

$$[Bits(c_1)|c_2].rk_{id_A,id_B}. \begin{bmatrix} -SK_{id_B} \\ I_{l \times l} \end{bmatrix} = [Bits(c_1)|c_2]. \begin{bmatrix} e_1 X & e_1 U_2 + e_2 - Power2(SK_{id_A,U_1}) \\ 0_{l \times mk} & I_{l \times l} \end{bmatrix} \begin{bmatrix} -SK_{id_B,U_2} \\ I_{l \times l} \end{bmatrix}$$

$$= [Bits(c_1)|c_2]. \begin{bmatrix} e_2 - Power2(SK_{id_A}) \\ I_{l \times l} \end{bmatrix}$$

$$= Bits(c_1)e_2 - Bits(c_1)Power2(SK_{id_A,U_1}) + c_2$$

$$= Bits(c_1)e_2 - c_1 SK_{id_A,U_1} + c_2$$

$$= Bits(c_1)e_2 - eSK_{id_A,U_1} + \bar{e} + m \lfloor \frac{q}{2} \rfloor$$

which will yield m if $Bits(c_1)e_2 - eSK_{id_A,U_1} + \bar{e}$ is less than $\lfloor \frac{q}{4} \rfloor$.

Since $e_2, e, \bar{e}, SK_{id_A,U_1}$ are from Gaussian distribution ψ_s so with some $s = \alpha_q$ it is possible that $Bits(c_1)e_2 - eSK_{id_A,U_1} + \bar{e}$ is less than $\lfloor \frac{q}{4} \rfloor$.

Theorem 3. *Lattice based identity based unidirectional* PRE *scheme is IND-p-CPA (semantic) secure assuming the decision* $LWE_{q,\chi}$ *is hard or* $Adv_{B,LWE_{q,\chi}}(n) = Adv_{\chi,A}(n)$.

Proof: Here proof is similar to the proof of [4,22]. We now show semantic security of *PRE*. We will show that if there exist a PPT adversary $\mathcal{A}$ that breaks unidirectional *PRE* scheme with some non-negligible probability then there must exist a PPT challenger $\mathcal{B}$ that solves decision LWE hard problem with non-negligible probability by simulating views of $\mathcal{A}$. Here CU denotes set of users for which adversary has made private key query (corrupted users) and HU denotes set of users for which adversary has not made private key query (honest users). For our proof, we make following assumptions.

1. We assume that for CU, adversary will directly ask (not like hash then private key query) private key query and challenger will return private key with hash of the identity of the user.
2. For HU, adversary will ask only hash query of the identity of the user.

Challenger (adversary $\mathcal{B}$) randomly chooses the matrices $A \in Z_q^{n \times m}$ and $X \in Z_q^{nk \times mk}$ sets the master public key is (A, X).

- Hash Queries: Whenever adversary A submits a hash query on $id_i \in HU$, challenger randomly chooses two matrices $U_{i,1} \in Z_q^{n \times l}$ and $U_{i,2} \in Z_q^{nk \times l}$ uniformly and returns $U_{i,1}, U_{i,2}$ to the adversary and stores $(id_1, (U_{i,1}, U_{i,2}))$ in a hash table (UHT).
- Whenever A submits a user secret key query for identity $id_j \in CU$, challenger $\mathcal{B}$ randomly choose two short matrices $e_{j,1} \in Z_q^{m \times l}$ and $e_{j,2} \in Z_q^{mk \times l}$ (short matrices means whose column vectors are short) from Gaussian distribution D and computes $U_{j,1} = Ae_{j,1}$ and $U_{j,2} = Xe_{j,2}$ as hash values of id_j. Challenger $\mathcal{B}$ returns $e_{j,1}, e_{j,2}$ as secret key and $U_{j,1}, U_{j,2}$ as hash values of the identity id_j and stores the tuple $(id_j, (U_{j,1}, U_{j,2}), (e_{j,1}, e_{j,2}))$ in key table (KT).

Re-Encryption Queries: Challenger $\mathcal{B}$ answers re-encryption key queries and re-encryption queries of the adversary $\mathcal{A}$ in following way.

- Whenever $\mathcal{A}$ submits a re-encryption key query for the the identities id_j and id_k such that $id_j, id_k \in HU$, challenger $\mathcal{B}$ randomly choose matrices $X_1 \in Z_q^{mk \times mk}$, $X_2 \in Z_q^{mk \times l}$ and returns

$$Q = \begin{bmatrix} X_1 & X_2 \\ 0_{l \times mk} & I_{l \times l} \end{bmatrix}$$

  to the challenger $\mathcal{B}$.
- Whenever $\mathcal{A}$ submits a re-encryption query for the identities id_j and id_k such that $id_j, id_k \in HU$, challenger $\mathcal{B}$ returns a random vector in $Z_q^{1 \times (mk+l)}$.
- Whenever $\mathcal{A}$ submits a re-encryption key query or a re-encryption query for the identities id_j and id_k such that $id_j, id_k \in CU$. Since private key is known to corrupted users so adversary himself can compute re-encryption key or re-encrypted ciphertext. (This query may not be required)

Challenge Ciphertext: Now adversary $\mathcal{A}$ submits a message m and challenged identity id^*. Challenger $\mathcal{B}$ retrieves the hash values $U^* = (U_{j,1}, U_{j,2})$ from the table UHT. Since Matrix A and matrix U^* are statistically close to uniform, challenger $\mathcal{B}$ obtains the m LWE samples from LWE oracle, which is parsed as $(A, c_1 = A^T s + e)$. Similarly challenger $\mathcal{B}$ again obtains the l LWE samples from LWE oracle, which is parsed as $(U_1^*, c_c = U_1^* s + x)$. Now challenger $\mathcal{B}$ computes $c_1^* = c_1$ and $c_2^* = c_2 + m \lfloor \frac{q}{2} \rfloor$ and sends $C^* = (c_1^*, c_2^*)$ to adversary $\mathcal{A}$. Adversary has to answer whether the challenged ciphertext is a valid ciphertext or a random ciphertext.

Phase 2: Adversary can ask query with some restriction same as in phase one.

Now adversary $\mathcal{A}$ outputs that challenged ciphertext is a valid ciphertext, then challenger will output that oracle O as pseudo-random LWE oracle. If adversary $\mathcal{A}$ outputs random ciphertext then adversary will output random LWE oracle. In other words if adversary $\mathcal{A}$ terminates with some output then challenger $\mathcal{B}$ terminates with same output and ends the simulation. So if adversary $\mathcal{A}$ breaks the scheme then there exists challenger $\mathcal{B}$ which solves decision LWE hard problem.

$Adv_{B,LWE_{q,\chi}}(n) = Adv_{\chi,A}(n)$. Hence our scheme is semantically secure.

Theorem 4. *Lattice based unidirectional* PRE *scheme is* master secret security *assuming the search* $LWE_{q,\chi}$ *is hard or* $Adv_{B,LWE_{q,\chi}}(n) = AdvMSS_{\chi,A}(n)$.

Proof: Here proof is similar to proof of [4,23]. We now show semantic security of unidirectional *PRE*. We will show that if there exist a PPT adversary $\mathcal{A}$ that can compute private key of the delegator D in our unidirectional *PRE* scheme with non-negligible probability then there must exist a PPT challenger $\mathcal{B}$ that solves LWE hard problem with non-negligible probability by simulating views of $\mathcal{A}$. Challenger (adversary $\mathcal{B}$) randomly chooses the matrices $A \in Z_q^{n \times m}$ and $X \in Z_q^{nk \times mk}$ sets the master public key is (A, X).

Challenger answers the hash query, private key query, re-encryption key query and re-encryption query as in the previous theorem.

Challenge Ciphertext: Now adversary $\mathcal{A}$ submits a message m and challenged identity id^*. Challenger $\mathcal{B}$ retrieves the hash values $U^* = (U_{j,1}, U_{j,2})$ from the table UHT. Since Matrix A and matrix U^* are statistically close to uniform, challenger $\mathcal{B}$ obtains the m LWE samples from pseudo-random LWE oracle, which is parsed as $(A, c_1 = A^T s + e)$. Similarly challenger $\mathcal{B}$ again obtains the l LWE samples from LWE oracle, which is parsed as $(U_1^*, c_c = U_1^* s + x)$. Now challenger $\mathcal{B}$ computes $c_1^* = c_1$ and $c_2^* = c_2 + m\lfloor \frac{q}{2} \rfloor$ and sends $C^* = (c_1^*, c_2^*)$ to adversary $\mathcal{A}$.

Now adversary $\mathcal{A}$ outputs private key SK_{id} of the target delegator, challenger $\mathcal{B}$ can compute e then s or in other words challenger can solve LWE hard problem. $Adv_{B,LWE_{q,\chi}}(n) = Adv_{\chi,A}(n)$. Hence our scheme is secure under *master secret security*.

5   Conclusion

We have proved that our scheme is not only semantically secure but also secure under *master secret security* model.

Acknowledgments. We would like to thank anonymous reviewers for their useful comments.

References

1. Agrawal, S., Boneh, D., Boyen, X.: Efficient Lattice (H)IBE in the Standard Model. In: Gilbert, H. (ed.) EUROCRYPT 2010. LNCS, vol. 6110, pp. 553–572. Springer, Heidelberg (2010)
2. Ajtai, M.: Generating hard instances of lattice problems (extended abstract). In: STOC, pp. 99–108. ACM (1996)
3. Alwen, J., Peikert, C.: Generating Shorter Bases for Hard Random Lattices. In: International Symposium on Theoretical Aspects of Computer Science (STACS 2009), pp. 75–86. IBFI Schloss Dagstuhl (2009)
4. Aono, Y., Boyen, X., Phong, L.T., Wang, L.: Key-private proxy re-encryption under LWE. In: Paul, G., Vaudenay, S. (eds.) INDOCRYPT 2013. LNCS, vol. 8250, pp. 1–18. Springer, Heidelberg (2013)
5. Applebaum, B., Cash, D., Peikert, C., Sahai, A.: Fast Cryptographic Primitives and Circular-Secure Encryption Based on Hard Learning Problems. In: Halevi, S. (ed.) CRYPTO 2009. LNCS, vol. 5677, pp. 595–618. Springer, Heidelberg (2009)
6. Ateniese, G., Fu, K., Green, M., Hohenberger., S.: Improved Proxy Re-encryption Schemes with Applications to Secure Distributed Storage. In: 12th Annual Network and Distributed System Security Symposium. LNCS, pp. 29–35. Springer (2005)
7. El Bansarkhani, R., Buchmann, J.: Improvement and Efficient Implementation of a Lattice-based Signature Scheme. In: Cryptology ePrint Archive (2013)
8. Blaze, M., Bleumer, G., Strauss, M.J.: Divertible protocols and atomic proxy cryptography. In: Nyberg, K. (ed.) EUROCRYPT 1998. LNCS, vol. 1403, pp. 127–144. Springer, Heidelberg (1998)
9. Boneh, D., Franklin, M.: Identity-Based Encryption from the Weil Pairing. In: Kilian, J. (ed.) CRYPTO 2001. LNCS, vol. 2139, pp. 213–229. Springer, Heidelberg (2001)
10. Cocks, C.: An Identity Based Encryption Scheme Based on Quadratic Residues. In: Honary, B. (ed.) Cryptography and Coding 2001. LNCS, vol. 2260, pp. 360–363. Springer, Heidelberg (2001)
11. Micciancio, D., Goldwasser, S.: Complexity of Lattice Problems: A Cryptographic Perspective, vol. 671. Kluwer Academic Publishers (2002)
12. Gentry, C.: A fully homomorphic encryption scheme. PhD thesis, Stanford University (2009)
13. Gentry, C., Peikert, C., Vaikuntanathan, V.: Trapdoors for hard lattices and new cryptographic constructions. In: STOC, pp. 197–206. ACM (2008)
14. Hoffman, K., Kunze, R.: Linear Algebra. Prentice-Hall, Inc. (1971)
15. Lindner, R., Peikert, C.: Better key sizes (and attacks) for LWE-based encryption. In: Kiayias, A. (ed.) CT-RSA 2011. LNCS, vol. 6558, pp. 319–339. Springer, Heidelberg (2011)
16. Micciancio, D., Peikert, C.: Trapdoors for Lattices: Simpler, Tighter, Faster, Smaller. In: Pointcheval, D., Johansson, T. (eds.) EUROCRYPT 2012. LNCS, vol. 7237, pp. 700–718. Springer, Heidelberg (2012)
17. Peikert, C.: An efficient and parallel gaussian sampler for lattices. In: Rabin, T. (ed.) CRYPTO 2010. LNCS, vol. 6223, pp. 80–97. Springer, Heidelberg (2010)
18. Regev, O.: On lattices, learning with errors, random linear codes, and cryptography. In: STOC, pp. 84–93. ACM (2005)
19. Shamir, A.: Identity-Based Cryptosystems and Signature Schemes. In: Blakely, G.R., Chaum, D. (eds.) CRYPTO 1984. LNCS, vol. 196, pp. 47–53. Springer, Heidelberg (1985)

20. Shor, P.W.: Polynomial-time algorithms for prime factorization and discrete logarithms on a quantum computer. SIAM Journal on Computing, 1484–1509 (1997)
21. Singh, K., Pandu Rangan, C., Banerjee, A.K.: Lattice based identity based proxy re-encryption scheme. Journal of Internet Services and Information Security (JISIS) 3(3/4), 38–51 (2013)
22. Singh, K., Rangan, C.P., Banerjee, A.K.: Cryptanalysis of Unidirectional Proxy Re-Encryption Scheme. In: The 2014 Asian Conference on Availability, Reliability and Security, AsiaARES 2014, Bali, Indonesia. LNCS, pp. 564–575. Springer (April 2014)
23. Xagawa, K.: Cryptography with Lattices. In: PhD Thesis. Department of Mathematical and Computing Sciences Tokyo Institute of Technology (2010)

A New Approach to Secrecy Amplification in Partially Compromised Networks (Invited Paper)

Radim Ošťádal[1], Petr Švenda[2], and Václav Matyáš[2]

[1] Government CERT, Czech Republic
[2] Masaryk University, Brno, Czech Republic
ostadal@mail.muni.cz, {svenda,matyas}@fi.muni.cz

Abstract. Usage of various key (pre-)distribution schemes (KDSs) in networks with an active attacker results in a partially compromised network where some fraction of keys used to protect link communication is known to the attacker. The secrecy amplification protocols were proposed to secure again some previously compromised communication links by using non-compromised paths to deliver new secure keys. Design of suitable secrecy amplification protocols remains a challenge in scenarios where a trade-off between necessary resources (e.g., energy necessary for transmission of message) and improvement in the number of secure links must be balanced. We inspect classes of secrecy amplification protocols known as node-oriented and group-oriented protocols proposed for use in wireless sensor networks (WSN).

We combine analysis of given protocol participant placement via a simulator and manual post-processing to provide a simpler, practically usable hybrid protocol with less steps and lower communication overhead, yet still better in terms of re-secured links than previously proposed protocols.

Keywords: Evolutionary algorithms, key establishment, secrecy amplification protocols, wireless sensor networks.

1 Introduction

Secure link communication is the building block for many security services maintained by a wireless sensor network (WSN). Secure link is usually achieved by a secret key shared between communicating parties, requiring suitable key management techniques. Common assumption in WSNs is the inevitability of a partial compromise in a network when nodes can be captured and keys extracted from the memory as no tamper resistance is usually assumed.

Our work targets scenarios where a link between nodes can be compromised yet the nodes themselves are not. A typical example comes with schemes based on symmetric cryptography, where the attacker learns a fraction of used keys, resulting in a partially compromised network. Substantial improvements in resilience against node capture or key exchange eavesdropping can be achieved

R.S. Chakraborty et al. (Eds.): SPACE 2014, LNCS 8804, pp. 92–109, 2014.

when a group of neighbouring nodes cooperates in an additional *secrecy ampli-fication* (SA) protocol after the initial key establishment protocol. This concept was originally introduced in [1] for the *key infection* plaintext key exchange, but can be also used for a partially compromised network resulting from node capture in probabilistic pre-distribution schemes [7]. A secrecy amplification pro-tocol can be executed to secure again some of the compromised links, resulting in a less compromised network. SA protocols were shown to be very effective, but for the price of a significant communication overhead. Our aim is to provide SA protocols that can secure a high number of links, but require only a small number of messages and are easy to execute and synchronize parallel executions in the real network – properties not found together in previously published SA protocols.

Also, we like to challenge the ways how performance of key distribution schemes is currently judged. If SA protocols are efficient enough to be used, performance of key distribution schemes should be also compared with the op-tion that an SA protocol will be applied.

The contributions of our work are: 1) Detailed analysis of impact of different node placement in previously published SA protocols; 2) design of a new class of SA protocols combining advantages of previously known SA protocols; and 3) a concrete efficient SA protocol outperforming previously published ones, together with its analytical and experimental evaluation.

This paper is organized as follows: the next section provides a short introduc-tion to wireless sensor networks and compromise patterns resulting from differ-ent KDSs and attack strategies. Section 3 highlights related security issues and provides an overview of related work on node and group oriented secrecy ampli-fication protocols. Section 4 describes the proposed approach of hybrid protocols taking the best from reviewed technique. Upper bound for secrecy amplification and our new manually constructed hybrid protocol are presented in Section 5. Section 6 provides a comparison with (so far) best node- and group-oriented protocols based on overall success rate. Conclusions are given in Section 7. The Appendix A provides detailed settings and observations of hybrid protocol prop-erties in terms of number of amplifications and messages.

2   Partial Network Compromise

A wide range of key distribution, establishment and management techniques were proposed (see [4] for an overview). Distinct key distribution schemes behave dif-ferently when a network is under attack targeted to disturb link key security. The impact on link key security differs based on the attack strategy used. Al-though various schemes significantly differ in the way how keys are distributed and managed, similar compromise patterns can be detected. A compromise pat-tern provides us with a conditional probability that link Y is compromised when other link X is compromised after a relevant attack.

The characteristics of a particular compromise pattern may significantly influ-ence the success rate of the secrecy amplification executed later. We will perform analysis of secrecy amplification protocols according to the following two possible compromise patterns, but our work can be extended to additional patterns as well.

2.1 Random Compromise Pattern

Random compromise pattern arises when a probabilistic key pre-distribution scheme [7] and later variants [3,6,8] are used and an attacker extracts keys from several randomly captured nodes.

In case of a node capture, all links to the captured node are compromised. If some probabilistic pre-distribution scheme like [3,7] is used, then some additional links between non-compromised nodes become compromised as well. Probabilistic key pre-distribution schemes exhibit almost uncorrelated pattern resulting from node capture and extraction of randomly selected keys.

2.2 Key Infection Compromise Pattern

Compromised networks resulting from key infection distribution [1] form the second inspected pattern. Here, link keys are exchanged in plaintext (no keys are pre-distributed) and an attacker can compromise them if the transmission can be recorded by an attacker's eavesdropping device. The weakened attacker model assumes that an attacker is not able to eavesdrop on all transmissions, yet has a limited number of restricted eavesdropping nodes in the field. The closer the link transmission is to the listening node and the longer the distance between link's peers, the higher the probability of a compromise. Typically, if the eavesdropping node is close to a legal node, most of the links to the latter can be compromised.

An eavesdropping of the exchanged key in the key infection approach [1] does not compromise nodes directly, but compromises links in the reach of eavesdropper's radio instead. Key infection distribution forms a significantly correlated pattern due to locality of eavesdropping – links close to the eavesdropper have a higher probability of being compromised.

3   Secrecy Amplification

Several secrecy amplification protocols were previously published and can be grouped according to general principles of their construction. In *multi-path key establishment*, node A generates q different random values and sends each one along a different path via node(s) C_i to node B, encrypted with existing link keys. This operation will be denoted as the PUSH protocol. All values combined together with the already existing key between A and B are used to create the new key value. An attacker must eavesdrop on all paths to compromise the new key value. A second method, called *multi-hop key amplification*, is basically a 1-path version of the multi-path key establishment with more than one intermediate node C_i.

3.1   Node-Oriented Protocols

Node-oriented security amplification protocols were firstly introduced in [1] and later enhanced and expanded in [5]. Node-oriented protocol is executed for all possible k-tuples of neighbours in the network. Note that the number of such k-tuples can be high, especially for dense networks (e.g., more than 10 direct neighbours) and resulting communication overhead is significant[1].

A variant of the PUSH protocol, called the PULL protocol, was presented in [5]. The initial key exchange is identical to the PUSH protocol. However, node C decides to help improving the secrecy of the key between nodes A and B instead of node A making such decisions as in the PUSH protocol. This in turn decreases the area affected by the attacker eavesdropping node and thus increases the number of non-compromised link keys (valid for key infection distribution).

The impact of a key composition mechanism called *mutual whispering* on subsequent amplification was also examined [5]. Mutual whispering is a key exchange where a pairwise key between A and B is constructed simply as $K_{12} = K_1 \oplus K_2$, where K_1 is the key whispered[2] from A to B and K_2 from B to A. Repeated iterations of the PULL protocols lead to a strong majority of secure links even in networks where up to 20% of nodes are the attackers' eavesdropping nodes. Note that the assumption that an attacker controls only a fraction of nodes (e.g., 10%) is reasonable, as an attacker must place his nodes before the network is deployed and therefore the density of the deployed legal network can be set to achieve the desired ratio. A detailed analysis of secrecy amplification protocols with respect to the network density and number of eavesdropping nodes was presented in [10].

One of the most advanced node-oriented protocols was defined in [11], using the method for automatic generation of secrecy amplification protocols, which utilized linear genetic programming (LGP) [2]. A detailed analysis showed that the protocol consists of previously defined mutual whispering, PUSH protocol, PULL protocol and also the multi-hop version of PULL amplification. We are using those protocols as a base for construction of more advanced hybrid protocols.

3.2   Group-Oriented Protocols

In group-oriented protocols, an identification of the parties in the protocol is no longer "absolute" (e.g., node number 1, 2, 3), but it is given by the relative distance from other parties (we are using the distance from two distinct nodes). It is assumed that each node knows the approximate distance to its direct neighbours. This distance can be approximated from the minimal transmission power needed to communicate with a given neighbour. If the protocol has to express the fact that two nodes N_i and N_j are exchanging a message over the intermediate

---

[1] E.g., (avg_neigh) * $(avg\_neigh - 1)$ * $msg\_per\_protocol\_execution$ for a three-party protocol, where avg_neigh is the average number of neighbours.

[2] Transmission is performed with the minimal radio strength necessary to communicate between two nodes, therefore nodes more distant from the sending node are not able to hear the transmission.

node N_k, only relative distances of such node N_k from N_i and N_j are indicated in the protocol (e.g., $N_{0.30\_0.70}$ is a node positioned 0.3 of the maximum transmission range from N_i and 0.7 from N_j). Based on the actual distribution of the neighbours, the node closest to the indicated distance(s) is chosen as the node N_k for a particular protocol run. There is no need to re-execute the protocol for all k-tuples (as was the case for node-oriented protocols) as all neighbours can be involved in a single execution, reducing the communication overhead significantly. See [11] for a detailed description of group-oriented protocols.

Note that inferring the relative distance from the received signal strength indication (RSSI) is usually a burden with errors resulting from the generally unreliable propagation of wireless signal and also as the relation between distance and RSSI is not linear. Relative distances used in group-oriented protocols are robust against moderate inaccuracies as a precise node position is not required for a protocol to succeed.

4 Hybrid Protocols

In this paper, we propose a new kind of protocols that combine advantages of both node- and group-oriented protocols. A protocol consists of several primitive instructions as described later in Section 5.1. Its construction is based on knowledge gained from analysis of node-oriented and group-oriented protocols.

Both mentioned types of secrecy amplification protocols covered in Section 3 have their advantages and disadvantages. As described previously, node-oriented protocols exhibit polynomial increase of messages with respect to the number of neighbours in the network. An additional issue is unknown number of direct neighbours and their placement. A protocol prepared for a fixed number of parties could fail due to lack of participants.

The group-oriented protocols do not share those issues and they show only a linear increase in messages sent with respect to the number of neighbours. The main difficulty is their complexity and complicated analysis of their behaviour. They consist of multiple times more instructions when compared with node-oriented protocols (e.g., the best performing group-oriented protocol presented in [9] has 41 instructions and might include cooperation of up to 34 nodes. Compare this to the PUSH protocol with 3 instructions and only 3 nodes involved.). Those are issues limiting practical implementation and further adoption.

Hybrid protocols proposed in this work show only a linear increase in messages sent with respect to the number of neighbours and do not require storing multiple values transmitted during the protocol execution, easing synchronization during parallel runs occurring in a real network. They are using relative distance from special nodes N_C and N_P in the same way as group-oriented protocols. They contain a lower number of instructions and their construction, analysis and implementation are simpler than for group-oriented protocols.

Steps of a hybrid protocol are as follows:

1. Every node in the network is separately and independently processed once, in the role of a central node N_C for each amplification iteration. Only direct neighbours of N_C might be involved in the protocol execution.
2. A separate protocol execution is performed once for each direct neighbour (node in the radio transmission range), this neighbour will have a special role in this execution and will be denoted as N_P (e.g., if there are 10 direct neighbours around N_C, then there will be only 10 protocol executions with the same central node N_C, each one with a different N_P).
3. The node N_P provides a list of distances from all its neighbours (as the minimal transmission power needed to communicate with a given neighbour) to node N_C. Based on the actual deployment of nodes, parties of the protocol are replaced by real identification of the nodes that are positioned as close as possible to the relative identification given by N_C and N_P in the protocol.
4. The key is updated after every protocol execution and only between nodes N_C and N_P. Also the memory slots of all participants are cleared.

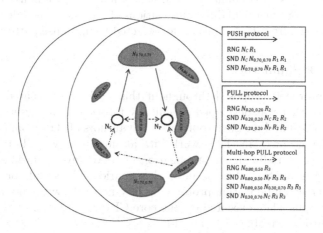

Fig. 1. An example of instructions of a basic hybrid secrecy amplification protocol. The PUSH, PULL and multi-hop version of PULL protocol are included. Selected node-relative identification (distance from N_C and N_P) of involved parties are displayed as the geographically most probable areas, where such nodes will be positioned. A probabilistic layout is shown for the case where the distance between nodes N_C and N_P is 0.5 of the maximal transmission range.

We construct protocols with application of knowledge from node-oriented protocols and statistical data about the most suitable placement of participating intermediate nodes. A hybrid protocol is executed for every pair of neighbouring nodes instead of every k-tuple as in node-oriented protocols. Other participating intermediate nodes are used for transmission of n different values for shared key update in the same fashion as previously described basic node-oriented protocols (mutual whispering, PUSH, PULL, multi-hop versions of PUSH and PULL). A visualisation of an example protocol can be seen in Figure 1. Participating intermediate nodes are not required to store any forwarded values and can erase them as soon as a message with the amplification value is forwarded to the next node towards destination. This allows for a simple synchronization even within large and dense WSNs. We incrementally improve the results of the protocol utilizing the greedy search approach for intermediate node(s) placement. All evaluations are performed on our reference network consisting of 100 legal nodes (7.5 legal neighbours on average) with originally 50% links compromised.

5   Optimal Node Placement

As was demonstrated in previous work, secrecy amplification protocols are able to provide a significant increase in secure links, e.g., from 50% of originally secured links to more than 90%. To achieve such an improvement, there is a considerable overhead in communication and on-node processing. In the subsequent section, we use a combination of different analysis techniques backed by large data sets about merits of different positions of intermediate nodes in hybrid protocols obtained from the simulator for selected compromise patterns.

5.1   Network Simulator

New hybrid protocols proposed throughout this work are evaluated using the same simulator that was developed specifically for security analysis of key distribution protocols and message routing by the authors of [11]. Commonly used simulators like ns2 or OMNeT++ work with an unnecessary level of details for our purposes (e.g., radio signal propagation or MAC layer collisions), significantly slowing evaluation of given network scenarios. The simulator is able to simulate a secrecy amplification protocol on fifty networks with 100 nodes each in about 3 seconds when executed on one core CPU @ 1.7 GHz.

The simulator is capable of performing:

- Random or patterned deployment of a network with up to 10^5 nodes together with neighbour establishment, secure links establishment and simple routing of messages.
- Evaluation of the number of secure links of probabilistic key pre-distribution protocols as described in [4]. Deployment of attacker's nodes and their eavesdropping impact on the network and evaluation of the number of secure links of published protocols for secrecy amplification of key infection approach (see [1] for details).

Protocols evaluated in the simulator are described in a metalanguage of proposed primitive instructions. Each party (a real node in network) in the protocol is modelled as a computing unit with a limited number of memory slots, where all local information is stored. Each memory slot can contain either a random value, encryption key or message. Protocol instructions were selected with the aim of describing all published secrecy amplification protocols and use only (cryptographic) operations available on real nodes.

The instruction set is as follows:

- NOP – No operation is performed.
- RNG N_a R_i – Generate a random value on node N_a into slot R_i.
- CMB N_a R_i R_j R_k – Combine values from slots R_i and R_j on node N_a and store the result to R_k. The combination function may vary on the application needs (e.g., a cryptographic hash function such as SHA-3).
- SND N_a N_b R_i R_j – Send a value from R_i on node N_a to slot R_j on N_b.
- ENC N_a R_i R_j R_k – Encrypt a value from R_i on node N_a using the key from R_j and store the result to R_k.
- DEC N_a R_i R_j R_k – Decrypt a value from R_i on node N_a using the key from R_j and store the result to R_k.

5.2   Upper Bound for Amplification Success

At first, an upper bound for amplification success (maximum number of secure links achievable by any sort of secrecy amplification protocol) can be established. A given link between nodes A and B is securable if there exists at least one secure path (no links on such a path are compromised) between nodes A and B via other nodes C_i.

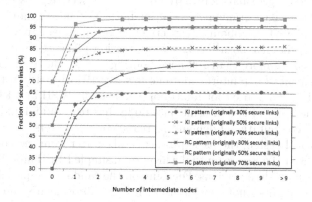

Fig. 2. Maximal possible increase in the number of secured links with dependency on the number of intermediate nodes. Results are displayed for both random compromise (RC) pattern and key infection (KI) compromise pattern. As can be seen, strong majority of secure links ($> 90\%$) can be obtained even when the initial network compromise is 50% (for RC pattern) or 70% (for KI pattern).

The upper bound of secured links can be achieved by a secrecy amplification protocol by sending fresh new keys via all possible paths between any two nodes. If there is a secure link, it will be used. However, there are two main practical limitations to such approach. First is the extraordinary high number of such paths even in a small network, resulting in unacceptable transmission overhead. Second is a high fragility to packet loss – as a network is usually not aware when particular links are compromised, fresh keys must be sent and combined together (e.g., via hash function) from all such paths – if even a single fresh key is lost, A and B will not be able to establish the same secure key value.

We used modified Floyd-Warshall algorithm to establish an upper bound for given network. The Floyd-Warshall algorithm is a graph analysis algorithm for finding the shortest paths in a weighted, directed graph. A single execution of the algorithm will find the shortest path between all pairs of vertices. As the precise compromise pattern for a given network is not known in advance (depends on an attacker, secrecy amplification protocol, exact placement of nodes, etc.), we perform multiple evaluations for different networks to obtain an average result. Details of used algorithm are available in Section A.

In the rest of this paper, we will focus more on the random compromise pattern as there are more key distribution schemes resulting in this pattern after an attack and also a bigger potential for improvement in fraction of secure links.

5.3   Intermediate Nodes Placement

We have used fifty random deployments of our reference network for the evaluation of the best placement of an intermediate node. We need to be able to address a sufficient number of distinct neighbours from two specific nodes N_C and N_P. We chose granularity of 0.01 and 0.03, respectively, as they allow us to address 10 000 (0.01 granularity used for both N_C and N_P) and 1 156 (0.03 granularity) different neighbours, respectively. Both numbers give us a satisfactory number of distinct positions in two-dimension plane as we do not expect the network density more than 100 neighbouring nodes. The granularity 0.01 is used for placement of one intermediate node w.r.t. PUSH and PULL protocols. The granularity 0.03 is used for multi-hop versions of PUSH and PULL protocols as the placement of two intermediate nodes has to be found and it presents (already high) computational demand increased by two orders.

In our protocol design, the basic protocols taken over from the node-oriented approach are used. Those are mutual whispering, simple PUSH and PULL protocols, and their multi-hop versions. Focusing on the random compromise pattern, mutual whispering does not provide us with any improvements and there is no difference between the PUSH and PULL protocol (see [5] for reasoning). The same holds also for multi-hop versions of these.

We incrementally select five intermediate nodes for PUSH and PULL protocols with the greedy search approach. Choosing the sixth node would give us only a negligible improvement with respect to the portion of secure links. We have evaluated every possible placement and the resulting number of secure links after the protocol execution. We were able to get the 83% of secure links with a single amplification. Final results are shown in Figure 6 in Appendix.

A different approach for analysis of multi-hop versions of PUSH and PULL protocol is necessary as it is not feasible to evaluate all possible particular results due to exponential state explosion with every additional intermediate node. We inspect three cases closely: 1) Specific placement of two nodes where the portion of secure links is biggest. 2) The average number of secure links calculated across all results for the first intermediate node placement is biggest. 3) The average number of secure links calculated across all results for the second intermediate node placement is biggest. In all cases, the best results were observed for placement of both intermediate nodes into the same position, effectively reducing the number of intermediate nodes. We interpret this in a way that a standard PUSH/PULL protocol gives us better or the same results as a multi-hop version of the PUSH/PULL protocol. The reason is that in the random compromise pattern, less intermediate hops mean a lower probability that compromised link will be used. Less intermediate hops also mean a lower number of all possible paths, but hybrid protocol is constructed so that not all paths are taken anyway.

A secrecy amplification protocol might be iterated multiple times for the same pair of nodes. As new links are secured in the first iteration, following iterations have a better starting position than the first one, potentially securing additional links. The final protocol works comparably with the node-oriented version of PUSH/PULL protocols on the random compromise pattern and consists of 5 independent sub-protocols (each corresponds to one PUSH/PULL protocol), resulting in 15 instructions. With initial 50% compromised links and two amplifications, we managed to get the network with 92.5% links secured, with three amplifications 94% secured links. When network has 40% initially compromised links, 91.9% links are secured after one amplification and 97.6% after three amplifications.

The search for intermediate node placement was conducted with simulations executing with only one amplification of particular basic protocols. As we expect more than one amplification of our final protocol (e.g., three) will be used (see results above), we also inspected difference when three amplifications are used for the search. Resulting graphs share the overall shape with those presented in Figure 6. The difference of the lowest and the highest success rate of the protocol is generally lower using three amplifications of the protocol than in the case of using only one, but overall difference is not significant enough to change instructions in the proposed protocols.

5.4 Constructing New Protocol

The resulting protocol is shown in Figure 3. There are still several ways for its optimization. We focus on minimization of the communication overhead. The tool we use is *protocol pruning*. Protocol pruning is a process of progressively removing every primitive instruction from the protocol and evaluating the change in the success ratio after a modified protocol execution. It gives us the loss of secured links when the instruction is removed from the protocol.

We were able to iteratively remove sub-protocols 4 and 5 with the success ratio loss of only 0.0012 when employing three amplifications. This means that the fraction of secured links is reduced only by 0.12 percent, which is negligible. Removing the first block means reduction by 0.9 percent, which is also a relevant trade-off given the fact that two messages are spared in every execution. We tested the final protocol on five hundred of deployments with an average success ratio 93.21% (secured links). Removing block two or three causes the success ratio loss of 17.0% or 14.5%, respectively.

#	instructions
0	RNG $N_{0.32\_0.85}$ R_1
1	SND $N_{0.32\_0.85}$ N_C R_1 R_1
2	SND $N_{0.32\_0.85}$ N_P R_1 R_1
3	RNG $N_{0.69\_0.98}$ R_2
4	SND $N_{0.69\_0.98}$ N_C R_2 R_2
5	SND $N_{0.69\_0.98}$ N_P R_2 R_2
6	RNG $N_{0.01\_0.39}$ R_3
7	SND $N_{0.01\_0.39}$ N_C R_3 R_3
8	SND $N_{0.01\_0.39}$ N_P R_3 R_3
9	RNG $N_{0.56\_0.70}$ R_4
10	SND $N_{0.56\_0.70}$ N_C R_4 R_4
11	SND $N_{0.56\_0.70}$ N_P R_4 R_4
12	RNG $N_{0.89\_0.01}$ R_5
13	SND $N_{0.89\_0.01}$ N_C R_5 R_5
14	SND $N_{0.89\_0.01}$ N_P R_5 R_5

#	instructions
0	RNG N_C R_2
1	SND N_C $N_{0.69\_0.98}$ R_2 R_2
2	SND $N_{0.69\_0.98}$ N_P R_2 R_2
3	RNG N_C R_3
4	SND N_C $N_{0.01\_0.39}$ R_3 R_3
5	SND $N_{0.01\_0.39}$ N_P R_3 R_3

Fig. 3. Best performing hybrid protocol (HP_{BEST})   **Fig. 4.** Final hybrid protocol (HP_{FINAL})

It is not efficient to remove more instructions as the success ratio loss becomes excessive. However, we can achieve a higher success ratio gain by increasing the number of repetitions of an amplification protocol. As we are taking the number of messages sent as the primary measure of how demanding a protocol is, we compare the efficiency of our final protocol (4 messages transmitted per protocol execution and 3 amplifications) with only one sub-protocol (2 messages transmitted per protocol execution and 6 amplifications). The best performing sub-protocol was the first one from Figure 3. It was able to secure nearly 90% links in the network, but this is worse than our original protocol. It is not possible to substitute any of the remaining instructions by amplifications preserving the performance of the protocol. Even if more amplifications would be able to do so, the communication overhead would exceed our final protocol.

To simplify synchronization of parallel protocol executions, we put full control over the protocol execution to the central node. As there is no difference between the PUSH and PULL protocol for the random compromise pattern, originally used PULL sub-protocols could be replaced by the PUSH ones. Both nonce generations are performed by the central node N_C and consequently transmitted to the intermediate node N_K. N_K only forwards the nonce to N_P and can forget it immediately. This will help with management of parallel protocol execution. The final protocol is shown in Figure 4.

We tested the performance on fifty larger networks with 1 000 nodes and initially with 50% links marked as compromised. The average number of neighbours was 7.5. The performance of the protocol was very similar as computed on smaller networks, with deviations of success ratio only around 0.5%.

6 Success Rate

The impact of the best known node- and group-oriented protocols together with our final hybrid protocol (as described in Section 4) for the random compromise pattern is compared in Figure 5. The NO_{BEST} performs slightly better than our hybrid protocol for the fraction of 20% initially secured links. For 40% and more, the HP_{FINAL} provides the best results among the tested protocols. The overall success rate is also very close to the theoretical reachable maximum computed by the modified Floyd-Warshall algorithm in Section 5.2.

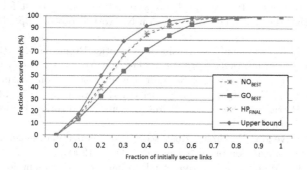

Fig. 5. An increase in the number of secured links after secrecy amplification protocols in the random compromise pattern. The best performing node-oriented protocol [11] is denoted as NO_{BEST}. The best performing group-oriented protocol [9] is denoted as GO_{BEST}. The pruned version of best hybrid protocol HP_{BEST} consists of 6 instructions (4 are SEND) is denoted as HP_{FINAL}. HP_{FINAL} is executed with 3 amplifications as it requires a comparable communication overhead. As can be seen, a strong majority of secure links (> 90%) can be obtained even when the initial network had one half of compromised links.

The more detailed comparison covering number of required messages, the impact of repeated secrecy amplifications and details of practical implementation for the TelosB hardware platform with the TinyOS 2.1.2 operating system and tested on our laboratory test-bed with 30 nodes positioned atop of nine interconnected offices can be found in Annex A.

7 Conclusions

Our work presented in this paper demonstrates that hybrid amplification protocols can provide better trade-off between security and efficiency than currently known approaches for secrecy amplification. Hybrid protocols show only a linear increase in messages sent with respect to the number of neighbours and do not require storing multiple values transmitted during the protocol execution. Proposed hybrid protocols also contain fewer instructions and their construction, analysis and implementation are simpler than for group-oriented protocols. The synchronization of the protocol steps and parallel execution on multiple nodes is easier than for previous approaches, making this approach practically usable on current platforms like TelosB as demonstrated by our prototype implementation.

Acknowledgments. This work was supported by the GAP202/11/0422 project of the Czech Science Foundation.

References

1. Anderson, R., Chan, H., Perrig, A.: Key infection: Smart trust for smart dust. In: 12th IEEE International Conference on Network Protocols, pp. 206–215. IEEE (2004)
2. Brameier, M.F., Banzhaf, W.: Linear Genetic Programming (Genetic and Evolutionary Computation). Springer-Verlag New York, Inc., Secaucus (2006)
3. Chan, H., Perrig, A., Song, D.: Random key predistribution schemes for sensor networks. In: IEEE Symposium on Security and Privacy, pp. 197–213 (2003)
4. Chan, H., Perrig, A., Song, D.: Wireless Sensor Networks. Kluwer Academic Publishers, Norwell (2004)
5. Cvrček, D., Švenda, P.: Smart dust security-key infection revisited. Electronic Notes in Theoretical Computer Science 157, 11–25 (2006)
6. Di Pietro, R., Mancini, L.V., Mei, A.: Random key-assignment for secure wireless sensor networks. In: 1st ACM Workshop on Security of Ad Hoc and Sensor Networks, pp. 62–71. ACM (2003)
7. Eschenauer, L., Gligor, V.D.: A key-management scheme for distributed sensor networks. In: 9th ACM Conference on Computer and Communications Security, Washington, DC, USA, pp. 41–47. ACM (2002)
8. Liu, D., Ning, P.: Establishing pairwise keys in distributed sensor networks. In: 10th ACM Conference on Computer and Communications Security, pp. 52–61. ACM Press (2003)
9. Smolka, T., Švenda, P., Sekanina, L., Matyáš, V.: Evolutionary design of message efficient secrecy amplification protocols. In: 12th European Conference on Genetic Programming, pp. 194–205 (2012)
10. Švenda, P., Matyáš, V.: Key distribution and secrecy amplification in wireless sensor networks, Technical report FIMU-RS-2007-05. Masaryk university, Czech Republic (2007)
11. Švenda, P., Sekanina, L., Matyáš, V.: Evolutionary design of secrecy amplification protocols for wireless sensor networks. In: Second ACM Conference on Wireless Network Security, pp. 225–236 (2009)

A   Protocol Evaluation

A.1   Upper Bound for Amplification Success - Details

Let us define the graph $G(V, E)$, where V represents the nodes in our WSN deployment and E represents neighbour relationships. After basic whispering (for the key infection compromise pattern) or after random key pre-distribution (for the random compromise pattern), we assign weight one to the edge between nodes N_i and N_j if and only if there exists a secure link key established between those nodes. If the link key is compromised, we assign weight equal to infinity.

After the Floyd-Warshall algorithm execution, we obtain the shortest path between all nodes and we can interpret the results as follows:

- If the nodes N_i and N_j are neighbours and there exists a shortest path between them, the link can be secured. The length of this path reduced by one is also the minimum number of intermediate nodes needed to secure the link.
- If the nodes N_i and N_j are neighbours and there is no shortest path calculated, the link cannot be secured.

We carried out several experimental calculations. Every calculation was conducted on fifty random deployments of our reference network. As can be seen in Figure 2, there is a significant difference between two inspected compromise patterns. In the random compromise pattern, we are able to secure significantly more link keys than in the key infection compromise pattern. We can explain this situation by the fact that in the key infection compromise pattern, the compromised links are concentrated in particular areas around eavesdropping nodes and it is more probable that such links cannot be secured. It can be also seen that the most benefit can be gained using two intermediate nodes. With more nodes, the increase in secure links fraction is very small.

A.2   Number of Amplifications

Different classes of secrecy amplification protocols use different capabilities to improve security throughout the network. A node-oriented protocol sends key updates via every possible neighbour or neighbours by a simple protocol. Group-oriented protocols share key updates inside the bigger group of cooperating nodes identified by relative distances. Hybrid protocols use sub-protocols (similarly to node-oriented), relative distances (similarly to group-oriented) and additionally utilize several repetitions of the whole process. Figure 7 shows the performance of particular protocols in our reference network with respect to the number of amplifications.

The most important observation is that with an increasing number of amplifications, the difference in success among distinct types of protocols is smaller, being negligible when four or more amplifications are used. That fact implies that protocol repetitions can substitute other methods used in node- and group-oriented protocols. We expect that three amplifications of a protocol will be a

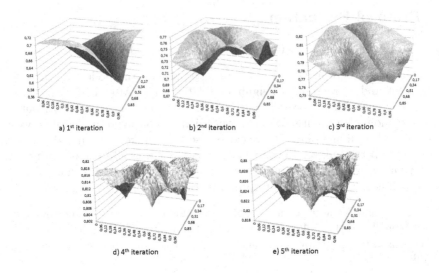

a) 1ˢᵗ iteration   b) 2ⁿᵈ iteration   c) 3ʳᵈ iteration

d) 4ᵗʰ iteration   e) 5ᵗʰ iteration

Fig. 6. Iterative search of intermediate nodes for PUSH/PULL protocols. Horizontal axis depicts distance from the node N_P, depth axis depicts distance from the node N_C, vertical axis represent the portion of secure links (quality of protocol with given position of nodes, scaled between 0 and 1). Based on our results, the first intermediate node is selected as $N_{0.32\_0.85}$ with the resulting success ratio 0.71 (a), second node as $N_{0.69\_0.98}$ with the success ratio 0.77 (b), third node as $N_{0.01\_0.39}$ with the success ratio 0.815 (c), fourth node as $N_{0.56\_0.70}$ with the success ratio 0.82 (d) and fifth node as $N_{0.89\_0.01}$ with the final success ratio of 0.83 (e).

proper compromise between a overall success of the hybrid protocol and the communication overhead it requires.

A.3 Number of Messages

The best performing node-oriented protocol was presented in [11]. The protocol consists of 10 instructions (6 are SEND) and requires participation of 4 different nodes. We will refer to it as NO_{BEST}. The best performing group-oriented protocol was presented in [9]. It has 41 instructions (24 are SEND) and might include cooperation of up to 34 nodes (but does not require such a number of distinct nodes). We will refer to is as GO_{BEST}. Our final hybrid protocol consists of 15 instructions (10 are SEND) before pruning and it might include cooperation of up to 7 nodes. We will refer to this protocol as HP_{BEST}. The pruned version of our protocol consists of 6 instructions (4 are SEND) and it might include cooperation of up to 4 nodes. We will refer to this protocol as HP_{FINAL}.

Figure 8 shows the number of messages sent by every node in protocol execution in our reference network with 7.5 legitimate neighbours on average. It can be seen that our final protocol has less messages sent with 5 amplifications than node- or group-oriented protocols with a single execution. As the communication

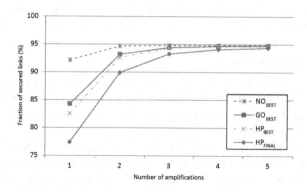

Fig. 7. Random compromise pattern (7.5 legal neighbours on average). Displayed results correspond to 50% originally compromised links. Node-oriented protocol performs better than others with only one amplification. Hybrid protocols perform comparably when a higher number of amplifications is performed.

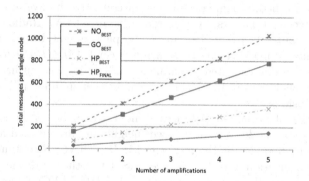

Fig. 8. Total number of messages per single node required to perform the best node-oriented and the best group-oriented secrecy amplification protocols (7.5 neighbours on average assumed). The hybrid protocol even with five amplifications sends considerably less messages than node or group oriented protocols with a single execution.

overhead is our primary metric for comparison of protocols, the proposed hybrid protocol gives more than 94% secure links (on average) from original 50% in our reference networks. This is a better result than node- or group-oriented protocol can provide with the same communication overhead.

The number of messages also depends on the number of participating parties and the average number of neighbours. Node-oriented protocols exhibit a polynomial increase of messages with respect to the number of neighbours in the network and an exponential increase of messages with respect to the number of communicating parties in the protocol execution. Group-oriented protocols exhibit only a linear increase of messages and the same dynamics holds for hybrid protocols. The growth in the number of messages depends on the count of SEND instructions within a protocol. This favours hybrid protocols even with a higher number of amplifications.

A.4   Test-Bed Results

To prove the practicality of the proposed protocol, we ran a prototype implementation for the TelosB hardware platform with the TinyOS 2.1.2 operating system and tested it in our laboratory network with 30 nodes positioned atop of nine interconnected offices.

Every node acts in three different roles according to a currently received message: *master* (being node N_C from the hybrid protocol), *slave* (being node N_P) and *forwarder* (being intermediate node). The implementation contains six phases executed mostly in parallel on all nodes in a network with a partial synchronization required only during the radio distance discovery:

1. A discovery of radio distance to neighbours – every node N_i periodically broadcasts *AM_MEASURE* message that is received together with the corresponding RSSI by its neighbours during the defined time-frame. Once broadcasting is finished, neighbours of N_i can compute the average RSSI value from the received packets, forming radio distance to N_i. Radio distance can be also computed from the RSSI of regular packets sent during ordinary network traffic, saving necessity to transmit special *AM_MEASURE* messages. This phase can be executed in parallel for all nodes with utilization of random back-offs between *AM_MEASURE* messages on different nodes to limit packet collisions.

2. A broadcast of measured distances to node's neighbours – once radio distances to other nodes are established, neighbours are notified about values measured by node N_i by the message *AM_DISTANCES* containing pairs of node's identification and its measured RSSI together with identification of measuring node. If node N_i receives the *AM_DISTANCES* message from a node that is its neighbour, measured values are stored locally. When node N_i receive measurements from all neighbours, next phase can be executed. Synchronization of remaining phases with other nodes is not required.

3. A computation of mapping to real nodes – mapping between nodes denoted in the hybrid protocol description and real nodes according to radio distances is performed locally. E.g., instead of node with $N_{0.69\_0.98}$ identification, a particular node N_i is selected. Note that mapping from the RSSI values distributed according to the logarithmic log-normal shadowing model of wireless signal propagation to the linear distance from a sending node is required. A different mapping model can be used where appropriate.

4. An execution of the hybrid protocol – node N_C executes the protocol as *master* to a selected neighbouring *slave* node N_P via intermediate *forwarder* nodes. Node N_C prepares its message with the sub-key as well as the routing path towards node N_P and sends it by the message *AM_SECAMPLIF*. Intermediate nodes act as simple forwarders with link transmission protected by already existing link keys. This phase can be executed in parallel for all nodes.

5. A verification phase – node N_C asks node N_P whether all sub-keys transmitted during the hybrid protocol execution or some were lost (e.g., due to packet loss) using message *AM_VERIFY*. If any sub-key is missing, a relevant sub-protocol for this sub-key is executed again.
6. A combination phase – all sub-keys, together with the existing link key between nodes N_C and N_P, are combined together using cryptographic hash function, forming the new shared link key. Optionally, a key confirmation can be executed before the old key is replaced by the new key value.

The hybrid protocol implementation has a small memory footprint – additional $(N*41)$ bytes of RAM are required (where N is the number of neighbours) and less then 3KB of additional code in EEPROM. Less then $(N*4*23 + N*2*5 + 28)$ bytes of payload divided into about $(N*6)$ messages are transmitted on average during hybrid protocol execution by every single node (including verification messages, but excluding messages send during radio distance discovery phase and retransmission of lost messages). When 10 neighbours on average are assumed, around 1 KB of payload is transmitted by every node during secrecy amplification by the proposed hybrid protocol. *Master* node stores the current state of the hybrid protocol executed with the selected *slave* node, the *slave* node stores only received sub-keys and *forwarder* node stores no additional value. Due to the parallelization possibility, execution of hybrid protocols from the same *master* to different *slave* nodes can be interleaved without having long message buffers on a single node.

Times required to finish different phases are highly dependent on the network density and the signal propagation characteristics of the surrounding environment resulting in a different packet loss ratio. The prototype implementation performed was intended to verify memory, computational, transmission and synchronization requirements, not to provide detailed performance results for different environments and settings. Still, reasonable estimates about time required to finish separate phases can be inferred from experiments performed with our laboratory test-bed.

The radio discovery (phase one) took most of the time to complete as multiple *AM_MEASURE* messages had to be sent from every node in the network to obtain a reliable averaged RSSI value. Required time is roughly minutes or tens of minutes to finish, depending on the required precision and network density (influencing the length of necessary random back-off to limit packet collisions). A broadcast of measured RSSI (phase two) is fast and requires only one or two messages, unless a high number of neighbours is present (more than 20). A mapping computation (phase three) is a fast local computation taking less than 1 second for a node with 10 neighbours and the optimized hybrid protocol with two sub-protocols described in Section 3. An execution of the optimized hybrid protocol (step four) takes 1-2 seconds, extending to tens of seconds when the packet loss is high and the verification phase (phase five) has to be executed repeatedly. Combination of received values by a hash function (phase six) is local and negligible.

Differential Power Analysis Attack on SIMON and LED Block Ciphers

Dillibabu Shanmugam, Ravikumar Selvam, and Suganya Annadurai

Hardware Security Research Group,
Society for Electronic Transactions and Security, India
{dillibabu,ravikumar,asuganya}@setsindia.net
http://www.setsindia.org/hardware.html

Abstract. Power analysis attack is one of the most important and effective side channel attack methods, that has been attempted against implementations of cryptographic algorithms. In this paper, we investigate the vulnerability of SIMON [5] and LED [16] lightweight block ciphers against Differential Power Analysis (DPA) attack. Firstly, we describe the power model used to mount the attack on Field Programmable Gate Array (FPGA) implementation of SIMON and LED block ciphers. Then, we proceed to experimentally verified DPA attack, which is the first successful DPA attack on the algorithms. Our attack retrieves complete 64-bit key of SIMON32/64 and LED-64 with a complexity of 176 and 2^{18} hypotheses respectively. Finally, we present our analysis on other versions of SIMON and LED. Our DPA results exhibits the weakness of algorithms, which emphasize the need for secure implementation of SIMON and LED.

Keywords: Lightweight block cipher, FPGA implementation, differential power analysis.

1 Introduction

Generally security analysis of block ciphers are performed in two directions. One is based on mathematical cryptanalysis; Other is based on analysis of leakage from cryptographic device termed as side-channel attacks. Mathematically strong crypto-primitives need not necessarily secure enough against side channel attacks(SCA). Therefore, it is essential to investigate ciphers in both directions towards the standardisation of the cipher.

Of all side-channel attacks, differential power analysis (DPA) attack found to be significantly successful against iterated block ciphers. DPA attack exploits the power consumed by the device when it performs cryptography operations. In 1999, Kocher et al. [19] showed that power analysis attack can efficiently reveal the secret key. Based on the knowledge of adversary about the implementation, leakage model is categorised in two classes of SCA, namely Profiled and Non-profiled. In profiled SCA, adversary has privilege to learn the precise leakage model in training phase in order to make use of on-the-fly attack

R.S. Chakraborty et al. (Eds.): SPACE 2014, LNCS 8804, pp. 110–125, 2014.
© Springer International Publishing Switzerland 2014

detection; whereas in non-profiled SCA, less precise model is used to mount the attack. Models of non-profiled SCA are Correlation Power Analysis (CPA), Mutual Information Analysis (MIA), algebraic side channel collision analysis were presented in [9,14,7]. Similarly, models of profiled SCA such as Template, Scholastic model, Linear Regression Analysis(LRA), Side Channel Cube Analysis and Algebraic SCA were published in [10,25,27,13,24].

Recently, in [22], information leakage through static power consumption of FPGA is exploited to mount DPA. By the advancement of technology, the static power consumption of CMOS circuit is almost equal to dynamic power consumption, which becomes a major concern for physical implementation. Static power consumption of LUTs, registers and connection switches of FPGA are investigated to mount higher order attacks. A.Moradi and F. X. Standaert [23] experimented Moments-Correlating Profile(MCP) and Moments-Correlating Collision(MCC) through statistical moments to explore the leakage of threshold implementation. The author suggest moments-correlating DPA as a natural candidate for leakage detection tests and advanced features for the evaluation of higher-order attacks.

After the advent of DPA, designers of cryptographic algorithm had started concentrating on the new design strategies to improve the defence quality against the attack. However, few algorithms are still vulnerable to DPA attack [30]. This motivated us to evaluate algorithms against DPA. The two familiar designs of lightweight block ciphers are Substitution- Permutation Networks (SPN) [6,8] and Feistel structure [17,26]. For analysis, we have taken SIMON and LED based on Feistel and SPN designs respectively.

SIMON and SPECK are two ultra lightweight block ciphers designed by U.S National Security Agency (NSA). SIMON is designed to provide optimal performance in hardware [4]. Linear, differential cryptanalysis and differential fault attacks were reported in [1,2,28]. Light Encryption Device (LED) is designed to be very compact in hardware compared to other lightweight block ciphers with similar design parameters. Differential attack [21] on reduced round of LED and fault attack [18] were reported recently.

In order to investigate the vulnerabilities of these algorithms against DPA, FPGA is the preferred platform due to its low cost and flexibility [11]. Therefore, we used customized I/O protocol [3] for SASEBO-G board, operated at 24 MHz, to practically verify our attack. SIMON and LED are implemented using Verilog Hardware Descriptive Language (HDL) in Xilinx FPGA (XC2VP7), where the drop voltage at a shunt resistor (1Ω) in the power line is measured. The oscilloscope captures the power trace at 2 Giga samples per second when the encryption starts.

Our Contribution. In this work, we present the power model chosen for power analysis attack on SIMON and LED. Then we present practically verified DPA attack on these algorithms using SASEBO-G board. Our attack reduces hypotheses complexity from 2^{64} to 176 and 2^{18} for SIMON and LED-64 respectively. We analyzed our approach, which is adoptable for other versions of SIMON and LED. To the best of our knowledge, this is the first DPA attack on SIMON and LED.

Outline. This paper is organised as follows. Section 2 describes, brief on SIMON, its hardware implementation, power model and DPA attack on its physical implementation. In Sect. 3, implementation details, power model and practical attack of LED are discussed in detail. Finally we conclude the paper in Sect. 4.

2   Differential Power Analysis on SIMON

This section provides a brief description of SIMON followed by a detailed description of the power model to mount DPA attack on SIMON. Then we present the experimental results and complexity of our attack.

2.1   Description of SIMON

SIMON is based on Feistel structure and the algorithm supports various block and key sizes. The version of SIMON is denoted as SIMON$2n/mn$, where $2n$ refers to the block size and mn refers to the key size. The n and m refer to word of 16, 24, 32, 48 or 64 and key word of 2,3 or 4 respectively. Feistel structure is an iterative structure with an internal function called round function. Single round function of SIMON is depicted in Fig. 1. A round function is defined as

$$\mathbf{R}_K(L^{i+1}, R^{i+1}) = (R^i \oplus f(L^i) \oplus K^i, L^i); \tag{1}$$
$$f(L^i) = (S^1(L^i) \ \& \ S^8(L^i)) \oplus S^2(L^i) \tag{2}$$

where, $i \in \{1, \cdots, T-1\}$,
T : Total number of rounds,
S^r: Left circular shift by r bits,
K^i: i^{th} round key,
$\oplus$: Bitwise *exclusive-or*,
$\&$: Bitwise *and*.

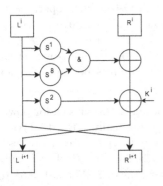

Fig. 1. SIMON Round Function

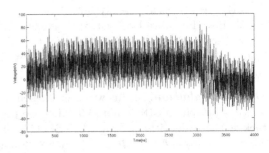

Fig. 2. Power consumption of SIMON32/64

FPGA Implementation of SIMON: SIMON32/64, refers 32-bit plaintext block with 64-bit key. The implementation takes 32 clock cycles to complete one block of encryption, that is one round is executed in one clock cycle. The algorithm requires three 16-bit registers and a few boolean operations (exclusive-or and *and* operations) as hardware space. Initially, the plaintext is divided into two halves and then loaded in two 16-bit registers, namely left and right registers. These two registers are updated for every round function. The 64-bit key (K) is divided into four 16-bit keys, which are loaded in 16-bit key register for the first four rounds. From fifth round onwards the round keys are generated using key scheduling algorithm, which is described in [5]. The first round 16-bit key is represented as K^1, second round key is represented as K^2 and so on. Hardware implementation of SIMON32/64 is as shown in Fig. 3.

Fig. 2 shows the power consumption of SIMON32/64 during one encryption and the trace pattern is high for 32 rounds.

2.2 Power Model

We used Hamming distance based power model to describe the power consumption, since this suits the power consumption of a FPGA implementation very well. In order to use the Hamming distance model, the state of a cell in the circuit before or after it processes the targeted intermediate result needs to be known [20]. The intermediate result is selected in such a way that it must be a function of plaintext/ciphertext and a portion of the key (k). The length of the relevant portion of the key must be as small as possible when compared to the original key (K) size of the algorithm, i.e. $|k| << |K|$. Therefore, complexity of attack is significantly lesser than the exhaustive key search space.

The power model described in this section is generic for all variants of SIMON. Therefore, the version of the algorithm is not specifically mentioned in this section. In the first round of SIMON, the key bits are exclusive-ored with the plaintext

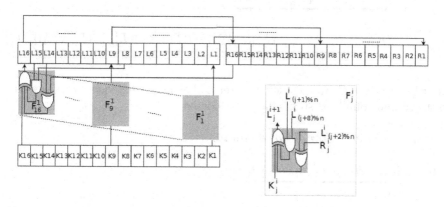

Fig. 3. Implementation module of SIMON32/64

and not diffused with the non-linear function. Key bits start diffusing with the state value in non-linear fashion from second round onwards. Therefore our targeted intermediate value to reveal key bits start from second round output. The power consumption of SIMON for i^{th} round can be represented as follows:

$$P_{total}^{i+1} = \sum_{j=1}^{n} L_j^i \oplus L_j^{i+1} + \sum_{j=1}^{n} R_j^i \oplus R_j^{i+1} \tag{3}$$

where index i refers to the round number and index j refers to bit position. In SIMON, n refers to the word size. The R register is directly mapped from previous state of L register. Therefore, the value of R register is not explicitly mentioned hereinafter. Each bit in the left register can be represented as follows:

$$L_j^{i+1} = K_j^i \oplus R_j^i \oplus L_{(j+2) \bmod n}^i \oplus (L_{(j+1) \bmod n}^i \,\&\, L_{(j+8) \bmod n}^i) \tag{4}$$

Therefore the Hamming distance model for the power analysis is given below:

$$HD = HW(L_j^{i+1} \oplus L_j^i) \tag{5}$$

2.3   Description of Our Attack

For the purpose of demonstration of power analysis attack, SIMON32/64 was chosen. Initially, Plaintext P is loaded in two 16-bit registers (R and L) as given in (6) and (7).

Initial Register value

$$R^1 = P_{16}, P_{15}, ...P_1 \tag{6}$$
$$L^1 = P_{32}, P_{31}, ...P_{17} \tag{7}$$

Register value after First round

$$L^2 = \underbrace{(K_{16}^1 \oplus R_{16}^1 \oplus L_{14}^1 \oplus (L_{15}^1 \& L_8^1))}_{L_{16}^2},$$
$$\underbrace{(K_{15}^1 \oplus R_{15}^1 \oplus L_{13}^1 \oplus (L_{14}^1 \& L_7^1))}_{L_{15}^2}, ... \underbrace{(K_1^1 \oplus R_1^1 \oplus L_{15}^1 \oplus (L_{16}^1 \& L_9^1))}_{L_1^2} \tag{8}$$

After the first round, value of left register L^2 has linear dependency on key bits, so the second round register value is considered.

Register value after Second round

$$L^3 = \underbrace{(K_{16}^2 \oplus R_{16}^2 \oplus L_{14}^2 \oplus (L_{15}^2 \& L_8^2))}_{L_{16}^3},$$
$$\underbrace{(K_{15}^2 \oplus R_{15}^2 \oplus L_{13}^2 \oplus (L_{14}^2 \& L_7^2))}_{L_{15}^3}, ... \underbrace{(K_1^2 \oplus R_1^2 \oplus L_{15}^2 \oplus (L_{16}^2 \& L_9^2))}_{L_1^3} \tag{9}$$

In (9), L_1^3 bit has non-linear function of L_{16}^2 and L_9^2, depends on key bits K_{16}^1 and K_9^1. Therefore, L_1^3 bit shall be considered as an intermediate result, as it satisfies the requirement to perform DPA. Hence, the first bit of (9), L_1^3, will be correlated with first bit of (8), L_1^2, for all possible hypothetical values for the key bits present in the equations. The bit L_1^3 involves four key bits $K_{16}^1, K_9^1, K_{15}^1, K_1^2$ and L_1^2 involves one key bit K_1^1. As a result, intermediate hypothetical value is correlated with captured power reveals 5-bit of key.

Similarly, L_2^3 is correlated with L_2^2. Here, bit L_2^3 involves four key bits K_{16}^1, K_{10}^1, K_2^1, K_2^2 and L_2^2 involves one key bit K_2^1. Whereas, K_{16}^1 and K_2^1 are known from first bit correlation. Consequently, number of hypothesis required for correlation is reduced from five to three bits. In order to reduce the complexity, same procedure is repeated for next six bits, L_3^3 to L_8^3 to reveal 24-bit key in the first two rounds. In the same way, remaining key bits are retrieved between round L^4 and L^3 as well as between round L^5 and L^4 with corresponding correlation bits as shown in Table 1.

2.4   Summary of Our Results

We recorded the power consumption of SIMON32/64 while it encrypts D (with minimum of 65,000 samples) randomly generated plaintexts using a fixed key K[1]. With the experimental set-up described in Sect.1, trace points were captured and stored in a matrix format.

Intermediate hypothetical value is calculated for D plaintexts using (8) and (9). Hypothetical power consumption value is calculated by taking Hamming distance between L_1^2 and L_1^3. Then the hypothetical power consumption value is correlated with the actual power consumption value. Fig. 4 shows the plot for 5-bit key hypothesis. The peak appears at 12, this means the correct key is 11 (because the index for key hypothesis in the plot starts from 1) with the correlation value of 0.01789. The correct key and its corresponding bit positions are given below.

Second bit of (9) is correlated with corresponding bit of (8) for key bits K_{10}^1, K_2^1, K_2^2. Fig. 5 shows peak value at 5 with the correlation value of 0.0201, this means key bit value is 4 and its corresponding individual bit values as shown above.

The same procedure is repeated for next six bits, L_3^3 to L_8^3, to reveal 24-bit key out of 32-bit in the first two rounds. In the same way, the key used in third and fourth rounds are also revealed. The overall complexity of attack to reveal complete 64-bit key is $2^7 + 2^5 + 2^4 = 176$ using DPA as shown in Table 1. The possibility of DPA attack on other versions of SIMON is presented in Appendix A.

---

[1] The key K that was used for experiment is K = [6 9 A 5 7 1 8 E C 3 8 1 5 A 6 9], represented in hexadecimal.

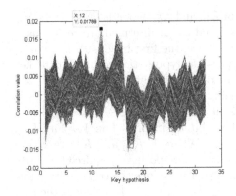

Fig. 4. First bit correlation between (8) and (9)

Fig. 5. Second bit correlation between (8) and (9)

K_{16}^1	K_{15}^1	K_9^1	K_1^1	K_1^2
0	1	0	1	1

K_{10}^1	K_2^1	K_2^2
1	0	0

Table 1. Attack complexity of SIMON32/64

Correlation between rounds	Correlation bits	Attack bits(Key)	Hypothesis
L^3, L^2	L_1^3, L_1^2	$K_{16}^1, K_{15}^1, K_9^1, K_1^1, K_1^2$	32
	L_2^3, L_2^2	K_{10}^1, K_2^1, K_2^2	8
	L_3^3, L_3^2	K_{11}^1, K_3^1, K_3^2	8
	L_4^3, L_4^2	K_{12}^1, K_4^1, K_4^2	8
	L_5^3, L_5^2	K_{13}^1, K_5^1, K_5^2	8
	L_6^3, L_6^2	K_{14}^1, K_6^1, K_6^2	8
	L_7^3, L_7^2	K_7^1, K_7^2	4
	L_8^3, L_8^2	K_8^1, K_8^2	4
L^4, L^3	L_1^4, L_1^3	$K_{16}^2, K_{15}^2, K_9^2, K_1^3$	16
	L_2^4, L_2^3	K_{10}^2, K_2^3	4
	L_3^4, L_3^3	K_{11}^2, K_3^3	4
	L_4^4, L_4^3	K_{12}^2, K_4^3	4
	L_5^4, L_5^3	K_{13}^2, K_5^3	4
	L_6^4, L_6^3	K_{14}^2, K_6^3	4
	L_7^4, L_7^3	K_7^3, K_8^3	4
L^5, L^4	L_1^5, L_1^4	$K_{16}^3, K_{15}^3, K_9^3, K_1^4$	16
	L_2^5, L_2^4	K_{10}^3, K_2^4	4
	L_3^5, L_3^4	K_{11}^3, K_3^4	4
	L_4^5, L_4^4	K_{12}^3, K_4^4	4
	L_5^5, L_5^4	K_{13}^3, K_5^4	4
	L_6^5, L_6^4	K_{14}^3, K_6^4	4
	$L_7^5, L_8^5, L_7^4, L_8^4$	K_7^4, K_8^4	4
	$L_9^5, L_{10}^5, L_9^4, L_{10}^4$	K_9^4, K_{10}^4	4
	$L_{11}^5, L_{12}^5, L_{11}^4, L_{12}^4$	K_{11}^4, K_{12}^4	4
	$L_{13}^5, L_{14}^5, L_{13}^4, L_{14}^4$	K_{13}^4, K_{14}^4	4
	$L_{15}^5, L_{16}^5, L_{15}^4, L_{16}^4$	K_{15}^4, K_{16}^4	4
Combined hypothesis			176

3 Differential Power Analysis of LED

In this section we describe a DPA attack on LED. Firstly, we give a brief description of LED and its hardware implementation. Then we describe a power model chosen for DPA attack and experimental verification of our attack is presented.

3.1 Description of LED

LED is based on a design principles of Advanced Encryption Standard (AES) [12]. The algorithm has a fixed block size of 64-bit, and key size of 64 or 128-bit. The version of LED is specified using its key size, namely, LED-64 and LED-128. LED operates on 4×4 row-major order matrix of nibbles, termed as state. The key size used for LED determines the number of iteration that have to be performed, which is called step function. The number of step functions required to convert given plaintext to ciphertext is eight for LED-64. A step function consists of four rounds, each round is combination of AddConstants, SubCells, ShiftRows, and MixColumnsSerial operations. The AddRoundKey is performed once in every four rounds which exclusive-ored with the state value.

AddConstants is a linear operation, where the state matrix is bitwise exclusive-ored with round constant as given in [16].

SubCells is a non-linear operation, where each nibble in the state matrix is replaced by a nibble generated using PRESENT Sbox [6]. ShiftRows is a linear operation, where row i of the state matrix is rotated i cell positions to the left, where i varies from 0 to 3.

MixColumnsSerial is also a linear operation presented in [16], where each column of the state matrix is multiplied by matrix ($M = A^4$, where A is a base matrix).

FPGA Implementation of LED: LED-64 takes 32 clock cycles to produce ciphertext, which means that a single round of operation is executed in one clock cycle. The implementation flow is depicted in Fig. 6.

The encryption starts with loading the plaintext in 64-bit data register, Data-Reg, which is updated for every round function output. The state value refers to the intermediate value computed during the transformation of data register value from one round to the next round. The selection signal sel chooses the AddRoundkey operation once in four rounds. In the first AddRoundkey, the key(K) is exclusive-ored with the plaintext that is stored in Data-Reg. Round function is implemented as combinational circuit and all four operations are

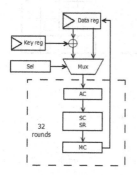

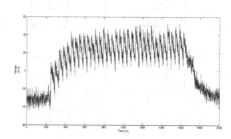

Fig. 6. Implementation of LED-64   **Fig. 7.** Power consumption of LED-64

computed in single clock cycle. In our implementation, the AddConstants(AC) operation fetches the corresponding pre-computed round constant value from the memory. SubCells(SC) and ShiftRows(SR) are implemented as a single module. SC is implemented through the characteristic equation as defined in [6]. The MixColumnsSerial(MC) takes the base matrix(A) for multiplication, which is multiplied four times with the state value.

Fig. 7 shows the power consumption of LED-64 during one encryption. It can be observed from Fig. 7 that the 32 patterns in the trace shows the 32 rounds of LED-64.

3.2   Power Model

We chose Hamming distance model for the reason mentioned in Sect. 2.2. In our attack, the targeted intermediate result is the first round output, which is the function of plaintext and key. In the first round, each input nibble of the S-box depends on a nibble of the key of LED. Each nibble in the output of first round depends on four nibbles of the key of LED as shown in Fig. 8. Based on this observation, we built suitable Hamming distance model for the attack. The targeted register is Data-Reg (as shown in Fig. 6) that stores the plaintext first and then stores the intermediate result after every round function.

3.3   Description of Our Attack

LED operates on row-major matrix, the elements of the state matrix are arranged as shown in Fig. 8, where a_0 denotes the most significant nibble and a_{15} denotes the least significant nibble. For AddConstants, SubCells and AddRoundKey operations every nibble is operated independently. In ShiftRows operation the position of nibbles are changed, which plays a major role in choosing plaintext positions for deriving power model.

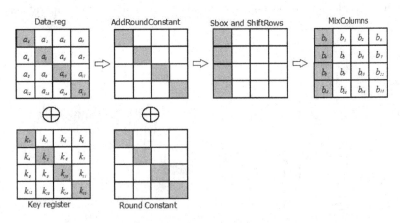

Fig. 8. Power model for first round attack

In each round, MixColumnsSerial diffuses four nibbles within the column. Hence the 64-bit state can be regarded as four small separate mappings each of which diffuses the nibbles of the corresponding column.

Since the MixColumnsSerial takes a column for multiplication and each output nibble depends on the values of the other nibbles of that particular column, the key hypothesis has to be performed for all four nibbles used in that column. The ShiftRows operation shuffles nibble row-wise before the MixColumnsSerial. Therefore, the plaintext and key position have to be chosen suitably, so that MixColumnsSerial gets a column for computing hypothetical intermediate value. From the above consideration, the state value for the first round attack is partitioned into four diagonals – The value $[a_0, a_5, a_{10}, a_{15}]$ forms the first column, $[a_1, a_6, a_{11}, a_{12}]$ the second column, $[a_2, a_7, a_8, a_{13}]$ the third and $[a_3, a_4, a_9, a_{14}]$ the fourth column respectively after ShiftRows operation.

As illustrated in Fig. 8, the first output nibble b_0 depends on the key value of k_0, k_5, k_{10} and k_{15} and its corresponding plaintext value. Therefore, we need to perform key hypothesis for 16-bit key (k_0, k_5, k_{10} and k_{15}) to derive the power model and hence the key search space has become 2^{16}. To reveal the entire 64-bit key, three more DPA attacks are necessary for the key positions [k_1, k_6, k_{11} and k_{12}], [k_2, k_7, k_8 and k_{13}] and [k_3, k_4, k_9 and k_{14}]. Therefore, the complexity of attack is $2^{16} \times 4 = 2^{18}$.

3.4 Summary of Our Results

We recorded the power consumption of LED-64 while it encrypts D (with minimum of 4000 samples) randomly generated plaintexts using a fixed key K[2]. With the experimental set-up described in Sect. 1, trace points were captured and stored in a matrix format for analysis. Based on the D plaintexts, the hypothetical intermediate values have been calculated by performing first round function of LED-64 for every plaintext and every possible choice of key. Since, the attack is performed for four nibbles, the key search space is 2^{16}.

The next step of the DPA attack is to map hypothetical intermediate value to a matrix of hypothetical power consumption values. In LED implementation, the first round output is stored in the same register as the plaintext. Therefore, hypothetical power consumption values can be calculated by taking Hamming distance between the corresponding plaintext position a_0, a_4, a_8 and a_{12} and the first round output nibbles b_0, b_4, b_8 and b_{12} as shown in Fig. 8.

Finally, the correlation coefficient between the hypothetical power consumption values of each key hypothesis and the recorded power traces are calculated as explained in [20,9]. A plot of the correlation matrix shows that a significant peak, that uniquely determines the correct key as shown in Fig. 9.

---

[2] We had chosen key $K = [0\ 1\ 2\ 3\ 4\ 5\ 6\ 7\ 8\ 9\ A\ B\ C\ D\ E\ F]$ as it is given in test vectors of [16]. Nevertheless, the attack was successful on other set of randomly chosen keys as well.

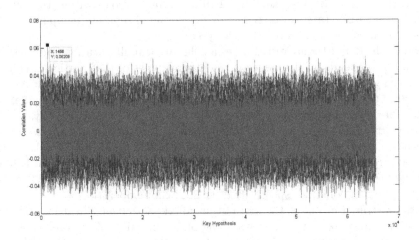

Fig. 9. Correlation Power Analysis result of LED-64

The correlation value is 0.0620 for the correct key $[0\ 5\ A\ F]^3$ at key positions k_0, k_5, k_{10} and k_{15} respectively. This process was repeated for three more diagonals to retrieve the complete key of LED-64. Therefore the attack complexity to retrieve the complete 64-bit key equals 2^{18}. DPA on other versions of LED is given in Appendix B.

4   Conclusion

In this paper, we presented the DPA attack on SIMON and LED with very less key search space. To retrieve 64-bit key, the required key search space for SIMON is 176 and LED is 2^{18}. Our results highlight the need of countermeasures against the proposed attack. Therefore suitable countermeasures have to be designed to resist against the attacks. Such countermeasures have to be analysed for these algorithms in terms of resources and throughput. The power model proposed in our attack is targeted for hardware implementations like FPGA, ASIC. However, the attack complexity may vary for other platforms.

Acknowledgments. This Research work was funded by Department of Atomic Energy (DAE), Govt. of India under the grant 12-R&D-IMS-5.01.0204.

We would like to thank Prem Laxman Das, Nalla Anandakumar, Vijayasarathy and anonymous reviewers for their useful comments.

---

[3] The peak appears at 1456 in the plot, since the MATLAB tool starts the plot from 1 rather than 0, the correct key value has to be reduced by one from the peak value, which is the decimal value of 0x05AF.

References

1. Alizadeh, J., Bagheri, N., Gauravaram, P., Kumar, A., Sanadhya, S.K.: Linear cryptanalysis of round reduced SIMON. IACR Cryptology ePrint Archive, 2013:663 (2013)
2. Alkhzaimi, H.A., Lauridsen, M.M.: Cryptanalysis of the SIMON family of block ciphers. Cryptology ePrint Archive, Report 2013/543 (2013), http://eprint.iacr.org/
3. Nalla Anandakumar, N., Dillibabu, S.: Correlation power analysis attack of AES on FPGA using customized communication protocol. In: Meghanathan, N., Wozniak, M. (eds.) CCSEIT, pp. 683–688. ACM (2012)
4. Aysu, A., Gulcan, E., Schaumont, P.: SIMON says, break the area records for symmetric key block ciphers on FPGAs. Cryptology ePrint Archive, Report 2014/237 (2014), http://eprint.iacr.org/
5. Beaulieu, R., Shors, D., Smith, J., Treatman-Clark, S., Weeks, B., Wingers, L.: The SIMON and SPECK Families of Lightweight Block Ciphers. Cryptology ePrint Archive, Report 2013/404 (2013), http://eprint.iacr.org/
6. Bogdanov, A.A., Knudsen, L.R., Leander, G., Paar, C., Poschmann, A., Robshaw, M., Seurin, Y., Vikkelsoe, C.: PRESENT: An Ultra-Lightweight Block Cipher. In: Paillier, P., Verbauwhede, I. (eds.) CHES 2007. LNCS, vol. 4727, pp. 450–466. Springer, Heidelberg (2007)
7. Bogdanov, A., Pyshkin, A.: Algebraic Side-Channel Collision Attacks on AES. Cryptology ePrint Archive, Report 2007/477 (2007), http://eprint.iacr.org/
8. Borghoff, J., Canteaut, A., Güneysu, T., Kavun, E.B., Knezevic, M., Knudsen, L.R., Leander, G., Nikov, V., Paar, C., Rechberger, C., Rombouts, P., Thomsen, S.S., Yalçin, T.: PRINCE - A Low-Latency Block Cipher for Pervasive Computing Applications - Extended Abstract. In: Wang, Sako (eds.) [29], pp. 208–225
9. Brier, E., Clavier, C., Olivier, F.: Correlation Power Analysis with a Leakage Model. In: Joye, M., Quisquater, J.-J. (eds.) CHES 2004. LNCS, vol. 3156, pp. 16–29. Springer, Heidelberg (2004)
10. Chari, S., Rao, J.R., Rohatgi, P.: Template attacks. In: Kaliski Jr., B.S., Koç, Ç.K., Paar, C. (eds.) CHES 2002. LNCS, vol. 2523, pp. 13–28. Springer, Heidelberg (2003)
11. Cryptography Research Inc. Protecting FPGAs from Power Analysis, http://www.cryptography.com/public/pdf/FPGASecurity.pdf. (accessed: July 2014)
12. Daemen, J., Rijmen, V.: Rijndael for AES. In: AES Candidate Conference, pp. 343–348 (2000)
13. Dinur, I., Shamir, A.: Side channel cube attacks on block ciphers. Cryptology ePrint Archive, Report 2009/127 (2009), http://eprint.iacr.org/
14. Gierlichs, B., Batina, L., Tuyls, P., Preneel, B.: Mutual information analysis. In: Oswald, E., Rohatgi, P. (eds.) CHES 2008. LNCS, vol. 5154, pp. 426–442. Springer, Heidelberg (2008)
15. Guo, J., Peyrin, T., Poschmann, A., Robshaw, M.: The LED Block Cipher. Cryptology ePrint Archive, Report 2012/600 (2012), http://eprint.iacr.org/
16. Guo, J., Peyrin, T., Poschmann, A., Robshaw, M.: The LED Block Cipher. In: Preneel, B., Takagi, T. (eds.) CHES 2011. LNCS, vol. 6917, pp. 326–341. Springer, Heidelberg (2011)
17. Hong, D., et al.: HIGHT: A New Block Cipher Suitable for Low-Resource Device. In: Goubin, L., Matsui, M. (eds.) CHES 2006. LNCS, vol. 4249, pp. 46–59. Springer, Heidelberg (2006)

18. Jovanovic, P., Kreuzer, M., Polian, I.: A Fault Attack on the LED Block Cipher. In: Schindler, W., Huss, S.A. (eds.) COSADE 2012. LNCS, vol. 7275, pp. 120–134. Springer, Heidelberg (2012)
19. Kocher, P.C., Jaffe, J., Jun, B.: Differential Power Analysis. In: Wiener, M. (ed.) CRYPTO 1999. LNCS, vol. 1666, pp. 388–397. Springer, Heidelberg (1999)
20. Mangard, S., Oswald, E., Popp, T.: Power analysis attacks - revealing the secrets of smart cards. Springer (2007)
21. Mendel, F., Rijmen, V., Toz, D., Varici, K.: Differential Analysis of the LED Block Cipher. In: Wang, Sako (eds.) [29], pp. 190–207
22. Moradi, A.: Side-channel leakage through static power should we care about in practice? Cryptology ePrint Archive, Report 2014/025 (2014), http://eprint.iacr.org/
23. Moradi, A., Standaert, F.-X.: Moments-Correlating DPA. Cryptology ePrint Archive, Report 2014/409 (2014), http://eprint.iacr.org/
24. Renauld, M., Standaert, F.-X., Veyrat-Charvillon, N.: Algebraic Side-Channel Attacks on the AES: Why Time also Matters in DPA. In: Clavier, C., Gaj, K. (eds.) CHES 2009. LNCS, vol. 5747, pp. 97–111. Springer, Heidelberg (2009)
25. Schindler, W., Lemke, K., Paar, C.: A stochastic model for differential side channel cryptanalysis. In: Rao, J.R., Sunar, B. (eds.) CHES 2005. LNCS, vol. 3659, pp. 30–46. Springer, Heidelberg (2005)
26. Shirai, T., Shibutani, K., Akishita, T., Moriai, S., Iwata, T.: The 128-Bit Block-cipher CLEFIA (Extended Abstract). In: Biryukov, A. (ed.) FSE 2007. LNCS, vol. 4593, pp. 181–195. Springer, Heidelberg (2007)
27. Standaert, F.-X., Malkin, T., Yung, M.: A unified framework for the analysis of side-channel key recovery attacks. In: Joux, A. (ed.) EUROCRYPT 2009. LNCS, vol. 5479, pp. 443–461. Springer, Heidelberg (2009)
28. Tupsamudre, H., Bisht, S., Mukhopadhyay, D.: Differential fault analysis on the families of SIMON and SPECK ciphers. Cryptology ePrint Archive, Report 2014/267 (2014), http://eprint.iacr.org/
29. Wang, X., Sako, K. (eds.): ASIACRYPT 2012. LNCS, vol. 7658. Springer, Heidelberg (2012)
30. Yalla, P.S.V.V.K.: Differential Power Analysis on Lightweight Implementations of Block Ciphers. George Mason University, Master's Thesis (2009)

A   Appendix

Attack complexity of other variants of SIMON: SIMON versions depend on values of m and n. Based on m, key is divided in to n word size and used in first m rounds of algorithm. For example, in SIMON 32/64, m is 4; from the above table it is clear that, we need to perform DPA up to $m+1$ rounds to retrieve complete 64-bit key. In the case of SIMON 48/72, m is 3, therefore $m+1$ rounds are required to reveal the key with the complexity of $(2^5+2^4+(2^3\times5)+(2^2\times24))=$ 184 shown in the Table 2. Similarly, in SIMON 96/96, m is 2; that means $m+1$ rounds are require to reveal the key. The attack complexity of SIMON 96/96 is $(2^5+(2^3\times5)+(2^2\times38))=$ 224, given in Table 3. This shows that our approach can be adoptable to attack all versions of SIMON.

Table 2. Attack complexity of SIMON48/72

Correlation between rounds	Correlation bits	Attack bits(Key)	Hypothesis
	L_1^3, L_1^2	$K_{24}^1, K_{23}^1, K_{17}^1, K_1^1, K_1^2$	32
	L_2^3, L_2^2	K_{18}^1, K_2^1, K_2^2	8
	L_3^3, L_3^2	K_{19}^1, K_3^1, K_3^2	8
	L_4^3, L_4^2	K_{20}^1, K_4^1, K_4^2	8
	L_5^3, L_5^2	K_{21}^1, K_5^1, K_5^2	8
	L_6^3, L_6^2	K_{22}^1, K_6^1, K_6^2	8
	L_7^3, L_7^2	K_7^1, K_7^2	4
L^3, L^2	L_8^3, L_8^2	K_8^1, K_8^2	4
	L_9^3, L_9^2	K_9^1, K_9^2	4
	L_{10}^3, L_{10}^2	K_{10}^1, K_{10}^2	4
	L_{11}^3, L_{11}^2	K_{11}^1, K_{11}^2	4
	L_{12}^3, L_{12}^2	K_{12}^1, K_{12}^2	4
	L_{13}^3, L_{13}^2	K_{13}^1, K_{13}^2	4
	L_{14}^3, L_{14}^2	K_{14}^1, K_{14}^2	4
	L_{15}^3, L_{15}^2	K_{15}^1, K_{15}^2	4
	L_{16}^3, L_{16}^2	K_{16}^1, K_{16}^2	4
	L_1^4, L_1^3	$K_{24}^2, K_{23}^2, K_{17}^2, K_1^3$	16
	L_2^4, L_2^3	K_{18}^2, K_2^3	4
	L_3^4, L_3^3	K_{19}^2, K_3^3	4
	L_4^4, L_4^3	K_{20}^2, K_4^3	4
	L_5^4, L_5^3	K_{21}^2, K_5^3	4
	L_6^4, L_6^3	K_{22}^2, K_6^3	4
	$L_7^4, L_8^4, L_7^3, L_8^3$	K_7^3, K_8^3	4
L^4, L^3	$L_9^4, L_{10}^4, L_9^3, L_{10}^3$	K_9^3, K_{10}^3	4
	$L_{11}^4, L_{12}^4, L_{11}^3, L_{12}^3$	K_{11}^3, K_{12}^3	4
	$L_{13}^4, L_{14}^4, L_{13}^3, L_{14}^3$	K_{13}^3, K_{14}^3	4
	$L_{15}^4, L_{16}^4, L_{15}^3, L_{16}^3$	K_{15}^3, K_{16}^3	4
	$L_{17}^4, L_{18}^4, L_{17}^3, L_{18}^3$	K_{17}^3, K_{18}^3	4
	$L_{19}^4, L_{20}^4, L_{19}^3, L_{20}^3$	K_{19}^3, K_{20}^3	4
	$L_{21}^4, L_{22}^4, L_{21}^3, L_{22}^3$	K_{21}^3, K_{22}^3	4
	$L_{23}^4, L_{24}^4, L_{23}^3, L_{24}^3$	K_{23}^3, K_{24}^3	4
Combined hypothesis			184

Table 3. Attack complexity of SIMON96/96

Correlation between rounds	Correlation bits	Attack bits(Key)	Hypothesis
	L_1^3, L_1^2	$K_{48}^1, K_{47}^1, K_{11}^1, K_1^1, K_1^2$	32
	L_2^3, L_2^2	K_{42}^1, K_2^1, K_2^2	8
	L_3^3, L_3^2	K_{43}^1, K_3^1, K_3^2	8
	L_4^3, L_4^2	K_{44}^1, K_4^1, K_4^2	8
	L_5^3, L_5^2	K_{45}^1, K_5^1, K_5^2	8
	L_6^3, L_6^2	K_{46}^1, K_6^1, K_6^2	8
	L_7^3, L_7^2	K_7^1, K_7^2	4
	L_8^3, L_8^2	K_8^1, K_8^2	4
	L_9^3, L_9^2	K_9^1, K_9^2	4
	L_{10}^3, L_{10}^2	K_{10}^1, K_{10}^2	4
	L_{11}^3, L_{11}^2	K_{11}^1, K_{11}^2	4
	L_{12}^3, L_{12}^2	K_{12}^1, K_{12}^2	4
	L_{13}^3, L_{13}^2	K_{13}^1, K_{13}^2	4
	L_{14}^3, L_{14}^2	K_{14}^1, K_{14}^2	4
	L_{15}^3, L_{15}^2	K_{15}^1, K_{15}^2	4
	L_{16}^3, L_{16}^2	K_{16}^1, K_{16}^2	4
	L_{17}^3, L_{17}^2	K_{17}^1, K_{17}^2	4
	L_{18}^3, L_{18}^2	K_{18}^1, K_{18}^2	4
	L_{19}^3, L_{19}^2	K_{19}^1, K_{19}^2	4
	L_{20}^3, L_{20}^2	K_{20}^1, K_{20}^2	4
	L_{21}^3, L_{21}^2	K_{21}^1, K_{21}^2	4
	L_{22}^3, L_{22}^2	K_{22}^1, K_{22}^2	4
	L_{23}^3, L_{23}^2	K_{23}^1, K_{23}^2	4
	L_{24}^3, L_{24}^2	K_{24}^1, K_{24}^2	4
L^3, L^2	L_{25}^3, L_{25}^2	K_{25}^1, K_{25}^2	4
	L_{26}^3, L_{26}^2	K_{26}^1, K_{26}^2	4
	L_{27}^3, L_{27}^2	K_{27}^1, K_{27}^2	4
	L_{28}^3, L_{28}^2	K_{28}^1, K_{28}^2	4
	L_{29}^3, L_{29}^2	K_{29}^1, K_{29}^2	4
	L_{30}^3, L_{30}^2	K_{30}^1, K_{30}^2	4
	L_{31}^3, L_{31}^2	K_{31}^1, K_{31}^2	4
	L_{32}^3, L_{32}^2	K_{32}^1, K_{32}^2	4
	L_{33}^3, L_{33}^2	K_{33}^1, K_{33}^2	4
	L_{34}^3, L_{34}^2	K_{34}^1, K_{34}^2	4
	L_{35}^3, L_{35}^2	K_{35}^1, K_{35}^2	4
	L_{36}^3, L_{36}^2	K_{36}^1, K_{36}^2	4
	L_{37}^3, L_{37}^2	K_{37}^1, K_{37}^2	4
	L_{38}^3, L_{38}^2	K_{38}^1, K_{38}^2	4
	L_{39}^3, L_{39}^2	K_{39}^1, K_{39}^2	4
	L_{40}^3, L_{40}^2	K_{40}^1, K_{40}^2	4
	$L_{41}^3, L_{42}^2, L_{41}^3, L_{42}^2$	K_{41}^2, K_{42}^2	4
	$L_{43}^3, L_{44}^2, L_{43}^3, L_{44}^2$	K_{43}^2, K_{44}^2	4
	$L_{45}^3, L_{46}^2, L_{45}^3, L_{46}^2$	K_{45}^2, K_{46}^2	4
	$L_{47}^3, L_{48}^2, L_{47}^3, L_{48}^2$	K_{47}^2, K_{48}^2	4
Combined hypothesis			224

B   Appendix

DPA on other versions of LED. LED-64 and LED-128 differs only by key size and so it differs only in AddRoundKey. LED-128 performs 48 rounds and the 128-bit key is divided into two parts $K = K_0 \| K_1$, and used alternatively for every four rounds. The first 64-bit key K_0 is retrieved using the same attack strategy employed for LED-64. After computing the first four rounds of operation using K_0, the next 64-bit key K_1 is retrieved.

The latest version of LED block cipher is published in [15]. This version is introduced to address the problem of using variable size keys, where the key size is not a multiples of 64-bit. This makes minor modification on both AddRoundKey(AK) and AddConstants(AC). In case of key size not in multiples of 64-bit, like 80- and 92-bit, the key is circularly appended to the second part of the key until it matches the required key size. In AddConstants, size of key denoted in eight bits are included in the first column of the matrix.

Our attack will work in the latest version of LED, as the round operation and its diffusion property remains same as the previous version. However, we have experimented with the same measurement set-up and power model described in Section 3 for the latest version of LED. The attack worked with the attack complexity of $(2^{18} + 2^6)$ for 80-bit key size.

LED can also be attacked from the last round. We have experimented with the same set of captured power traces, the attack was successful with the same complexity.

In our attack on LED the data register is updated for every round. The implementation can be serialised by updating the data register for every operation in a round as prescribed in [16]. In that case, if the intermediate result is chosen after the SubCells operation, then the key search space shall be reduced to 2^8 from 2^{18} to reveal 64-bit key.

Khudra: A New Lightweight Block Cipher for FPGAs

Souvik Kolay and Debdeep Mukhopadhyay

Dept. of Computer Science and Engineering
Indian Institute of Technology Kharagpur, India
{souvik1809,debdeep.mukhopadhyay}@cse.iitkgp.ernet.in

Abstract. The paper shows that designing lightweight block ciphers for the increasingly popular Field Programmable Gate Arrays (FPGAs) needs a new revisit. It shows that due to the underlying FPGA architecture many popular techniques for lightweight block ciphers which work on Application Specific Integrated Circuits (ASICs) does not apply to FPGAs. The paper identifies new methods and design criteria for lightweight block ciphers operating on FPGAs. Using these guidelines, a new block cipher *Khudra* based on the recursive Feistel structure is designed, which has a 64 bit block size and 80 bits of key. Rigorous cryptanalysis, ranging from linear and differential cryptanalysis to more powerful attacks like impossible differential, related key attacks etc. have been performed to justify that 18 rounds of *Khudra* provide sufficient security margin. Finally, the cipher has been implemented in two different flavors, *Khudra-I* and *Khudra-II*, on low cost FPGAs like Xilinx Spartan-III XC3S400 and extensively compared with other contemporary ciphers like PRESENT, Piccolo and compact implementations of other standard cipher like AES, Camellia etc. The implementation results show that *Khudra* requires at least around 45% less slices and 29% less AT product compared to round wise implementation of any of the contemporary lightweight block cipher.

Keywords: Lightweight, Block Cipher, FPGAs, Efficient Implementation.

1 Introduction

With the rapid increase of pervasive devices, lightweight cryptography has become a hot topic today. The area of cryptography, which deals with the design, analysis and implementation of cryptographic algorithms for devices with extremely constrained resources is formally termed as *lightweight cryptography*. Designing this kind of cryptographic algorithms always require a trade-off between security, efficiency and resources. As lightweight ciphers are constrained by area, power, and cost, application specific design opportunities in ASIC and amenability to mass productions makes ASIC a popular choice for lightweight crypto-systems. But ASIC chips cannot be reconfigured or modified. On the other hand, Field-programmable gate array (FPGAs) can be reconfigured or upgraded after manufacture. Although ASICs are popular choice for lightweight cryptography, recent low cost FPGAs make them an alternative for battery powered devices (WSN)[31]. Low cost FPGAs seem ideal for the customer producing small amount of WSN or RFIDs. The reconfiguration feature of FPGAs, allowing in-house update of

R.S. Chakraborty et al. (Eds.): SPACE 2014, LNCS 8804, pp. 126–145, 2014.
© Springer International Publishing Switzerland 2014

design, is suited for several applications. With the growing popularity of FPGAs for networking applications, designing lightweight cipher helps to add more functionality and security.

In ASIC designs for lightweight cryptography, the libraries are specially designed. In those cases the synthesizer is forced to use the particular gates, having less GE. For example, Piccolo [27] uses a particular type of cell for XOR and XNOR, not available in UMC18 used by PRESENT [6]. However on FPGAs all designs are mapped to Look-up-Tables (LUTs). Further the number of LUTs largely depend on the number of input variables in the function. To demonstrate this, four 4×4 S-boxes with different GE, has been implemented in Xilinx Spartan 3 FPGA and the result is compared in Table 1. Even though their properties and GE are different, all of them take same number of LUTs. So a cipher which possesses less Gate Equivalence in ASIC, may not necessarily have smaller footprint in case of FPGA implementations. A compact design of a cipher on FPGA, typically follows serialized implementation (use of same module repeatedly). Serialized implementation reduces the area-time(AT) product which is also not desirable even for lightweight devices [8]. A further constraint is to remove the memory elements in the design. This necessitates further strategies for realizing lightweight ciphers on FPGAs.

In this paper, first we show that the strategies used for traditional lightweight ASIC implementation are not suitable for FPGAs. Then we propose new general strategies for designing block ciphers on FPGAs. Keeping these strategies in mind, we propose a new lightweight block cipher for FPGAs, *Khudra*, which encrypts 64 bit plaintext using 80 bit keys. *Khudra* provides sufficient security not only against the classical cryptanalysis but also against the more stronger attacks like MIME and related-key differential attacks. The implementation of *Khudra* not only consumes less resource on FPGAs but also produces good throughput without using any BRAMs. The results have been found to out-perform two of the most popular lightweight block ciphers designed for ASIC (namely PRESENT and Piccolo) and other compact implementation of well known block ciphers. To the best of our knowledge, this is the first reported work in designing a new lightweight cipher specifically for the growingly popular FPGA platforms.

The paper is organized as follows : Section 2 discusses the existing lightweight block ciphers along with their optimization strategies used for ASIC implementation. Section 3 discusses the broad design ideas, followed by detailed design principles in section 4. The security analysis of *Khudra* has been discussed in section 5. Section 6 presents the hardware implementation details of *Khudra* and comparison with the compact FPGA implementation of some well known block ciphers. Finally, we summarize the work done and conclude in section 7.

Table 1. Comparison of Different S-boxes

Implementation Platform	PRESENT[6]	MIBS[28]	LBlock[39]	Piccolo[27]
ASIC (GE)	28	24	22	12
FPGA (SLICE)	2	2	2	2

2   Related Works

Almost all the lightweight block ciphers are targeted for ASIC implementations. Here is a list of some lightweight block ciphers: compact implementation of AES [4] and DES [21], Kasumi [38], mCrypton [10], HIGHT [13], DESL and DESXL [18], CLEFIA [35], PRESENT [6], Puffin [20], MIBS [28], KATAN [11], Klein [41], TWINE [37], LED [23] and Piccolo [27] etc. Generally, these ciphers use at least one of the following strategies for lightweight implementation in ASICs:

> **A:** SPN structure with bit permutation.
> **B:** Feistel 'F-Function' with less Gate Equivalence.
> **C:** S-box with less Gate Equivalence.
> **D:** Using less register in the design.

Table 2. Comparison among the Lightweight Block Ciphers

Cipher	Structure Adopted	Strategies Used	Cipher	Structure Adopted	Strategies Used
AES[1]	SPN	C	CLEFIA	Feistel	B
PRESENT	SPN	A, C	MISTY	Feistel	B
Puffin	SPN	A, C	Kasumi	Feistel	B
LED	SPN	C, D	Twine	Feistel	B, C
DESL, DESXL	Feistel	B	MIBS	Feistel	B, C
HIGHT	Feistel	B	Piccolo	Feistel	B, C, D

Table 2 shows the strategies used in the lightweight block ciphers for the ASIC implementations. The reason for adopting these strategies are as follows:

A: Substitution-Permutation Network(SPN) consists of a Substitution layer followed by a permutation layer. A bit permutation in hardware comes free of cost, because it can be done by just a 'wiring'. Hence, the use of bit permutation as the Permutation layer definitely reduces the area.

B, C: Both these two strategies directly reduce the Gate Equivalence.

D: In ASICs, a register consumes much more 'GE/per bit' than any 'logic gates'. Additionally, implementation results of these lightweight ciphers show that the area consumed only by the registers can be up to 55% of the total area of the whole design. In round wise implementation, registers are generally required for storing intermediate data in data processing part and key scheduling part. Latest lightweight block ciphers like LED and Piccolo use 'no key schedule' and 'multiplexer based key schedule' respectively, which does not require any register to implement the key schedule.

Some techniques have been proposed in [31] for the serialized implementations of two well known lightweight block ciphers: HIGHT and PRESENT on FPGAs, These implementations reduce the slice requirements about 2 times but require 4.7 and 8 times more clock cycles than the round-wise implementations of HIGHT and PRESENT respectively. For this reason, area-time product decreases significantly. In [17], involutive

---

[1] Compact implementation of AES [4].

ciphers ICEBERG has been proposed specifically for FPGA implementation. There are also few compact implementations on FPGAs of some well known traditional block ciphers, like AES [22,32,40], Serpent[1], Camellia [30] and Misty[29]. These implementations generally use some special techniques for serialization to occupy less slices on FPGAs.

3 Goals and Methods for Designing Lightweight Ciphers on FPGAs

In this section, first we discuss the design constraints for lightweight implementation on FPGAs. We argue that lightweight block ciphers mentioned on table 2 will not produce equivalently lightweight designs on FPGAs. Based on these observations, we propose a new design strategy for lightweight cryptography on FPGAs and show how it is applied to our new lightweight block cipher, *Khudra*.

3.1 Motivation of Designing Lightweight Ciphers for FPGAs

For compact design, serialized architectures are often used in both ASICs and FPGAs. In this technique, the same hardware is used repeatedly in some clock cycles to process one block of data. Thus, it definitely reduces the area in both platforms, but also reduces the throughput significantly. Hence, it is not a good option for lightweight cryptography, where throughput also now comes into consideration [8]. Let us review the ASIC strategies discussed in section 2 with respect to the FPGA platforms.

A: In both ASIC and FPGA, bit permutation can be implemented by simple wiring (if there is no routing congestion). So, this strategy reduces the area requirement in both cases.

B, C: For ASICs, less gates are desirable, while for FPGAs, less LUTs are desirable. Strategies B and C are both targeted for ASICs. As discussed in Section 1 and Table 1, the FPGA resources namely slices which are comprised of LUTs, depend on the number of inputs of a function. This rules out any optimization due to the choice of S-boxes with less gates as used in PRESENT and Piccolo to be effective in reducing LUTs on FPGA. Similarly the choice of suitable diffusion layers have no effect in reducing LUTs.

D: An n-input LUT can map any combinatorial logic with n input variables and the flip-flops inside the slice are used to design any sequential circuit. For FPGAs the ratio between the registers and the LUTs are crucial. While applying strategy D, if a design require more LUTs than flip-flops, then some slice will be occupied only to use the LUTs in the slice. Thus use of less register in the design may leads to unutilized flip-flops in some slices.

The above reasons show that except strategy A, none of them are useful for lightweight implementations on FPGAs. From table 2 we can see that all the block ciphers with SPN structure adopt strategy C and all ciphers with the Feistel Structure adopts strategy B. Besides some of these adopt strategy D. Hence, we can say that for lightweight FPGA implementation, most of the strategies do not work. Thus, an existing lightweight cipher may not be equally lightweight on FPGAs. Furthermore, it also motivates to develop block ciphers which are secured and are also lightweight on FPGA platforms.

3.2 Lightweight Strategy for FPGA Implementation

Smaller and cheaper FPGAs, that are suitable for lightweight implementation, normally contain LUTs that has only one output pin. So any function that produces an output of n bits and each of the output bit is dependent on at least 2 input bits, cannot be implemented using less than n LUTs on these FPGAs. Generally, two design strategies are followed for designing block cipher: Substitution - Permutation Network (SPN) and Feistel Network. A lower bound of the LUT requirements for implementing both these structures on FPGAs is provided, considering the plaintext size of n bits and key size of k.

SPN Structure:

> *Key XORing:* n bit key XORing has been done in this step, thus requires n LUTs.
> *Substitution Layer:* It is a $n \times n$ function, thus requires at least n LUTs.
> *Permutation Layer:* This step can be realized using bit permutation, thus no LUT is needed.

Feistel Structure:

> *Key XORing:* At least $n/2$ bit key XORing has been done in this step, thus requires at least $n/2$ LUTs.
> *F-Function:* Inside this function substitution and diffusion layer is used.
> *Substitution Layer:* At least $n/2$ bit substitution layer is used in this step, thus requires at least $n/2$ LUTs.
> *Diffusion Layer:* It is a $m \times n/2$ mapping, where $2 \leq m \leq n/2$, so this step will also require at least $n/2$ bit LUTs.
> Permutation Layer: It is the default Feistel Permutation, which requires $n/2$ XORs, thus the LUT requirement is $n/2$.

Here, we have not considered the Key-scheduling, which also require significant amount of LUTs. Further, as the encryption is done in some rounds, $n+k$ bit registers and $n+k$ number of 2 : 1 mux is also required for the feedback of message and keys of the previous round. For this purposes, $n + k$ flip-flops and $n + k$ LUTs are required. Thus, total number of LUTs required is at least $3 \times n + k$ and register is at least $n + k$. Generally, an FPGA slice contains equal number of LUTs and Flip-Flops, so finally in most of the slices only the LUTs are used and Flip-Flops remained unused.

From this observation, we can say that number of slices can be reduced if we can decrease the LUT requirements by utilizing some more flip-flops. For this reason, we have denoted the ratio between total number of LUT utilization and total number of Flip-Flop utilization as ($R_{LUT/FF}$) and propose the following strategy for **balancing LUTs and Flip-Flops:**

– *To choose a new design for which number of LUTs reduces, number of flip-flops increases and the ratio ($R_{LUT/FF}$) is close to 1.*

Note that $R_{LUT/FF} = 1$ does not produce the smallest implementation, but reduce the number of under utilized slices. The novelty of the work shows that such design criteria leads to a compact architecture yet not fully serialized, thus having promising throughput.

3.3   Proposed Cipher Architecture Based on the Strategies

Data Processing Part. For the same block size, Feistel structure with 'SP F-function' uses half of the number of S-boxes than SPN, but due to the use of costly diffusion(permutation) layer, both of the structures require almost same resources. Therefore, we plan to use the Feistel structure in our design to reduce the number of S-boxes but without using any extra diffusion layer. Feistel structure has two parts: F-function and a Feistel permutation. Inside the F-function of a Feistel structure, two types of approaches are generally used: SP and SPS. SP provides one substitution layer followed by a permutation layer and SPS provides one substitution layer followed by a permutation layer and followed by another substitution layer. Realizing the F-function of our Feistel structure, we have used r rounds of Feistel structure recursively inside the F-function. A simple n block Feistel permutation requires only $n/2$, 2 input XORs, where as for the same block size, Camellia type of diffusion layer (used in MIBS) or MDS matrix (used in Clefia and Piccolo) requires much more area. Instead, by using the proposed recursive architecture, we reduce both the number of S-boxes and resource requirement for the permutation layer. The number of rounds: r, inside the F-function is decided, considering both security and efficiency. As the F-function is computed in

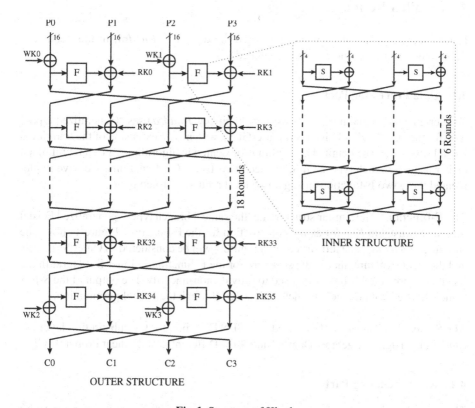

Fig. 1. Structure of Khudra

rounds, the intermediate values are stored in some registers. As discussed, these registers improve the utilization of the slices, by reducing the wastage of the FFs in the slices. The further advantage is the reduction in the LUTs. Thus the ratio $R_{LUT/F-F}$ reduces and slice utilization also reduces. Hence we propose the design of a new lightweight cipher, *Khudra*, with this recursive design structure.

Key Scheduling Part. For key scheduling, recently proposed lightweight block ciphers either have chosen simple multiplexer based key-schedule or no key-schedule. Both of these techniques do not require any register for storing the master keys or the round keys but the master keys should be hold in the input pins, throughout the entire encryption process. As the low cost FPGAs, generally comes with limited number of I/O pins, so this strategy is not very much suitable for lightweight implementation on FPGAs. Again, the above mentioned strategy also occupy only LUTs and no FFs (as there is no need of registers). Keeping these facts in mind, we have planned to used a shift-register base key-schedule, which require less number of LUTs and more FFs. As for the data processing part, *Khudra* require more LUTs compared to FFs, so the planned key-schedule will improve the overall $R_{LUT/F-F}$ ratio.

4   Detailed Design

Having discussed the ideas which governed the design of *Khudra*, in this section, a detailed description of the design is provided.

4.1   Data Processing Part

To encrypt a 64 bit plaintext block using a 80 bit key, *Khudra* uses "Generalized type-2 transformations" [19] of Feistel Structure(GFS), which is an extension of the traditional Feistel Structure. The detailed algorithm is presented in algorithm 2. For a 64 bit block cipher using 4 branch type-2 GFS, we need two 16×16 F-Functions. We have implemented these two F-functions using a two level recursive structure.

The F-function. The similar structure i.e. the same 4 branch type-2 generalized Feistel Structure is used in *Khudra* as the construction for the F-Function. Figure 1 shows the structure of *Khudra*. The left structure in Figure 1 will be considered as Outer Structure, and the right structure, that is the structure for the F-function as Inner Structure. In the inner structure, 4×4 S-boxes are used to provide non-linearity. The output of the S-box is then XORed with the next branch and passed through the Feistel permutation.

The S-box. In *Khudra*, we have used PRESENT's S-box for the substitution layer because of its 'Higher Algebraic Degree' and 'Low Differential and Linear Probability' [6].

4.2   Key Scheduling Part

The key scheduling part of *Khudra* takes a master key of 80 bits and generates 16 bit round-keys $RKi(0 \leq i < 36)$ and 16 bit whitening keys $WKi(0 \leq i < 4)$. Initially, input keys are stored in a 80 bit key register K and represented as $k_0||k_1||k_2||k_3||k_4$, where each k_i is of 16 bits for $0 \leq i < 5$). Whitening keys (WKi) and round keys (RKi) are generated according to algorithm 1. RCi denotes the 16 bit round constant and $i_{(6)}$ is the 6 bit representation of the round counter i.

Algorithm 1. Key Scheduling (k_0, k_1, k_2, k_3, k_4)

$WK0 \leftarrow k_0, WK1 \leftarrow k_1, WK3 \leftarrow k_3, WK4 \leftarrow k_4$
for $i \leftarrow 0$ *to* 35 **do**
  $\quad RCi \leftarrow \{0||i_{(6)}||00||i_{(6)}||0\}$
  $\quad RKi \leftarrow k_{i \bmod 5} \oplus RCi$
end

Algorithm 2. Encryption

Input: Plaintext $P[63:0]$ and Round Key $RK[36][15:0]$
Output: Ciphertext $C[63:0]$
begin
  for $i = 0$ *to* 17 **do**
    $\quad tp_3[15:0] \leftarrow P[63:48], \; tp_1[15:0] \leftarrow P[31:16]$;
    $\quad$ **for** $j = 0$ *to* 5 **do**
      $\quad\quad tq_3[3:0] \leftarrow P[63:60], \; tq_1[3:0] \leftarrow P[55:52]$;
      $\quad\quad P[63:60] \leftarrow S(P[63:60]) \oplus P[59:56]$;
      $\quad\quad P[55:52] \leftarrow S(P[55:52]) \oplus P[51:48]$;
      $\quad\quad P[59:56] \leftarrow tq_1[3:0], \; P[51:48] \leftarrow tq_3[3:0]$;
      $\quad\quad tr_3[3:0] \leftarrow P[31:28], \; tr_1[3:0] \leftarrow P[23:20]$;
      $\quad\quad P[31:28] \leftarrow S(P[31:28]) \oplus P[27:24]$;
      $\quad\quad P[23:20] \leftarrow S(P[23:20]) \oplus P[19:16]$;
      $\quad\quad P[27:24] \leftarrow tr_1[3:0], \; P[19:16] \leftarrow tr_3[3:0]$;
    $\quad$ **end**
    $\quad P[63:48] \leftarrow P[63:48] \oplus P[47:32] \oplus RK[2 \times i + 1][15:0]$;
    $\quad P[31:16] \leftarrow P[31:16] \oplus P[15:0] \oplus RK[2 \times i][15:0]$;
    $\quad P[47:32] \leftarrow tp_1[15:0], \; P[15:0] \leftarrow tp_3[15:0]$;
  end
end

---

5 Security Analysis

In this section, we will discuss the security analysis of *Khudra* against some popular attacks, like differential cryptanalysis, linear cryptanalysis, impossible differential attack, differential-linear attack, algebraic attack, boomerang type attacks, slide key attack and related key attack.

5.1 Differential Cryptanalysis (DC) and Linear Cryptanalysis (LC)

In order to measure the resistance of *Khudra* against linear and differential cryptanalysis, we have calculated the minimum number of so called 'active S-boxes', and their differential or linear approximation probabilities. An exhaustive search has been performed using the properties mentioned in Appendix A to compute the number of active S-boxes. For the inner structure of *Khudra*, we have found at least 6 active S-boxes in the differential and linear characteristics. These S-boxes have both differential and linear probability of 2^{-2}. So, the F-function of *Khudra* has a differential and linear probability $2^{(-2) \times 6} = 2^{-12}$. Then, we have computed the minimum number of 'active F-Functions' in both differential and linear characteristics. Table 3 shows the number of 'active F-Functions', with the varying number of rounds. From this table, We see that 6 rounds of *Khudra* have at least 6 'active F-Functions'. Combining the probabilities of these 6 'active F-Functions', *Khudra* consisting of at least 6 rounds has no differential or linear characteristics whose probabilities are more than 2^{-72}. Thus, we conclude that the full round of *Khudra*, which have both the linear and differential properties of 2^{-216}, is sufficiently secure against both linear and differential cryptanalysis.

Table 3. Minimum number of active F-Functions in Single-key and Related-key settings

No. of rounds:	1	2	3	4	5	6	7	8	9	10	11	12	13	14	15	16	17	18
Min # active Single-key	0	1	2	3	4	6	6	7	8	9	10	12	12	13	14	15	16	18
F-Functions Related-key	0	0	0	1	2	3	3	3	4	5	6	6	7	7	8	9	9	10

5.2 Impossible Differential Cryptanalysis (IDC)

Impossible Differential Cryptanalysis is one of the most powerful attack for Feistel Structure, due to its slow diffusion and use of smaller S-boxes in the F-function. To show the resistance against this kind of attack, first we have considered 16-bit truncated differential followed by 4-bit truncated differential. To search for the impossible differential, we have followed the steps mentioned in [25]. We have found that for 16-bit truncated differential, 7 rounds of *Khudra* has no impossible differential. While for 4-bit truncated differential, 10 rounds of *Khudra* has no impossible differential. Based on these observations, we have tried to attack 11 rounds of *Khudra* with the impossible differential found after 9 round. The detailed attacking methodology has been described in Appendix B. In this case, the number of chosen plain text required is 2^{57} and the time complexity for finding RK_{19} and RK_{21} is around 2^{61} encryptions for 11 round of *Khudra*. Hence, we claim full round *Khudra* has immunity against the impossible differential cryptanalysis.

5.3 Truncated Differential Attacks (TDA)

Truncated differential cryptanalysis is a general technique for the analysis of block ciphers with byte oriented structure [26]. To find the best round-reduced truncated differentials we have used the approach mentioned in [3] combined with the following standard assumptions:

1. S-boxes have no effect on the probability because they cannot change an active nibble into an non-active nibble and vice versa.
2. XOR can cancel two active nibbles with probability 2^{-4}.

Table 4. Round-wise best truncated differential probabilities (TDP) of *Khudra*

Number of Rounds	1	2	3	4	5	6	7	8	9	10
Best 4-bit TDP	0	2^{-12}	2^{-24}	2^{-40}	2^{-56}	2^{-84}	2^{-84}	2^{-96}	2^{-108}	2^{-124}
Lower bound on best TDP	0	$2^{-11.7}$	$2^{-23.4}$	2^{-39}	$2^{-54.6}$	$2^{-81.9}$	$2^{-81.9}$	$2^{-93.6}$	$2^{-105.3}$	$2^{-120.9}$

Second row of the table 4 provides the best 4 bit truncated differential probabilities (TDP) with the varying number of rounds. Further, we consider a more stronger scenario, where the attacker can even control the difference within a nibble. In this case, we assume that each time attacker able to cancel two active nibbles with the difference that has the maximum probability. For Present's s-box the maximum probability is $\frac{1}{15} \approx 2^{3.9}$. Using this over estimation, we have computed the best truncated differential probability and results has been provided in the third row of the table 4. For both of this cases, we can see that no truncated differential exists after 6 rounds of *Khudra*. Thus, we can conclude that the full round *Khudra* has sufficient security margin against truncated differential attacks.

5.4 Differential-Linear Cryptanalysis

Differential-Linear Cryptanalysis was proposed by Langford and Hellman in [34]. In this technique, the attacker utilizes the differential characteristic for the first part of the cipher and linear approximation for the remaining part of the cipher. '*Letting p be a probability of a certain differential characteristic and letting q be a probability of a certain linear approximation, the complexity of the differential-linear cryptanalysis would have the complexity order of about p^2q^2 [33]*'. As discussed in Appendix , any round of *Khudra* has the same 'Differential' and 'Linear' probability. So, if p be the differential probability for the first part of the cipher, and q be the linear probability for the remaining part of the cipher, we can say that q is also the differential probability of the remaining part of the cipher. Thus, the full round differential probability can be at most pq, which is greater than p^2q^2 (as, $0 \leq p \leq 1$ and $0 \leq q \leq 1$). Therefore, we can say that for *Khudra*, differential-linear cryptanalysis is weaker than the differential cryptanalysis.

5.5 Boomerang Type Attacks (BA)

Various kinds of boomerang attacks like 'The Boomerang' [12], 'Amplified Boomerang' [24] and 'Rectangle Attack' [16] have been proposed. These attacks divide the cipher into two sub-ciphers, then find a boomerang quartet with high probability. To show the resistance against these kind of attacks, we have computed the number of differential active F-Function in each sub-cipher. From table 5, we can see that any combination of two sub-ciphers of 8 round *Khudra* has at least 6 active F-Functions. Again, an F-Function of *Khudra* has differential probability of 2^{-12}. So, the highest probability boomerang quartet of 8 round *Khudra* can have the probability at most 2^{-72}. Likewise, the full round *Khudra*, has the highest probability boomerang quartet of at most 2^{-192}, and thus provide enough immunity against the boomerang type attacks.

Table 5. # active F-functions for all combinations of sub-ciphers on 8 round *Khudra*

# rounds in sub-cipher1 / active f-function:	1/0	2/1	3/2	4/3
# rounds in sub-cipher2 / active f-function:	7/6	6/6	5/4	4/3
Total #active F-function after 8 rounds:	6	7	6	6

5.6   Key Scheduling Attacks

Slide Attack and Related Key Attack. Two well known attacks on the key-scheduling algorithm, namely slide [2] and related key attacks [14], use the simple relations and similarities among the round-keys to get the actual master key. To remove the *self-similarity* in the key scheduling algorithm, in each round, we have different round constants, generated by the round counter. This strategy makes *Khudra* secure against these two key-scheduling attacks.

Related-Key Differential Cryptanalysis (RDC). In related-key differential cryptanalysis, adversary can control the difference both in plaintext and key-schedule to cancel out differences in data processing part. In order to show the resistance of *Khudra* against these kind of attacks, we have calculated the minimum number of 'active F-functions' in related-key settings. Table 3 shows the number of 'active F-Functions' in the related-key settings, with the varying number of rounds. 11 rounds of *Khudra* has at least 6 'active F-Functions'. Thus, we conclude that the full round of *Khudra* is secure against related-key differential cryptanalysis.

Related-Key Boomerang Attacks (RBA). We also consider boomerang and rectangle attacks [9] in related-key settings. To show the resistance against these kind of attacks, we have computed the number of differential active F-Function in each sub-cipher in the related-key settings. From table 3, we can see that any combination of full round *Khudra* has at least 6 active F-Functions. So, the highest probability boomerang quartet of 14 round *Khudra* can have the probability at most 2^{-72} and thus provide enough immunity against related-key boomerang type attacks.

Meet-in-the-Middle Attack (MITM). The recently proposed 3-subset meet-in-the-middle attack works well for block cipher with simple key schedule and slow diffusion. The computational complexity (C_{comp}) of the attack can be bounded by the following estimation [5]:

$$C_{comp} = 2^{|A_0|}(2^{|A_1|} + 2^{|A_2|}) + (2^{l-m} + 2^{l-m-b} + 2^{l-m-2b} + \cdots)$$

The notations are used as mentioned in [5]. We have performed an exhaustive search on 12 round *Khudra* as discussed in section 5.6 previously for calculating the first part of the equation (shown in bold font). The computational complexity is found to be at least 2^{80} for any case. Hence, we can rule out a possibility for such an attack.

Table 6. Comparison of the Security Margin

Cipher	DC	LC	IDC	BA	RDC	RBA	MITM
PRESENT[6]	25 rounds (2^{-100})	28 rounds (2^{-43})	Not Reported	Not Reported	Not Reported	Not Reported	Not Reported
Piccolo[27]	7 rounds $(2^{-65.1})$	8 rounds 2^{-64}	7 round (4 bit TD)	9 rounds $(2^{-65.1})$	14 rounds $(2^{-65.1})$	17 rounds $(2^{-65.1})$	19 rounds $(> 2^{80})$
Khudra	6 rounds (2^{-72})	6 rounds 2^{-72}	9 round (4 bit TD)	8 rounds (2^{-72})	11 rounds (2^{-72})	14 rounds (2^{-72})	12 rounds $(> 2^{80})$

Table 6 provides number of rounds required for PRESENT, Piccolo and *Khudra* to achieve sufficient security margin against different kinds of attacks. In the table, the entries corresponding to the attacks best on linear and differential cryptanalysis (DC, LC, IDC, BA, RDC, RBA) mention the probability for linear or differential trail. While that for MITM mentions the computational complexity. This discussion shows that full round *Khudra* provides security margin comparable to PRESENT and Piccolo.

6   Implementation Details and Comparison

Having analyzed the security of *Khudra*, now comes the vital step of implementing the cipher in hardware. In this section, first we will describe the architecture for FPGA implementation along with the comparison of the implementation result with some of the lightweight ciphers for ASICs and other compact implementations of standard well known block ciphers.

6.1   FPGA Implementations

Data Processing Part. Figure 2 shows an overall block diagram of the hardware implementations of the outer structure of *Khudra*. In figure, X denotes the 64 bit plaintext input and Y denotes 64 bit state of the cipher, which is updated in every round. The architecture exactly follows the structure of *Khudra* as shown in fig. 1. 'F-Function' of *Khudra* can be implemented in various ways. Here, we have shown two different ways to implement the 'F-function' and depending on that, we have named two variants of *Khudra*: *Khudra-I* and *Khudra-II*. '2r Feistel' and '3r Feistel' block contains hardware for the 2 and 3 rounds of the 'inner structure' respectively.

In our implementation, to use more flip-flops and minimize the use of LUTs, we have first computed the 'F-function' of *Khudra*, in some clock cycles and the value is stored in a 16 bit register. Adopting this strategy, we do not need dedicated hardware for the whole 'F-function', thus we can save some LUTs. In the 'F-function' of *Khudra - I*,

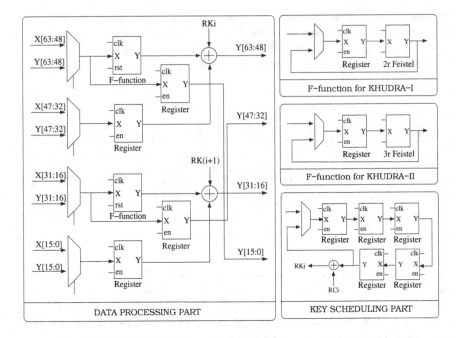

Fig. 2. Block Diagram for Hardware Implementation

due to the '2r Feistel', we need 3 clock cycles to compute the 'F-function', as the inner structure of Khudra has 6 rounds. Similarly, in case of *Khudra-II* we need 2 clock cycles to compute the 'F-function'. After the computation of the 'F-function', this value is used in the 'Outer Structure'. Hence, to complete the whole encryption process, we need $14 \times 3 = 42$, $14 \times 2 = 28$ clock cycles respectively for *Khudra-I* and *Khudra-II*. It can be noted that by incrementally unrolling the serialized implementation, $R_{LUT/FF} = 1$ can be reached, but throughput reduces drastically. In [8], Poschmann et al. have shown that beyond certain point, minimizing the area using serialization does not produce the best result in terms of AT product. This is the reason for not using hardware for one round of the inner structure to compute the 'F-function'.

Key Scheduling Part. As discussed earlier, to reduce the i/o port requirement we have implemented the key scheduling part using shift register. To load the master key in the register, our design requires 5 clock cycles. Note that these extra 5 clock cycles only require if user wants to change the keys, do not require for every encryption if the key is same. This shift register base implementation reduces the requirements of the multiplexer and also increases the requirements of registers, which improve the $R_{LUT/FF}$ ratio.

6.2   Implementation Results and Comparison

We have implemented both the variants of *Khudra* in Verilog on the *Spartan-III XC3S400* (Package FG456 with speed grade -5) FPGA core from Xilinx. In table 7, we have compared the implementation results of *Khudra* with HIGHT, PRESENT and Piccolo on the same FPGA device. First two rows of the table 7 shows the fully serialized implementation results of HIGHT and PRESENT. Though the slice requirement reduces due to the serialized implementation but AT product increases significantly. The next two rows show the round wise implementation results of PRESENT and Piccolo. This comparison shows the improvement on the ratio $R_{LUT/FF}$ over these two ciphers. Due to the recursive structure, our design requires less LUTs compared to PRESENT and Piccolo but requires more flip-flops. One slice of *Spartan-III XC3S400* contains two LUTs and two slice flip-flops. So it is also clear from the result that any of the two implementations of *Khudra*, does not need any additional flip-flops except the available flip-flops on the occupied slice. Thus, this increase in the number of flip-flops, has no adverse effect on the resource requirements of the cipher. Further, we have compared the implementation result of *Khudra* with some other compact implementations of popular block ciphers in table 8. In this comparison, we can clearly see that *Khudra* has less slice requirements as well as AT product than any of these block ciphers.

Table 7. Comparison with Lightweight Ciphers

Cipher	LUTs	Flip-Flop	$R_{LUT/FF}$	Area (Slice)	Cycles per block	Throughput @ 100 kHz (kbits)	AT Product (slice × cycles)
PRESENT [31]	159	114	1.39	**117**	256	25	**29, 952**
HIGHT [31]	132	25	5.28	**91**	160	40	**14, 560**
PRESENT [7]	350	154	2.27	**202**	32	200	**6, 464**
Piccolo	374	73	5.12	**235**	27	237	**6, 345**
Khudra-I*	214	182	1.17	**112**	54	118.5	**6, 048**
Khudra-II*	240	181	1.32	**128**	36	177.8	**4, 602**

* Though the number of Flip-Flops are more compared to others, it does not require any extra Slice as the $R_{LUT/FF}$ ratio is greater than 1

Table 8. Comparison of Khudra with Well known Block Ciphers

Cipher	Platform and Implementation Strategy	Block Size (bits)	Area (slice)	Cycles per block	Throughput @ 100 kHz (kbits)	AT Product (slice × cycles)
ICEBERG [17]	Virtex-II, L	64	**631**	34	188.2	**21, 454**
ICEBERG [17]	Virtex-II, L(R)	64	**526**	34	188.2	**17, 884**
AES [22]	XC2S30, S	128	**393**	534	23.9	**209, 862**
AES [32]	XC2S30, S(R)	128	**222***	46	278	**10, 212**
Camellia [30]	XC3S50, S	128	**318**	875	14.63	**278, 250**
Camellia [30]	XC3S50, S(R)	128	**214**	875	14.63	**1462.89**
Khudra-I	XC3S400	64	**112**	54	118.5	**6, 048**
Khudra-II	XC3S400	64	**128**	36	177.8	**4, 602**

L: Loop Architecture [17], S: Serialize Architecture, (R): Block RAM based implementation

* The equivalent slice implementation requires 522 slices [36]

7 Conclusion

In this paper, we have shown that the strategies for designing lightweight block cipher on ASICs are not suitable for FPGAs. Further, we have identified new methods and design criteria for designing lightweight block ciphers on FPGAs. Using these guidelines, this paper puts forward an idea of a new lightweight block cipher, *Khudra*, using a recursive Feistel structure, which uses 80 bit keys to encrypt 64 bit data. Extensive security analysis have also been provided to justify the security of the scheme against conventional attacks. The paper suggests new criteria based on the parameter, $R_{LUT/FF}$ to develop lightweight FPGA implementations for ciphers, and shows how the architecture for *Khudra* achieves the same. Finally, the comparisons with well known lightweight ciphers and compact implementations of standard ciphers have been provided to demonstrate the benefits of the method.

References

1. Elbirt, A.J., Paar, C.: An FPGA implementation and performance evaluation of the Serpent block cipher. In: FPGA, pp. 33–40 (2000)
2. Biryukov, A., Wagner, D.: Advanced Slide Attacks. In: Preneel, B. (ed.) EUROCRYPT 2000. LNCS, vol. 1807, pp. 589–606. Springer, Heidelberg (2000)
3. Biryukov, A., Nikolic, I.: Security Analysis of the Block Cipher CLEFIA (2012), http://www.cryptrec.go.jp/estimation/techrep_id2202-2.pdf
4. Moradi, A., Poschmann, A., Ling, S., Paar, C., Wang, H.: Pushing the Limits: A Very Compact and a Threshold Implementation of AES. In: Paterson, K.G. (ed.) EUROCRYPT 2011. LNCS, vol. 6632, pp. 69–88. Springer, Heidelberg (2011)
5. Bogdanov, A., Rechberger, C.: A 3-Subset Meet-in-the-Middle Attack: Cryptanalysis of the Lightweight Block Cipher KTANTAN. In: Biryukov, A., Gong, G., Stinson, D.R. (eds.) SAC 2010. LNCS, vol. 6544, pp. 229–240. Springer, Heidelberg (2011)
6. Bogdanov, A.A., Knudsen, L.R., Leander, G., Paar, C., Poschmann, A., Robshaw, M.J.B., Seurin, Y., Vikkelsoe, C.: PRESENT: An Ultra-Lightweight Block Cipher. In: Paillier, P., Verbauwhede, I. (eds.) CHES 2007. LNCS, vol. 4727, pp. 450–466. Springer, Heidelberg (2007)
7. Poschmann, A.: Lightweight Cryptography - Cryptographic Engineering for a Pervasive World. IACR Cryptology ePrint Archive 2009, 516 (2009)
8. Poschmann, A., Robshaw, M.J.B.: On Area, Time, and the Right Trade-Off. In: Susilo, W., Mu, Y., Seberry, J. (eds.) ACISP 2012. LNCS, vol. 7372, pp. 404–418. Springer, Heidelberg (2012)
9. Biham, E., Dunkelman, O., Keller, N.: Related-key boomerang and rectangle attacks. In: Cramer, R. (ed.) EUROCRYPT 2005. LNCS, vol. 3494, pp. 507–525. Springer, Heidelberg (2005), http://dx.doi.org/10.1007/11426639_30
10. Lim, C.H., Korkishko, T.: mCrypton – A Lightweight Block Cipher for Security of Low-Cost RFID Tags and Sensors. In: Song, J.-S., Kwon, T., Yung, M. (eds.) WISA 2005. LNCS, vol. 3786, pp. 243–258. Springer, Heidelberg (2006)
11. De Cannière, C., Dunkelman, O., Knežević, M.: KATAN and KTANTAN — A Family of Small and Efficient Hardware-Oriented Block Ciphers. In: Clavier, C., Gaj, K. (eds.) CHES 2009. LNCS, vol. 5747, pp. 272–288. Springer, Heidelberg (2009)
12. Wagner, D.: The Boomerang Attack. In: Knudsen, L.R. (ed.) FSE 1999. LNCS, vol. 1636, pp. 156–170. Springer, Heidelberg (1999)
13. Hong, D., et al.: HIGHT: A New Block Cipher Suitable for Low-Resource Device. In: Goubin, L., Matsui, M. (eds.) CHES 2006. LNCS, vol. 4249, pp. 46–59. Springer, Heidelberg (2006)

14. Biham, E.: New Types of Cryptanalytic Attacks Using Related Keys. J. Cryptology 7(4), 229–246 (1994)
15. Biham, E.: On Matsui's Linear Cryptanalysis. In: De Santis, A. (ed.) EUROCRYPT 1994. LNCS, vol. 950, pp. 341–355. Springer, Heidelberg (1995)
16. Biham, E., Dunkelman, O., Keller, N.: The Rectangle Attack - Rectangling the Serpent. In: Pfitzmann, B. (ed.) EUROCRYPT 2001. LNCS, vol. 2045, pp. 340–357. Springer, Heidelberg (2001)
17. Standaert, F.-X., Piret, G., Rouvroy, G., Quisquater, J.-J.: FPGA implementations of the ICE-BERG block cipher. Integration, the VLSI Journal 40(1), 20–27 (2007), Embedded Cryptographic Hardware,
    http://www.sciencedirect.com/science/article/pii/
    S016792600500060X
18. Leander, G., Paar, C., Poschmann, A., Schramm, K.: New Lightweight DES Variants. In: Biryukov, A. (ed.) FSE 2007. LNCS, vol. 4593, pp. 196–210. Springer, Heidelberg (2007)
19. Hoang, V.T., Rogaway, P.: On Generalized Feistel Networks. In: Rabin, T. (ed.) CRYPTO 2010. LNCS, vol. 6223, pp. 613–630. Springer, Heidelberg (2010),
    http://dx.doi.org/10.1007/978-3-642-14623-7_33
20. Cheng, H., Heys, H.M., Wang, C.: PUFFIN: A Novel Compact Block Cipher Targeted to Embedded Digital Systems. In: DSD, pp. 383–390 (2008)
21. Verbauwhede, I., Hoornaert, F., Vandewalle, J., DeMan, H.J.: Security and Performance Optimization of a new DES Data Encryption Chip. IEEE Journal of Solid-State Circuits 23, 647–656 (1988)
22. Kaps, J.-P., Sunar, B.: Energy Comparison of AES and SHA-1 for Ubiquitous Computing. In: EUC Workshops, pp. 372–381 (2006)
23. Guo, J., Peyrin, T., Poschmann, A., Robshaw, M.: The LED block cipher. In: Preneel, B., Takagi, T. (eds.) CHES 2011. LNCS, vol. 6917, pp. 326–341. Springer, Heidelberg (2011)
24. Kelsey, J., Kohno, T., Schneier, B.: Amplified Boomerang attacks Against Reduced-Round MARS and Serpent (2000)
25. Kim, J., Hong, S., Sung, J., Lee, C., Lee, S.: Impossible Differential Cryptanalysis for Block Cipher Structures. In: Johansson, T., Maitra, S. (eds.) INDOCRYPT 2003. LNCS, vol. 2904, pp. 82–96. Springer, Heidelberg (2003)
26. Knudsen, L.R.: Truncated and higher order differentials. In: Preneel, B. (ed.) FSE 1994. LNCS, vol. 1008, pp. 196–211. Springer, Heidelberg (1995)
27. Shibutani, K., Isobe, T., Hiwatari, H., Mitsuda, A., Akishita, T., Shirai, T.: *Piccolo*: An Ultra-Lightweight Blockcipher. In: Preneel, B., Takagi, T. (eds.) CHES 2011. LNCS, vol. 6917, pp. 342–357. Springer, Heidelberg (2011)
28. Izadi, M., Sadeghiyan, B., Sadeghian, S.S., Khanooki, H.A.: MIBS: A New Lightweight Block Cipher. In: Garay, J.A., Miyaji, A., Otsuka, A. (eds.) CANS 2009. LNCS, vol. 5888, pp. 334–348. Springer, Heidelberg (2009)
29. Matsui, M.: New Block Encryption Algorithm MISTY. In: Biham, E. (ed.) FSE 1997. LNCS, vol. 1267, pp. 54–68. Springer, Heidelberg (1997)
30. Yalla, P., Kaps, J.-P.: Compact FPGA implementation of Camellia. In: FPL, pp. 658–661 (2009)
31. Yalla, P., Kaps, J.-P.: Lightweight Cryptography for FPGAs. In: ReConFig, pp. 225–230 (2009)
32. Chodowiec, P., Gaj, K.: Very Compact FPGA Implementation of the AES Algorithm. In: Walter, C.D., Koç, Ç.K., Paar, C. (eds.) CHES 2003. LNCS, vol. 2779, pp. 319–333. Springer, Heidelberg (2003)
33. SONY: The 128-bit Blockcipher CLEFIA: Security and Performance Evaluations,
    http://www.sony.net/Products/cryptography/clefia/download/
    data/clefia-eval-1.0.pdf

34. Langford, S.K., Hellman, M.E.: Differential-Linear Cryptanalysis. In: Desmedt, Y.G. (ed.) CRYPTO 1994. LNCS, vol. 839, pp. 17–25. Springer, Heidelberg (1994)
35. Shirai, T., Shibutani, K., Akishita, T., Moriai, S., Iwata, T.: The 128-Bit Blockcipher CLE-FIA (Extended Abstract). In: Biryukov, A. (ed.) FSE 2007. LNCS, vol. 4593, pp. 181–195. Springer, Heidelberg (2007)
36. Good, T., Benaissa, M.: AES on FPGA from the Fastest to the Smallest. In: Rao, J.R., Sunar, B. (eds.) CHES 2005. LNCS, vol. 3659, pp. 427–440. Springer, Heidelberg (2005)
37. Suzaki, T., Minematsu, K., Morioka, S., Kobayashi, E.: TWINE: A Lightweight, Versatile Block Cipher. In: ECRYPT Workshop on Lightweight Cryptography, vol. 2011, pp. 148–169 (November 2011)
38. Hoang, V.T., Rogaway, P.: Design Principles of the KASUMI Block Cipher. IACR Cryptology ePrint Archive 2010, 301 (2010)
39. Wu, W., Zhang, L.: LBlock: A Lightweight Block Cipher. IACR Cryptology ePrint Archive 2011, 345 (2011)
40. Zhang, X., Parhi, K.K.: High-speed VLSI architectures for the AES algorithm. IEEE Trans. VLSI Syst. 12(9), 957–967 (2004)
41. Gong, Z., Nikova, S., Law, Y.W.: KLEIN: A new family of lightweight block ciphers. In: Juels, A., Paar, C. (eds.) RFIDSec 2011. LNCS, vol. 7055, pp. 1–18. Springer, Heidelberg (2012)

A Exhaustive Search Procedure for Active S-boxes and Active F-Functions

Active S-boxes in Differential Characteristic: In the inner structure of Khudra, there are four branches, each of the branch contains four bits. For each branch, we will consider two cases: the differential of a branch containing all zero bits and the differential containing at least one non-zero bits. We will use the following properties:

- Due to the bijectiveness of s-boxes, whenever a non zero branch differential is passed through a s-box, it will produce another non-zero branch differential. In other words we can say, if the input differential of a s-box is non-zero, then the output differential will also be non-zero.
- If a branch containing zero differential value is XORed with another branch containing zero differential value, it will produce a zero differential value.
- If only one of the branch involved in the XOR contains a non-zero differential value, it will produce a non-zero differential branch value.
- If a branch containing non-zero differential value is XORed with another branch containing non-zero differential value, it will produce a zero differential value(if the input differential of two branches values are equal) or it will produce a zero differential value(if the input differential of two branches values are not equal).

Using these four conditions, an exhaustive search has been performed to compute the number of active s-boxes in the inner structure.

Active S-boxes in Linear Characteristic: In case of linear characteristic, whenever a branch X splits into two branches Y and Z, the mask value of X becomes the XOR of the mask value of Y and Z. Again if $X = Y \oplus Z$, mask value of all three becomes same[15]. The propagation of mask value in a linear characteristic is same as the propagation of difference in a differential trail with the role of XOR and branching being interchanged. Thus the number of linear active s-boxes is exactly same as the number of differential active s-boxes.

Active F-Functions in Differential and Linear Characteristic: Now as the F-Functions are also bijective and the inner structure is identical with the outer structure. So, the same techniques can also be applied for the exhaustive search of the minimum number of active 'F-functions' in the differential characteristic. Further, due to the previously mentioned reason, minimum number of active 'F-functions' in the linear characteristics will be exactly same as the differential characteristics.

B Impossible Differential Attack on *Khudra*

As discussed earlier, to show the resistance against this kind of attack, we have performed an automated search using the algorithm mentioned in [25]. The only differentials that are found to be impossible after 9 rounds are:

$$[0_{(16)}, 0_{(16)}, 0_{(16)}, \alpha_{in(16)}] \nRightarrow [0_{(16)}, 0_{(16)}, \alpha_{out(16)}, 0_{(16)}]$$

Table 9. Differential values for $\alpha_{in(16)}$ and $\alpha_{out(16)}$

$\alpha_{in(16)}$	$\alpha_{out(16)}$	$\alpha_{in(16)}$	$\alpha_{out(16)}$
1	16, 32, 48, 64, 80, 96, 112, 128, 144, 160, 76, 192, 208	2	16, 32, 48, 64, 80, 96, 112, 128, 144, 160, 176, 192, 224
3	16, 32, 48, 64, 80, 96, 112, 128, 144, 160, 176	4	16, 32, 48, 64, 80, 96, 112, 128, 144, 160, 192, 208, 224
5	16, 32, 48, 64, 80, 96, 112, 128, 144, 192, 208	6	16, 32, 48, 64, 80, 96, 112, 128, 160, 192, 224
7	16, 32, 48, 64, 80, 96, 112	8	16, 32, 48, 64, 80, 96, 128, 144, 160, 176, 192, 208, 224
9	16, 32, 48, 64, 80, 128, 144, 160, 176, 192, 208	10	16, 32, 48, 64, 96, 128, 144, 160, 176, 192, 224
11	16, 32, 48, 128, 144, 160, 176	12	16, 32, 64, 80, 96, 128, 144, 160, 192, 208, 224
13	16, 64, 80, 128, 144, 192, 208	14	32, 64, 96, 128, 160, 192, 224

where $0_{(16)}$ denotes 16-bit zero difference, $\alpha_{in(16)}$ and $\alpha_{out(16)}$ denote 16-bit non-zero difference. Table 9 shows the differential values for $\alpha_{in(16)}$ and $\alpha_{out(16)}$. To demonstrate the best possible attack using these 9 round differential, here we are considering $\alpha_{in(16)} = 1$ and $\alpha_{out(16)} = 112$. The reasons for choosing this impossible difference are as follows:

1. If $\alpha_{in(16)} = 1$, then there is only one brunch with non-zero input difference as the Hamming weight of 1 is 1. Now as we are considering 4-bit truncated differential, so we need to induce input difference in $1 \times 4 = 4$ bits, which is easier from the attacker point of view. Note that $\alpha_{in(16)}$ can also be 2, 4 and 8 for the same reason.
2. While choosing the output difference, we need to pick the one with highest Hamming weight so that we can rule out more bits of round keys which can lead to this impossible output difference. Here we have chosen $\alpha_{out(16)} = 112$, which has Hamming weight of 3. Again in this case, we can pick $\alpha_{out(16)} = 192$, which also has Hamming weight of 3.

Key Recovery Attack on 11-round *Khudra*. We choose the impossible differential of input difference $[0_{(16)}, 0_{(16)}, 0_{(16)}, [0_{(4)}, 0_{(4)}, 0_{(4)}, X]]$ and output difference $[0_{(16)}, [0_{(16)}, [0_{(4)}, Y_1, Y_2, Y_3], 0_{(16)}]$ after 9 rounds, where $0_{(16)}$ and $0_{(4)}$ denote 16 bit and 4 bit zero difference respectively, X, Y_1, Y_2, Y_3 are 4-bit non-zero difference. This difference will become $[0_{(16)}, [0_{(4)}, Y_1, Y_2, Y_3], \beta_{(16)}, 0_{(16)}]$ after 10 rounds and it will become $[[0_{(4)}, Y_1, Y_2, Y_3], \beta_{(16)}, \gamma_{(16)}, 0_{(16)}]$ after 11 rounds. Here $\beta_{(16)}$ and $\gamma_{(16)}$ represents $2^{12} - 1$ values that can be obtained as the output difference of the 'F-function' of *Khudra*, for the input difference $[0_{(4)}, Y_1, Y_2, Y_3]$ and $\beta_{(16)}$ respectively. The probability of obtaining such plaintext-ciphertext pair is $1/2^{16} \times (2^{12} - 1)/2^{16} \times (2^{12} - 1)/2^{16} \times (2^{12} - 1)/2^{16} \approx 2^{-28}$.

Round key of 10-th round, RK_{19} and 11 round RK_{21} can be derived as follows:

1. Guess an element in the key space of RK_{19} and RK_{21}
2. Using the collected ciphertexts and the guessed key values, calculate the output differences of the 'f-function', denoted by ΔF_1 and ΔF_2 respectively.
3. Check whether the following conditions are satisfied:

$$\Delta F_1 \oplus \beta = 0$$
$$\Delta F_2 \oplus \gamma = 0$$

4. If the condition above are satisfied, the guessed key value is not correct. Eliminate the key from the key space.

The probability that an element in the key space survives the check with such a pair is $1 - 2^{-28}$. Therefore, let N be the number of pairs required for narrowing down the candidates to 16-bit correct key, RK_{19} and RK_{21}. So, we have

$$2^{32}(1 - 2^{-28})^N = 1$$

N is about $2^{33.16}$. Hence, the number of required chosen plaintext pairs is $2^{28} \times 2^{33.16} = 2^{61.16}$. If we choose two different plaintexts from a set of 2^4 plaintexts (referred as structures) for which the first three branch and the first 12 bits of the last branch are fixed, we can make $_{2^4}C_2 \approx 2^{6.9}$ pairs. In other words, it is possible to obtain the number of ciphertext pairs that are required for the attack by choosing $2^{61.16-6.9} = 2^{54.26}$ structures. Hence, RK_{19} can be obtained by using $2^{54.26} \times 2^4 = 2^{56.26}$ chosen plaintexts. So, the time complexity required for the attack is as follows:

- For obtaining ciphertexts: 2^{57} encryptions.
- For reducing the key candidates: $2^{33.16} \times 2^{32} = 2^{65.16}$ F-function computation $> 2^{61}$ encryptions, where $2^{33.16}$ is for choosing ciphertext pairs and 2^{32} is for guessing RK_{19} and RK_{21}.

Khudra. Hence, the overall time complexity is 2^{61} encryptions.

B.1   ASIC Implementations

We have estimated the gate equivalence (GE) for the ASIC implementation of *Khudra* following the architecture shown in figure 3. The GE for each component is estimated according to the $0.13\mu m$ standard cell library used for implementing Piccolo, where Scan Flip-Flop=6.25 GE, XOR=2 GE, D Flip-Flop=4.5 GE and Mux (2 : 1)=2 GE [27]. The estimated gate equivalence for each module of *Khudra* has been shown in table 10. Further, the modules of *Khudra*, can be implemented using lesser GE than provided in the table 10. For example, we have considered the GE of a 4 : 1 MUX is equivalent to the GE of 3 2 : 1 MUX, whereas the first should take lesser area in actual implementation.

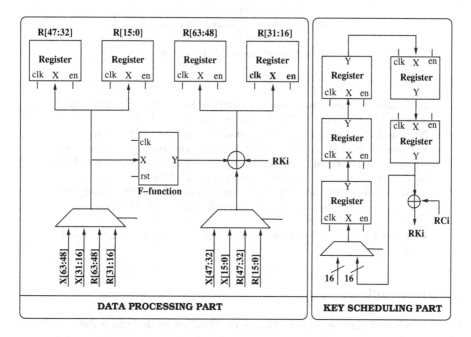

Fig. 3. Block Diagram for Hardware Implementation

Table 10. Area Requirement for ASIC Implementation

Module	Component	Utilized	GE	Module	Component	Utilized	GE
Data State	Scan Flip-Flop	32	200.00	Key State	Scan Flip-Flop	16	100.00
	2:1 MUX	64	128.00		D Flip-Flop	64	288.00
	D Flip-Flop	32	144.00	Key-XOR	XOR	16	32.00
Diffusion	XOR	16	32.00	Round Const.	XOR	16	32.00
F-Function	S-box	12	288.00	**Key**			
	XOR	48	96.00	**Schedule**			**452.00**
Data				**Control**			
Processing			**888.00**	**Logic**			**22.00**
				Total			**1362.00**

FNR: Arbitrary Length Small Domain Block Cipher Proposal

Sashank Dara and Scott Fluhrer

Cisco Systems, Inc,
170 West Tasman Drive, San Jose,
CA 95314, USA
{sadara,sfluhrer}@cisco.com

Abstract. We propose a practical flexible (or arbitrary) length small domain block cipher, *FNR* encryption scheme. FNR denotes **F**lexible **N**aor and **R**eingold. It can cipher small domain data formats like IPv4, Port numbers, MAC Addresses, Credit card numbers, any random short strings while preserving their input length. In addition to the classic Feistel networks, Naor and Reingold propose usage of Pair-wise independent permutation (PwIP) functions based on Galois Field $GF(2^n)$. Instead we propose usage of random $N \times N$ Invertible matrices in $GF(2)$.

Keywords: Feistel Networks, Luby Rackoff, block ciphers, length preserving.

1 Introduction

There is a compelling need for privacy of sensitive fields before data is shared with any cloud provider, semi-trusted vendors, partners etc. Network telemetry data, transaction logs etc. are often required to be shared for benefiting from variety of *Software-as-Service* applications like security monitoring etc. Such sensitive data fields are of well defined data formats like NetFlow, IPFIX etc. For example Port(16), IPv4(32), MAC (48) , IPv6 (128) etc.

While designing privacy for sensitive fields, it may be desirable to preserve the length of the inputs, in order to avoid any re-engineering of packet formats or database columns of existing systems. Traditional AES-128/256 encryption would encrypt plaintext (of any smaller lengths) to result in a 128 bit ciphertext with the aid of padding. Expansion of ciphertext length may be undesirable for said reasons.

Small domain block ciphers are useful tool in designing privacy of sensitive data fields of smaller length (<128 bits). In addition to the classic Feistel networks, Naor and Reingold propose usage of *Pair-wise Independent Permutation (PwIP)* functions based on Galois Field $GF(2^n)$ in first and last rounds of LR constructions. It is proven to provide additional randomness and security. But $GF(2^n)$ representations for arbitrary lengths of inputs is difficult in practice. We propose usage of invertible matrices to provide a neat and generic way to achieve Pair-wise independence for any arbitrary length.

R.S. Chakraborty et al. (Eds.): SPACE 2014, LNCS 8804, pp. 146–154, 2014.

2 Prior Art

Luby Rackoff Constructions are considered seminal work in formalizing secure block cipher design [6]. They have been subjected to rigorous theoretical analysis and well laid security bounds are established. Further variable input length block ciphers have been proposed in [3],[10]. These constructions require multiple application of original block cipher in order to make them arbitrary length block ciphers. This makes them computationally intensive and inefficient. Design of ciphers for arbitrary domains were also proposed in [4]. The *Prefix Cipher, Cycle Walking* mentioned in their work would be very expensive in practice. The *Generalized Feistel Network* approach mentioned in their work uses DES as PRF. RC5 has features for arbitrary domain lengths but it is patented. Elastic block cipher design has been proposed in [5] but they are not subjected to rigorous independent analysis.

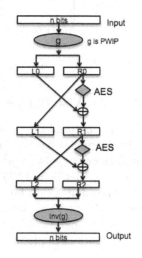

Fig. 1. Two Round NR

Feistel Networks also form the foundational blocks for Format Preserving Encryption(FPE). FPE has been studied rigorously theoretically [2]. A white paper is available from Voltage Inc. [13] which has good overview. A very good synopsis is given by Rogaway [11]. Few modes of FPE have been recently proposed for NIST standardization [1].

Usage of *Pair-wise* Independent Permutations in LR constructions was first proposed by Naor and Reingold [7] as shown in the figure 1. While their techniques are based on performing operations in $GF(2^n)$ we propose to operate on invertible matrices. This makes our scheme flexible enough to perform on any arbitrary input fields.

2.1 Definitions

2.2 Secrets

There are various secret keys used in FNR.

1. **Key:** A 128 bit long secret key, K, is needed. This is used internally by *Pseudo Random Function (PRF)* i.e AES algorithm. This is generated by a good entropy source or derived by using good key derivative function from a user supplied password.
2. **Tweak:** A tweak, T, is like *salt* or *IV*. In practice, A string is supplied by the user, as tweak, which is then encoded as fixed length binary string using some cryptographic hash function.

3. **A, B** are two matrices. A is invertible binary matrix of $N \times N$ dimension. B is binary vector of $1 \times N$ dimension. Where N denotes number of bits in the input. Both A,B should be uniformly distributed and randomly generated.

$$A_{n,n} = \begin{pmatrix} a_{1,1} & a_{1,2} & \cdots & a_{1,n} \\ a_{2,1} & a_{2,2} & \cdots & a_{2,n} \\ \vdots & \vdots & \ddots & \vdots \\ a_{n,1} & a_{n,2} & \cdots & a_{n,n} \end{pmatrix} \quad where \quad a_{i,j} \in \{0,1\} \quad \forall i,j \in \{1 \cdots n\} \quad (1)$$

$$B_{1,n} = \begin{pmatrix} b_{1,1} & b_{1,2} & \cdots & b_{1,n} \end{pmatrix} \quad where \quad b_{1,j} \in \{0,1\} \quad \forall j \in \{1 \cdots n\} \quad (2)$$

2.3   Pair-Wise Independent Permutation (PwIP)

It is combinatorial construction to achieve a uniformly distributed permutation of given input. It has the property that for any two distinct inputs x, y, and any two distinct outputs x^1, y^1, the probability that $x^1 = \text{PwIP}(x)$ and $y^1 = \text{PwIP}(y)$ is uniform, that is, is $1/((2^n) * (2^n - 1))$ independent of x, y, x^1, y^1.

Let the input X be a binary vector of n bits length, considered as 1 X N matrix, then $PwIP_{A,B}(X)$ as defined below gives a uniformly distributed permutation. The matrix operations $*, \oplus, \div$ are performed in GF(2). Also instead of bit-wise XOR operation, modular addition could be used too.

$$X_{1,n} = \begin{pmatrix} x_{1,1} & x_{1,2} & \cdots & x_{1,n} \end{pmatrix} \quad where \quad x_{1,i} \in \{0,1\} \quad \forall i \in \{1 \cdots n\} \quad (3)$$

$$PwIP_{A,B}(X) = (X \times A) \oplus B \text{ where } A,B \text{ are defined in 1 and 2} \quad (4)$$

Inverse PwIP. The inverse of such a *PwIP* is defined as follows. *Note:* In case modular addition is used while performing *PwIP*, then Addition and Subtraction are same in Galois Field, GF(2).

$$PwIP_{A,B}^{-1}(Y) = ((Y \oplus B) \times A^{-1}) \quad (5)$$

2.4   Feistel Networks

Feistel is symmetric structure to construct block ciphers. One round of Feistel is a $2n$ bit permutation δ, with an n bit round function as defined below

$$\delta_f(L, R) = (R, L \otimes f(R)) \quad where |L| = |R| = n \quad (6)$$

An r round Feistel network is simply the composition of r one round Feistel structures, transforming r n-bit functions $f_1, f_2...f_r$ into a $2n$ bit permutation.

$$\delta_{f_1,f_2....f_r}(L, R) = \delta(f_1) \circ \delta(f_2) \circ ....\delta(f_r) \quad (7)$$

The security of PRP constructed by a Feistel Network based scheme relies on security of underlying PRF (i.e round function) [6]. The security guarantee depends on ensuring a different round function for each round. We propose using AES in ECB mode as the round function. Now to ensure the output is distinct in each round, we could use unique round key or by ensuring the inputs to the round function is distinct for each round. We achieve this by mixing a *round_const* for each round to the input to to PRF.

$$round\_const_r = \{\texttt{0x00, 0x03, 0x0c, 0x0f, 0x30, 0x33, 0x3c}\} \quad where \quad r \in \{1,7\} \tag{8}$$

2.5 Encryption

The inputs to encryption algorithm are plaintext P, that needs to be encrypted, a secret key K, a tweak T and the matrices A,B. The output of an encryption function is n bits of ciphertext C.

Overview Input plaintext is subjected to *PwIP* to get a uniformly distributed permutation of the same. This follows by a Feistel network of $r = 7$ rounds. The output of the Feistel network is subjected to $PwIP^{-1}$. The final output is then considered as ciphertext. The algorithm for the same is described in Algorithm.1.

Algorithm 1. FNR Encryption Algorithm

    Inputs : key k, char* tweak,Matrix A, Matrix B, bitvector plain, integer n
              `/* n is max number of bits and even                    */`
    Output: bitvector cipher
              `/* cipher and plain are of same bit length              */`
1 **Function** $Encrypt(k,\ tweak,\ plain,\ n)$ **is**
2 **begin**
3   **if** $(|plain| \neq n)$ **then** return $\perp$;
4   bitvector d $= PwIP$(A,B,plain,n);
5   **while** $i < r$ **do**
6   **begin**
7   left = d[0..n/2] ;
8   right = d[n/2 .. n-1] ;
9   left = right ;
10   right = left $\otimes AES_{key}(round\_const_i \parallel tweak \parallel right)$;
11   d = left $\parallel$ right ;
12   i++;
13   **end**
14   bitvector cipher $=PwIP^{(-1)}$(A,B,d,n);
15   return cipher;
16 **end**

2.6 Decryption

The inputs to decryption algorithm are ciphertext C, secret key K, tweak T and the matrices A,B. The output is plaintext P.

Overview. The algorithm is very similar to encryption except that the processing is done in reverse way. The algorithm for the same is described in Algorithm.2 . The differences with encryption algorithm can be observed as shown in line 11

3   Security

Security of LR schemes under went rigorous analysis by the community over many years. Also usage of *PwIP* is later proven to mitigate basic linear and differential cryptanalysis [14].

3.1   Round Functions

If assume that the AES output for any given input is uniformly distributed, that means that the AES output bits we actually use in the Feistel will be independent between even and odd rounds (even if the attacker could engineer a collision with probability 1; the fact that the collision probability between even and odd round is actually considerably smaller turns out to be irrelevant). As we add the round constants as defined in equation.8 as last byte to the input to AES

Algorithm 2. FNR Decryption Algorithm

```
      Inputs : key k, char* tweak,Matrix A, Matrix B, bitvector cipher, integer n
                   /* n is max number of bits and even                      */
      Output: bitvector plain
                   /* both cipher and plain are n bits                      */
    1 Function Decrypt(k, tweak, cipher, n) is
    2 begin
    3 |   if (|cipher| ≠ n) then return ⊥;
    4 |   /* perform pair wise permutation                                  */
    5 |   bitvector d = PwIP(A,B,cipher,n);
    6 |   while i < r do
    7 |   begin
    8 |   |   left = d[0..n/2] ;
    9 |   |   right = d[n/2 .. n-1] ;
   10 |   |   left = right ;
   11 |   |   right = left ⊗AESₖ(round_const(r−i) || tweak || right)
   12 |   |   d = left || right ;
   13 |   |   i++ ;
   14 |   end
   15 |   /* perform inverse of permutation                                 */
   16 |   bitvector plain = PwIP^(−1)(A,B,d,n);
   17 |   return plain;
   18 end
```

Line 11: $right = left \otimes AES_k(round\_const_{(r-i)} \| tweak \| right)$

Line 16: $bitvector\ plain = PwIP^{(-1)}(A,B,d,n)$

3.2   Round Count

A minimum of 7 rounds are needed to mitigate adaptive chosen plaintext and chosen ciphertext attacks due to Patarin's proof [9].

The security measure of block ciphers is based on the probability with which an attacker can distinguish the ciphertext from a random text. Although our *PwIP* is different from theirs, without loss of generality, detailed proof given in [7] holds good for FNR.

If r is round count, n is number of bits of input domain, m is number of queries an attacker needs to make, then the security measure for FNR, is defined as in Equation.9.

$$(r/2 * m^2/2^{(1-1/r)*n}) \, where \, r \geq 4 \tag{9}$$

It is to be noted that without the use of *PwIP* functions the security measure of pure Feistel Networks due to Patarin's proof [8] is defined as in Equation.10

$$5 * (m^3)/(2^n) \tag{10}$$

So for example an input domain of 32 bits and round count of 7, it requires approximately 8757 pairs of plaintext and ciphertext. Where as without the use of *PwIP* functions attacker just needs around 950 pairs of plaintext and ciphertext.

4 Implementation

4.1 Feistel Network

Our reference implementation is slightly different from most implementations of LR, in that we don't divide the block into two separate halves; instead, we use the even bits as one half and the odd bits as other half, and we don't swap them; instead, we alternate between rounds which half we use as the input to our random function, and which half we XOR the output of the random function into. Since we have an odd number of rounds ($r = 7$), this all works out.

Nits: if the block we're encrypting has an odd number of bits, this is strictly speaking an unbalanced Feistel (if unbalanced only by a single bit). In addition, if we're encrypting a single bit, this really isn't a Feistel at all (because one half is empty).

4.2 Performance

The performance of the algorithms have been benchmarked in Figure.2. The graphs are plotted for both AES and AES-NI instructions as options for internal PRP. The benchmarking is performed an virtual machine that runs Ubuntu 12.4 with 8 GB RAM on an Intel Sandy Bridge Generation of Processor's with 4 vCPU's. The source code is available under LGPLv2[12].

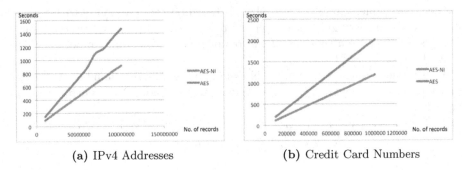

(a) IPv4 Addresses   (b) Credit Card Numbers

Fig. 2. Performance of FNR

4.3   Test Vectors

For generating the below test vectors, the key used is *'0000000000000000'* and tweak used is *'tweak-is-string'*. Tweak is an arbitrary length string which is expanded into a fixed length form. Note that even though same secrets are used, the results might vary due to the choice of A,B Matrices used in PwIP function.

The test vectors for various IPv4 Addresses, Credit Card numbers are given in Table.1 and Table.2. Each IPv4 is ranked as 32 bit integer before it is encrypted, the resultant ciphertext is a 32 bit integer which is de-ranked into a dotted notation. Each CC number is ranked as 15 digit number by dropping the LUHN_CHECKSUM. The ranked integer is then encrypted to get a ciphertext that is again 15 digit number. Such integer is de-ranked by appending a LUHN_CHECKSUM at the end into a valid Credit card number.

Table 1. Test Vectors for IPv4 Addresses

Plain Text		Cipher Text	
Raw(Dotted)	*Ranked(Integer)*	*Raw(Integer)*	*De-ranked(Dotted)*
192.168.1.0	3232235776	2676870780	159.141.206.124
192.168.1.1	3232235777	2129658955	126.240.4.75
192.168.1.2	3232235778	3505438271	208.240.190.63
192.168.1.3	3232235779	3073749301	183.53.177.53
192.168.1.4	3232235780	2962433103	176.147.36.79

Table 2. Test Vectors for Credit Card numbers

Plain Text		Cipher Text	
Raw	*Ranked*	*Raw*	*De-ranked*
4556584414106354	455658441410635	975846115884519	9758461158845197
4486224784662570	448622478466257	716640796278824	7166407962788248
4929883910358398	492988391035839	665162088006340	6651620880063403
4929880239524890	492988023952489	932731766659682	9327317666596825
4916550835157636	491655083515763	949857941349711	9498579413497119

5   Conclusions

In this paper we proposed a flexible and practical arbitrary block domain cipher. We provide the reference implementation's performance results, test vectors. Also we provided examples of how to preserve formats of few data types like IPv4 addresses and Credit card numbers. Our work is flexible variant of Naor and Reingold's work. We recommend using this block cipher for domain sizes 32 bits to 128 bits. FNR does not provide authentication and integrity. FNR does not provide any semantic security when used in ECB mode (like all other deterministic modes)

Acknowledgments. We sincerely thank our colleagues Dr. David McGrew, Anthony Grieco, Dr.Zulfikar Ramzan, for their crucial suggestions, improvements in our work. Also we acknowledge exhaustive comments, corrections and suggestions from Dr. Praveen Gauravaram (Tata Consultancy Services Innovation Labs), Dr. Kapali Viswanathan (Hewlett-Packard), Dr. Saugat Majumdar (Aruba Networks).

The reference implementation is written by Scott Fluhrer and demo applications were written by Kaushal Bhandankar. Many bug fixes, patches, code review performed by our colleagues Olve Maudal, Anand Verma, Mohit Kumar and Abhishek Singh.

References

1. Bellare, M., Rogaway, P., Spies, T.: The ffx mode of operation for format-preserving encryption (draft 1.1) Manuscript (standards proposal) submitted to NIST (February 2010)
2. Bellare, M., Ristenpart, T., Rogaway, P., Stegers, T.: Format-preserving encryption. In: Jacobson Jr., M.J., Rijmen, V., Safavi-Naini, R. (eds.) SAC 2009. LNCS, vol. 5867, pp. 295–312. Springer, Heidelberg (2009)
3. Bellare, M., Rogaway, P.: On the construction of variable-input-length ciphers. In: Knudsen, L.R. (ed.) FSE 1999. LNCS, vol. 1636, pp. 231–244. Springer, Heidelberg (1999)
4. Black, J.A., Rogaway, P.: Ciphers with arbitrary finite domains. In: Preneel, B. (ed.) CT-RSA 2002. LNCS, vol. 2271, pp. 114–130. Springer, Heidelberg (2002)
5. Cook, D.L.: Elastic block ciphers. PhD thesis, Columbia University (2006)
6. Luby, M., Rackoff, C.: How to construct pseudorandom permutations from pseudorandom functions. SIAM Journal on Computing 17(2), 373–386 (1988)
7. Naor, M., Reingold, O.: On the construction of pseudorandom permutations: Luby rackoff revisited. Journal of Cryptology 12(1), 29–66 (1999)
8. Patarin, J.: Improved security bounds for pseudorandom permutations. In: Proceedings of the 4th ACM Conference on Computer and Communications Security, pp. 142–150. ACM (1997)
9. Patarin, J.: Luby-rackoff: 7 rounds are enough for formula_image security. In: Boneh, D. (ed.) CRYPTO 2003. LNCS, vol. 2729, pp. 513–529. Springer, Heidelberg (2003)

10. Patel, S., Ramzan, Z., Sundaram, G.S.: Efficient constructions of variable-input-length block ciphers. In: Handschuh, H., Hasan, M.A. (eds.) SAC 2004. LNCS, vol. 3357, pp. 326–340. Springer, Heidelberg (2004)
11. Rogaway, P., Tweet, D.: Format-preserving encryption (2010)
12. Fluhrer, S., Dara, S.: Reference Implementation of FNR (2014), https://github.com/sashank/libfnr
13. Spies, T.: Format preserving encryption. Unpublished white paper. Database and Network Journal (December 2008), Format preserving encryption: www.voltage.com
14. Vaudenay, S.: Decorrelation: a theory for block cipher security. Journal of Cryptology 16(4), 249–286 (2003)

AEC: A Practical Scheme for Authentication with Error Correction

Abhrajit Sengupta[1], Dhiman Saha[1], Shamit Ghosh[1],
Deval Mehta[2], and Dipanwita Roy Chowdhury[1]

[1] Department of Computer Science and Engineering, IIT Kharagpur, India
{abhrajit.sengupta,dhimans,shamit.ghosh,drc}@cse.iitkgp.ernet.in
[2] Department of Space, Space Application Center, Ahmedabad, India
m_deval@sac.isro.gov.in

Abstract. We present a Message Authentication Code (MAC) with integrated error correction capability, called AEC. The MAC itself can detect/correct errors upto a certain limit and provides an estimate of the number and location of the errors. The security of AEC lies in the random selection of the underlying error correcting code (ECC). In this work, we propose a new on-the-fly solution to this problem of random ECC selection, making it highly secure. Moreover, this solution combined with the simple and regular structure of Cellular Automata (CA) based ECC, makes it highly suitable for efficient hardware implementation. Detailed FPGA implementations of both standalone and compact variants of AEC, are presented on the Spartan-3 FPGA platform. The compact implementation has low area footprint and high throughput making it particularly suitable for resource constrained applications. To the best of our knowledge this is the only practical design of an ECC-MAC scheme.

Keywords: MAC, ECC, Cellular Automata, Mersenne Prime.

1 Introduction

Message Authentication Code (MAC), also referred to as a keyed hash function, is a cryptographic primitive that verifies the integrity of data and the authenticity of its sender. However, as traditional MACs are susceptible to any alteration in the message, even simple channel noises are detrimental to its functionality, causing straightaway rejection of authentic messages. Though this is preferable in some situations, many of the less information-sensitive applications, such as image and other multimedia communications, can allow few errors occurred during transmission. The message should be rejected only if large number of errors are present, indicating a probable attempt of forgery. But, classical MAC algorithms do not convey any information about the number or location of the errors. This concludes the need for a MAC construction technique with integrated error correction property that offers some resilience against random channel noises, especially in environments where latency is a concern or resources are limited.

R.S. Chakraborty et al. (Eds.): SPACE 2014, LNCS 8804, pp. 155–170, 2014.

Krawczyk [1] first exploited the idea of constructing MAC with error correction capabilities. He used Cyclic Redundancy Code(CRC) to construct the hash function and proved it to be *unconditionally secure* if used with a *perfect* one-time pad. But this is a purely theoretical construction and lacks any equivalent realization in practical applications. Later, Liu and Boncelet came up with a series of ideas in [2–4], for noisy message authentication. Though NTMAC [2] works well with a modest number of errors, it suffers from a higher collision rate. The CRC-NTMAC [3] and BCH-NTMAC [4] schemes try to improve upon NTMAC, but no optimal choice of parameters are given. Moreover, as the security of these two schemes is directly related to the secrecy of the *pseudo-random* partitioning of the message, it is particularly hard to achieve in hardware. The authors suggested two ways to achieve this, but neither of them suffices for efficient implementation, as one of them depends on *true*-random number generator and the other suffers from a collision attack. Further in [5], Bhaumik and Roy Chowdhury proposed a Reed Solomon Code based alternative, extricating the use of a true-random number generator. It was shown to be resistant against any existential MAC forgeries if used with a *randomly* selected ECC. However, the authors did not mention any efficient technique for the *random* selection of a generator polynomial cum the ECC. One obvious choice to accomplish this is by storing all possible polynomials in memory and selecting one of them at random based on the secret key. But the space complexity of this approach is exponential in the degree of the polynomial, making it unrealizable in hardware. Additionally, storing of polynomials in memory is not a viable option as it gets vulnerable to several side-channel attacks like cache attack or cold-boot attack [6].

In this paper, we offer a solution to this problem by presenting a practical and secure integrated ECC-MAC design, named AEC. We show how by combining a certain number theoretic result with theory of cellular automata, such a design can be accomplished. Here, we capitalize on the fact that the simple and regular structure of CA based ECC is highly efficient in hardware both in terms of area and speed, to construct an efficient implementation of our design, missing in related work of [5]. Moreover, we also present a customized version of our design tailored for highly resource constrained environments. The contribution of this work can be summarized as below:

– A secure hardware efficient integrated ECC-MAC scheme
– New secret key based approach for randomized selection of CA based ECC
– Detailed implementation of both standalone and compact unit on FPGA

The rest of the paper proceeds as follows. Section 2 describes the proposed scheme for authentication with integrated error correction. The security of the scheme is evaluated in Section 3. Details of the hardware architecture is furnished in Section 4 and Section 5 presents the implementation cost on FPGA. Finally, the paper is concluded in Section 6.

2 Design of AEC: Authentication with Integrated Error Correction

In this section, we present the design of an authentication scheme with integrated error correction capability, suitable for practical applications. We reiterate the fact that our ECC is based on CA (refer Appendix A), making it highly efficient in hardware. The authentication algorithm works in two different stages, MAC-GENeration stage and the MAC-VERification stage.

MAC Generation

The MAC generation process starts with sharing two keys k_1 and k_2 between the sender and the receiver before the initiation of a session. At first, the data goes through a optional padding phase if necessary and partitioned into blocks of size w (w is the number of the cells in the cellular automata, used for error correction). Now, with the help of key k_1, a CA based error correcting code is selected, which serves the purpose of forward error detection/correction. Next, the checkbytes computed by the ECC, are mixed with key k_2 in a non-linear fashion by NMix to get the MAC. This MAC value is then transmitted to the receiver along with the data as (Message, MAC) pair. The MAC generation process is depicted in Fig. 1, and Algorithm 1 shows the detail.

Algorithm 1. MAC-GEN(t, m, k_1, k_2) $\quad\triangleright |m| \leq 2^w, |k_1| = w - 1, |k_2| = w$

1: **procedure** PREPROCESS(m)

2: $\quad m' \leftarrow \mathcal{P}(m)$ $\quad\triangleright \begin{cases} \mathcal{P} \text{ is the padding function} \\ |\mathcal{P}(m)| = w \times n, n \in \mathbb{Z}^+ \end{cases}$

3: $\quad \{m_1, m_2, \cdots, m_n\} \leftarrow \mathcal{B}(m')$ $\quad\triangleright \mathcal{B}$ partitions m' into n blocks

4: **end procedure**

5: **procedure** SELECT RANDOM CA(k_1)

6: $\quad r_1 \leftarrow$ prefixed linear CA rule[1] $\quad\triangleright |r_1| = w - 1$

7: $\quad s \leftarrow C_{r_1}(k_1)$ $\quad\triangleright$ Apply CA with rule r_1, CA initialized with seed k_1

8: $\quad \mathcal{S} \leftarrow \{1, s, 1\}$

9: $\quad$ **while** IRREDUCIBLE$(\mathcal{S})$ = FALSE **do** $\quad\triangleright$ Rabin's Test [7]

10: $\quad\quad s \leftarrow C_{r_1}(s)$

11: $\quad\quad \mathcal{S} \leftarrow \{1, s, 1\}$

12: $\quad$ **end while**

13: $\quad r_2 \leftarrow$ SYTHESIZECA$(\mathcal{S})$

14: $\quad$ **return** r_2 $\quad\triangleright r_2$ is the randomly selected CA

15: **end procedure**

16: **procedure** COMPUTE MAC$(\mathcal{B}(m'), r_2, t, k_2)$

17: $\quad c_i \leftarrow$ CA ENCODER$(\mathcal{B}(m'), t, i), \quad 0 \leq i \leq 2t - 1$

18: $\quad mac_i \leftarrow$ NMIX(c_i, k_2) $\quad\triangleright$ NMix is a non-linear function

19: $\quad$ **return** MAC $\leftarrow \{mac_0, mac_1, \cdots, mac_{2t-1}\}$

20: **end procedure**

---

[1] r_1 is any maximal length 90,150 CA rule.

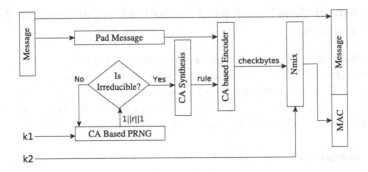

Fig. 1. MAC generation at the Sender

MAC Verification

At the receiving end, verification of the MAC is performed to detect the presence of errors in the transmitted data, if any. At first, checkbytes C are recomputed from the received data. This step is identical to the checkbyte computation procedure described in the MAC generation process. In parallel to this, the received MAC is subjected to the inverse of the non-linear transformation (INMix) to get back the original checkbytes C' transmitted by the sender. Next, the received checkbytes C' and the computed checkbytes C are passed to the CA based decoder to find out if the transmitted message has arrived correctly, or not. If all of the syndromes are zero, the message is readily accepted as its error-free. However, if any error creeps in, a decision is to be taken depending on the number of words in error. If the number of errors are greater than the error correction capability of the code, it leads to straightaway rejection of the message. Otherwise, its corrected and subsequently accepted. The whole process is depicted in Fig. 2, and Algorithm 2 shows the detail.

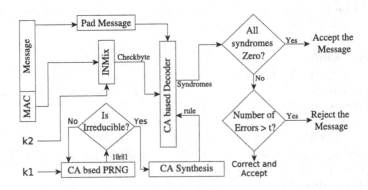

Fig. 2. MAC verification at the Receiver

Algorithm 2. MAC-VER(m, MAC, t, k_1, k_2)

1: PREPROCESS(m)
2: SELECT RANDOM CA(k_1)
3: $C \leftarrow$ CA ENCODER$(\mathcal{B}(m'), t, i)$, $0 \leq i \leq 2t - 1$ ▷ $C = \{c_0, c_1, \cdots, c_{2t-1}\}$
4: $C' \leftarrow$ INVERSE NMIX(mac_i) ▷ $C' = \{c'_0, c'_1, \cdots, c'_{2t-1}\}$
5: $X \leftarrow C \oplus C'$ ▷ $X = \{x_0, x_1, \cdots, x_t\}$ is the syndrome
6: $X' \leftarrow \{x_i : x_i \neq 0\}$
7: **if** $X' = \varnothing$ **then**   ▷ All zero syndrome
8:     **return** Accept
9: **else**
10:     **if** No. of Errors $> t$ **then**
11:         **return** Reject   ▷ More that t errors, so discard m
12:     **else**
13:         Correct and Accept
14:     **end if**
15: **end if**

2.1   Random Selection of CA with Key k_1

In this section, we describe how to randomly select a CA with the help of key k_1 and still make efficient implementation of it. It is to be noted that if the checkbytes are also used to provide authenticity, it will be vulnerable to simple forgeries if a fixed known ECC is used. In their work [5], Bhaumik and Roy Chowdhury acknowledged the importance of randomly selecting a linear code, but failed to account for an efficient technique for accomplishing that. Straightforward way of achieving that could be storing of all possible generator polynomials over a field and then selecting one of them at random with the help of secret key. But, the space complexity of this approach is exponential in the degree of the polynomial, rendering it infeasible for any practical applications. In favor of this statement, we highlight that for any prime q and any positive integer n, there are $\left(\frac{\phi(q^n-1)}{n}\right)$ number of primitive polynomials over the field $GF(q^n)$ where ϕ is the Euler's Totient function. This implies that in order to meet the present day security standard of 80-bit, $\left(\frac{\phi(2^{80}-1)}{80}\right) \approx 10^{25}$ units of disk space would be required, which is beyond practical limits. Herein, lies the main contribution of AEC, which constitutes a complete on-the-fly solution to the problem of randomly choosing a linear code.

To come up with an efficient solution, we exploit the work of Cattel and Muzio [8], where they presented a detailed method for the synthesis of a one-dimensional linear hybrid CA from a given irreducible polynomial. But, to be able to use such CA based ECC, one must first find a *maximum-length* CA i.e. having a period[2] of $(2^n - 1)$, n being the number of cells in the CA. To tackle this issue, we exploit another important result in [9], where the authors claimed that if a given irreducible polynomial is primitive, then the synthesized CA will be unique as

---

[2] The no of iterations after which a CA returns to its initial state.

well as of *maximum-length*. This result is interesting, since it maps the problem of randomly selecting a linear code to the problem of finding a primitive polynomial over a finite field. However, finding primitive polynomials in large finite fields is a non-trivial problem. The verification of primitive polynomials and its associated complexity is too costly to implement either in software or in hardware, and hence, not suitable for any practical application. The fastest known algorithms for testing primitivity of polynomials of degree n require the factorization of $(2^n - 1)$ to be known beforehand, in addition to finding a primitive root over the defining field. To overcome this, we use the result given by the following theorem, which establishes a one-to-one correspondence between primitive and irreducible polynomials.

Theorem 1. *If $2^r - 1$ is a prime number (Mersenne Prime) then all degree-r irreducible polynomials are also primitive* [10].

The result furnished in Theorem 1 reduces the hard problem of finding a primitive polynomial to the easier problem of finding an irreducible polynomial. Once such a w $(2^w - 1 \in \mathbb{P})$ is fixed, one can choose any irreducible polynomial of degree w, and synthesize it into a maximum-length CA using the technique described in [8].

Due to the arguments stated above, random CA based ECC selection turns out to be equivalent to selecting an irreducible polynomial randomly. Next, we illustrate how to select an irreducible polynomial at random with the help of secret key k_1. First, we fix $GF(2^w)$ as the extension field in accordance with Theorem 1. A polynomial $f(x) = \sum b_i \cdot x^i, 0 \le i \le w$ over $GF(2^w)$ is represented as the bit string $\{b_w, b_{w-1}, \cdots, b_0\}$. Now, the key k_1 serves as the seed to a PRNG (in this work, CA based PRNG [11,12] is used). A $(w-1)$-bit CA based PRNG produces random patterns of $(w-1)$ bits, to which 1 is concatenated at either end to get a pattern of $(w+1)$ bits. The reason behind prepending 1 is quite straightforward as the polynomials are monic[3]. The appending of 1 at the LSB is also trivial; otherwise, x will be a non-trivial factor of the polynomial, implying it not irreducible. The polynomial corresponding to the resulting bit-pattern is subjected to Rabin's irreducibility test [7]. This whole process continues until we find an irreducible polynomial. Finally, this irreducible polynomial is synthesized into an equivalent maximum-length CA according to [8]. This step corresponds to SELECT RANDOM CA(k_1) in Algorithm 1.

Estimate of Success of IRREDUCIBLE($\mathcal{S}$)**.** We now give an estimate of the number of trials before which the random polynomial generated by the PRNG passes the irreducibility test. Let us first calculate the total number of irreducible polynomials of degree n over a field $\mathbb{F}_q$. This is given by the following formula

$$I_n = \frac{1}{n} \sum_{k|n} \mu(k) q^{n/k}, \quad \mu \to \text{Möbius function. [13].}$$

---

[3] Highest degree coefficient is 1.

It follows that $q^n - 2q^{n/2} \leq nI_n \leq q^n$. Therefore, a fraction very close to $\left(\frac{1}{n}\right)$ of the polynomials of degree n over any finite field $\mathbb{F}_q$ are irreducible. Therefore, the expected running time of this step is linear in the degree of the polynomial being tested. Once the CA has been synthesized, we can proceed to the encoding phase of the CA based ECC.

2.2 Calculation of Checkbytes and Subsequent Error Correction

After a suitable maximum-length CA is selected, it is used for the calculation of checkbytes which helps to keep track of transmission errors. But before any computation begins, the data goes through a optional padding phase to make it a multiple of word-size(w), where $w : 2^w - 1 \in \mathbb{P}$ and partitioned into blocks of size equal to w. This corresponds to procedure PREPROCESS(m) of Algorithm 1. After this, the data is passed to the CA based Encoder for the computation of checkbytes. CA based ECC is widely used in literature for its simplicity and efficiency in hardware [9]. The checkbytes and syndromes for a t-word error correcting code, where each word is n-bit long, can be generated using an n-cell maximum-length[4] CA in the following manner:

$$C_i = \bigoplus_{j=0}^{N-1} T^{i \times (N-1-j)}[B_j], \quad \begin{cases} i = \{0, 1, \cdots, 2t - 1\}; \\ B = [B_0, B_1, \cdots, B_{N-1}]; \\ T \text{ is the characteristic matrix of the CA} \end{cases} \tag{1}$$

$$S_i = C_i \oplus C_i' \quad 0 \leq i \leq 2t - 1 \quad \begin{cases} C_i \text{ is the received checkbyte} \\ C_i' \text{ is the checkbyte computed} \end{cases}$$

Locating and subsequent correction of the erroneous byte(s) using CA are further discussed in [9]. In this paper, we have worked with single-word error correcting and double-word error locating code.

Now, we elaborate how the choice of t i.e. the error correction capability of the code, relates to the security of the scheme. Here, the inherent belief lies on the fact that in wireless transmission systems, burst errors are more common in nature, and are confined to a small part of the data. Thus, it can at most affect a few words of information rather than spanning over the whole data. However, if some intentional tampering or some outright forgery happens, the chances are more that it will be spanned throughout the data. This causes a large number of errors and the message is discarded accordingly. This leads to the careful choice of t by the user.

2.3 Generating MAC Using ECC

Finally, we describe how the checkbytes computed in the previous section also serves the purpose of authentication. However, due to its linear nature check-bytes alone are not sufficient enough to provide authentication, as it's linear

---

[4] CA having a period of $(2^n - 1)$.

property makes it susceptible to several well known cryptanalysis techniques like linear/differential cryptanalysis. However, a *non-linear* operation can prevent these type of threats, making it secure. So, for this purpose, we have taken NMix [14] as the nonlinear key mixing function in our design.

Justification of Using NMix. The choice of NMix is driven by the fact that it is a non-linear *bent* function, i.e. it is as different as possible from all linear or *affine* functions and thus, naturally hard to approximate.

The proposed scheme involves calculation of checkbytes using ECC which is known to be linear. The following equations show how an adversary can mount a successful forgery for a message by exploiting this linear property . From Eq.(1) we get that,

$$C_i = B_{N-1} \oplus T^i([B_{N-2}] \oplus T^i([B_{N-3}] \oplus \cdots \oplus T^i([B_1] \oplus T^i([B_0])) \cdots)$$
$$= L_i(B) \tag{2}$$

As T is a matrix operator is can be viewed as a linear transformation L_i on input B. Suppose, we have another pari (B', C') known to the attacker.

$$C'_i = L_i(B') \tag{3}$$

Now from, Eq. (2) and (3) we get,

$$C_i \oplus C'_i = L_i(B) \oplus L_i(B')$$
$$= L_i(B \oplus B') \qquad \text{[Since } L_i \text{ is a linear operator]}$$

Thus, with only two known message-mac pair (B, C) and (B', C'), the attacker is able to forge mac C'' for a third message B'', where $B'' = B \oplus B'$ and $C'' = C \oplus C'$. This attack is valid for any combination of two or more messages. Due to this reason, nonlinearity has been introduced in our design, so that Eq.(2) and (3) does not hold any longer. This is due to the fact that,

$$\text{NMix}(X, r) \oplus \text{NMix}(Y, r) \neq \text{NMix}(X \oplus Y, r)$$

Now, as shown at line 18 of COMPUTE MAC in Algorithm 1, NMix is applied to the checkbytes $C \leftarrow \{c_0, c_1, \cdots, c_t\}$ with key k_2 as the random pad r to get the $MAC \leftarrow \{mac_0, mac_1 \cdots, mac_t\}$ as output. These MAC values along with the message, is then sent to the receiver as the authenticator. However, for different messages the value of r (say, by some PRNG) must be changed as otherwise it may be vulnerable to some key recovery attack. At the other end, after receiving the MAC, the receiver applies inverse NMix on it to get back the checkbytes C. These checkbytes are then passed to the CA based decoder for subsequent error detection/correction, described in the previous section. It is to be noted that applying non-linear mixing may propagate the error to multiple bits within a single word. However, as CA based decoder deals with word-errors rather than bit-errors, NMix does not affect the error correction property of the code.

3   Security Analysis

This section summarizes the formal security arguments of AEC against state-of-the-art cryptanalysis techniques and proves the robustness of the scheme.

3.1   Linear Cryptanalysis

Linear Cryptanalysis (LC) tries to exploit the high bias that may be present amongst message bits, MAC bits and key bits. The approach is based on finding *affine* approximation to the action of the MAC scheme to derive the key. Since ECC is linear in nature, it alone offers little or no resilience against LC and thus used with a non-linear *bent* function NMix to resist it.

In [14] the bias of best linear approximation of NMix was shown to 2^{-i}, where $2 \leq i \leq w$. Thus, the probability of recovering key bits by linear approximation of NMix is bounded by the following equation

$$Pr[\text{LC(NMix)}] = \frac{1}{2} \times \frac{1}{2^2} \times \frac{1}{2^3} \cdots \times \frac{1}{2^w} = 2^{(-1) \times \Sigma_{i=1}^{w}} \leq \frac{1}{2^w}$$

3.2   Differential Cryptanalysis

Differential Cryptanalysis (DC) is a general form of cryptanalysis technique which studies how the differences in an input can affect the resultant difference at the output. It is usually a chosen message-MAC attack, discovering any non-random behavior exhibited by the MAC and exploiting such properties to recover the key. In AEC, differential resistance is provided by the non-linear mixing function Nmix, which has been shown to be resistant against any kind of DC technique in [14]. It is known that the best linear approximation of the differential terms decreases exponentially in case of NMix. Suppose, for a particular instance, the input difference is denoted by ΔX and the output difference by ΔY for a fixed key $\mathcal{K}$. Then, the $Pr(\Delta Y | \Delta X)$ is bounded by 2^{-w} (same argument holds as that of LC), where w is the length of the word.

3.3   Other Attacks

Birthday Attack : The effort required for a successful birthday attack against AEC is $2^{n/2}$, n being the length of the MAC output, and hence is infeasible in current scenario for reasonable choices of n.

MAC Forgery : The success of MAC forgery is directly related to the success of linear/differential cryptanalysis technique and is thus upper bounded by 2^{-w}, w being the length of the word.

Generator Polynomial Recovery : The generator polynomial recovery, which seems to be the most suitable of all the attacks, requires computational effort of $\left(\frac{\phi(2^w - 1)}{w} \right)$, w being the word-size.

Table 1 summarizes the bounds on the complexity of all the generic attacks against AEC, while Table 4 in Appendix B gives statistical analysis of the MAC function against the NIST Test Suite. Here, w denotes the word-size of AEC.

Table 1. Computational Effort Required for Different Attacks against AEC

Attack Name	$w = 61$	$w = 89$	$w = 127$
Linear Cryptanalysis	2^{61}	2^{89}	2^{127}
Differential Cryptanalysis	2^{61}	2^{89}	2^{127}
Birthday Attack	2^{122}	2^{178}	2^{254}
MAC Forgery Attack	2^{61}	2^{89}	2^{127}
Generator Polynomial Recovery	2^{55}	2^{82}	2^{120}

4   Architectural Design

This section presents the detailed hardware architecture of proposed AEC scheme. It has been implemented in two different ways, standalone and resource constrained implementation.

Standalone Implementation

In a standalone implementation, the device is a transceiver unit, comprising of both a transmitter and a receiver as shown in Fig. 3. Though this unit is capable of functioning without having to rely on any other central authority, the downside is, it is much slower than its highest possible operating frequency.

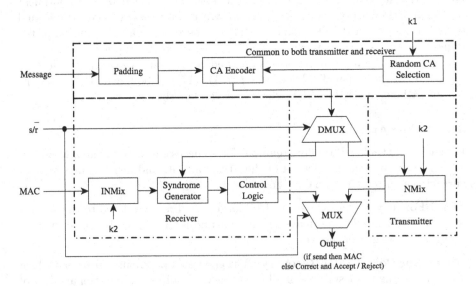

Fig. 3. Standalone Implementation

Resource Constrained Implementation

In this implementation, the functionality of SELECT RANDOM CA has been separated from the transceiver shown in Fig. 4. For communication, the transceiver relies on a central authority for the generation of maximum-length CA. The central authority performs the SELECT RANDOM CA as described in Algorithm 1 and sends the rule itself as the key to the transceiver. This design strategy is much faster as it leverages the transceiver from synthesizing a maximum-length CA, which is the slowest and heaviest component in the design of AEC. Logic diagrams for the encoder, decoder and Nmix are produced in Appendix C.

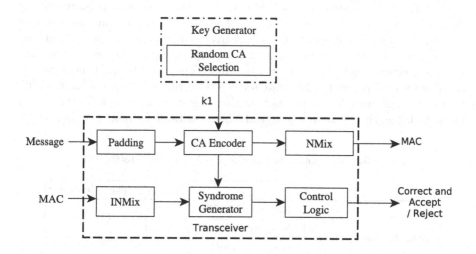

Fig. 4. Separate Key Generator and Transceiver

5   Results

The design has been implemented and verified in **Xilinx Spartan-3 (XC3S1500-4FG676C)** FPGA platform. Table 2 compares the communication overhead of AEC with generic composition of HMAC and then CA based ECC. We have chosen Keccak as the hash primitive in the HMAC construction. The choice of Keccak is motivated by the fact that it has been adopted as the latest SHA-3 standard. Hence, it is important to verify how AEC performs when compared with a state-of-the-art algorithms like Keccak. Here, t denotes the number of error correction capability and w signifies the word size of AEC. From the table it immediately gets clear that AEC reduces the overhead almost by a factor of two. It is known that for hash length of $2n$ bits Keccak offers n-bit security. So, for comparison, hash value nearest to the double of the word size of AEC is chosen so that both systems have similar levels of security.

Table 2. Comparison of Communication Overhead

t	AEC			HMAC then ECC		
	w=89	w=127	w=521	Keccak-224	Keccak-256	Keccak-512
1	178	254	1042	356	508	2084
2	267	381	1563	445	635	2605
3	356	508	2084	534	762	3126

Table 3 shows the hardware requirements for both types of implementations, Standalone and Resource constrained environments. It shows the complexity of AEC with RS(255,251) code implemented using CA. For a standalone system the key generator is a part of the transceiver unit and hence, no separate result is given. Moreover, it can be seen, that separating the key generator from the transceiver largely improves performance. This kind of implementation is suitable for environments where latency is a concern, as we can see the separate transceiver has much higher throughput than the standalone unit. To the best of our knowledge, this is the first practical scheme suitable for real life applications.

Table 3. Implementation Summary in Xilinx XC3S1500 FPGA

		Transceiver	Key Generator
Standalone System	Number of LUTs	8121	-
	Number of Slices	5048	-
	Frequency (MHz)	81	-
	Throughput (Mbit/s)	0.871	-
Resource Constrained	Number of LUTs	1866	4936
	Number of Slices	986	3250
	Frequency (MHz)	121	81
	Throughput (Mbit/s)	163	0.330

6   Conclusion

This paper presents a new MAC algorithm for message authentication with error correction capabilities. The proposed work overcomes the weaknesses and limitations of previous works by proposing a low cost architectural design of the proposed scheme. It also introduces a new efficient technique for random selection of an error correcting code making it secure. The security analysis of AEC has been carried out against well-known generic attacks to show the robustness of the scheme.

References

1. Krawczyk, H.: LFSR-based hashing and authentication. In: Desmedt, Y.G. (ed.) CRYPTO 1994. LNCS, vol. 839, pp. 129–139. Springer, Heidelberg (1994)
2. Boncelet Jr., C.G.: The ntmac for authentication of noisy messages. IEEE Transactions on Information Forensics and Security 1(1), 35–42 (2006)
3. Liu, Y., Boncelet, C.G.: The crc–ntmac for noisy message authentication. IEEE Transactions on Information Forensics and Security 1(4), 517–523 (2006)
4. Liu, Y., Boncelet, C.G.: The bch-ntmac for noisy message authentication. In: 2006 40th Annual Conference on Information Sciences and Systems, pp. 246–251 (March 2006)
5. Bhaumik, J., Roy Chowdhury, D.: An integrated ecc-mac based on rs code. Transactions on Computational Science 4, 117–135 (2009)
6. Alex Halderman, J., Schoen, S.D., Heninger, N., Clarkson, W., Paul, W., Cal, J.A., Feldman, A.J., Felten, E.W.: Least we remember: Cold boot attacks on encryption keys. In: USENIX Security Symposium (2008)
7. Rabin, M.O.: Probabilistic algorithms in finite fields. SIAM J. Comput. 9, 273–280 (1979)
8. Cattell, K., Muzio, J.C.: Synthesis of one-dimensional linear hybrid cellular automata. IEEE Transactions on Computer-Aided Design of Integrated Circuits and Systems 15(3), 325–335 (1996)
9. Chaudhuri, P.P., Roy Chowdhury, D., Nandi, S., Chattopadhyay, S.: Additive Cellular Automata: Theory and Applications. IEEE Computer Society Press (1997)
10. Golomb, S.W.: Shift register sequences (1967)
11. Comer, J.M., Cerda, J.C., Martinez, C.D., Hoe, D.H.K.: Random number generators using cellular automata implemented on fpgas. In: 2012 44th Southeastern Symposium on System Theory (SSST), pp. 67–72 (March 2012)
12. Wolfram, S.: Random sequence generation by cellular automata. Advances in Applied Mathematics 7(2), 123–169 (1986)
13. Mignotte, M.: Mathematics for Computer Algebra. Springer (1992)
14. Bhaumik, J., Roy Chowdhury, D.: Nmix: An ideal candidate for key mixing. In: SECRYPT, pp. 285–288 (2009)

A   Basics of Cellular Automata

Cellular Automata (CA) is a linear finite state machine composed of 1-dimensional array of n-cells. The state of a cell changes its value at discrete time steps, governed by some predefined rule which uniquely characterizes the CA. In this paper, we assume all CAs having 3-neighborhood property. However, it turns out that out of 2^{2^3} possible boolean functions, only two *linear* functions are of prime interest viz., rule 90 and 150 (ascertained from the decimal value of their position in function table). The state of i-th cell at time instant t can be expressed as:

$$s_i^{(t+1)} = s_{i-1}^{(t)} \oplus d_i \cdot s_i^{(t)} \oplus s_{i+1}^{(t)}, \quad d_i = \begin{cases} 0, & \text{if } d_i \rightarrow \text{rule 90} \\ 1, & \text{if } d_i \rightarrow \text{rule 150} \end{cases}$$

Thus, a CA rule can be completely specified by an n-tuple $R = [d_1, d_2, ...d_n]$. The transition function $f : \{0,1\}^n \rightarrow \{0,1\}^n$ of an n-cell CA can be represented by a $n \times n$ square matrix T, referred to as the characteristic matrix of the CA. The detailed theory of CA can be found in [9].

CA is widely used in literature for its error correction property as it is highly efficient as well as being very easy to implement in hardware. A t-word error correcting code, where each word is n-bit long, can be generated with the help of an n-cell *maximum-length*[5] cellular automata. The $2t$ checkbytes are generated by running the CA for $N(\leq 2^n - 1)$ cycles, while sequentially feeding the N information words, where N is the block length in number of words. The expression for the i-th checkbyte is given below.

$$C_i = \bigoplus_{j=0}^{N-1} T^{i \times (N-1-j)}[B_j], \quad \begin{cases} i = \{0, 1, \cdots, 2t-1\}; \\ B = [B_0, B_1, \cdots, B_{N-1}]; \\ T \text{ is the characteristic matrix of the CA} \end{cases} \tag{4}$$

In decoder, the syndrome corresponding to the i-th checkbyte, S_i is computed using the expression given below.

$$S_i = C_i \oplus C_i' \quad 0 \leq i \leq 2t-1 \quad \begin{cases} C_i \text{ is the received checkbyte} \\ C_i' \text{ is the checkbyte computed} \end{cases}$$

One or more non-zero syndromes signify the presence of errors in the received data. Locating and subsequent correction of the erroneous byte(s) using CA are further discussed in [9].

B   Statistical Analysis of the MAC Function

In this model, statistical analysis of the MAC function has been carried out against the NIST Statistical Test Suite and Table 4 summarizes the results. The tests are performed by taking the MAC values for 10,000 messages for a fixed key and length of each MAC is 356-bits.

---

[5] CA having a period of $(2^n - 1)$.

Table 4. Results of NIST Statistical Test Suite

Test Name	Status
Frequency (Monobit) Test	Pass
Frequency Test within a Block	Pass
Runs Test	Pass
Discrete Fourier Transform (Spectral) Test	Pass
Non-overlapping Template Matching Test	Pass
Overlapping Template Matching Test	Pass
Serial Test	Pass
Approximate Entropy Test	Pass
Cumulative Sums (Cusum) Test	Pass

C Architecture of Encoder

In this paper, the scheme has been implemented taking word size of 89-bits due to aforementioned arguments. Here, we present the architecture of CA based RS(255,251) Encoder in Fig. 5. Checkbytes C_0, C_1, C_2 and C_3 are generated by running CA-I, CA-T ,CA-T^2 and CAT^3 respectively for 251 cycles, while sequentially feeding the information bytes (Starting from D_0 to D_{250}). The characteristic matrix of one such CA, CA-T is shown in Fig. 6. The architecture of decoder is essentially same as encoder.

After, generation of checkbytes they are mixed with key k_2 in a nonlinear manner by NMix, which is given in Fig. 7. As the architecture of inverse NMix is same as that of forward Nmix it is omitted.

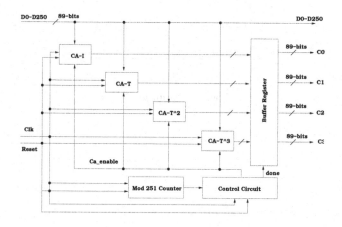

Fig. 5. Architecture of RS(255,251) Encoder

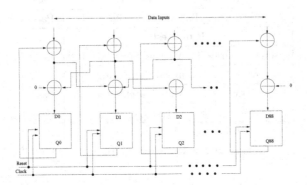

Fig. 6. Internal architecture of CA with characteristic matrix T

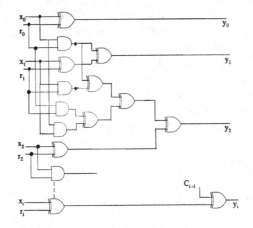

Fig. 7. Logic Diagram for NMix [5]

Yet Another Strong Privacy-Preserving RFID Mutual Authentication Protocol

Raghuvir Songhela and Manik Lal Das

DA-IICT, Gandhinagar, India
{songhela_raghuvir,maniklal_das}@daiict.ac.in

Abstract. Radio Frequency IDentification (RFID) systems are gaining enormous interests in industry due to their vast applications such as supply chain, access control, inventory, transport, health care and home appliances. Although tag identification is the primary security goal of an RFID system, privacy issue is equally, even more important concern in the RFID system because of pervasiveness of RFID tags. Over the years, many protocols have been proposed for RFID tags' identification using symmetric key cryptography and other primitives. Many of them have failed to preserve tags' privacy. In order to achieve privacy and to provide scalability and anti-cloning features of RFID system, public-key primitives should be used in an RFID authentication protocol [1]. In this paper, we present a mutual authentication protocol for RFID systems using elliptic curves arithmetic. The proposed protocol provides *narrow-strong* and *wide-weak* privacy under standard complexity assumption.

Keywords: RFID System, Mutual Authentication, Tracking Attack, Elliptic Curve Cryptography, Privacy, Un-traceability.

1 Introduction

Radio Frequency IDentification (RFID) systems have found enormous applications in industry such as supply chain management, access control system, inventory control, transport system, health care, home appliances, object tracking, and so on. An RFID system consists of a set of tags, one or more readers and a back-end server. Typically, all the readers are connected with the back-end server. The communication channel between the readers and the back-end server is assumed to be secure. For simplicity, the reader and the back-end server can be considered as a single entity, we consider it "a reader". A tag is basically a microchip with limited memory along with a transponder. Based on RFID chip capacity, RFID tags can be divided into three types - Active, Passive and Battery-Assisted Passive (Semi-Passive). Passive tags are less expensive and they can be made small enough to fit on almost any product. A passive tag does not have a power source. It only transmits a signal upon receiving RF energy emitted from a reader in its proximity. Active and semi-passive tags have internal batteries to power their circuits. An active tag uses its battery to broadcast radio waves to a reader, whereas a semi-passive tag gets activated in the presence of

R.S. Chakraborty et al. (Eds.): SPACE 2014, LNCS 8804, pp. 171–182, 2014.

an RFID reader and relies on the reader to supply the power for broadcasting the message. A reader is a device used to interrogate RFID tags. The reader consists of one or more transceivers which emit radio waves.

Although tags' authentication is the main goal of RFID system, the system should guarantee that tags are not being tracked by attackers with a motive of compromising privacy of tag-enabled objects. Furthermore, RFID authentication protocols should preserve operational and cryptographic properties like system scalability and security against cloning and tracking attacks. Recent works in RFID authentication protocols suggest that public-key cryptography (PKC) primitives are necessary to address these requirements [2], [1]. In particular, ECC (Elliptic Curve Cryptography) arithmetic is preferred over other PKC algorithms because of its smaller key size and existence of efficient algorithms for elliptic curve arithmetic.

Privacy of tags has become an important issue in the RFID system. Privacy can be termed in two concepts: anonymity and un-traceability [3]. The real ID of a tag must not be known by others to achieve anonymity. To achieve un-traceability, the equality or inequality of two tags must be impossible to ascertain. Therefore, un-traceability is a stronger privacy requirement than anonymity. Several theoretical models have been proposed so far which address the privacy of RFID systems [4], [5], [6], [2]. The privacy model of Vaudenay [2] was one of the first and most complete privacy models that featured the notion of strong privacy. According to [2], if an attacker has access to the result of the tag's authentication (accept or reject) in a reader, he is defined as a wide attacker. Otherwise, he is a narrow attacker. If an attacker is able to extract the tag's secret and still that tag remains active in the set of tags, then he is a strong attacker. If the tag is inactive after the corruption by the attacker then he is a weak attacker. Therefore, a wide-strong attacker is defined as the most powerful.

In this paper, we present a mutual authentication protocol for RFID system using ECC arithmetic, which provides *narrow-strong* and *wide-weak* privacy under standard complexity assumption. We compare the proposed mutual authentication protocol with similar works and show that the protocol is efficient and provides strong privacy in comparison to other protocols.

The remainder of this paper is organized as follows. In section 2, we discuss preliminaries and security and privacy properties of RFID system. In section 3, we review some ECC-based RFID security protocols. In section 4, we present our protocol. We analyze the proposed protocol in section 5. We conclude the paper with section 6.

2   Preliminaries

2.1   Elliptic Curves and Computational Assumptions

An elliptic curve E over a field F is a cubic curve with no repeated roots [7]. The general form of an elliptic curve is $Y^2 + a_1XY + a_3Y = X^3 + a_2X^2 + a_4X + a_5$, where $a_i \in F$, $i = 1, 2, \cdots, 5$. The set $E(F)$ contains all points $P(x, y)$ on the curve, such that x, y are elements of F along with an additional point called the point at infinity ($\mathcal{O}$). The set $E(F)$ forms an Abelian group under elliptic curve point addition operation with ($\mathcal{O}$) as the additive identity. For all $P, Q \in E(F)$, let F_q be a finite field with order of a prime number q. The number of points in the elliptic curve group $E(F_q)$, represented by $\#E(F_q)$, is called the order of the curve E over F_q. The order of a point P is the smallest positive integer r, such that $rP = \mathcal{O}$. Without loss of generality, the elliptic curve equation can be simplified as $y^2 = x^3 + ax + b \pmod{q}$, where $a, b \in F_q$ satisfy $4a^3 + 27b^2 \neq 0$, if the characteristic of F_q is neither 2 nor 3. There are mainly three operations on ECC, namely point addition, scalar multiplication of a point and map-to-point operation, which are commonly used in security protocols.

Elliptic Curve Discrete Logarithm Problem: Elliptic Curve Discrete Logarithm Problem (ECDLP) is a standard assumption upon which ECC-based cryptographic algorithm can rely. The ECDLP is stated as: Given two elliptic curve points P and Q ($= xP$), where x is sufficiently large, finding scalar x is an intractable problem with best known algorithms and available computational resources. x is called the discrete logarithm of Q to the base P.

Decisional Diffie-Hellman (DDH) Assumption: Let P be a generator of $E(F_q)$. Let $x, y, z \in_R Z_q$ and $A = xP$, $B = yP$. The DDH assumption states that: The distribution $\langle A, B, C(= xyP) \rangle$ and $\langle A, B, C(= zP) \rangle$ is computationally indistinguishable.

2.2 Security and Privacy Properties of RFID System

An RFID system must meet following security and operational properties [2], [8].

Security: Ensuring That Fake Tags are Rejected. *Authentication*: Authentication of tag ensures its legitimacy to reader. Depending on application requirement, tags' authentication or tag-reader mutual authentication is achieved in RFID system.

Integrity: Integrity allows a reader to detect data tampering/alteration upon receiving data from a tag. As tag-reader communication takes place over radio waves, RFID security protocol must ensure data integrity property.

Privacy: Ensuring That Privacy of Legitimate Tags is not Compromised. RFID tags are small and thus, can be attached to consumer goods, library books, home appliances for identification and tracking purposes. In case of any misuse (e.g., stolen RFID-enabled items), the reader can trigger an appropriate message to seller/vendor/owner of the item. The use of radio waves makes adversary's task easy for eavesdropping tag-reader communication and thereby, the information relating to the tag is an easy target of the adversary. Furthermore, the tag of an object can be tracked or monitored wherever the object is lying.

Resistance: Ensuring That the Protocol is Secure Against Cloning. If a group of tags share the same secret key and use it for the authentication, then it will be possible for an attacker to clone all tags in the group once any single tag of the group is cracked by him. It can also cause the tracking problem, as the attacker can decrypt the exchanged messages. Therefore, secret information should be pertinent only to a single tag so that an attacker cannot use revealed secret information to clone other tags but the cracked one.

Forward/Backward Un-traceability: Ensuring That the Cracked Tag Cannot Be Tracked from Its Past or Future Sessions. Suppose, a tag is cracked and the private key of that tag is stolen by an attacker. A protocol satisfies the feature of the forward/backward un-traceability if the attacker is unable to decode the messages of the previous/future protocol runs initiated by the same tag.

3   Related Works

In recent times, many RFID protocols have been devised using public key cryptographic primitives in order to prevent tracking attacks [9], [10], [11], [12]. In particular, elliptic curve cryptography (ECC) [7] has been realized in RFID authentication protocols [13], [12], [8], [14], [15], [16], [17], [18], [19], [3]. Many RFID protocols use the concept of the Schnorr [20] identification protocol, where, the prover acts as the tag and the verifier acts as the reader. The RFID protocol which is based on the Schnorr protocol might not preserve the privacy of tag, as the goal of the Schnorr protocol is to identify the communicating principal. Lee *et al* [12] proposed an RFID authentication protocol, known as EC-RAC (Elliptic Curve based Randomized Access Control), claiming that it is secure against tracking attack. However, the claim is not correct as shown in [16] and [17]. Subsequently, randomized Schnorr protocol [16], revised EC-RAC [8] (we refer here EC-RAC mutual authentication version only, termed it as EC-RAC-4) have been proposed to eliminate tracking attacks. Later, attacks on revised EC-RAC have been found [21]. Both randomized Schnorr and EC-RAC-4 protocols are *narrow-strong* privacy-preserving, but not *wide-weak* privacy-preserving. Lee *et al* then proposed low-cost untraceable authentication protocols [3] claiming narrow-strong and wide-weak privacy. However, it is found that the protocol in [3] suffers from man-in-the-middle attack [19].

4   The Proposed Protocol

The protocol has two phases – Setup and Authentication. The Setup phase is a one-time computation, configured with tags and reader before they are deployed into the field. The Authentication phase is invoked when tag and reader start communication.

Protocol's Goal and Assumptions: The protocol aims to provide mutual authentication along with *narrow-strong* and *wide-weak* privacy. If there are more than one readers in the RFID system then all the readers share the same private key. If we keep the private keys different then all the tags need to store the public keys of all the readers, which is not preferred. Moreover, privacy is preserved even if the private key is kept same across all the readers. In the protocol, it is assumed that, before mutual authentication, the tag should have the public key of the reader. The reader should also have access to the public key of all tags. In our protocol, we consider active tags who can initiate communication with a reader. We further assume that communicating tags have similar computing resource that we have in contactless smart cards [22].

4.1 Setup Phase

Setup phase is implemented only once, before the deployment of the tags and the reader. Let P be the base point of an admissible elliptic curve. The reader shares its public key Y $(=yP)$ with all the tags and stores its private key y securely with it. Each tag shares its public key X $(=xP)$ with the reader (which gets stored in back-end server) and stores its private key x securely with it.

4.2 Authentication Phase

The Authentication phase works as follows.

Tag $\rightarrow$ Reader : r_{t_1}, K, T_1

The tag chooses random numbers k and r_{t_1}. Then it computes

1. $r_s \leftarrow f(r_{t_1}, [kY])$
2. $K \leftarrow kP$
3. $T_1 \leftarrow r_s x Y$

Here, $[P]$ indicates the x-coordinate of the Elliptic Curve point P. To avoid the man-in-the-middle attack as shown in [19], the value of k should be different from the multiples of order of Y on the elliptic curve and zero. $f()$ is a cryptographic pseudo-random function. Tag sends r_{t_1}, K, T_1 to the reader.

Reader $\rightarrow$ Tag : T_2

Upon receiving tag's message $< r_{t_1}, K, T_1 >$, the reader first computes $f(r_{t_1}, [yK])$ (say r'_s). It checks whether $T_1 y^{-1} r'^{-1}_s = X$. If it holds, then tag's authentication is confirmed. Reader now computes $T_2 \leftarrow y r'_s K$ and sends it to the tag.

After receiving reader's response, the tag checks whether $T_2 k^{-1} r_s^{-1} = Y$. If it holds, then the reader authentication is confirmed.

In order to get the value of X, the reader requires the access of the list of public keys of all the tags. If the reader finds the derived value matching with any entry in the list, the communicating tag is considered as authentic one. The protocol is depicted in Figure 1.

5 Analysis of the Protocol

5.1 Narrow-Strong Privacy

A narrow attacker does not have access to the **result** of authentication of the tag. It is noted that the outcome of the **result** query is a bit indicating successful/unsuccessful authentication of the tag at the reader side. A strong attacker

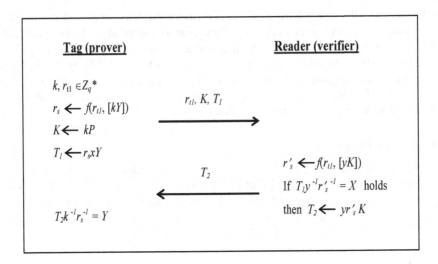

Fig. 1. The Proposed Protocol

can corrupt a tag and still that tag remains in the set of the valid tags, that is, the tag can communicate with the reader even after it has been corrupted by the attacker. A narrow-strong attacker has properties of narrow attacker and strong attacker both. Suppose, the attacker has cracked tag and has retrieved the private key x of tag. Now, any of the tags starts a new protocol run with the reader. The attacker can manipulate messages sent by this tag. Given the messages sent by this tag, the narrow-strong attacker has to determine whether this tag is the same which is cracked by him or not with the probability significantly greater than $1/2$ to carry a successful attack.

The messages exchanged in our protocol are r_{t_1}, T_1, K and T_2, where K is a random ephemeral elliptic curve (EC) point, r_{t_1} is a random number generated by the tag, and T_2 is a EC point generated by the reader. It is easy to see that these three messages do not include any information about the tag. Message T_1 contains the private key of the tag (x), public key of the reader (Y) and the random number (r_s) which depends on r_{t_1} and k. It is computationally infeasible to link message T_1 with any particular tag, as r_s is a result of one-way pseudo-random function which takes two arguments. Out of these two arguments, r_{t_1} is communicated in plain text form to the reader. However, the attacker can not learn r_s without knowing k. Although $K = kP$, the attacker can not get any clue of k from K, as it is an ECDLP, an intractable problem. As a result, the attacker can not calculate the value of r_s, which is used to calculate T_1. Therefore, even if the attacker knows the private key of a tag, x, it does not help him in decrypting T_1 as he does not have value of r_s. Therefore, given a private key of any tag and a message set sent by some other tag to the reader, the attacker can not determine if the protocol run was initiated by the corrupt tag or uncorrupt tag.

5.2   Wide-Weak Privacy

The attacks on protocols in [3] observed in [19] use the fact that the reader sends the random number in plain form to the tag, which can be modified by the attacker. In our protocol, we have taken care of this and the protocol provides wide-weak privacy as proved below.

A wide-weak attacker has properties of both, wide attacker and weak attacker. A weak attacker can not corrupt a tag. A wide attacker has one-bit extra information compared to a narrow attacker: the decision of the reader whether to accept a tag or not (result of the tag authentication). This extra bit of information can be used by a wide-weak attacker to perform a tracking attack. The goal of a wide-weak attacker is to determine if two sets of protocol instance originate from the same tag. One of these sets contains authentic messages from the past. We denote the source (i.e. the tag) of these messages by tag A. The other set contains the messages of tag B. The tracking attack is successful when the attacker can determine the (in)equality of these two tags with a probability significantly greater than $1/2$.

The attacker has four messages from the protocol run initiated by tag A. We denote them by $r_{t_1}^A$, T_1^A, K^A and T_2^A. We also denote the messages sent by tag B to the reader by $r_{t_1}^B$, T_1^B and K^B. Before the messages from the protocol run of tag B reaches the reader, the attacker can manipulate them. Based on the result of the authentication of tag B, the attacker tries to guess whether both tags are same or not. Both the tags are same if x^A and x^B are same. Note that K^A and K^B are two random points on EC and contain no information about the tag. The same argument applies to $r_{t_1}^A$ and $r_{t_1}^B$ as both of them are random numbers. We now prove that this protocol is wide-weak privacy-preserving by the method of the contradiction. Suppose, the proposed protocol is not wide-weak privacy-preserving and the attacker manipulates messages sent by tag B to the reader and from the result of the tag authentication by the reader, it can determine if tag A and B are equal or not with probability greater than $1/2$. Following three scenarios may arise.

Modification in $r_{t_1}^B$: The Attacker Changes the Value of $r_{t_1}^B$ Which is Sent from the Tag B to the Reader. Suppose, the attacker replaces $r_{t_1}^B$ with $r_{t_1}^{'}$. However, he can not pass T_1^B validation at the server end. The reason for the same is r_{t1}^B is used for calculating r_s^B, which in turn is used to calculate T_1^B. But, to calculate r_s^B by its own, the attacker has to retrieve the value of k^B from K^B, which he can not do because of the ECDLP hardness problem. Now suppose, he selects his own ephemeral random number $k^{'}$, calculates $K^{'}$ and replaces K^B with K'. However, he can not calculate a valid $T_1^{'}$ to replace T_1^B, because $T_1^{'}$ should have involvement of the private key x^B of the tag B. But, the attacker does not have the information of the private key of the tag B. Therefore, the attacker can not generate the valid pair of messages in this case and hence attack is not feasible.

Modification in K^B: The Attacker Changes the Value of K^B Which is Sent from the Tag B to the Reader. Suppose, the attacker does not change the value of r_{t1}^B and keeps it as it was sent originally by the tag B. As mentioned in the previous point, if the attacker tries to replace K^B by selecting his own K', then he has to calculate a valid T_1'. However, without knowing the private key of the tag B, he can not calculate a valid T_1', and the attack can not take place.

Modification in T_1^B: The Attacker Changes the Value of T_1^B Which is Sent from the Tag B to the Reader. Suppose, the attacker modifies T_1^B by adding T_1^A or any T_1 message intercepted from the previous run of the protocol. Suppose, the tag A and tag B are same. As tag A and tag B are same, $x^B = x^A$ and the following condition will hold.

$$r_s^B x^B Y(= T_1^B) + r_s^A x^A Y(= T_1^A) = (r_s^B + r_s^A) x^B Y$$

Now, for successful authentication at the reader end, the attacker has to replace r_{t1}^B by r_{t1}' and/or K^B by K' such that the reader gets the value of r_s as $(r_s^B + r_s^A)$. If the attacker successfully derives these values and if the reader authenticates the tag B then the attacker can conclude that tag A and tag B are same. If the reader does not authenticate the tag B then the attacker can conclude that both the tags are different.

In order to derive the values of the r_{t1}' and/or K', the attacker has to retrieve the value of $(r_s^B + r_s^A)$ from the message which was resulted after addition of two messages, that is, $(r_s^B + r_s^A) x^B Y$. However, this can not be done, as the attacker has to solve the ECDLP which he can not, with the best available algorithms and resources. Therefore, the attacker can not retrieve the value of $(r_s^B + r_s^A)$, and the attack is not possible. Similarly, if both the tags are not same then the following condition will hold.

$$r_s^B x^B Y(= T_1^B) + r_s^A x^A Y(= T_1^A) = (r_s^B x^B + r_s^A x^A) Y$$

Here, the attacker has to replace the values of r_{t1}^B and/or K^B such that the reader gets the value of r_s as $(r_s^B x^B + r_s^A x^A)$. But the attacker can't retrieve the value of $(r_s^B x^B + r_s^A x^A)$ from the $(r_s^B x^B + r_s^A x^A) Y$ as it is an ECDLP, an intractable problem. Therefore, in both the cases modification in T_1^B does not help the attacker to carry a successful attack. Our initial assumption stated that the attacker can manipulate the messages sent by the tag B and can break wide-weak privacy. As we have shown above, the attacker is unable to carry out wide-weak attack by manipulating messages. These results show that the initial assumption was false and the proposed protocol provides the wide-weak privacy.

5.3 Forward/Backward Un-traceability

Suppose the attacker cracks the tag and reveals all the information pertinent to that tag. However, the attacker cannot track the tag in the past communications. The tag chooses two random numbers r_{t_1} and k. r_{t_1} is sent in plain text form by the tag to the server and hence accessible to the attacker. However, the attacker cannot decrypt the value of T_1 due to dependence of T_1 on r_s. The r_s is calculated by passing two parameter values to the pseudo-random function, out of which first one r_{t_1} is accessible to the attacker. But, to calculate the second parameter, the attacker has to calculate k from K $(=kP)$, which is ECDLP, an intractable problem. As attacker cannot calculate the value of r_s, he cannot operate inverse functions on T_1 and cannot get clue whether the communication has been originated from the same tag or not. In the similar way, backward un-traceability can be proved in which the attacker cannot track the tag in the future communications. Therefore, the proposed protocol provides both forward and backward un-traceability.

5.4 Anti-Cloning and Replay Prevention

Cloning is an important issue when an RFID system is relying on group key management. In case of group key, if one tag is cracked then the attacker can forge other tags of the group of the system as all tags within the group use the same key for communication. In our protocol, the attacker is unable to forge the other tags of the system. However, if the attacker crack a tag and retrieve its private key along with the other parameters pertinent to that tag then he can clone that tag to the system. The protocol also prevents replay attempts, as a new session must be composed of a random number chosen by the tag, which has to be validated by the reader with tag's previous sessions' state stored in it.

5.5 Computational Cost

We provide the computational cost of the protocols in Table 1. The notations used in the Table 1 indicate as follows: PM - Point Multiplication; PA - Point Addition. The low-cost untraceable authentication protocol [3] provides only tag authentication and requires three point multiplications on each side. It requires one point addition on the server side. However, it does not provide mutual authentication. Moreover, the protocol is not wide-weak privacy-preserving [19]. The EC-RAC-4 [8] requires four point multiplication operations on each side. It also requires one point addition on the server side. EC-RAC-4 provides only narrow-strong privacy and not wide-weak privacy. Moreover, EC-RAC-4 is vulnerable to tracking attack [21].

The proposed protocol requires four and three point multiplication on the tag and the reader side, respectively. The protocol doesn't require any point addition operation on either side. However, the pseudo-random function is used on each side to generate a random number from two arguments. When compared to low-cost untraceable authentication protocol [3], the proposed protocol requires one more point multiplication on the tag side and requires pseudo-random function on each side. But, the proposed protocol provides the mutual authentication as well as wide-weak privacy whereas the former one does not. In comparison to EC-RAC-4 [8] (which supports mutual authentication), the proposed protocol takes one less point multiplication and one less point addition operation on the server side. In addition, the proposed protocol provides wide-weak privacy

Table 1. Comparison of computational cost

Performance ⇒ Protocol ⇓	Tag side comp.	Reader side comp.
Low-cost untraceable Protocol [3]	3 PM	3 PM + 1 PA
EC-RAC-4 [8]	4 PM	4 PM + 1 PA
Proposed Protocol	4 PM	3 PM

whereas the former does not. However, the proposed protocol requires pseudo-random function computation on each side. Therefore, the proposed protocol is computationally comparable with other protocols, and it also provides wide-weak privacy along with mutual authentication.

5.6   Communication Cost

Table 2 depicts the communication cost of the protocols in terms of the total number of parameters sent by the tag and the reader in one protocol run. The notations used in the Table 2 indicate as follows: m_r - scalar number; m_{ec} - EC point. Low cost untraceable protocol [3] and EC-RAC-4 [8] - each consists of three messages in a protocol run. In these protocols, the tag sends two messages and the reader sends one message in a protocol run. Whereas, our protocol is a two-message protocol in which the tag and the reader sends one message each in entire protocol run. EC-RAC-4 [8], the tag sends three EC points; the reader sends one scalar number and one EC point. Whereas, in our protocol, the tag sends two EC points and one scalar number, and the reader sends one EC point only. As a result, our protocol takes less communication cost than EC-RAC-4 [8] (as it is reasonable to assume that the size of the random number is less than size of EC point). Furthermore, the proposed protocol is scalable as the computation amount is fixed and independent of the number of tags.

Table 2. Comparison of the communication cost

Comparison ⇒ Protocol ⇓	Tag side comm.	Reader side comm.
Low-cost untraceable Protocol [3]	$2\ m_{ec}$	$1\ m_r$
EC-RAC-4 [8]	$3\ m_{ec}$	$1\ m_r + 1\ m_{ec}$
Proposed Protocol	$1\ m_r + 2\ m_{ec}$	$1\ m_{ec}$

6   Conclusions

We have proposed a new RFID mutual authentication protocol. The proposed protocol provides wide-weak and narrow-strong privacy with less computational load compared to [8], [3]. The proposed protocol resists to all attacks that occur in EC-RAC variants and other related protocols. The performance analysis provided in tables 1 and 2 showed that the proposed protocol is comparable to related RFID authentication protocols, and it preserves privacy of the tags.

References

1. Burmester, M., Medeiros, B., Motta, R.: Robust Anonymous RFID Authentication with Constant Key Lookup. In: Proc. of ACM Symposium on Information, Computer and Communications Security (ASIACCS 2008), pp. 283–291 (2008)
2. Vaudenay, S.: On Privacy Models for RFID. In: Kurosawa, K. (ed.) ASIACRYPT 2007. LNCS, vol. 4833, pp. 68–87. Springer, Heidelberg (2007)
3. Lee, Y.K., Batina, L., Singelee, D., Verbauwhede, I.: Low-cost Untraceable Authentication Protocols for RFID (extended version). In: Proc. of the ACM Conference on Wireless Network Security (WiSec 2010), pp. 55–64 (2010)
4. Avoine, G.: Adversarial Model for Radio Frequency Identification. IACR Cryptology ePrint Archive, Report no.49 (2005)
5. Juels, A., Weis, S.: Defining Strong Privacy for RFID. IACR Cryptology ePrint Archive, Report no.137 (2006)
6. Ng, C.Y., Susilo, W., Mu, Y., Safavi-Naini, R.: RFID Privacy Models Revisited. In: Jajodia, S., Lopez, J. (eds.) ESORICS 2008. LNCS, vol. 5283, pp. 251–266. Springer, Heidelberg (2008)
7. Hankerson, D., Menezes, A., Vanstone, S.: Guide to Elliptic Curve Cryptography. Springer (2004)
8. Lee, Y.K., Batina, L., Verbauwhede, I.: Untraceable RFID Authentication Protocols: Revision of EC-RAC. In: Proc. of the IEEE International Conference on RFID, pp. 178–185 (2009)
9. Wolkerstorfer, J.: Is Elliptic-curve Cryptography Suitable to Secure RFID Tags? In: Proc. of the Workshop on RFID and Light-weight Cryptography (2005)
10. Tuyls, P., Batina, L.: RFID-tags for Anti-counterfeiting. In: Pointcheval, D. (ed.) CT-RSA 2006. LNCS, vol. 3860, pp. 115–131. Springer, Heidelberg (2006)
11. Batina, L., Guajardo, J., Kerins, T., Mentens, N., Tuyls, P., Verbauwhede, I.: Public-key Cryptography for RFID-tags. In: Proc. of the IEEE International Workshop on Pervasive Computing and Communication Security, Persec 2007 (2007)
12. Lee, Y.K., Sakiyama, K., Batina, L., Verbauwhede, I.: Elliptic Curve based Security Processor for RFID. IEEE Transactions on Computer 57(11), 1514–1527 (2008)
13. Okamoto, T.: Provably Secure and Practical Identification Schemes and Corresponding Signature Schemes. In: Brickell, E.F. (ed.) CRYPTO 1992. LNCS, vol. 740, pp. 31–53. Springer, Heidelberg (1993)
14. Hein, D., Wolkerstorfer, J., Felber, N.: ECC Is Ready for RFID – A Proof in Silicon. In: Avanzi, R.M., Keliher, L., Sica, F. (eds.) SAC 2008. LNCS, vol. 5381, pp. 401–413. Springer, Heidelberg (2009)
15. Oren, Y., Feldhofer, M.: A Low-resource Public-key Identification Scheme for RFID Tags and Sensor Nodes. In: Proc. of the ACM Conference on Wireless Network Security, pp. 59–68 (2009)
16. Bringer, J., Chabanne, H., Icart, T.: Cryptanalysis of EC-RAC, a RFID Identification Protocol. In: Franklin, M.K., Hui, L.C.K., Wong, D.S. (eds.) CANS 2008. LNCS, vol. 5339, pp. 149–161. Springer, Heidelberg (2008)
17. Deursen, T., Radomirovic, S.: Attacks on RFID Protocols. IACR Cryptology ePrint Archive, Report no.310 (2008)
18. van Deursen, T., Radomirović, S.: EC-RAC: Enriching a Capacious RFID Attack Collection. In: Ors Yalcin, S.B. (ed.) RFIDSec 2010. LNCS, vol. 6370, pp. 75–90. Springer, Heidelberg (2010)
19. Fan, J., Hermans, J., Vercauteren, F.: On the Claimed Privacy of EC-RAC III. In: Ors Yalcin, S.B. (ed.) RFIDSec 2010. LNCS, vol. 6370, pp. 66–74. Springer, Heidelberg (2010)

20. Schnorr, C.-P.: Efficient Identification and Signatures for Smart Cards. In: Brassard, G. (ed.) CRYPTO 1989. LNCS, vol. 435, pp. 239–252. Springer, Heidelberg (1990)
21. Deursen, T., Radomirovic, S.: Untraceable RFID Protocols are not Trivially Composable: Attacks on the Revision of EC-RAC. IACR Cryptology ePrint Archive, Report no.332 (2009)
22. ISO/IEC 14443-4:2008(E), Identification cards – Contactless integrated circuit cards – Proximity cards – Part 4: Transmission protocol,
    `https://www.iso.org/obp/ui/#iso:std:iso-iec:14443:-4:ed-2:v1:en`
    (retrieved September 2013)

Boosting Higher-Order Correlation Attacks by Dimensionality Reduction

Nicolas Bruneau[1,2], Jean-Luc Danger[1,3], Sylvain Guilley[1,3],
Annelie Heuser[1,*], and Yannick Teglia[2]

[1] TELECOM-ParisTech, Crypto Group, Paris, France
[2] STMicroelectronics, AST division, Rousset, France
[3] Secure-IC S.A.S., Rennes, France

Abstract. Multi-variate side-channel attacks allow to break higher-order masking protections by combining several leakage samples. But how to optimally extract all the information contained in all possible d-tuples of points? In this article, we introduce preprocessing tools that answer this question. We first show that maximizing the higher-order CPA coefficient is equivalent to finding the maximum of the covariance. We apply this equivalence to the problem of trace dimensionality reduction by linear combination of its samples. Then we establish the link between this problem and the Principal Component Analysis. In a second step we present the optimal solution for the problem of maximizing the covariance. We also theoretically and empirically compare these methods. We finally apply them on real measurements, publicly available under the DPA Contest v4, to evaluate how the proposed techniques improve the second-order CPA (2O-CPA).

Keywords: Bi-variate attacks, second-order correlation power analysis (2O-CPA), principal component analysis, interclass variance, covariance vector.

1 Introduction

For more than a decade now Side-Channel Attacks (SCA [6]) have been an important threat against embedded systems. As a consequence protection techniques and countermeasures have been an important research topic. Data masking [9] is one of the most popular protection technique. These schemes have in turn been the target of higher-order SCA [24,18].

In some particular masking implementations, the two shares [16] depending on the same mask leak at different moments (e.g., in software). Second-order attacks that combine two different time samples are called *bi-variate SCA*. When the masking scheme uses d shares, *multi-variate SCA* are still able to reveal the secret key by combining leakage samples corresponding to each of the d shares.

---

* Annelie Heuser is a Google European fellow in the field of privacy and is partially founded by this fellowship.

R.S. Chakraborty et al. (Eds.): SPACE 2014, LNCS 8804, pp. 183–200, 2014.

Note that, depending on the implementation and the measurement setup each share may leak in multiple samples.

To enhance the results of SCA several preprocessing tools can be used. In the case of *bi-variate SCA* it is particularly interesting to take into account all the information spread over the time. Indeed, the number of possible pairs increases quadratically in the number of leakage samples. For example, if the first share leaks over T_1 samples and the second share over T_2 samples, we could perform a *bi-variate SCA* on $T_1 \times T_2$ possible combined points. So, taking into account all these leaks may undoubtedly increase the efficiency of an attack.

More generally, to break $(d-1)$-order masking schemes the attacker needs to combine d samples corresponding to d shares. So, if T_i is the number of samples which leak the i-th share then the attacker could perform *multi-variate SCA* on $\prod_{1 \leq i \leq d} T_i$ different d-tuples. In other words, the number of possible d-tuples to perform *multi-variate SCA* is in $O(T^d)$ where T is the number of samples each share leaks (and assuming that each share is leaking the same number of samples, i.e., $\forall i \in [\![1, d]\!], T_i = T$).

Many methods have been presented in the area of SCA to combine the information spread over time: the Principal Component Analysis (PCA) for dimensionality reduction [1] for Template attacks [7] but also as a preprocessing tool [2] for DPA [13]. Recently in [11] Hajra and Mukhopadhyay present an approach based on match filters to find the optimal preprocessing. Other methods have been designed to combine samples from different acquisitions ([22,20]). Additionally, PCA has also been used as a distinguisher in [21]. Some other methods could be applied like the Canonical Correlation Analysis [17] to improve CPA [6]. Interestingly, all these methods lead to a dimensionality reduction.

Another approach to improve the efficiency of SCA is to find the optimal model. A *linear-regression* approach may be used. In [17] Oswald and Paar introduce optimization algorithms to determine numerically the optimal linear combination before CPA. By choosing a different objective we can give a formal expression for the result of the optimization problem, and then have an optimal method without any utilization of sophisticated optimization algorithms that would require "parameter settings", which could be costly in time. Still, we notice that the approach in [17] and our could be advantageously combined.

Our Contributions. In this paper we tackle the question *how to optimally combine the information spread over multiple time samples, for HO-CPA attacks of arbitrary order?* We present the optimal preprocessing method and express it as a generic synthetic formula. By linking the PCA to the problem of maximizing the result of the CPA we are able to evaluate the presented method. We compare these two methods theoretically and prove that they are optimal under some assumptions. We then compare these methods empirically as preprocessing tools to boost 2O-CPA attacks on a first-order masking scheme. In particular, we test these methods on real measurements (DPA contest v4 [23]). In summary, we show that taking into account all possible pairs of leakage points will significantly improve the effectiveness of 2O-CPA, in one attack.

Outline of the Paper. The rest of the paper is organized as follows. In Sect. 2 we present our case study and a theoretical comparison between PCA and the covariance method as a method to obtain the optimal preprocessing for second-order CPA. The attacks are then applied on a real masked implementation in Sect. 3. Sect. 4 provides another case study to apply these methods as preprocessing tools. Finally, conclusions and perspectives are drawn in Sect. 5.

2 Theoretical Optimal Preprocessing Function

2.1 Case Study

Let us assume that each measurement trace can be seen as a vector of points. So the leakage of the measurements can be defined as: $L = (L_t)_{t \in T}$ where $L_t = S_t + N_t$, S_t being the part of the leakage which is linked to the internal operation processed on the target component and N_t being the noise that assumed to be independent of L_T. It can be noted that, we simply refer to interval $[\![1, T]\!]$ as T, whenever there is no risk of confusion. It can also be assumed that these traces are centered and also reduced, i.e., $\mathbb{E}[L_t] = 0 \ \forall t$ and $\mathsf{Var}[L_t] = 1 \ \forall t$. Note that, the attacker is always able to center by removing the empirical mean and reduce by dividing the empirical standard deviation.

Let Z be the internal variable (depending on the sensitive variable) manipulated during the algorithm and let f define the leakage model. In the case of CPA, a transformation of the initial data (preprocessing) may increase the correlation coefficient. To consider all information contained in L an option would be to use a linear transformation as a prepossessing. Note that, combining all points by a weighted sum leads to a dimensionality reduction. More precisely,

$$\max_{\alpha} |\rho[L \cdot \alpha, f(Z)]|, \tag{1}$$

where ρ is the Pearson coefficient, α is a vector in $\mathbb{R}^T$ and $\cdot$ the scalar product.

Remark 1. The solution of $\max_{\alpha} |\rho[L \cdot \alpha, f(Z)]|$ is also a solution of $\max_{\alpha} \rho[L \cdot \alpha, f(Z)]^2$.

Remark 2 (EIS (Equal Images under the Same key) assumption [19]). The only part of the correlation that allows to distinguish the key is the covariance.

After the preprocessing we do not need to normalize by the variance of the traces, because we compare key guesses between each other for a given time sample not on a direct scale. So, as seen in Remark 2 the normalization by the variance does not impact the way we distinguish the key. Thus, we can simply focus on maximizing the following equation:

$$\max_{\|\alpha\|=1} \mathsf{Cov}[L \cdot \alpha, f(Z)]^2. \tag{2}$$

As the covariance is not bounded we introduce the constraint $\|\alpha\| = 1$ where $\|\cdot\|$ is the Euclidean norm, namely $\|\alpha\| = \sqrt{\alpha \cdot \alpha}$.

In this section we assume that the attacker has a "learning device" with a fixed key on which he is unrestricted in the number of acquisitions, which is typically more than the required number to successfully perform the attack. As a consequence we can reasonably assume that the attacker knows the key on the learning device and he is able to identify the zones of interest in $[\![1, T]\!]$ where the internal variable leaks. Moreover, he is able to estimate the weights of the linear combination (see Eq. (2)) on the learning device. In the rest of this study we call this step the "learning phase". In the final step the attacker targets another device that is expected to leak in a similar way as the learning one. However, on the device under attack he is no longer able to acquire an unlimited amount of traces. In particular, in this "attack phase" his main goal is to retrieve the secret key using only the minimum number of traces.

2.2   Principal Component Analysis

A classical way to recombine information with linear combinations is to apply PCA [12]. Let us define X as a set of data that is composed of N vectors of size T. Accordingly, we write X as an $N \times T$ matrix.

Definition 1. *The PCA is an orthonormal linear projection of the data, which maximizes the variance of the projected subspace of dimension $T' \leq T$. More formally, we search the projection which maximizes the variance of the projected data. For the first dimension of the subspace this leads to:*

$$\max_{\|u_1\|=1} \mathrm{Var}\left[X u_1\right] = \max_{\|u_1\|=1} {}^t u_1 {}^t X X u_1.$$

For the second dimension, as we want an orthonormal projection, this yields:

$$\max_{\substack{\|u_2\|=1 \\ u_2 \cdot u_1 = 0}} {}^t u_2 {}^t X X u_2.$$

The process is iterated for each dimension $T' \leq T$.

Remark 3. In general, most of the variance lays within a few dimensions (i.e., much less than T).

Proposition 1. *The solution of the problem in Def. 1 is the T' eigenvectors of X associated to the T' maximal eigenvalues.*

Proof. The proof can be found in [12].   □

As the problem of maximizing the covariance depends on the expected leakage model the preprocessing is defined such that it takes f into account. This implies that the given preprocessing methods are model-dependent. We can explicit the Proposition 1:

Proposition 2. *If we link our measurements L to their conditional expectations $\mathbb{E}[L|f(Z)]$ knowing a model $f(Z)$, then the PCA yields the principal direction:*

$$\max_{\|\alpha\|=1} \text{Var}\left[\mathbb{E}[L|f(Z)] \cdot \alpha\right].$$

This result means that the eigenvector of largest eigenvalue is the projection that maximizes the inter-class variance.

Proof. Let $f_1, f_2, \ldots, f_N$ the values that $f(Z)$ can take. Then, the lines of matrix X are $\mathbb{E}[L|f(Z) = f_1]$, $\mathbb{E}[L|f(Z) = f_2]$, ..., $\mathbb{E}[L|f(Z) = f_N]$. Apply Proposition 1. □

2.3 Preprocessing on Modulated Side Channel Traces

Definition 2. *Let us now define a modulated trace as a trace in which each time sample can be expressed as a modulation of a model (static in time) plus an independent noisy part:*

$$L = (\beta_t f(Z) + N_t)_{t \in T} = f(Z)\beta + (N_t)_{t \in T}, \tag{3}$$

where β is a vector in $\mathbb{R}^T$ and each N_t is drawn from an independent identical distribution $\mathcal{N}$. In specific, the variance of the noise does not depend on the time sample $t \in T$.

Theorem 1. *In the case of modulated traces the solution of PCA is equivalent to maximizing the covariance (Eqn. (2)). More precisely, if $L = (\beta_t f(Z) + N_t)_{t \in T}$ then*

$$\alpha \in \underset{\|\alpha\|=1}{\text{argmax}} \, \text{Cov}[L \cdot \alpha, f(Z)]^2 \iff \alpha \in \underset{\|\alpha\|=1}{\text{argmax}} \, \text{Var}[\mathbb{E}[L|f(Z)] \cdot \alpha].$$

Proof. The proof is given in Appendix A. □

In a particular case of Theorem 1 we can explicitly describe α.

Lemma 1. *If α and β are linearly dependent, we have:*

$$\frac{\beta}{\|\beta\|} \in \underset{\|\alpha\|=1}{\text{argmax}} \, \text{Cov}[L \cdot \alpha, f(Z)]^2 . \tag{4}$$

Proof. The proof is given in Appendix B. □

After projection into the new reduced space the covariance matrix will be zero everywhere except at $(0,0)$. Moreover, all the variance should be contained in the first principal direction, thus, we do not need to take the other eigenvectors into consideration.

As β does not depend on a particular model we also maximize the covariance for wrong keys in the same proportion as the covariance for the good key. Thus we do not change the way we distinguish the good key from the wrong ones (the relative distinguishing margin is unchanged [25]). However, the dimensionality reduction leads to an improvement of the attack by increasing the signal-to-noise ratio (SNR). We define the SNR as the variance of the signal divided by the variance of the noise. This definition of SNR coincides with the Normalized Inter-Class Variance (NICV [5,4]).

Lemma 2. *If the noise N_t is identically distributed (i.d.) for all t, then the noise is unchanged by any linear combination of unitary norm.*

Proof. By hypothesis, $\mathsf{Var}\left[(N_t)_{t \in T} \cdot \alpha\right] = \|\alpha\|^2 \mathsf{Var}\left[\mathcal{N}\right] = \mathsf{Var}\left[\mathcal{N}\right]$.　　□

Proposition 3. *If the noise N_t is i.d. for all t, then the signal-to-noise ratio is maximum after the projection:*

$$\frac{\max\limits_{t \in T} \mathsf{Var}\left[\beta_t f(Z)\right]}{\mathsf{Var}\left[\mathcal{N}\right]} \leq \frac{\max\limits_{\|\alpha\|=1} \mathsf{Var}\left[\mathbb{E}\left[L|f(Z)\right] \cdot \alpha\right]}{\mathsf{Var}\left[\mathcal{N}\right]}.$$

Proof. By definition of α we have $\max\limits_{t \in T} \mathsf{Var}\left[\beta_t f(Z)\right] \leq \max\limits_{\|\alpha\|=1} \mathsf{Var}\left[\mathbb{E}\left[L|f(Z)\right] \cdot \alpha\right]$. Besides, by lemma 2, the numerator of the SNR does not depend on our preprocessing, since is satisfies $\|\alpha\| = 1$.　　□

Remark 4. In the case of modulated traces the PCA gives the solution of a matched-filter [14].

2.4　Covariance Vector as a Preprocessing Method

In the general case when the model is not known or in the presence of noise, the variance may not only be contained in the first eigenvector [2]. Therefore, it may be useful to also take the other directions of the PCA into account. Note that, we still obtain an optimal function to reduce the dimensionality before conducting a CPA under the same leakage model assumption.

Proposition 4.

$$\left(\frac{\mathsf{Cov}\left[L_t; f(Z)\right]}{\|(\mathsf{Cov}\left[L_t; f(Z)\right])_{t \in T}\|}\right)_{t \in T} \in \underset{\|\alpha\|=1}{\mathrm{argmax}}\, \mathsf{Cov}\left[L \cdot \alpha, f(Z)\right]^2$$

Proof. The proof is given in Appendix C.　　□

　　So, the normalized covariance is the optimal preprocessing method to maximize the value of the covariance when using linear combinations of traces points. In the rest of this study we call this method the "covariance method" and the result the "covariance vector".

Remark 5. Note that, the model of the actual leakage of the traces is not used in the proof of Appendix C. The results are therefore applicable for any leakage model such as the one presented in [10].

2.5 Discussion

The previous subsection shows that the projection of the differential traces on the covariance vector gives a solution to the problem of maximizing the covariance after dimensionality reduction (i.e., after having learned the best linear form). This method is better than the state-of-the-art, where each tuple of samples is processed on its own (see the *big picture* in Fig. 1); it can be seen as a generalization to higher-order attacks of [11]. Some other preprocessing tools have been proposed to reduce the dimensionality and enhance the quality of the CPA. The PCA [2] is a known way to preprocess the data to reduce the dimension and increase the efficiency of attacks. As defined in Sect. 2.3, PCA is directly linked to the maximization problem, which is also underlined by our empirical results given in Sect. 3.

Oswald and Paar showed in [17] that the best linear combination ("best" in the sense of separating the highest peaks from the nearest rival) can be approached by numerical resolutions. The model presented in [11] is not totally applicable to our study case. If we are in the case of modulated traces, the expectation over each sample of the combined traces could be null. In this case the method presented is not directly suitable.

The point of this study is not to exhibit a better method for dimensionality reduction but to show that we can solve this problem in an easier way by using the vector of covariance.

Other preprocessing methods can be used before any dimensionality reduction such as reduction filtering using a Fourier or a Hartley transform [3].

3 Empirical Results

In Sect. 2 we defined two preprocessing methods (the PCA and the "covariance method"). They were described in general, but can also apply to second-order CPA; the only difference is that the interval $[\![1,T]\!]$ where samples live is replaced by the Cartesian product $[\![1,T_1]\!] \times [\![1,T_2]\!]$, where T_1 and T_2 are the window lengths containing the leakage of the two shares. Accordingly, the leakage L is the suitable combination (e.g., the centered product [18]) of samples from each window, which is reflected in the model (See for instance Eqn. (5) and (6)). We will now compare these two methods on real measurements. These methods combine in one point the information spread over several points. The more samples to combine, the more the dimensionality reduction increases the success of the attacks.

3.1 Implementation of the Masking Scheme

To evaluate these two methods we use the publicly available traces of the DPA contest v4 [23], which uses a first order low-entropy masking protection applied on AES called Rotating S-box Masking (RSM). In RSM only sixteen Substitution boxes (S-boxes) are used and all the sixteen outputs of SubBytes are masked by

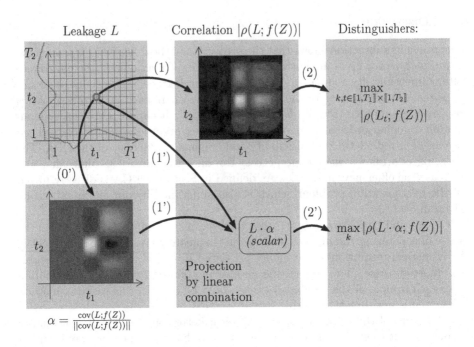

Fig. 1. Big picture of the "covariance method". The usual 2O-CPA computes a correlation for each pair (t_1, t_2) of leakage (step (1)), and then searches for a maximum over the keys and the time instances (step (2)). Our new method obtains a "covariance vector" (termed α) on a "learning device" (step (0')), and then first projects the leakage L on α (step (1')), before looking for the best key only while maximizing the distinguisher (step (2')). Notice that the model $f(Z)$ depends implicitly on the key guess k.

a different mask. We take great in this paper to exploit second-order leakage (in particular, we avoid the first-order leakage identified by Moradi et al. [15]). Moreover, the same mask is used for the AddRoundKey operation where it is XORed to one plaintext byte P and in the SubBytes operation where it is XORed with the S-box output depending on another plaintext byte P'. As a consequence a bi-variate CPA can be built by combining these two leaks knowing P and P'. The leakage model in this case is given by:

$$f(Z) = \mathbb{E}\left[(w_H(P \oplus M) - 4) \cdot (w_H(\mathtt{Sbox}[P' \oplus K] \oplus M) - 4) \,|\, P, P', K\right], \quad (5)$$

where P, P', K are two bytes of the plaintext and a byte of the key respectively, together noted $Z = (P, P', K)$, and where $w_H(\cdot)$ is the Hamming weight function and the expectation is taken over K. We denote this combination as (XOR, S-Boxes).

Moreover, we also define another way to combine points in order to compensate the mask. As only sixteen different masks in RSM are used, also a link between the masks used at the output of the S-boxes exists. Accordingly, the combination of the outputs of two different S-boxes are not well balanced and we could consider an attack depending on two different S-Boxes which use two different masks. In this case the leakage model for the bi-variate CPA is:

$$f(Z) = \mathbb{E}\left[(w_H(\texttt{Sbox}[P \oplus K] \oplus M) - 4) \cdot (w_H(\texttt{Sbox}[P' \oplus K'] \oplus M') - 4) \,|\, P, P', K, K'\right]. \tag{6}$$

In this equation, which we denote as (S-Boxes, S-Boxes), P and K (resp. P' and K') are the plaintext and key bytes entering the first (resp. the second) S-Box, and Z is a shortcut for the quadruple (P, P', K, K'). We notice that there exists a deterministic link between M and M'; M and M' belong to some subset $\{m_0, m_1, \ldots, m_{15}\}$ of $\mathbb{F}_2^8$. We assume that M enters S-box $0 \leq i \leq 15$ and M' S-box $0 \leq i' \leq 15$. Then when $M = m_{\mathsf{offset}}$ for some $0 \leq \mathsf{offset} \leq 15$, we have that $M' = m_{\mathsf{offset}+i'-i \mod 16}$.

3.2 Leakage Analysis

We assume that the adversary is able to identify the area where the two operations leak during the "learning phase". In order to analyze the leakage of the two operations, we first calculate the covariance of the traces when the mask is known using 25000 measurements.

Figure 2a presents the absolute value of the covariance between the points where the mask is XORed with the plaintext and the leakage model $w_H(P \oplus M \oplus K) - 4$. The covariance is computed for all key guesses K, where the wrong keys are plotted in grey and the correct key in red. Note that, as we target an XOR operation the maximum of the absolute value of the covariance is reached for two key guesses, namely the correct one and its opposite. It is quite clear, in Fig. 2a, that the traces are reasonably modulated (as per Def. 2); consequently, the relative distinguishing margin is constant over all the whole trace (as underlined in Sec. 2.3). In the sequel, we use as leakage for the first share $w_H(P \oplus M) - 4$ instead of $w_H(P \oplus M \oplus K) - 4$. As the second share is key-dependent, this choice allows us to restrict ourselves to one key search instead of two.

Figure 2b presents the covariance between the points where the output of an S-box leaks and the leakage model $w_H(\texttt{Sbox}[P' \oplus K] \oplus M) - 4$.

In both cases the mask leaks over several points; 50 samples represent less than 1 clock cycle. In this case the leakage is not uniformly spread over the points, thus it is reasonable to use a weighted sum to reduce the dimensionality of the data.

As the two leakages do not depend on the same operations their shapes are different. Interestingly, the distance between the correct key (red) and the next rival (grey) is much smaller in Figure 2a than in Figure 2b, Indeed the covariance plotted in Figure 2a is computed using a leakage depending on AddRoundKey, whereas the covariance plotted in Figure 2b is computed using a leakage caused by SubBytes. More precisely, the second plot corresponds to a time window when the value of the S-box output is moved during the ShiftRows operation that follows SubBytes.

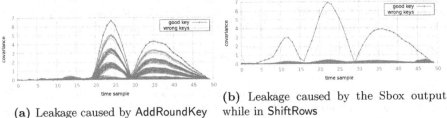

(a) Leakage caused by AddRoundKey

(b) Leakage caused by the Sbox output while in ShiftRows

Fig. 2. Covariance absolute value, for (a) XOR and (b) S-box

Figure 3a (resp. 3b) presents the covariance between the points where the output of an S-box leaks and the leakage model $w_H(\mathtt{Sbox}[P \oplus K] \oplus M) - 4$ (resp. $w_H(\mathtt{Sbox}[P' \oplus K'] \oplus M') - 4$). It can be noticed that the leakages of two different S-boxes indeed differ. The reason of this difference is that the two leakages are not due to the execution of the same operations. Figure 3b shows the covariance between the leakage of the S-box output due to the ShiftRows operation that follows and the corresponding model, whereas Figure 3a shows the covariance between the leakage due to the SubBytes operations and the corresponding model. As *looking-up* and *moving* a byte are different operations, they leak differently.

3.3 Experimental Protocol

In this experiment we select two windows of 50 points corresponding to the leakage of the two shares. Then all possible pairs of points have been combined using the centered product function [18]. In all the experiments, the preprocessing method and the 2O-CPA are applied on these "combined" traces. We compare 2O-CPA with and without preprocessing.

We used the 50000 first traces of the DPA contest v4 for the learning phase and the remaining for the attack phase. To compute the success rate we repeated the experiment as many times as we could due to the restricted amount of traces.

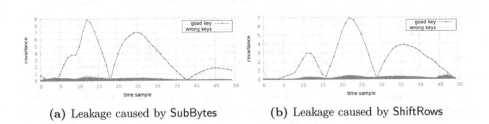

(a) Leakage caused by SubBytes

(b) Leakage caused by ShiftRows

Fig. 3. Covariance absolute value, for (a) S-box and (b) S-box+ShiftRows

Note that, several attacks using profiling or semi-profiling have been published in the Hall of Fame of the DPA contest v4. Most of these attacks are specially adapted to the vulnerabilities of the provided implementation or the particularities of RSM. However, our proposed preprocessing tools do not particularly target RSM, moreover, they are generic and could be applied to any masking scheme leaking two shares.

3.4 Comparison of the Two Preprocessing Methods and Classical Second-Order CPA

First of all, for the (XOR, S-Boxes) combination we see in Fig. 4 that the preprocessing improves the efficiency of the attacks. We need less than 200 measurements to reach 80% of success with the covariance or PCA preprocessing while we need more than 275 measurements for the classical 2O-CPA, which gives an improvement of 30%.

Figure 5 shows a 3-D representations of the vectors using the PCA (which returns the first eigenvector) and the covariance method (which returns the

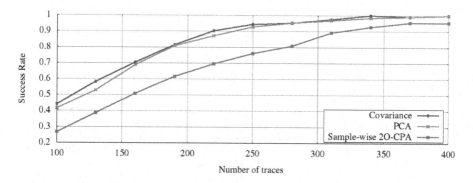

Fig. 4. Comparison between the classical second-order CPA and second-order CPA with preprocessing using (XOR, S-Boxes)

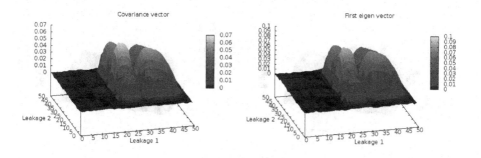

Fig. 5. Comparison between covariance vector and the first eigenvector

covariance vector). The larger the value on the z-axis of Fig. 5 and 7, the higher the contribution (weight) of this point. The axes "leakage 1" and "leakage 2" represent the part depending on the two leakages of XOR (Fig. 2a) and S-box (Fig. 2b) operations in the combined traces. We can see in Figure 5 that the two methods highlight the same points of the combined traces and have the same shape (approximately the same values). Thus, the two methods give similar results in terms of success rate, which is confirmed by Figure 4.

As can be seen in Figure 6, in case of the (S-Boxes, S-Boxes) combination we need around 275 traces to reach 80% of success for the 2O-CPA after the two preprocessing methods, while the raw 2O-CPA needs around 550 traces to succeed. So, using the preprocessing method decreases the number traces to perform the attack by 50%. It can be seen that the two methods yield apparently exactly the same results, which means that we are precisely in the framework of Theorem 1: the display traces that are almost perfectly modulated by one static leakage model.

One explanation of the effectiveness of the preprocessing can be found in Figure 7. There are much more leaking points in the same window size when we

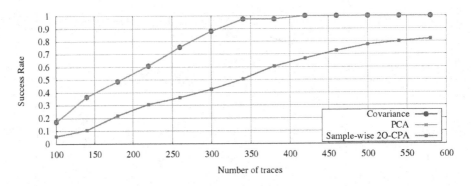

Fig. 6. Comparison between the classical second-order CPA and second-order CPA with preprocessing using (S-boxes, S-Boxes)

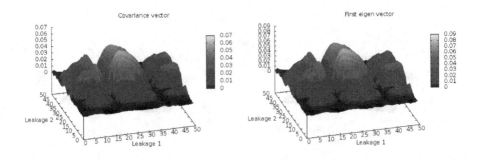

Fig. 7. Comparison between the covariance vector and the first eigenvector

combine two S-boxes. It can be seen in Sect. 3.5 that another explanation can be the fact that when we apply these preprocessing methods the attacks are less sensitive to the noise.

3.5   How is the Preprocessing Linked to the Noise?

We have theoretically shown in Proposition 3 that the presented preprocessing methods improve the SNR. We now empirically verify this results. In each point we add Gaussian noise to mimic real noisy measurements. We perform this experiment on the same points and with the same model as used for Figure 4.

Figure 8a shows that using preprocessing methods improves second-order CPA in presence of noise. In this case we added Gaussian noise with a standard deviation of 3. The attacks after preprocessing need around 225 measurements to reach 80% of success whereas the 2O-CPA needs more than 550 measurements. Thus, preprocessing leads to a gain over 50%. As shown in Figure 4 the gain was close to 30% without noise.

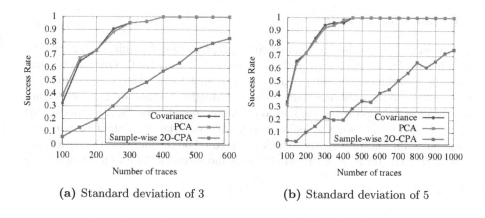

(a) Standard deviation of 3   (b) Standard deviation of 5

Fig. 8. Comparison between 2O-CPA with preprocessing method and without in presence of Gaussian noise, with a standard deviation of 3 for (a) with a standard deviation of 5 for (b)

In Figure 8b we can see that for Gaussian noise with a standard deviation of 5 the gain is more than 75%. Indeed the 2O-CPA after preprocessing needs around 250 traces reach 80% of success rate whereas for 2O-CPA 1000 measurements are not sufficient.

So this kind of preprocessing by dimensionality reduction is well designed against noisy implementation where the noise is not correlated with the time or the data.

4   On the Fly Preprocessing

We have defined a case study when the attacker owns a "learning device". As a consequence he is able to acquire a sufficient number of measurements to well estimate the covariance matrix for the PCA and the covariance vectors. However, the attacker might not always have this powerful tool.

As seen in Subsect. 3.4 even for a small number of traces for the learning phase we have a significant improvement when we use preprocessing methods. We therefore evaluate these tools also as "on the fly" preprocessing methods.

4.1   Case Study

We now model a less powerful attacker who does not have a "learning device" and estimates the value of the coefficient of the linear transformation directly on the traces used for the attack. Because the key is unknown the preprocessing method has to be computed for each key hypothesis. Finally, the adversary applies the covariance between the transformed data and the model depending on the key hypothesis. In this experiment we use the 10000 first traces of the DPA contest to compute the success rate which results in 25 repetitions.

4.2   Empirical Results

Figure 9a illustrates the success rate after preprocessing for different sizes of the learning set for PCA (green) and the covariance vector (red). One can observe that the covariance method performs better than PCA when a low number of traces is used during the learning phase, accordingly, this method is a good choice as a "on the fly" preprocessing method. The reason why the PCA method needs more measurements for the learning than the covariance method to reach its maximum efficiency during the attack phase could be the fact that the covariance matrix (see the term $^t X X$ in Def. 1) needs more traces to be well estimated.

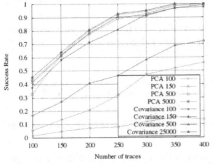 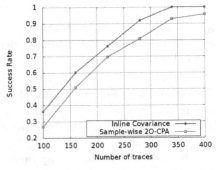

(a) Comparison between covariance and PCA depending on the size of the learning base

(b) Comparison between covariance in line preprocessing and 2O-CPA

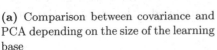

Fig. 9. Evaluation of inline preprocessing methods

Figure 9b shows that with the "on the fly" preprocessing we can perform 2O-CPA using 225 measurements. This represents a gain of 18% compared to raw (sample-wise) 2O-CPA.

5 Conclusions and Perspectives

In this article we presented the covariance method as an optimal preprocessing method for second-order CPA. By using all possible leakage points our method improves the efficiency of the attacks and as the number of combined leakage points grow quadratically, thus our preprocessing method is well adapted for *bi-variate CPA*. We further theoretically linked the PCA to the problem of maximization of the covariance. We demonstrated theoretically the result of the covariance method to be the optimal linear combination for maximizing the covariance and underlined empirically that this method improves the result of *bi-variate CPA*.

Compared to 2O-CPA, the attack based on the optimal covariance method is significantly improved, particularly in presence of noise and when the number of leaking points is important. This is partly explained by the fact the optimal covariance considers all the relevant sampling points, whereas the 2O-CPA considers only the best pair of samples and does not exploit the other interesting pairs.

We have also shown that the optimal covariance method is more efficient than PCA when the learning phase is performed on the fly. All the results have been validated by experiences on real traces corresponding to masking implementation of the DPA contest v4. As a consequence dimensionality reduction by linear combination is well adapted to the case of *multi-variate CPA*. Moreover, the higher the order of masking, the more efficient the attack after preprocessing.

In our future work we will extend the previous results on other implementations which are less favorable to attacker, e.g., with more noise. Also we plan to compare the method presented in this article and the method presented in [11] in these cases. We will additionally apply these methods on different masking scheme especially on higher-order masking schemes.

References

1. Archambeau, C., Peeters, E., Standaert, F.-X., Quisquater, J.-J.: Template Attacks in Principal Subspaces. In: Goubin, L., Matsui, M. (eds.) CHES 2006. LNCS, vol. 4249, pp. 1–14. Springer, Heidelberg (2006)
2. Batina, L., Hogenboom, J., van Woudenberg, J.G.J.: Getting more from pca: First results of using principal component analysis for extensive power analysis. In: Dunkelman (ed.) [8], pp. 383–397
3. Belgarric, P., et al.: Time-Frequency Analysis for Second-Order Attacks. In: Francillon, A., Rohatgi, P. (eds.) CARDIS 2013. LNCS, vol. 8419, pp. 108–122. Springer, Heidelberg (2014)

4. Bhasin, S., Danger, J.-L., Guilley, S., Najm, Z.: NICV: Normalized Inter-Class Variance for Detection of Side-Channel Leakage. In: International Symposium on Electromagnetic Compatibility (EMC 2014/Tokyo), May 12-16. IEEE (2014), Session OS09: EM Information Leakage. Hitotsubashi Hall (National Center of Sciences), Chiyoda, Tokyo, Japan.

5. Bhasin, S., Danger, J.-L., Guilley, S., Najm, Z.: Side-channel Leakage and Trace Compression Using Normalized Inter-class Variance. In: Proceedings of the Third Workshop on Hardware and Architectural Support for Security and Privacy, HASP 2014, pp. 7:1–7:9. ACM, New York (2014)

6. Brier, E., Clavier, C., Olivier, F.: Correlation Power Analysis with a Leakage Model. In: Joye, M., Quisquater, J.-J. (eds.) CHES 2004. LNCS, vol. 3156, pp. 16–29. Springer, Heidelberg (2004)

7. Chari, S., Rao, J.R., Rohatgi, P.: Template Attacks. In: Kaliski Jr., B.S., Koç, Ç.K., Paar, C. (eds.) CHES 2002. LNCS, vol. 2523, pp. 13–28. Springer, Heidelberg (2003)

8. Dunkelman, O. (ed.): CT-RSA 2012. LNCS, vol. 7178. Springer, Heidelberg (2012)

9. Goubin, L., Patarin, J.: DES and Differential Power Analysis. The "Duplication" Method. In: Koç, Ç.K., Paar, C. (eds.) CHES 1999. LNCS, vol. 1717, pp. 158–172. Springer, Heidelberg (1999)

10. Hajra, S., Mukhopadhyay, D.: Pushing the limit of non-profiling dpa using multivariate leakage model. IACR Cryptology ePrint Archive, 2013:849 (2013)

11. Hajra, S., Mukhopadhyay, D.: On the Optimal Pre-processing for Non-profiling Differential Power Analysis. In: Prouff, E. (ed.) COSADE 2014. LNCS, vol. 8622, pp. 161–178. Springer, Heidelberg (2014)

12. Jolliffe, I.T.: Principal Component Analysis. Springer Series in Statistics (2002) ISBN: 0387954422

13. Kocher, P.C., Jaffe, J., Jun, B.: Differential Power Analysis. In: Wiener, M. (ed.) CRYPTO 1999. LNCS, vol. 1666, pp. 388–397. Springer, Heidelberg (1999)

14. Messerges, T.S., Dabbish, E.A., Sloan, R.H.: Investigations of Power Analysis Attacks on Smartcards. In: USENIX — Smartcard 1999, Chicago, Illinois, USA, May 10-11, pp. 151–162 (1999)

15. Moradi, A., Guilley, S., Heuser, A.: Detecting Hidden Leakages. In: Boureanu, I., Owesarski, P., Vaudenay, S. (eds.) ACNS 2014. LNCS, vol. 8479, pp. 324–342. Springer, Heidelberg (2014)

16. Nikova, S., Rijmen, V., Schläffer, M.: Secure hardware implementation of nonlinear functions in the presence of glitches. J. Cryptology 24(2), 292–321 (2011)

17. Oswald, D., Paar, C.: Improving side-channel analysis with optimal linear transforms. In: Mangard, S. (ed.) CARDIS 2012. LNCS, vol. 7771, pp. 219–233. Springer, Heidelberg (2013)

18. Prouff, E., Rivain, M., Bevan, R.: Statistical Analysis of Second Order Differential Power Analysis. IEEE Trans. Computers 58(6), 799–811 (2009)

19. Schindler, W., Lemke, K., Paar, C.: A Stochastic Model for Differential Side Channel Cryptanalysis. In: Rao, J.R., Sunar, B. (eds.) CHES 2005. LNCS, vol. 3659, pp. 30–46. Springer, Heidelberg (2005)

20. Souissi, Y., Bhasin, S., Guilley, S., Nassar, M., Danger, J.-L.: Towards Different Flavors of Combined Side Channel Attacks. In: Dunkelman (ed.) [8], pp. 245–259

21. Souissi, Y., Nassar, M., Guilley, S., Danger, J.-L., Flament, F.: First Principal Components Analysis: A New Side Channel Distinguisher. In: Rhee, K.-H., Nyang, D. (eds.) ICISC 2010. LNCS, vol. 6829, pp. 407–419. Springer, Heidelberg (2011)

22. Standaert, F.-X., Archambeau, C.: Using Subspace-Based Template Attacks to Compare and Combine Power and Electromagnetic Information Leakages. In: Oswald, E., Rohatgi, P. (eds.) CHES 2008. LNCS, vol. 5154, pp. 411–425. Springer, Heidelberg (2008)

23. TELECOM ParisTech SEN research group. DPA Contest (4th edn.) (2013–2014), http://www.DPAcontest.org/v4/

24. Waddle, J., Wagner, D.: Towards Efficient Second-Order Power Analysis. In: Joye, M., Quisquater, J.-J. (eds.) CHES 2004. LNCS, vol. 3156, pp. 1–15. Springer, Heidelberg (2004)

25. Whitnall, C., Oswald, E.: A Fair Evaluation Framework for Comparing Side-Channel Distinguishers. J. Cryptographic Engineering 1(2), 145–160 (2011)

A Proof of Theorem 1

Proof. On the one side we have

$$\text{Cov}\left[L \cdot \alpha, f(Z)\right] = \left(\text{Cov}\left[S_t + \mathcal{N}_t, f(Z)\right]\right)_{t \in T} \cdot \alpha$$
$$= \left(\text{Cov}\left[S_t, f(Z)\right]\right)_{t \in T} \cdot \alpha$$
$$= \left(\mathbb{E}\left[S_t f(Z)\right]\right)_{t \in T} \cdot \alpha \ .$$

The other side yields $\text{Var}\left[\mathbb{E}\left[L|f(Z)\right] \cdot \alpha\right] = \text{Var}\left[(S_t)_{t \in T} \cdot \alpha\right]$. Now if $S_t = \beta_t f(Z)$, then we have for both sides

$$\begin{cases} \text{Cov}\left[L \cdot \alpha; f(Z)\right]^2 &= (\alpha \cdot \beta)^2 \, \mathbb{E}\left[f(Z)^2\right]^2, \\ \text{Var}\left[\mathbb{E}\left[L|f(Z)\right] \cdot \alpha\right] &= \text{Var}\left[(\alpha \cdot \beta) \, f(Z)\right] = (\alpha \cdot \beta)^2 \, \mathbb{E}\left[f(Z)^2\right], \end{cases}$$

which proves equivalence. □

B Proof of Lemma 1

Proof.

$$\underset{\|\alpha\|=1}{\text{argmax}} \, \text{Cov}\left[L \cdot \alpha, f(Z)\right]^2 = \underset{\|\alpha\|=1}{\text{argmax}} \, (\alpha \cdot \beta)^2 \, \mathbb{E}\left[f(Z)^2\right]^2$$

$$= \underset{\|\alpha\|=1}{\text{argmax}} \, (\alpha \cdot \beta)^2, \text{ because } \mathbb{E}\left[f(Z)^2\right]^2 > 0.$$

By the Cauchy-Schwarz theorem, we have: $(\alpha \cdot \beta)^2 \leqslant \|\alpha\|^2 \times \|\beta\|^2$, where equality holds if and only if α and β are linearly dependent, i.e., $\alpha = \lambda \beta$. Accordingly, if $\|\alpha\| = 1$ we have $\lambda = \frac{1}{\|\beta\|}$, which gives us the required solution. □

C Proof of Proposition 4

Proof.

$$\mathrm{Cov}\left[L \cdot \alpha, f(Z)\right] = \left(\mathrm{Cov}\left[L_t; f(Z)\right]\right)_{t \in T} \cdot \alpha .$$

Similar to the proof of Lemma 1, we use the Cauchy-Schwarz inequality. In particular,

$$\left(\left(\mathrm{Cov}\left[L_t; f(Z)\right]\right)_{t \in T} \cdot \alpha\right)^2 \leqslant \|\alpha\|^2 \times \|\left(\mathrm{Cov}\left[L_t; f(Z)\right]\right)_{t \in T}\|^2.$$

We have the equality,

$$\left(\left(\mathrm{Cov}\left[L_t; f(Z)\right]\right)_{t \in T} \cdot \alpha\right)^2 = \|\alpha\|^2 \times \|\left(\mathrm{Cov}\left[L_t; f(Z)\right]\right)_{t \in T}\|^2,$$

if and only if $\alpha = \lambda \left(\mathrm{Cov}\left[L_t; f(Z)\right]\right)_{t \in T}$.
So, if $\|\alpha\| = 1$ we have $\lambda = \frac{1}{\|\left(\mathrm{Cov}\left[L_t; f(Z)\right]\right)_{t \in T}\|}$.   □

Analysis and Improvements
of the DPA Contest v4 Implementation

Shivam Bhasin[1], Nicolas Bruneau[1,2], Jean-Luc Danger[1,3], Sylvain Guilley[1,3],
and Zakaria Najm[1]

[1] TELECOM-ParisTech, Crypto Group, Paris, France
[2] AST division, Rousset, France
[3] Secure-IC S.A.S., Rennes, France

Abstract. DPA Contest is an international framework which allows researchers to compare their attacks under a common setting. The latest version of DPA Contest proposes a software implementation of AES-256 protected with a low-entropy masking scheme. The masking scheme is called Rotating Sbox Masking (RSM) which claims first-degree security. In this paper, we review the attacks submitted against DPA Contest v4 implementation to identify the common loop holes in the proposed implementation. Next we propose some ideas to improve the existing implementation to resist most of the proposed attacks at affordable performance overhead. Finally we compare our implementation with the original proposal in terms of complexity and side-channel leakage.

Keywords: Side Channel Attacks, DPA Contest, Low Entropy Masking Schemes, Shuffling.

1 Introduction

Physical systems are now an integral part of our life. Such systems use embedded computers and sensors to perform desired computation based on feedback from physical processes and vice-versa. Some typical application of physical systems are in domains like health management, traffic management, data-centers, power-grids, etc. Given the critical nature of applications, it becomes an attractive target for all kinds of attacks. This brings in the need for security and privacy.

A common solution to security threats is to use cryptography. Modern cryptographic algorithms are based on strong mathematical problems and are considered secure from a theoretical view point. On the other hand, when these algorithms are implemented in a physical systems, they become vulnerable. These attacks which compromise the physical implementation of cryptography are known as physical attacks or "Side-Channel Attacks" (SCA [1,2]). In such cases, designers resort to countermeasures. Countermeasures for SCA tend to modify the implementation in a way that the mere basis of SCA is removed. Having said that, a perfect countermeasure is not possible to design. This is because certain non-linearities in the target device which are not under the control of designer leave the countermeasure imperfect. Therefore a common trend

R.S. Chakraborty et al. (Eds.): SPACE 2014, LNCS 8804, pp. 201–218, 2014.

in SCA countermeasure research is to make the design harder to attack, given the design constraints. In this paper, we focus on symmetric ciphers that run as software codes on embedded computers.

Common countermeasures for software implementations of ciphers are masking and shuffling [3,4]. Another lesser studied countermeasure for software implementations is hiding [5]. All the countermeasures come at a significant cost overhead in terms of memory, time or both. Hiding based countermeasure makes the leakage uniform and independant of the data processed. Shuffling is a simple countermeasure which plays on randomizing the order of operations of the cipher. Masking on the other hand uses a random value called "mask" which is mixed with the sensitive data. The mixing is done by using different operations like XOR, addition, multiplication etc. Out of the three countermeasures for software implementations, masking is the most studied one.

Recently, researchers have started looking into the lightweight solutions for SCA countermeasures. These countermeasures are designed to resist not all but a selection of important and powerful attacks. One such countermeasure is Rotating Sbox Masking (RSM) which is a type of Low-Entropy Masking Scheme (LEMS). RSM was initially proposed for hardware implementations [6] and further tuned for software targets in [7]. We choose RSM because it has been studied widely by researchers worldwide under the framework of DPA Contest [8]. DPA Contest allows researchers to apply their attacks on a common set of available side-channel traces, in order to find the best attacks. During the fourth version of the contest i.e. DPA Contest v4 (DPACv4 [9]) the target was a AES-256 implementation protected with RSM running on an ATMEL AVR-163 microcontroller. Both the implementation and the traces were made available as a part of the framework.

In this paper, we review the attacks proposed in DPACv4 framework to identify the common pitfalls of the proposed implementation. Next we try to propose an improved implementation of RSM which does not suffer from some of the obvious and noted pitfalls. The rest of the paper is organised as follows: Sec. 2 provides general background on DPA contest and its latest version and RSM. In Sec. 3, we review the attacks proposed under the framework of DPACv4 with prime focus on non-profiled attacks to identify the main pitfalls in the implementations. A proposition to improve the original implementation of DPACv4 is given in Sec. 4 followed by security evaluation in Sec. 5. Finally conclusions are drawn in Sec. 6. Technical proofs are in appendix.

2   General Background

2.1   DPA Contest

DPA Contest is an international contest which allows researchers from all over the world to compete on a common ground. It was launched in 2008 and since then four versions of the contest have completed. The first version of the contest targeted an unprotected DES implementation running on a ASIC fabricated in ST 130 nm technology. Version 2 of the contest targeted a unprotected AES implementation running on an FPGA platform [25]. The database of traces of both implementations was made available online, with a goal to find the attack which recovers the secret key using minimum number of traces. The next version of the contest (v3) was an acquisition competition which focused on finding the best measurement setup. The latest or the fourth version of the contest was launched last year. This contest targets a protected AES-256 implementation on a 350 nm metal-3 layer ATMEL AVR-163 microcontroller. Protection applied is RSM which is a LEMS and discussed in next subsection.

2.2   Masking and RSM

Masking splits sensitive data $Z \in \mathbb{F}_2^n$ into $(d+1)$ variable random shares, noted $\boldsymbol{R} = (R_i)_{i \in [\![0,d]\!]}$, in such a way that the relation $R_0 \perp \cdots \perp R_d = Z$ is satisfied for a group operation $\perp$ [10].. Typically, $\perp = \oplus$, the exclusive-or (XOR) operation. Such schemes claim d^{th}-order security. When a cryptographic algorithm is modified to introduce masking, two computations are performed: masked sensitive and mask compensation computation. In software, this computation is performed in serial. The linear operations can be easily masked. Masking the non-linear sbox S involves computing $S(Z) \oplus M'$ from the variables $M, Z \oplus M$ and M' (new mask) without compromising with SCA resistance.

GLUT [11], a proposed solution, pre-computes a look-up table, associated to the function $S' : (X, Y, Y') \mapsto S(X \oplus Y) \oplus Y'$. This approach is very expensive in practice. Rotating Sbox Masking (RSM) is based on precomputed table look-ups at the same time reducing the area overhead of GLUT. The optimization comes from reusing sboxes and removal of computation of mask compensation. RSM is a LEMS but the low-entropy is covered for by carefully choosing the mask set M. From a security point of view, M is chosen such that the jth order moment of the conditional leakage $L^j | Z = z$ given a guess on the sensitive variable Z are all the same for $j = 1, 2, \cdots, d$. Thus only an attack of order $(d+1)$ can succeed. Under this constraint, the masks set M must be an orthogonal array of strength d [12].

The unmasking and masking which is integrated into the precomputed masked sbox removes the need for computation of corresponding mask compensation. The set of chosen mask M can be a public parameter however M should be shifted by a random offset before each encryption. The linear operations are masked by a simple XOR operation with precomputed constants applied at the end of each round. For a linear operation P, a mask m_i can be computed as $P(m_i) \oplus m_i$ on the fly or stored precomputed in memory. We refer interested readers to [6], [7] and [13] for details of RSM and its security analysis.

2.3   DPACv4 Implementation

DPACv4 targets an AES-256 implementation protected with RSM. It was mostly written in the C language, and compiled using avr-gcc. The overall algorithm running on the smartcard is described in Alg. 4 in Appendix A.

A quick glossary for Alg. 4 is as follows:

- $\mathsf{MaskedSubBytes}_i(X) = \mathsf{SubBytes}(X \oplus M_i) \oplus M_{i+1}$
- $\mathsf{MaskCompensation}_{\mathsf{offset}} = \mathsf{Mask}_{\mathsf{offset}} \oplus \mathsf{MixColumns}(\mathsf{ShiftRows}(\mathsf{Mask}_{\mathsf{offset}}))$
- $\mathsf{MaskCompensationLastRound}_{\mathsf{offset}} = \mathsf{Mask}_{\mathsf{offset}} \oplus \mathsf{ShiftRows}(\mathsf{Mask}_{\mathsf{offset}})$

The MaskedSubBytes operation firstly calls the 8 sboxes with even index followed by remaining 8 sboxes with odd index. The $\mathsf{Mask}_{\mathsf{offset}}$ operation applies 16 mask bytes to 16 state bytes according to the computed index. The mask set used for DPACv4 is:

$$M_{i \in \llbracket 0,15 \rrbracket} = \{\mathsf{0x00, 0x0f, 0x36, 0x39, 0x53, 0x5c, 0x65, 0x6a,}$$
$$\mathsf{0x95, 0x9a, 0xa3, 0xac, 0xc6, 0xc9, 0xf0, 0xff}\} \ .$$

3   Summary of Attacks Presented in DPACv4

Since the launch of DPACv4 in July 2013, 28 attacks have been submitted and evaluated. The results of all these attacks along with their brief description is available on the website of the contest. In general, the submitted attacks can be classified in two categories: *profiling based attacks* and *non-profiling based attacks*.

Some of the attacks submitted under the DPACv4 framework proved to be very efficient. For instance, in the profiling based attack category, 14 attacks have been proposed. The best attack in this category can break the implementation and recover the secret key with **a single trace** (attack phase). On the other hand, for the non-profiling based attacks, the best attack takes as low as **14 side-channel traces** to recover the secret key. In the following we focus on non-profiling attacks.

The first attack which is a univariate correlation power attack (CPA [2]) was proposed by Moradi et al. [14]. This attack exploits a vulnerability which arises from a basic design error. A vulnerability in RSM arises when a sbox input x_i masked with mask m_i, is written over by a sbox output y_i masked with m_{i+1} in the same register. The activity of the register can be written as $(x_i \oplus y_i) \oplus (m_i \oplus m_{i+1})$. Now under the RSM countermeasure both the mask m_i and m_{i+1} are balanced. The set of mask for RSM belong to a code and carefully chosen to satisfy certain properties and provide desired security. However, the composite mask $m_i \oplus m_{i+1}$ turns out to be unbalanced. This unbalance leads to a first-order leakage which can be exploited by a simple univariate CPA.

The next attack by Kanghong et al. unrolls in two steps. In the first step, the attacker tries to guess the value of initial offset used for each encryption. The attackers exploit the fact that the Hamming weight HW of mask $m_0 \oplus m_{15}$ is 8, while for all other mask combinations $(m_i \oplus m_{i+1})$ it is 4. This difference in Hamming weight can be observed in DPACv4 traces and the temporal location of this maximum difference gives an idea of the offset. In the second and final step, an attacker can group all traces with the same offset and launch a univariate

CPA attack to recover the secret key. Kanghong et al. used 69 traces to recover the key.

Thereafter several attacks exploiting the same vulnerability were proposed. Each time the method to determine the offset was novel. Junrong et al. propose two attack using maximal difference to determine the offset and recovering the key in 110 traces. Zhou et al. use maximal difference and pattern matching to determine the secret key in 14 traces. Next , Nakai et al. retrieve the offset using F-Test followed by a CPA to find the key in 43 traces. Another attacker who remains anonymous uses a first order CPA to first recover the offset followed by a DPA to find the key.

Two more attacks belonging to the non-profiled category were proposed under DPACv4. Zhou et al. attacked RSM using a second order CPA attacks. This attack exploited the joint leakage which came from combination of sbox output with input mask m_i and plaintext blinding with mask m_{i+1}. Although the individual leakages of plaintext blinding and sbox output are masked, the joint leakage becomes unmasked, which can be exploited by a CPA attacks. The other attack was a collision attack. Firstly the attacks detects collision using Pearson's correlation to compute the 15 key differences between first byte and other 15 bytes of the key. Next the whole key can be recovered by a simple brute force attack.

Apart from the DPA Contest framework, few other attacks were published on the implementation proposed in DPACv4. Kutzner et al. [21] proposed several attacks on the hardware and software implementations of RSM. Considering the software implementation (as of DPACv4), two attacks were proposed. The first attack guesses the offset followed by univariate CPA. In other words, it exploits the same vulnerability as majority of the attacks. The second attack proposed was by Kutzner et al. is indeed unique. It exploits a property called **constant difference** in the RSM mask. Authors discovered that the difference in mask between m_i and m_{i+8} is constant. In other words, $m_i \oplus m_{i+8}$ is constant. This property was used to mount a $1^{st} - order$ correlation enhanced collision attack [15] to recover the secret key. A third (simulated) attack was presented on hardware RSM in the same paper [21]. We noticed that this attack can also be a potential threat to software implementation of RSM. It exploits the fact that the mask m_i used by sbox S_0 in the first round is same as used by S_7 in last round, which allows collision attacks.

Few other papers were also published which attacked the DPACv4 traces. Belgarric et al. [16] demonstrated practical bivariate attacks (using preprocessing tools like Discrete Hartley Transform) by attacking in frequency domain. Moreover, Ye et al. [17] proposed a couple of attacks based on mutual information and collisions to exploit LEMS like RSM. All the attacks in those two papers were possible owing to the fact that the attacker is aware of the predictable sequence of AES operations.

To summarize the threats exploited by attacks submitted in DPACv4, we can identify four implementation pitfalls:

1. The mask (m_i, m_{i+1}) although balanced by itself, were not balanced when XORed together $((m_i \oplus m_{i+1}))$.

2. Mask (m_0, m_{15}) have a higher Hamming distance than other mask, which leaks the the value of the offset.
3. As the offset is incremented by a constant in every round, it lead to predictable sequence of operations which can be exploited by collision attacks.
4. The unaltered and predictable sequence of operations allows combination of points, thereby leading to second-order CPA and collision attacks.

4   Proposition for Improving DPACv4 Implementation

In this section, we propose some improvements to the original DPACv4 implementation based on our know-how of its pitfalls. These pitfalls are discussed and analyzed in the previous section. As stated earlier, designing a perfect countermeasure is not possible. Trying to thwart all attacks at once is not an obvious task. Of course, some solutions proposed by Rivain and Prouff [18] and Coron [19] can be applied. However, it would lead either to explosion in implementation cost. In the following, we attempt to boost the security level of the AES RSM implementation at reasonable cost overhead. We discuss each of the pitfall in detail and make an attempt to fix it.

The first pitfall arises from the fact that the value $m_i \oplus m_{i+1}$ exist in the implementation, directly or indirectly. As stated earlier the mask m_i and m_{i+1} are balanced, but the value $m_i \oplus m_{i+1}$ is unbalanced. We analysed the code of DPACv4 implementation. The original code was written in C language. It is compiled using `avr-gcc` to generate assembly code. If we check the original C code, $m_i \oplus m_{i+1}$ is never computed itself. However on compilation with `avr-gcc` certain instances of such nature may occur. `avr-gcc` reuses several general purpose registers and 2-stage pipeline to optimize the design. Suppose there exist a value $x \oplus m_i$ in a register or pipeline. This value is followed by $y \oplus m_{i+1}$. The side-channel activity at next clock will correspond to $x \oplus y \oplus m_i \oplus m_{i+1}$, which is unbalanced.

Now looking into the DPACv4 implementation, the result of plaintext blinding $x_i \oplus m_i$ stored in a register is overwritten by its sbox output MaskedSubBytes($x_i \oplus m_i$). The latter term can be written as SubBytes(x_i) $\oplus m_{i+1}$ It is well known that the activity of the register follows the value update model i.e. $x_i \oplus$ SubBytes(x_i) $\oplus m_i \oplus m_{i+1}$. Thus the accidental $m_i \oplus m_{i+1}$ leakage occurs which can be exploited in side-channel.

A straightforward way to avoid accidental computation of the form $m_i \oplus m_{i+1}$ in the implementation flow, is to rewrite the complete code in assembly language. However writing assembly code is a tedious and error-prone task. A common practice is to write only the sensitive modules of the code in assembly. This is considered as best practice to avoid any surprises from compilation. Another precaution which must be taken at this stage is register precharge. If we precharge every general purpose register to '0' value before writing in a new value, we can avoid all leakages of form $m_i \oplus m_{i+1}$. By ensuring these two conditions, one can get rid of accidental univariate leakage like the one presented in [14].

The second pitfall identified in DPACv4 implementation is that the value of offset is leaked in side-channel. In fact, the mask ($m_0 = 0x00, m_{15} = 0xFF$) have considerable higher Hamming distance of 8. All other adjacent masks have a Hamming distance of 4, which can be identified in side-channel traces The fact that, after each sbox, offset $\leftarrow$ offset $+ 1$, allows to retrieve the offset since there is a constant temporal distance between mask $0x00$ and $0xFF$. We consider this vulnerability to be very serious as it was exploited by most of the attacks submitted under DPACv4. Once the offset is know to the attacker, the attacker can easily sort the traces with same offset. Same offset for a set of traces translates to same mask values *i.e.* a constant mask denoted by m_k. Since the mask is constant, the Pearson correlation $\rho(x \oplus m_k, y)$ simplifies to $\rho(x, y)$. This is equivalent to a totally unmasked implementation.

To protect against such attacks, we propose to use a random offset for each sbox. Although we use a random offset for each sbox, the basic set of 16 mask remains unchanged. Therefore all the security proofs which apply to RSM also apply to our implementation. The random offset is applied by using a random array of 16 independent indices. This array is generate to address the array of 16 masks independently for each sbox. Unlike the original implementation, this implementation can (sometimes) use same mask for multiple sboxes. Moreover by using independant offset for each sbox, we also solve the problem of collision attacks as proposed in [21]. The correlation-enhanced collision attack [21] exploits the fact that $SubBytes(x_i+k_i) = SubBytes(x_{i+8})+k_{i+8}+0x95$. By randomizing the manipulation of mask of indices i and $i + 8$, this attack is no more possible, as m_i and m_{i+8} will not have same temporal distance. Similarly in [21] the collision attack exploiting the first and last round becomes irrelevant. The overhead associated with this countermeasure is that the set of MaskCompensation becomes very large to store in the memory. To solve this problem we compute the MaskCompensation on the fly which has a time penalty as overhead.

Finally, there were certain bivariate and higher order attacks proposed under the framework of DPACv4. In [7], authors tweak the original RSM scheme for software implementation to claim first degree security. Thus if higher order attacks work on RSM, it is as expected. There are two possible ways to boost the security level of this implementation. The first way is to modify the masking scheme in order to resist higher-order attacks [20]. On the other hand, one can combine countermeasures to boost the security level while keeping overhead in check. We choose the second method and use shuffling [4] as an additional countermeasure. As the prime targets of SCA are first and last rounds of AES, we only shuffle the order of sbox execution of first and last round of the AES. This shuffling is performed by drawing a random permutation for indices of execution of sboxes for first and last round for each encryption. In the middle rounds, the sboxes are executed as before i.e. 8 even sbox indices followed by remain 8 odd indices. Since the window of execution of the concerned sboxes will change, the selection of trace windows for combination will not be easy. For the same reason, attack proposed in [17] becomes impractical.

The attacks on DPAcv4 and the corresponding countermeasures proposed in this section are all summarized in Tab. 1.

Table 1. Attacks on DPACV4 implementation and corresponding countermeasures proposed in this article

Attacks \ Countermeasures		ASM (instead of C)	Registers precharge	One mask per sbox	Shuffling
First-order attack	[14]	x	x		
Recover the offset	[9]			.	x
Collision on the sbox	[21]			x	x
Collision 1st-last rounds	[21]			x	x
Bivariate attacks	[16]				x
MIA	[17]				x

4.1 Target Platform

To analyze our implementation we use the same platform as of DPACv4. The target is a 8-bit AVR microcontroller Atmega163 embedded in a smartcard. It contains 16Kb of in-system programmable flash, 512 bytes of EEPROM, 1Kb of internal SRAM and 32 general purpose working registers. The smartcard is read using a simple reader interface mounted on SASEBO-W board and controlled by Xilinx Spartan-VI FPGA. The traces are acquired using a LeCroy WaveRunner 6100A oscilloscope using an EM probe. The acquisition bandwidth is 200 MHz and the sampling rate $F_S = 500$ MS/s.

4.2 Implementation

The proposed implementation is written in assembly language and carefully checked to avoid most identified pitfalls. This implementation takes the well optimized Rijndael furious and DPACV4 implementations as references.

Tab. 2 compares the unprotected Rijndael furious and DPACv4 implementations with our improved design. Please note that the numbers includes the cost of key expansion as well as the embedded OS used in DPACV4. Rewriting the sensitive part in assembly actually accelerated the proposed design compared to original one. Please note that Tab. 2 does not take into account the cost of embedded CSPRNG which is used to generate the randomness needed for the shuffled masking scheme. We make sure that the blinding operation is performed in a specific order to avoid some horizontal attacks. Also, direct manipulation of private shares with known variables is avoided. For example the key should first be blinded with the random mask before blinding the plaintext. The improved algorithm running on the smartcard is described in Alg. 1.

Algorithm 1. Modified AES implementation to overcome pitfalls of DPACv4.

Input : 16-bytes Plaintext $X \llbracket X_0, X_1 \cdots X_{15} \rrbracket$,
 SubKeys, 15 16-bytes constants $\mathsf{RoundKey}[r]$, $r \in \llbracket 0, 14 \rrbracket$,
 16 masks of 8 bit, called $\mathsf{Mask}[]$
Output: 16-bytes Ciphertext $X \llbracket X_0, X_1 \cdots X_{15} \rrbracket$

```
/* Draw 16 4-bit (uniformly random, unknown) offset[] for the key
blinding */
```

```
/* Draw of 2 shuffling functions (uniformly random permutations),
Shuffle0, Shuffle13 : [0,15] → [0,15], bijective */
```

$\mathsf{RoundKey}[0] \leftarrow \mathsf{RoundKey}[0] \oplus \mathsf{Mask}[\mathsf{offset}[]]$

```
                         /* All rounds but the last one */
```
for $r \in \llbracket 0, 12 \rrbracket$ **do**
 $X = X \oplus \mathsf{RoundKey}[r]$ `/* AddRoundKey */`
 if $r = 0$ **then**
  for $i \in \mathsf{Shuffle0}(\llbracket 0, 15 \rrbracket)$ **do**
   $X_i = \mathsf{MaskedSubBytes}_{\mathsf{offset}[i]+r}(X_i)$
  end
 else
  for $i \in \llbracket 0, 15 \rrbracket$ **do**
   $X_i = \mathsf{MaskedSubBytes}_{\mathsf{offset}[i]+r}(X_i)$
  end
 end
 $X = \mathsf{ShiftRows}(X)$
 $X = \mathsf{MixColumns}(X)$
 for $i \in \llbracket 0, 15 \rrbracket$ **do**
  $\mathsf{MaskCompensation}[i] =$
  $\mathsf{ShiftRows}(\mathsf{MixColumns}(\mathsf{Mask}[\mathsf{offset}[i]+(r+1)])) \oplus \mathsf{Mask}[(\mathsf{offset}[i]+(r+1))]$
 end
 $X = X \oplus \mathsf{MaskCompensation}[]$
end

```
                         /* Last round */
```
$X = X \oplus \mathsf{RoundKey}[13]$
for $i \in \mathsf{Shuffle13}(\llbracket 0, 15 \rrbracket)$ **do**
 $X_{\mathsf{Shuffle}[i]} = \mathsf{MaskedSubBytes}_{\mathsf{offset}[i]+13}(X_i)$
end
$X = \mathsf{ShiftRows}(X)$
$X = X \oplus \mathsf{RoundKey}[14]$

```
                         /* Ciphertext unmasking */
```
for $i \in \llbracket 0, 15 \rrbracket$ **do**
 $\mathsf{MaskCompensationLastRound}[i] =$
 $\mathsf{ShiftRows}(\mathsf{Mask}[\mathsf{offset}[i]+14]) \oplus \mathsf{Mask}[(\mathsf{offset}[i]+14)]$
end
$X = X \oplus \mathsf{MaskCompensationLastRound}[]$

Table 2. Cost Complexity of the original (DPACv4) over the new implementation and Rijndael Furious

Architecture	Rijndael Furious	Original (protected)	Improved (protected)	Overhead
Code Size (bytes)	2596	11136	17847	60%
RAM (bytes)	1	8	12	50%
Number of cycles	3579	113600	16004	−86%

4.3 Shuffling Algorithms

To generate the shuffle, we propose two algorithms:

1. the first one (Alg. 2) generates a full entropy permutation of $[\![0, 2^n - 1]\!]$, and works in $\mathcal{O}(n^2 \log(2^n))$ time;
2. the second one (Alg. 3) generates a low entropy permutation of $[\![0, 2^n - 1]\!]$, but works in linear time $\mathcal{O}(n)$.

Alg. 2 redraws numbers repeatedly till there is no collision. Notice that we suggest to draw numbers in $\{0, 1, \ldots, 2^n - 1\}$, because it is easy to draw uniformly n bits. Instead, randomly drawing numbers in an interval is not trivial (applying a "modulo" would break the uniformity).

Lemma 1. *The expected running time of Alg. 2 is $2^n \sum_{m=1}^{2^n} \frac{1}{m}$, that is equivalent to $\mathcal{O}(2^n \log(2^n))$ for large values of n.*

Proof. See Appendix B.

Algorithm 2. Full Entropy Shuffling

---

   input : None
   output: A permutation $\mathbb{F}_2^n \mapsto \mathbb{F}_2^n$

   Initialize a vector of 2^n elements of $\mathbb{F}_2^n$;
   for $\omega \in \{0, 1, \ldots, 2^n - 1\}$ **do** // Scrambling
      | $r \leftarrow_{\mathcal{R}} \mathcal{U}([\![0, 2^n - 1]\!])$;
      | **while** $r \in S[0, i - 1]$ **do**
      | | $r \leftarrow_{\mathcal{R}} \mathcal{U}([\![0, 2^n - 1]\!])$;
      | **end**
      | $S[i] \leftarrow r$;
   end
   return S

Alg. 3 is inspired from the key scheduling of RC4.

Algorithm 3. Low Entropy Shuffling

---

input : $k[2^n]$, an array of 2^n elements of $\mathbb{F}_2^n$
output: A permutation $\mathbb{F}_2^n \mapsto \mathbb{F}_2^n$

$S[2^n]$, an array of 2^n elements of $\mathbb{F}_2^n$;
for $\omega \in \{0, 1, \ldots, 2^n - 1\}$ **do** // Initialisation
$\quad$| $S[\omega] \leftarrow \omega$
end
$j \leftarrow 0$ **for** $\omega \in \{0, 1, \ldots, 2^n - 1\}$ **do** // Scrambling
$\quad$| $j \leftarrow j + S[\omega] + k[\omega mod2^n]$;
$\quad$| swap($S[\omega], S[j]$) ;
end
return S

---

5   Security Evaluation

We acquired 32K side-channel traces for the proposed implementation using the setup described above. The plaintexts and the key used were same as of DPACv4. The main aim is to check for any first-order or univariate leakage present in the implementation. To do so, we rely on leakage detection technique. More precisely we use Normalized Inter-Class Variance (NICV [22]). NICV detects any univariate leakage present in the side-channel traces and does not depend on a leakage model. It is computed with respect to public parameters like plaintext or ciphertext. NICV is expressed as:

$$NICV = \frac{\mathsf{Var}\left[\mathbb{E}\left[Y|X\right]\right]}{\mathsf{Var}\left[Y\right]},$$

where Y denotes side-channel traces and X represent a chosen part of plaintext or ciphertext. We compute NICV with respect to a input plaintext byte for the collected traces. The results are shown in Fig 1(a). It can be deduced from Fig 1(a), that no univariate leakage is present in the improved implementation in the SubBytes and further. We can see two big peaks during the initial AddRoundKey in figure which indicate presence of a possible univariate leakage. We further investigated the peak using a univariate CPA attacks. Indeed these peaks correspond to the loading of the raw plaintext byte into different section of the card i.e. memory and ALU. This leakage does not contain any information about the key used and therefore not sensitive. We can also see this non-sensitive leakage on the NICV computed on traces of the original implementation of DPACv4 as shown in Fig 1(b). Moreover in Fig. 1(b), we detect a univariate leakage related to the plaintext during the SubBytes operation. Such leakage can be sensitive. We further investigated the leakage in the SubBytes of original DPACv4 implementation. It turned out to be the same leakage as exploited by Moradi et al [14].

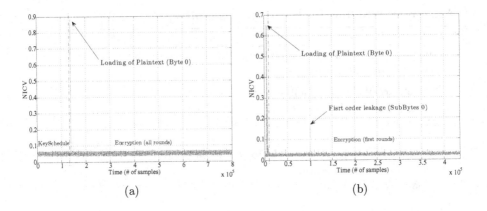

Fig. 1. NICV computed on the (a) proposed implementation; (b) original implementation of DPACv4

Next we investigate the leakage corresponding to the offset. In order to show that our new implementation is less prone to folding attacks than the DPACV4 implementation we check that traces contains less leakage points related to the offset value. We computed NICV with respect to the 4 bit offset used in the first implementation. We can see in Fig. 2 that there are 48 significant peaks. Those leakage points corresponds to the loading of the single 4 bit offset index used to address the mask table, the sBox and the mask correction table. If the device leaks in value, a single folding attack on one of those leakage point can be sufficient to recover the full key. If the offset is partially leaked at each leakage point , the attacker can exploit multiple leakage point to mount more robust folding attacks.

Then we computed NICV with respect to the first 4-bit offset of 16 on our new implementation. The results are shown in Fig 3. We can see three big peaks. Those tree peaks corresponds to the loading of the index that is used to read the mask,the sBox and the mask correction table in memory. Those leakage are sensitive because it provide information on the byte of mask used to blind the key. However, it is no longer possible to mount horizontal attacks since each byte of mask is selected by a different random 4 bit offset. Knowing those leakage point can however be used to mount "folding" type attacks, provided that the target leaks in value. If the target appears to leak in value, 16 folding attacks are however not sufficient to recover the full key because the attacker should also fold the dataset depending the 16 4-bit random shuffle. If the offset values are partially leaked , only 3 leakage point per offset nibble are available to guess the leaked value, which is not sufficient.

5.1   Insight on Horizontal Attacks

In this section, we compare a full entropic sbox masking against improved RSM proposed in Sec 4. A way to mask the non linear sbox is to use sbox

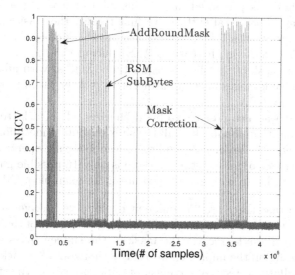

Fig. 2. NICV computed on the first 4 bit offset of the proposed implementation (first round + KeySchedule)

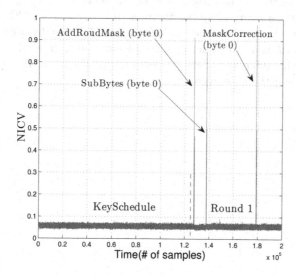

Fig. 3. NICV computed on the first 4 bit offset of the DPACV4 implementation (first round + KeySchedule)

recomputation [23]. As presented in [24] this kind of masking scheme can be defeated by using "horizontal" attacks to first recover the mask and then performing first order attacks. These attacks are possible due to the fact that the mask is used 256 times (in the case of AES) during the sbox recomputation. Mainly the input mask of the sbox is sequentially XORed with all the possible values in $\mathbb{F}_2^8$. These leakages allow an attacker to recover the value of the mask using for example a CPA.

In DPACv4, it was also possible to build "horizontal" attacks to recover the random offset, and then the mask of all the sbox outputs. Indeed for each plaintext byte there was the leakage depending on the following operation: $x_i \oplus m_i$. Then as the sequence of mask is known there is only 16 possible guesses, corresponding to 16 masks, to recover the mask using for example a CPA.

Remark 2. Note that there are 256 different exploitable leakages in the case of the sbox recomputation and only 16 for RSM. But the results of the "horizontal" attacks on RSM allows to recover the mask of the sixteen bytes of the states whereas (depending on the implementation) the "horizontal" attack on the sbox recomputation allows to recover the mask of only one byte of the state.

In our proposition, a random offset is used to mask each byte and it is no longer possible to perform "horizontal" attack. Indeed it is necessary to guess 16^{16} values. Moreover, the shuffling makes the attack even more difficult as it is necessary to guess the 16! possible orders of plaintext.

The Success Rate is given by the formula [10]: $SR = 1 - e^{-n \times k}$ where n is the number of traces, in our case the number of different leakages depending on the mask, and k is a first order exponent (obtained from a Chernov bound). Figure 4 shows the difference of the success rate for the recovering the mask for improved RSM and the sbox recomputation.

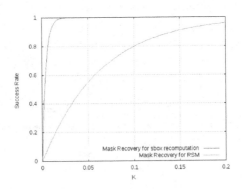

Fig. 4. Difference of Success Rate for normal sbox recomputation vs our proposition of RSM

Remark 3. The sbox recomputation can also be done in a random order but it is necessary to generate a permutation on 256 value. This generation could be costly (see Alg. 2 and 3).

6   Conclusions and Perspectives

LEMS has its own advantages and shortcomings. An example of LEMS was proposed in DPACv4, where researchers from all over the world were able to attack a common implementations. 18 profiled and non-profiled attacks were proposed revealing 4 major pitfalls of the proposed implementation. In this paper, we analyze these pitfalls and propose an improved implementation. Our results demonstrate that it is possible to resist the non-profiled attacks at an overhead of 27% in code size, 50% in memory and 1.5% in computation time.

Disclaimer

The exact specifications of the improved implementation of the DPA contest v4 will be posted on the official website and related social media [9].

Acknowledgments. Authors are grateful to Guillaume Duc for the animation of the DPA contests, and to all the DPA contest participants, who made these competitions live and very active.

References

1. Kocher, P.C., Jaffe, J., Jun, B.: Differential Power Analysis. In: Wiener, M. (ed.) CRYPTO 1999. LNCS, vol. 1666, pp. 388–397. Springer, Heidelberg (1999)
2. Brier, E., Clavier, C., Olivier, F.: Correlation Power Analysis with a Leakage Model. In: Joye, M., Quisquater, J.-J. (eds.) CHES 2004. LNCS, vol. 3156, pp. 16–29. Springer, Heidelberg (2004)
3. Herbst, C., Oswald, E., Mangard, S.: An AES Smart Card Implementation Resistant to Power Analysis Attacks. In: Zhou, J., Yung, M., Bao, F. (eds.) ACNS 2006. LNCS, vol. 3989, pp. 239–252. Springer, Heidelberg (2006)
4. Rivain, M., Prouff, E., Doget, J.: Higher-Order Masking and Shuffling for Software Implementations of Block Ciphers. Cryptology ePrint Archive, Report 2009/420 (2009), http://eprint.iacr.org/2009/420
5. Rauzy, P., Guilley, S., Najm, Z.: Formally Proved Security of Assembly Code Against Leakage. IACR Cryptology ePrint Archive 2013, 554 (2013)
6. Nassar, M., Souissi, Y., Guilley, S., Danger, J.L.: RSM: a Small and Fast Countermeasure for AES, Secure against First- and Second-order Zero-Offset SCAs. In: DATE, Dresden, Germany, pp. 1173–1178. IEEE Computer Society (2012) (TRACK A: "Application Design", TOPIC A5: "Secure Systems")
7. Bhasin, S., Danger, J.L., Guilley, S., Najm, Z.: A Low-Entropy First-Degree Secure Provable Masking Scheme for Resource-Constrained Devices. In: Proceedings of the Workshop on Embedded Systems Security, WESS 2013, Montreal, Quebec, Canada, pp. 7:1–7:10. ACM, New York (2013), doi:10.1145/2527317.2527324

8. TELECOM ParisTech SEN research group: DPA Contest (1st edn.) (2008–2009), http://www.DPAcontest.org/
9. TELECOM ParisTech SEN research group: DPA Contest (4th edn.) (2013–2014), http://www.DPAcontest.org/v4/
10. Chari, S., Jutla, C.S., Rao, J.R., Rohatgi, P.: Towards Sound Approaches to Counteract Power-Analysis Attacks. In: Wiener, M. (ed.) CRYPTO 1999. LNCS, vol. 1666, pp. 398–540. Springer, Heidelberg (1999)
11. Prouff, E., Rivain, M.: A Generic Method for Secure SBox Implementation. In: Kim, S., Yung, M., Lee, H.-W. (eds.) WISA 2007. LNCS, vol. 4867, pp. 227–244. Springer, Heidelberg (2008)
12. Hedayat, A.S., Sloane, N.J.A., Stufken, J.: Orthogonal Arrays, Theory and Applications. Springer series in statistics. Springer, New York (1999) ISBN 978-0-387-98766-8
13. Grosso, V., Standaert, F.-X., Prouff, E.: Low Entropy Masking Schemes, Revisited. In: Francillon, A., Rohatgi, P. (eds.) CARDIS 2013. LNCS, vol. 8419, pp. 33–43. Springer, Heidelberg (2014)
14. Moradi, A., Guilley, S., Heuser, A.: Detecting Hidden Leakages. In: Boureanu, I., Owesarski, P., Vaudenay, S. (eds.) ACNS 2014. LNCS, vol. 8479, pp. 324–342. Springer, Heidelberg (2014)
15. Clavier, C., Feix, B., Gagnerot, G., Roussellet, M., Verneuil, V.: Improved Collision-Correlation Power Analysis on First Order Protected AES. In: Preneel, B., Takagi, T. (eds.) CHES 2011. LNCS, vol. 6917, pp. 49–62. Springer, Heidelberg (2011)
16. Belgarric, P., et al.: Time-Frequency Analysis for Second-Order Attacks. In: Francillon, A., Rohatgi, P. (eds.) CARDIS 2013. LNCS, vol. 8419, pp. 108–122. Springer, Heidelberg (2014)
17. Ye, X., Eisenbarth, T.: On the Vulnerability of Low Entropy Masking Schemes. In: Francillon, A., Rohatgi, P. (eds.) CARDIS 2013. LNCS, vol. 8419, pp. 44–60. Springer, Heidelberg (2014)
18. Rivain, M., Prouff, E., Doget, J.: Higher-Order Masking and Shuffling for Software Implementations of Block Ciphers. In: Clavier, C., Gaj, K. (eds.) CHES 2009. LNCS, vol. 5747, pp. 171–188. Springer, Heidelberg (2009)
19. Coron, J.-S.: Higher Order Masking of Look-Up Tables. In: Nguyen, P.Q., Oswald, E. (eds.) EUROCRYPT 2014. LNCS, vol. 8441, pp. 441–458. Springer, Heidelberg (2014)
20. Rivain, M., Prouff, E.: Provably Secure Higher-Order Masking of AES. In: Mangard, S., Standaert, F.-X. (eds.) CHES 2010. LNCS, vol. 6225, pp. 413–427. Springer, Heidelberg (2010)
21. Kutzner, S., Poschmann, A.: On the Security of RSM — Presenting 5 First- and Second-order Attacks. In: Prouff, E. (ed.) COSADE 2014. LNCS, vol. 8622, pp. 299–312. Springer, Heidelberg (2014)
22. Bhasin, S., Danger, J.L., Guilley, S., Najm, Z.: Side-channel Leakage and Trace Compression Using Normalized Inter-class Variance. In: Proceedings of the Third Workshop on Hardware and Architectural Support for Security and Privacy, HASP 2014, pp. 7:1–7:9. ACM, New York (2014)
23. Akkar, M.-L., Giraud, C.: An Implementation of DES and AES, Secure against Some Attacks. In: Koç, Ç.K., Naccache, D., Paar, C. (eds.) CHES 2001. LNCS, vol. 2162, pp. 309–318. Springer, Heidelberg (2001)

24. Tunstall, M., Whitnall, C., Oswald, E.: Masking Tables – An Underestimated Security Risk. In: Moriai, S. (ed.) FSE 2013. LNCS, vol. 8424, pp. 425–444. Springer, Heidelberg (2014)
25. Clavier, C., Danger, J.-L., Duc, G., Abdelaziz Elaabid, M., Gérard, B., Guilley, S., Heuser, A., Kasper, M., Li, Y., Lomné, V., Nakatsu, D., Ohta, K., Sakiyama, K., Sauvage, L., Schindler, W., Stöttinger, M., Veyrat-Charvillon, N., Walle, M., Wurcker, A.: Practical improvements of side-channel attacks on AES: feedback from the 2nd DPA contest. Journal of Cryptographic Engineering, 1–16 (2014)

A   Algorithm of DPACv4 Implementation

The algorithm running on the smartcard for DPACv4 is described in Alg. 4.

Algorithm 4. AES implementation used for the DPACv4 (Source: [9]).

Input   : 16-bytes Plaintext X $[\![X_0, X_1 \cdots X_{15}]\!]$,
              Key, 15 16-bytes constants $\mathsf{RoundKey}[r]$, $r \in [\![0, 14]\!]$
Output: 16-bytes Ciphertext X $[\![X_0, X_1 \cdots X_{15}]\!]$

Draw a random offset, uniformly in $[\![0, 15]\!]$
$X = X \oplus \mathsf{Mask}_{\mathsf{offset}}$ /* Plaintext blinding */

                              /* All rounds but the last one */
for $r \in [\![0, 12]\!]$ do
$\quad$ $X = X \oplus \mathsf{RoundKey}[r]$ /* AddRoundKey */
$\quad$ for $i \in [\![0, 15]\!]$ do
$\quad\quad$ $X_i = \mathsf{MaskedSubBytes}_{\mathsf{offset}+i+r}(X_i)$
$\quad$ end
$\quad$ $X = \mathsf{ShiftRows}(X)$
$\quad$ $X = \mathsf{MixColumns}(X)$
$\quad$ $X = X \oplus \mathsf{MaskCompensation}_{\mathsf{offset}+1+r}$
end

                              /* Last round */
$X = X \oplus \mathsf{RoundKey}[13]$
for $i \in [\![0, 15]\!]$ do
$\quad$ $X_i = \mathsf{MaskedSubBytes}_{\mathsf{offset}+13+r}(X_i)$
end
$X = \mathsf{ShiftRows}(X)$
$X = X \oplus \mathsf{RoundKey}[14]$

                              /* Ciphertext unmasking */
$X = X \oplus \mathsf{MaskCompensationLastRound}_{\mathsf{offset}+14}$

B   Proof of Lemma 1

The running time of Alg. 2 is probabilistic because of the conditional redraws at line 2. Let i, $0 \le i < 2^n$, be the number of values already chosen. Then, a uniformly drawn value r in $[\![0, 2^n - 1]\!]$ is a new value with probability $(2^n - i)/2^n$. If it is not a new value, then j redraws are required, with probability

$$\left(\frac{i}{2^n}\right)^j \times \frac{2^n - i}{2^n} \; .$$

Thus, the average number of random number drawing is:

$$1 + \sum_{j=1}^{+\infty} j \left(\frac{i}{2^n}\right)^j \times \frac{2^n - i}{2^n}$$

$$= 1 + \sum_{j=1}^{+\infty} j \left(\frac{i}{2^n}\right)^{j-1} \times \frac{(2^n - i)i}{2^{2n}}$$

$$= 1 + \frac{i}{2^n - i} \; .$$

because $\frac{1}{(1-x)^2} = \sum_{i=1}^{\infty} i x^{i-1}$ for all $x \in \mathbb{R}$ such that $|x| < 1$.

Thus, the average time of Alg. 2 is

$$\sum_{i=0}^{2^n - 1} 1 + \frac{i}{2^n - i}$$

$$= 2^n + \sum_{m=1}^{2^n} \frac{2^n - m}{m} \qquad (m \leftarrow 2^n - i)$$

$$= 2^n \sum_{m=1}^{2^n} \frac{1}{m} \; .$$

Now,

$$\lim_{N \to +\infty} \sum_{m=1}^{N} \frac{1}{m} - \ln N = -\gamma \; ,$$

where γ is the Euler-Mascheroni constant ($\gamma \approx 0.577$). Thus, the average running time of Alg. 2 is equivalent to $2^n \ln(2^n)$ when n tends to the infinity.

Some Randomness Experiments on TRIVIUM

Subhabrata Samajder and Palash Sarkar

Applied Statistics Unit
Indian Statistical Institute
203, B.T.Road, Kolkata, India - 700108
{subhabrata_r,palash}@isical.ac.in

Abstract. The first output bit of TRIVIUM can be considered to be a boolean function of 80 key and 80 IV variables. Choose n ($n \leq 30$) of the key variables and set the other variables to constant values. This gives an n-variable boolean function. In this work, we experimentally find examples of such boolean functions which deviate from a uniform random n-variable boolean function in a statistically significant manner. This improves upon the previously reported experimental 'non-randomness' result using the cube testing methodology by Aumasson et al in 2009 for TRIVIUM restricted to 885 rounds. In contrast, we work with full TRIVIUM and instead of using the cube methodology we directly find the algebraic normal form of the restricted version of the first output bit of TRIVIUM. We note, however, that our work does not indicate any weakness of TRIVIUM. On the other hand, the kind of experiments that we conduct for TRIVIUM can also be conducted for other ciphers.

Keywords: stream ciphers, TRIVIUM, statistical test, non-randomness.

1 Introduction

TRIVIUM is a hardware oriented synchronous stream cipher that was submitted to the Profile II (hardware) of the eSTREAM competition by Christophe De Cannière and Bart Preneel [DCP]. TRIVIUM maintains an internal state of size 288 bits. The state is subdivided into 3 shift registers of sizes 93, 84 and 111 bits each. It uses a simple quadratic state update function with 3 AND operations as the only non-linear operations per round. There are 1152 initialization rounds. During the key generation, at each step, the state is updated and a single key bit is produced. This key bit is the XOR of 6 state bits. Over the years TRIVIUM has received much attention from the research community due to its simple structure. However, there is still no known attack on full version of TRIVIUM which works better than exhaustive search.

To gain a better understanding of the full cipher, scaled-down variants, such as Bivium A and Bivium B [Rad06], have been studied. Both Bivium A and Bivium B use two shift registers as their internal state unlike TRIVIUM which uses three. The attacks on TRIVIUM can be broadly classified into two categories. The first type analyses the scaled-down variants (Bivium A and Bivium B [Rad06]) and tries to extrapolate their results to the full TRIVIUM. The second approach has

R.S. Chakraborty et al. (Eds.): SPACE 2014, LNCS 8804, pp. 219–236, 2014.

been to study the reduced-round variants of the cipher, i.e., TRIVIUM with 'r' rounds of key initialization where $r \leq 1152$.

Early results on reduced-round variants of TRIVIUM can be found in [TK07] and [Vie07]. In [TK07], Turan et al used Matsui's linear cryptanalysis method to get a linear approximation with a bias 2^{-31} for 288 rounds of key initialization. Whereas in [Vie07], Vielhaber used an IV resynchronization attack with 2^6 IV's to break 576 rounds of TRIVIUM. Englund et al in [EJT07], experimentally showed statistical weakness in the keystream of TRIVIUM when reduced to 736 rounds of key initialization. In [O'N07], O'Neal claimed that TRIVIUM with 1152 rounds of key initialization may not be secure and proposed that the initialization rounds for TRIVIUM should be increased to $4 \times 1152 = 4608$ rounds. Fischer et al in [FKM08] used a framework for chosen IV statistical distinguishing analysis of stream ciphers to extract few key bits of TRIVIUM when reduced to 672 rounds of key initializations.

The cube attack was proposed in [DS09] by Dinur et al and used to recover the key after 767 initialization rounds. The attack required 2^{45} bit operations and the authors showed that this can be further reduced to 2^{36} bit operations. In [ADMS09], Aumasson et al introduced a new class of attacks called cube testers and developed distinguishers for 790 rounds of TRIVIUM with 2^{30} complexity and were able to detect non-randomness over 885 rounds in 2^{27} complexity, improving on the original 767-round cube attack.

Recently in [FV13], Fouque and Vannet increased the number of attacked initialization rounds by improving the time complexity of computing cube. They were able to find a key recovery attack requiring 2^{39} queries for 784 initialization rounds and were also able to provide another key recovery attack up to 799 rounds with a complexity of 2^{40} for queries and 2^{62} for the exhaustive search part. In their attack, they used the Moebius Transform to improve on the time taken in the pre-processing stage of cube attack.

Our Results: The motivation for our work is the discovery of non-randomness after 885 rounds of TRIVIUM reported in [ADMS09]. We briefly discuss this result. The input key and IV variables are divided into two groups called cube variables (CV) and superpoly variables (SV). Suppose $g(x_1, \ldots, x_c; y_1, \ldots, y_s)$ denotes the boolean function representing the first keystream bit of TRIVIUM. There are $c + s$ input variables, where $CV = \{x_1, \ldots, x_c\}$ and $SV = \{y_1, \ldots, y_s\}$. Then superpoly s_{CV} of g corresponding to a cube of size c is defined as

$$s_{CV}(y_1, y_2, \ldots, y_s) = \bigoplus_{(x_1, x_2, \ldots, x_c) \in \mathbb{F}_2^c} g(x_1, x_2, \ldots, x_c; y_1, y_2, \ldots, y_s),$$

which is an s-variable boolean function in the variables SV. The details about the non-randomness of 885 rounds of TRIVIUM reported in [ADMS09] is a bit sketchy. We try to provide some more details. A cube of size 27 of IV variables mentioned in [DS09] was considered. Set all other IV variables to 0. It was *experimentally* discovered that in the superpoly corresponding to this cube, the key variables 1, 4 and 5 are neutral (i.e., changing their values does not affect the outcome of the polynomial). It is mentioned that the zero key was used which would imply that all key bits other than 1, 4 and 5 were set to zero. It was argued that the discovery of such a polynomial in the structure of TRIVIUM is an evidence of non-randomness. This claim is also well accepted in the literature.

In general terms the above example can be viewed as follows. Let $g(x_1, \ldots, x_c;$ $y_1, \ldots, y_s)$ be the first output bit of TRIVIUM (after 885 rounds). The authors discover a transformation Φ such that the key bits 1, 4 and 5 are neutral for the boolean function $\Phi(g)$. The transformation Φ consists of applying the cube, setting IV and the other key bits to 0.

The above kind of experimentally discovered 'non-randomness' after 885 rounds reported in [ADMS09] forms the motivation for our work. We ask the question as to whether it is possible to experimentally discover some kind of 'non-randomness' in full TRIVIUM. As above, if g denotes the boolean function representing the first output bit, our goal is to discover a transformatiion Ψ such that the boolean function $\Psi(g)$ shows some statistically quantifiable deviation from a uniform random function. The Ψ that we consider does not involve evaluating a cube. The function g depends on 80 key and 80 IV variables. The transformation Ψ consists of choosing n key variables and setting the other key and IV variables to constant values. As a result $\Psi(g)$ is a boolean function on n variables. We are able to experimentally obtain examples of $\Psi(g)$ whose deviation from a uniform boolean function is statistically significant. Here n is a parameter which is at most 30.

The main computational challenge is to obtain the algebraic normal form (ANF) of $\Psi(g)$. For this we discuss two methods. The first one symbolically evolves TRIVIUM over the full 1152 rounds. This requires a fast algorithm for multiplying two boolean functions given by their ANFs and for this task we use the implementation reported in [Sam13]. The second method proceeds by first obtaining the truth table representation for $\Psi(g)$ and then using the Moebius transformation to obtain the ANF. Either of the methods yields both the ANF and also the truth table representation of $\Psi(g)$.

Suppose u^* is a uniform random boolean function of n variables. The weight of u^* is a random variable with mean 2^{n-1}. Given a probability α, there is an interval I_α such that the weight of u^* is in I_α with probability at least α. We say that $\Psi(g)$ is unbalanced at level α if its weight lies outside the internal I_α. Similar notions of algebraic unbalancedness for $\Psi(g)$ can be defined with respect to the total number of monomials in the ANF of $\Psi(g)$ and also with respect to the number of monomials of degree d in the ANF of $\Psi(g)$. We also define a notion of unbalancedness over an l-dimensional uniform random vectorial boolean function $\tilde{u}^*$. Further details of the corresponding statistical tests are provided later.

In this work, we experimentally find concrete examples of $\Psi(g)$ for $n = 10, 20$ and 30 which are unbalanced, algebraically unbalanced with respect to the total number of monomials and also with respect to monomials of certain specific degrees. We further provide give concrete examples of $\Psi(\tilde{g})$ for $n = 20, 30$ (where $\tilde{g}$ denotes an l-dimensional vectorial boolean function) which are unbalanced. These results are obtained for level α corresponding to more than

99% probability. For lower values of α, we are able to obtain examples of $\Psi(g)$ which simultaneously fail several of the statistical tests. Our experiments consist of randomly selecting the n key variables and choosing the values for the other $160 - n$ key and IV variables. This in effect randomly chooses the transformation Ψ. The reported results are obtained by randomly choosing possibilities for Ψ several thousands of times.

We make no claims that our results exhibit a weakness of TRIVIUM. There are two implications of our work. First, our results show that to experimentally discover some 'non-random' polynomial in the structure of TRIVIUM, the complicated cube analysis technique of [ADMS09] is unnecessary. Instead one can simply look at the boolean function representing the first output bit by setting $160 - n$ of the input variables to constant values. Second, our work discovers 'non-randomness' in TRIVIUM after the full 1152 rounds of initialization whereas [ADMS09] reported results only after 885 rounds.

The method described here is not particular to TRIVIUM. It can be applied to any cipher. Whether the results will be similar to that obtained for TRIVIUM is not clear and exploring this can form possible future work.

Related Work: We are not the first to consider applying statistical tests to the algebraic normal form of the output bits of a stream cipher. An early work by Filio [Fil02] and later follow-up in [Saa06] had explored this possibility. Our approach, however, differs from that of [Fil02,Saa06] in the following way. The work considered the ANFs of the first N output bits of a stream cipher and investigated the distribution of monomials of degree d in these ANFs for $d \leq 3$. The study was thus aggregated and unlike the specific 'non-randomness' example reported in [ADMS09].

2   A Brief Description of TRIVIUM

TRIVIUM maintains a 288-bit internal state "S" denoted by $S = (s_1, s_2, \ldots, s_{288})$ and uses two algorithms, namely a key initialization algorithm, which we call the key and IV setup, and a key stream generation algorithm. The state S is further divided into 3 shift registers, namely $S_1 = (s_1, s_2, \ldots, s_{93})$, $S_2 = (s_{94}, s_{95}, \ldots, s_{177})$ and $S_3 = (s_{178}, s_{179}, \ldots, s_{288})$.

2.1   Key and IV Setup

The algorithm is initialized by loading an 80-bit key into the first 80-bits of the state S, i.e., $s_1, s_2, \ldots, s_{80}$ and an 80-bit IV into the state bits $s_{94}, s_{95}, \ldots, s_{173}$ and setting all remaining bits to 0, except for s_{286}, s_{287}, and s_{288}, which are set to 1. Each round of the iterative process extracts the values of 15 specific state bits and uses them to update 3 bits of the state. This is repeated for $4 \times 288 = 1152$ times. This can be summarized by the following pseudo-code (Algorithm 1):

Algorithm 1: TRIVIUM - Key and IV Setup

$(s_1, s_2, \ldots, s_{93}) \leftarrow (K_1, K_2, \ldots, K_{80}, 0, \ldots, 0)$
$(s_{94}, s_{95}, \ldots, s_{177}) \leftarrow (IV_1, IV_2, \ldots, IV_{80}, 0, 0, 0, 0)$
$(s_{178}, s_{179}, \ldots, s_{288}) \leftarrow (0, \ldots 0, 1, 1, 1)$
for $i = 1$ *to* $4 \cdot 288$ **do**
    $t_1 \leftarrow s_{66} \oplus s_{91} \cdot s_{92} \oplus s_{93} \oplus s_{171}$
    $t_2 \leftarrow s_{162} \oplus s_{175} \cdot s_{176} \oplus s_{177} \oplus s_{264}$
    $t_3 \leftarrow s_{243} \oplus s_{286} \cdot s_{287} \oplus s_{288} \oplus s_{69}$
    $(s_1, s_2, \ldots, s_{93}) \leftarrow (t_3, s_1, \ldots, s_{92})$
    $(s_{94}, s_{95}, \ldots, s_{177}) \leftarrow (t_1, s_{94}, \ldots, s_{176})$
    $(s_{178}, s_{179}, \ldots, s_{288}) \leftarrow (t_2, s_{178}, \ldots, s_{287})$
end

2.2 Key Stream Generation

The key stream generation algorithm is similar to that of the key initialization algorithm except that at each round, a single bit which is a linear function of six state bits, is output before the state update. This process repeats itself until the requested $N \leq 2^{64}$ bits of key stream is generated. The complete description is given by the following pseudo-code (Algorithm 2):

Algorithm 2: TRIVIUM - Key Stream Generation

for $i = 1$ *to* N **do**
    $t_1 \leftarrow s_{66} \oplus s_{93}$
    $t_2 \leftarrow s_{162} \oplus s_{177}$
    $t_3 \leftarrow s_{243} \oplus s_{288}$
    $z_i \leftarrow t_1 \oplus t_2 \oplus t_3$
    $t_1 \leftarrow t_1 \oplus s_{91} \cdot s_{92} \oplus s_{171}$
    $t_2 \leftarrow t_2 \oplus s_{175} \cdot s_{176} \oplus s_{264}$
    $t_3 \leftarrow t_3 \oplus s_{286} \cdot s_{287} \oplus s_{69}$
    $(s_1, s_2, \ldots, s_{93}) \leftarrow (t_3, s_1, \ldots, s_{92})$
    $(s_{94}, s_{95}, \ldots, s_{177}) \leftarrow (t_1, s_{94}, \ldots, s_{176})$
    $(s_{178}, s_{179}, \ldots, s_{288}) \leftarrow (t_2, s_{178}, \ldots, s_{287})$
end

---

3 Algebraic Normal Forms of the Output Bits of TRIVIUM

Let us denote the key K by $(k_1, k_2, \ldots, k_{80})$ and the IV by $(iv_1, iv_2, \ldots, iv_{80})$. If instead of bits, we consider the key and the IV as variables then the state is initialized as follows:

$$(s_1, s_2, \ldots, s_{93}) \leftarrow (k_1, k_2, \ldots, k_{80}, 0, \ldots, 0),$$

$$(s_{94}, s_{95}, \ldots, s_{177}) \leftarrow (iv_1, iv_2, \ldots, iv_{80}, 0, 0, 0, 0),$$

$$(s_{178}, s_{179}, \ldots, s_{288}) \leftarrow (0, \ldots 0, 1, 1, 1).$$

During each state update these state bits get multiplied and added in the boolean function ring defined over the variables K and IV. Thus, considering each state bit as a boolean function in $80 + 80 = 160$ variables, one can view each state update as performing 3 multiplications (1 for each $t_i, i = 1, 2, 3$.) and 9 additions (3 for each $t_i, i = 1, 2, 3$.). Addition is just bitwise XOR, whereas multiplication is that of two boolean functions given by their ANF's.

Handling the ANF of a boolean function on 160 variables is infeasible. Hence, we reduce the number of variables in the following manner. The key and IV bit positions which are to be treated as variables are randomly selected. These selected bit positions are then renamed as variables $k_1, k_2, \ldots, k_{n_k}$ and $iv_1, iv_2, \ldots, iv_{n_{iv}}$, such that $n_k + n_{iv} = n$. We work with $n \leq 30$. The rest of the key and IV bit positions are then set randomly to either 0 or 1. The outputs bits of TRIVIUM can then be considered to be boolean functions of n variables. We provide two methods to compute the ANFs of the output bits.

3.1   Method - 1

A symbolic computation of TRIVIUM is carried out where the state bits are treated as polynomials in $k_1, k_2, \ldots, k_{n_k}$ and $iv_1, iv_2, \ldots, iv_{n_{iv}}$. As a result, the first output bit which is the bitwise XOR of six state bits, namely $s_{66}, s_{93}, s_{162}, s_{177}, s_{243}$ and s_{288} is also a polynomial in these variables.

The main time-consuming step in the above symbolic computation is that of multiplying the ANFs of two boolean functions. We used the implementation MultANF$_{64}$ of multiplication described in [Sam13]. Using this algorithm, two 30-variable boolean functions can be multiplied in less than 2 seconds on a 3 GHz processor. Carrying out the simulation of full 1152 rounds of TRIVIUM with $n = 30$ requires 3456 multiplications and the entire computation requires about one-and-half hours.

The complexity of Method - 1 is dominated by the number of multiplications of two n-variable boolean functions. We know from [Jou09] that the complexity for multiplying two n-variable boolean functions in their ANF is of the order of $3n2^n$. TRIVIUM uses 3 multiplications at each round. Therefore the total complexity of Method - 1 when used to evaluate an r-round variant of TRIVIUM (TRIVIUM with r rounds of key initializations) is of the order of $9rn2^n$.

3.2   Method - 2

The second method first constructs the truth table of the first output bit z_1 which is a polynomial in n variables as mentioned above. A fast implementation of TRIVIUM is used to evaluate z_1 on all possible 2^n input combinations. This provides the truth table representation of z_1. This is converted into the ANF format using the Moebius transformation (see [Jou09] for a description of this algorithm).

The complexity of Method - 2 when used to evaluate r-round variant of TRIVIUM is 2^n computations of r-round TRIVIUM plus the cost required to convert the truth table of an n-variable boolean function into its corresponding ANF. And the cost for the conversion of the truth table to its ANF is $\mathcal{O}(n2^n)$.

3.3 Complexity of the Cube Tester

Let the IV variables be divided into two parts the cube variables (CV) and the superpoly variables (SV). All the key variables are also treated as SV. Consider an r-round variant of TRIVIUM, i.e., TRIVIUM with r rounds of key initialization. The cube tester [ADMS09] selects the cube variables from the 80 available IV variables. It treats the remaining key and IV variables as SV. It further divides the SV variables into two parts. Let us call the first part of variables as the function variables (FV) and retain the name SV for the second part of variables. In the cube testers for TRIVIUM mentioned in [ADMS09] the SV variables are all set to zero whereas the FV variables are set to fixed random values. Then 2^{CV} many executions of r-round TRIVIUM is used to find the value of the superpoly at (SV, FV). This is repeated for N different choices of FV. Therefore, to test one particular superpoly the attacker needs $N \times 2^{CV}$ executions of r-round TRIVIUM. In their paper [ADMS09] the authors had mainly concentrated on the cubes that were listed in the appendix of [DS09]. As mentioned in the paper the maximum size of FV and CV considered are 5 and 30 respectively. Therefore in order to compute the complete truth table of a 5-variable function the cube tester has to compute 2^{35} r-round variant of TRIVIUM.

4   Some Elementary Statistics

Let $X_1, \ldots, X_n$ be independent Bernoulli distributed random variables with $\Pr[X_i = 0] = p$. Then $X = X_1 + \cdots + X_N$ follows $\mathsf{Bin}(N, p)$ with expected value Np. Given a probability α, there is an interval I_α which is symmetric about the mean, such that $\Pr[X \in I_\alpha] \geq \alpha$. If N is large enough, then the binomial distribution is well approximated by the normal distribution and it is quite routine to use the normal approximation to obtain $\Pr[X \in I_\alpha]$. Further, given α, the interval I_α is found by converting to standard normal and then using tables for the standard normal distribution.

Denote by u^* a uniform random n-variable polynomial. For our study, we will follow the above statistical approach for u^* in the following settings.

Total Number of Monomials in u^*: Any particular monomial occurs in u^* with probability $1/2$ and is independent of the occurrence of any other monomial. If we denote the 2^n possible monomials of n variables as $m_0, \ldots, m_{2^n-1}$, then we have 2^n random variables $X_0, \ldots, X_{2^n-1}$ where X_i is 1 if m_i is present in u^* and 0 otherwise. The random variables $X_0, \ldots, X_{2^n-1}$ are independent Bernoulli distributed variables with $\Pr[X_i = 1] = 1/2$. The number of monomials in u^* is $X = X_0 + \cdots + X_{2^n-1}$ and follows $\mathsf{Bin}(2^n, 1/2)$.

Number of Monomials of Degree d in u^*: Consider the number of monomials of degree d in u^*. There are a total of $\binom{n}{d}$ such monomials. In a manner similar to the above case, the number of monomials of degree d in u^* follows $\mathsf{Bin}\left(\binom{n}{d}, 1/2\right)$.

Weight of u^*: For any input, the output of u^* is 0 or 1 with probability $1/2$ and this is independent of the output of u^* on any other input. So, as in the case of total number of monomials, the weight of u^* follows $\mathsf{Bin}(2^n, 1/2)$.

Determining Whether a Given Polynomial is 'Non-random': Given a particular n-variable boolean function f, we can compute the total number of monomials in f. If the number of monomials turns out to be 'significantly' away from 2^{n-1}, then this is usually taken as an indication of some kind of non-randomness in f. We will use the term algebraically unbalanced to express the idea that the total number of monomials in f deviates significantly from the expected number of monomials in a uniform random polynomial.

Statistical tests will be conducted as follows. For a probability α, we first compute the interval I_α such that the total number of monomials in u^* will be in I_α with probability at least α. Then the total number of monomials in the given function f is calculated. If this lies outside the interval I_α, then we say that the function f fails the algebraic balancedness test for probability α, or that f is algebraically unbalanced at level α written as AU_α.

In a similar manner we conduct tests on f for monomials of degree d and the weight of f. Given an α, the interval I_α for the weight of f will be the same as that for the total number of monomials. On the other hand, when considering monomials of degree d, the interval $I_\alpha^{(d)}$ will depend on d. This is because the number of trials in the binomial distribution corresponding to monomials of degree d is $\binom{n}{d}$. If the number of monomials of degree d in f is outside the interval $I_\alpha^{(d)}$, then we will say that f is d-algebraically unbalanced at level α, written as d-AU_α. Similarly, if the weight of f is outside the interval I_α, then we say that f is unbalanced at level α, written as U_α.

5 Unbalancedness over First l Output Bits

This section generalizes the test for unbalancedness of a boolean function f to vectorial boolean functions of dimension l. An l-dimensional vectorial boolean function is defined as $\tilde{f} : \mathbb{F}_2^n \to \mathbb{F}_2^l$, such that

$$\tilde{f}(x_1, \ldots, x_n) = (f_1(x_1, \ldots, x_n), f_2(x_1, \ldots, x_n), \ldots, f_l(x_1, \ldots, x_n))$$

where each $f_i(x_1, x_2, \ldots, x_n)$, $i = 1, 2, \ldots, l$ are n-variable boolean functions. Denote a uniform random vectorial boolean function by $\tilde{u}^*$, where each of its co-ordinates u_i^*, $i = 1, 2, \ldots, l$ behaves as uniformly and independently distributed n-variable polynomials.

Statistics Involved: Let $X_{i,j} \in \{0, 1\}$, $i \in \{1, 2, 3, \ldots, l\}$ and $j \in \{1, 2, 3, \ldots, N\}$, denote mutually independent random variables with $X_{i,j} \sim \mathsf{Ber}(p_i)$ for all $j \in \{1, 2, \ldots, N\}$. Let $X_i = \sum_{j=1}^N X_{i,j}$, $i \in \{1, 2, 3, \ldots, l\}$. Then $X_1, X_2, \ldots, X_l$ are independently distributed with each $X_i \sim \mathsf{Bin}(N, p_i)$. For sufficiently large N, X_i's are well approximated by normal distribution with mean Np_i and variance

$Np_i(1 - p_i)$. Let $Y_i = \frac{X_i - Np_i}{\sqrt{Np_i(1-p_i)}}$. Then the random variables $Y_1, Y_2, \ldots, Y_l$ and hence $Y_1^2, Y_2^2, \ldots, Y_l^2$ are mutually independent with each $Y_i \sim \mathcal{N}(0, 1)$ and $Y_i^2 \sim \chi^2(1)$ (Chi-squared distribution with 1 degree of freedom). Therefore $\sum_{i=1}^{l} Y_i^2 \sim \chi^2(l)$ (Chi-squared distribution with l degree of freedom). For a given α and l degrees of freedom, we therefore can get an interval $I_\alpha = [0, \chi^2(l)_\alpha]$ such that $\Pr\left[\sum_{i=1}^{l} Y_i^2 \in I_\alpha\right] = \alpha$.

Weight of $\tilde{u}^*$: For any input and any coordinate i ($i \in \{1, 2, \ldots, l\}$), the output of u_i^* is 0 or 1 with probability $1/2$ and this is independent on any other input and coordinate i. For a given coordinate i we denote the 2^n ($= N$) possible outputs of the n-variable boolean function u_i^* as $X_{i,0}, X_{i,1}, \ldots, X_{i,2^n-1}$, where $X_{i,j}$ is 1 if the jth output of u_i^* is 0 and 0 otherwise. Given i, the random variables $X_{i,0}, X_{i,1}, \ldots, X_{i,2^n-1}$ are independent Bernoulli distributed variables with $\Pr[X_{i,j} = 1] = 1/2$. Thus the number of zeros in the 2^n outputs of u_i^* is $X_i = \sum_{j=0}^{2^n-1} X_{i,j}$ and follows $\mathsf{Bin}(2^n, 1/2)$. For $n \geq 5$, X_i's are well approximated by $\mathcal{N}(2^{n-1}, 2^{n-2})$. Hence, the mutually independent random variables $Y_i^2 = \left(\frac{X_i - 2^{n-1}}{\sqrt{2^{n-2}}}\right)^2 \sim \chi^2(1)$ for all $i \in \{1, 2, \ldots, l\}$. Therefore, $\sum_{i=1}^{l} Y_i^2 \sim \chi^2(l)$.

Determining a l-Dimensional Vectorial Boolean Function to Be 'Non-random': Given an l-dimensional vectorial boolean function $\tilde{f}$ in variables $x_1, x_2, \ldots, x_n$, we construct its l-dimensional truth table. For each of the 2^n possible values of the variables $x_1, x_2, \ldots, x_n$, we consider the corresponding values of $\tilde{f}(x_1, x_2, \ldots, x_n)$. This corresponds to the l-dimensional truth table of $\tilde{f}$. Each coordinate i of this l-dimensional truth table individually corresponds to the truth table of f_i. Let n_i denote the number of zeros in the truth table corresponding to f_i. Compute $\sum_{i=1}^{l} \left(\frac{n_i - 2^{n-1}}{\sqrt{2^{n-2}}}\right)^2$ For a given α and l, if $\sum_{i=1}^{l} \left(\frac{n_i - 2^{n-1}}{\sqrt{2^{n-2}}}\right)^2 > \chi^2(l)_\alpha$ then we say that the l-dimensional vectorial boolean function $\tilde{f}$ is unbalanced at level α, written as $\mathsf{U}_{l,\alpha}$

6   Searching for (Algebraically) Unbalanced Polynomials

As mentioned earlier, the first output bit of Trivium can be written as a boolean function of 80 key and 80 IV variables. Since, it is infeasible to handle 160-variable boolean functions, we have used the following strategy to search for unbalanced polynomials.

1. Fix n to be an integer which is at most 30.
2. Out of the 80 key variables, choose n key variables.
3. Set the remaining $80 - n$ key variables and 80 IV variables to random binary values. This defines the first output bit to be a function f of the n key variables.

4. Use either Method-1 or Method-2 to obtain both the truth table representation and the algebraic normal form of the first output bit.

5. Determine whether f is AU_α, $d\text{-}\mathsf{AU}_\alpha$, U_α or $\mathsf{U}_{l,\alpha}$. For all the test except $\mathsf{U}_{l,\alpha}$ we have used 6 values $\alpha_1, \ldots, \alpha_6$ with $\alpha_i = 1 - 1/2^{i+1}$ to conduct the tests. These values roughly correspond to 75%, 87.5%, 93.75%, 96.88%, 98.44% and 99.22% probabilities respectively. For $\mathsf{U}_{l,\alpha}$ the value of α was set at 99.5%.

Note that the above method randomly searches for a function f which fails one or more of the tests. For a fixed n, Steps 2 and 3 above perform the task of selecting an f; Step 4 performs the task of generating the ANF of f; and finally Step 5 performs the test on f. If f fails one or more of the tests, then this f is reported.

The tests for different values of α are not independent. For $i > j$, $\alpha_i > \alpha_j$ and so, $I_{\alpha_i} \supset I_{\alpha_j}$. As a consequence, if a function f is AU_{α_i} then it is also AU_{α_j}. Similar comments hold for $d\text{-}\mathsf{AU}_\alpha$ and U_α.

6.1   Experimental Results

The experiments were conducted by taking values of $n = 10, 20$ and 30. Table 1 gives some polynomials for $n = 10, 20, 30$, which are U_{α_6}, i.e., these polynomials are unbalanced at level α_6. In the Table the column "Key Variables" indicate the key bit positions that were treated as variables. The columns "Key Constant" and "IV Constant" gives the values of $80 - n$ and 80 bits of the key and IV bits which were set to constant values.

Consider once more what it means for a polynomial to be unbalanced at level α_6. With probability α_6, i.e., with about 99% probability, the weight of a uniform random function will be in the interval I_{α_6}. Here we report examples of f whose weight lies outside the interval I_{α_6}. This indicates significant unbalancedness.

Table 1. Table showing list of polynomials which are U_{α_6}. The values given in the table are for $n = 10, 20, 30$ and 1152 key initialization rounds of TRIVIUM.

n	Key Variables	Key Constant	IV Constant	Number of 0's
		OX452D5AA716418A9CC	OXBC925DE125682B159CB4	465
		OX1476803AD7850AD36	OXA1D62667224E6CF221CF	465
		OX31D5EC5914E3D922F	OXE24571405777B5521A	555
	1, 4, 22, 38, 42, 44, 53, 56, 61, 78	OX54CD8D3B53FC0A114	OXD4702BB150946D98D944	556
10		OX238009F2E69728CB8	OX68131089DB607D1981F1	556
		OX53DB1C63D36BB4FD2	OXCF5050997F8601AB88EF	558
		OX42F216A6B2AFCEC17	OX30E66D573F151F784B58	560
		OX17485DC470A73061E	OXD54A1D5A59055062EFB6	571

Continued on next page

Table 1 – *Continued from previous page*

n	Key Variables	Key Constant	IV Constant	Number of 0's
20	15, 16, 20, 27, 31, 37, 41, 45, 58, 73	OX27F50AF693342B6F9	OX706CCD7801037A0A49	437
	0, 1, 9, 10, 14, 19, 27, 29, 41, 42, 52, 55, 62, 64, 68, 69, 71, 75, 78, 79	OX3625E972822DB6A	OXB2D91DF4E87047E9B8C6	522657
		OX80F5C4876AADE17	OXA380363693475CFCCEB	522768
		OXB7521EE35C15C4B	OX309D70CFFD406A96299A	522860
		OXBCEFBB60D3A6BAF	OXB0EC6893275307067F03	522862
		OXCD8AC4B29BEE0B1	OX1DFF5B9FFE4363C2F1A3	522902
30	1, 4, 7, 9, 10, 12, 13, 14, 15, 21, 25, 27, 30, 31, 32, 33, 34, 44, 52, 54, 55, 56, 58, 59, 62, 66, 69, 70, 74, 79	OX290C10B0294D2	OX586A33527C2928DDE2C6	536920658
	7, 15, 20, 21, 22, 26, 29, 30, 32, 33, 34, 41, 42, 49, 52, 54, 55, 56, 57, 59, 60, 63, 64, 65, 66, 72, 75, 76, 78, 79	OX1FD41217D312F	OXC8C051B0D49C69D1A7DD	536822130
		OX12C5E491E4B6F	OX99E4748853D60D6617EC	536920867

Table 2, gives some polynomials for $n = 10, 20, 30$, which are AU_{α_6}, i.e., these polynomials are algebraically unbalanced at level α_6. Further, the entries d in the column "Monomial Degrees" indicate that the corresponding function is also $d\text{-}\mathsf{AU}_{\alpha_6}$. The entry "None" in the column "Monomial Degrees" means that the corresponding function is not $d\text{-}\mathsf{AU}_{\alpha_6}$ for any value of $d = 2, 3, \ldots, n - 2$. Again we note that the reported functions show algebraic unbalancedness at a level corresponding to 99.22% probability which indicates a significant deviation.

Table 2. Table showing list of polynomials which are AU_{α_6}. Some of them are also $d\text{-}\mathsf{AU}_{\alpha_6}$. The values given in the table are for $n = 10, 20, 30$ and 1152 key initialization rounds of TRIVIUM.

n	Key Variables	Key Constant	IV Constant	Monomial Degrees
10	1, 4, 22, 38, 42, 44, 53, 56, 61, 78	OX37FE4B0255D1D295C	OXD70079FAE0F0308EC206	6, 8
		OX457B6B0466DE7552E	OXD167CC3093E7E699466	None
		OX0484EB9A3E80085D	OX9B10785F6BF67CA8D5CB	None
		OX243E3DFA82D00EE44	OXB4526FDF61F96D7FCAE3	None
	15, 16, 20, 27, 31, 37, 41, 45, 58, 73	OX5EE252240CE406D5	OX3F0E2249DE7C031CF797	None
20	0, 1, 9, 10, 14, 19, 27, 29, 41, 42, 52, 55, 62, 64, 68, 69, 71, 75, 78, 79	OX56B4A18579E0D3E	OXAC576EF0BDDE67E72619	None
		OXFC12A46241151AD	OX10E6744E590F46973ADD	13
		OXADC520A5DA98587	OX77EC7B17675B6489CAD8	None
		OXC6AFA4B133A47F7	OX61207A01BCC272B683F9	None
		OX43ED55256B3CFF5	OX822E158DE22B7390747F	None
		OXAA1BE875BC0B948	OXE49D3F5E9DF3726567A	10
		OX44B684623514BE0	OX9CB0767A4B911C07655B	13
		OXF9BB1A903D2B55A	OXBEFF617BF05E74ED8172	11
30	7, 15, 20, 21, 22, 26, 29, 30, 32, 33, 34, 41, 42, 49, 52, 54, 55, 56, 57, 59, 60, 63, 64, 65, 66, 72, 75, 76, 78, 79	OXE65F1294C96A	OXEB482AFBDFE04F8DAD56	14
		OX128D80C2688E3	OX3CF5643BE9AD30EAC0C8	None
		OX199D831A8D833	OX9F7651D0129823F00C61	None
		OX1DBD945A6AD33	OXDB855A93A2834AC2FE5C	15

Experiments to test $U_{l,\alpha}$ were done by taking values of $n = 20, 30$ and $l = 8$. Tests were done by setting $\alpha = 0.995$. Table 3 gives examples of polynomials which are $U_{8,0.995}$ for $n = 20, 30$. For $n = 20$, we found 4 such polynomials whereas for $n = 30$ we found 6 polynomials.

Table 3. Table showing $U_{8,0.995}$ polynomials for $n = 20, 30$

n	Key Variables	Key Constant	IV Constant
20	0, 4, 10, 11, 18, 19, 20, 21, 29, 30, 32, 35, 38, 41, 42, 43, 45, 56, 66, 69	0XE83EDFD172DA59E	0XD6985433DD11269B7EEC
		0X8976F5F031C8922	0X7F8322315CFB6675E72C
		0X671FA8E37FA1559	0X52CCAD8EF5C7C69766A
		0X25FB47658CE713C	0X73D27D4741280A814760
30	0, 2, 3, 4, 7, 8, 12, 19, 23, 26, 30, 33, 35, 37, 38, 39, 42, 43, 44, 49, 54, 58, 60, 62, 63, 64, 65, 70, 72, 76	0X3646D112845B2	0XB1E95646DCFA6FF10729
		0X259294BDB83A1	0X6028CA379F720ABC080
		0X11C4515398DDF	0XCEB11DDCCDCE6CD72BC1
		0X188CF40F48433	0XE2F81539EA2F476236B3
	0, 1, 5, 6, 7, 12, 13, 14, 21, 24, 36, 37, 40, 43, 47, 52, 55, 56, 58, 61, 63, 64, 65, 68, 72, 73, 75, 77, 78, 79	0X1067524FF3553	0XD91F545A23C53ADC5796
		0X2588D2C38E8BF	0X388A1E1866F8247F8D51

We note that our experiments did not find any polynomial which simultaneously fail the tests for balancedness, total number of monomials and monomials of certain degrees at level α_6. On the other hand, as we go down from level α_6 to level α_1, the experiments find more and more examples of polynomials simultaneously failing the tests for balancedness, total number of monomials and monomials of certain degree. Some examples are noted below and the details are given in the appendix.

1. Table 5 (Appendix A) gives a few polynomials which simultaneously fails the test for balancedness and the test for the total number of monomials at level α_4. In addition, the table also gives the monomial degrees for which the test fails. We found 3 polynomials for $n = 10$ and 2 polynomials for $n = 30$ which had failed the test. However, we did not find any example for $n = 20$.
2. Tables 4, 5, 6, 7, 8 (Appendix A) give examples of polynomials which simultaneously fail the three tests at levels $\alpha_5, \alpha_4, \alpha_3, \alpha_2$ and α_1, respectively. In case of $\alpha = \alpha_5$, we can see from Table 4 that corresponding to $n = 10$ we have only two polynomials which failed the tests, whereas we could not find any such examples for $n = 20, 30$. However, when the value of α was relaxed to α_1, we found 45, 61 and 28 polynomials for $n = 10, 20$ and 30, respectively. Due to space constraint Table 8 gives 27 and 38 polynomials corresponding to $n = 10$ and 20 (for the full table refer to [SS14]). The tables also show a steady increase in the number of monomials of a particular degree failing the test as α decreases.

7   Conclusion

In this paper, we have reported results of experiments conducted on the boolean function representing the first output bit of full TRIVIUM. These results show that by suitably restricting some of the input variables to constant values, it is possible to obtain polynomials which deviate from a uniform random polynomial in a statistically quantifiable manner. Our results may be considered as showing some kind of 'non-randomness' in full TRIVIUM. This is to be contrasted with the experimental evidence of 'non-randomness' after 885 rounds reported in [ADMS09] using the complicated machinery of cube testers. We note on the one hand, that our results do not indicate any weakness in TRIVIUM, and on the other hand, that similar tests can be carried out on other ciphers.

At this point, we do not have any theoretical explanations for the experimentally obtained observations. Looking for such observations can form the task of future research.

References

ADMS09. Aumasson, J.-P., Dinur, I., Meier, W., Shamir, A.: Cube Testers and Key Recovery Attacks on Reduced-Round MD6 and Trivium. In: Dunkelman, O. (ed.) FSE 2009. LNCS, vol. 5665, pp. 1–22. Springer, Heidelberg (2009)

DCP. De Cannière, C., Preneel, B.: Trivium-specifications. eSTREAM, ECRYPT Stream Cipher Project, Report 2005/030 (2005)

DS09. Dinur, I., Shamir, A.: Cube Attacks on Tweakable Black Box Polynomials. In: Joux, A. (ed.) EUROCRYPT 2009. LNCS, vol. 5479, pp. 278–299. Springer, Heidelberg (2009)

EJT07. Englund, H., Johansson, T., Sönmez Turan, M.: A Framework for Chosen IV Statistical Analysis of Stream Ciphers. In: Srinathan, K., Rangan, C.P., Yung, M. (eds.) INDOCRYPT 2007. LNCS, vol. 4859, pp. 268–281. Springer, Heidelberg (2007)

Fil02. Filiol, É.: A New Statistical Testing for Symmetric Ciphers and Hash Functions. In: Deng, R.H., Qing, S., Bao, F., Zhou, J. (eds.) ICICS 2002. LNCS, vol. 2513, pp. 342–353. Springer, Heidelberg (2002)

FKM08. Fischer, S., Khazaei, S., Meier, W.: Chosen IV Statistical Analysis for Key Recovery Attacks on Stream Ciphers. In: Vaudenay, S. (ed.) AFRICACRYPT 2008. LNCS, vol. 5023, pp. 236–245. Springer, Heidelberg (2008)

FV13. Fouque, P.-A., Vannet, T.: Improving Key Recovery to 784 and 799 Rounds of Trivium Using Optimized Cube Attacks. In: Moriai, S. (ed.) FSE 2013. LNCS, vol. 8424, pp. 502–517. Springer, Heidelberg (2013)

Jou09. Joux, A.: Algorithmic cryptanalysis. CRC Press (2009)

O'N07. O'Neil, S.: Algebraic Structure Defectoscopy. In: Special ECRYPT Workshop–Tools for Cryptanalysis (2007)

Rad06. Raddum, H.: Cryptanalytic Results on Trivium. Technical Report 2006/039, eSTREAM, ECRYPT Stream Cipher Project, Report (2006), http://www.ecrypt.eu.org/stream/papersdir/2006/039.ps

Saa06. Saarinen, M.-J.O.: Chosen-IV Statistical Attacks on eSTREAM Stream Ciphers. In: Proc. Stream Ciphers Revisited SASC (2006)

Sam13.   Samajder, S., Sarkar, P.: Fast Multiplication of the Algebraic Normal Forms of Two Boolean Functions. In: Budaghyan, L., Helleseth, T., Parker, M.G. (eds.) WCC 2013, pp. 373–385 (2013),
http://www.selmer.uib.no/WCC2013/pdfs/Samajder.pdf

SS14.   Samajder, S., Sarkar, P.: Some randomness experiments on trivium. Cryptology ePrint Archive, Report 2014/211 (2014), http://eprint.iacr.org/

TK07.   Turan, M.S., Kara, O.: Linear Approximations for 2-round TRIVIUM. In: Proc. First International Conference on Security of Information and Networks (SIN 2007), pp. 96–105 (2007)

Vie07.   Vielhaber, M.: Breaking One.Fivium By AIDA: An Algebraic IV Differential Attack. Technical Report 2007/413, Cryptology ePrint Archive, Report (2007), http://eprint.iacr.org/2007/413

A   Tables

Table 4. Table showing list of polynomials which are both AU_{α_5} and U_{α_5}. Some of them are also d-AU_{α_5}. The values given in the table are for $n = 10, 20, 30$ and 1152 key initialization rounds of TRIVIUM.

n	Key Variables	Key Constant	IV Constant	Monomial Degrees
10	1, 4, 22, 38, 42, 44, 53, 56, 61, 78	OX37BDD3EAD0BAFABC0	OXDB565D9DB98F4E3389C5	None
		OX47E214EB5727E04C9	OXD34F684B1055DAECE93	7

Table 5. Table showing list of polynomials which are both AU_{α_4} and U_{α_4}. Some of them are also d-AU_{α_4}. The values given in the table are for $n = 10, 20, 30$ and 1152 key initialization rounds of TRIVIUM.

n	Key Variables	Key Constant	IV Constant	Monomial Degrees
10	1, 4, 22, 38, 42, 44, 53, 56, 61, 78	OX37BDD3EAD0BAFABC0	OXDB565D9DB98F4E3389C5	None
		OX47E214EB5727E04C9	OXD34F684B1055DAECE93	7
		OX4547D85442C8D68CF	OXD08829A188F6241E7C2D	5, 8
30	7, 15, 20, 21, 22, 26, 29, 30, 32, 33, 34, 41, 42, 49, 52, 54, 55, 56, 57, 59, 60, 63, 64, 65, 66, 72, 75, 76, 78, 79	OX11D3963CFE658	OXE9F618EC66862A0DEB4E	12
		OX191766116C74F	OX1E8B7D71045E0F56A4EA	4, 24

Table 6. Table showing list of polynomials which are both AU_{α_3} and U_{α_3}. Some of them are also d-AU_{α_3}. The values given in the table are for $n = 10, 20, 30$ and 1152 key initialization rounds of TRIVIUM.

n	Key Variables	Key Constant	IV Constant	Monomial Degrees
10	1, 4, 22, 38, 42, 44, 53, 56, 61, 78	OX37BDD3EAD0BAFABC0	OXDB565D9DB98F4E3389C5	None
		OX47E214EB5727E04C9	OXD34F684B1055DAECE93	2, 7
		OX4547D85442C8D68CF	OXD08829A188F6241E7C2D	5, 8
20	0, 1, 9, 10, 14, 19, 27, 29, 41, 42, 52, 55, 62, 64, 68, 69, 71, 75, 78, 79	OX6725535534737CA	OXDDAE21B901422A1643A	None
		OXDDAE21B901422A1643A	OXF51C70E932C18D17D41	None

Continued on next page

Table 6 – *Continued from previous page*

n	Key Variables	Key Constant	IV Constant	Monomial Degrees
30	7, 15, 20, 21, 22, 26, 29, 30, 32, 33, 34, 41, 42, 49, 52, 54, 55, 56, 57, 59, 60, 63, 64, 65, 66, 72, 75, 76, 78, 79	OX11D3963CFE658	OXE9F618EC66862A0DEB4E	12
		OX3C25D092EFEF9	OXEE0C5AA49BA676F04E05	14, 15
		OX613242AFA99E	OX74996C308B57426EC1FF	4, 13
		OX191766116C74F	OX1E8B7D71045E0F56A4EA	4, 24

Table 7. Table showing list of polynomials which are both AU_{α_2} and U_{α_2}. Some of them are also d-AU_{α_2}. The values given in the table are for $n = 10, 20, 30$ and 1152 key initialization rounds of TRIVIUM.

n	Key Variables	Key Constant	IV Constant	Monomial Degrees
10	1, 4, 22, 38, 42, 44, 53, 56, 61, 78	OX37BDD3EAD0BAFABC0	OXDB565D9DB98F4E3389C5	3, 4
		OX47E214EB5727E04C9	OXD34F684B1055DAECE93	2, 7
		OX4547D85442C8D68CF	OXD08829A188F6241E7C2D	4, 5, 8
		OX22C82FA5C4FF1FFA7	OX8E6C7CCC6DA42DE02582	6
		OX46F73734324A8C3CF	OXED6F602BFE6161C4B002	5, 7, 8
		OX548E1A39B23F3483B	OX2C2B1447188F2DF15053	6, 8
		OX52A20EB6B6861FD2B	OX69EF224FC6FB72AC6C37	2, 3
		OX243E3DFA82D00EE44	OXB4526FDF61F96D7FCAE3	5, 6
		OX21FEF73EB0DC5739A	OX7598278A31B96B6E06F5	3
		OX36B1281D43A9240B3	OXE58A191A1E6C333C8EFD	3, 5
		OX1185DD59742FE8169	OX89B62A60C21C42A0E6B2	4,
		OX37FE4B0255D1D295C	OXD70079FAE0F0308EC206	6, 7, 8
20	0, 1, 9, 10, 14, 19, 27, 29, 41, 42, 52, 55, 62, 64, 68, 69, 71, 75, 78, 79	OX6725535534737CA	OXDDAE21B901422A1643A	8, 12, 15, 17
		OXC481FD7BC1F523	OXC37057969DFB005C79DC	5, 6, 8, 9
		OXDF7305B0CFDB228	OXC9C17DF5198908297669	8
		OX3480FFC0AD084D6	OXF51C70E932C18D17D41	9, 15
		OX80A26F93FFE786E	OX49025F652E977970AAA3	3, 5, 6, 9
		OX99997304FBA97AB	OX91A0123D835369D66539	3, 10, 11
		OX1438B4C6E410610	OXEC881E225AE17BE12D06	6, 16
		OX2B8619E6B23FD69	OXF24C75F66F5957352674	None
		OX2E93E577A837AAC	OXF50C2B06C5B100F1D712	2, 14
		OXFDAFFE872B1ECA6	OX63F0791A5BD92EA49167	2, 7, 10
		OX1E15EFE0723A1A0	OXAFF45320480C32FE05AD	11, 12, 13, 14, 17
		OX94252897FEBA	OX40B53BED60BA2A4EF7BD	7
		OX5A4644E0DCF37F1	OXAFE71BE0360E0C918B9C	3, 9, 13
		OXAA07D7C6F262C91	OX4F821468B1891D2AD371	2, 3, 4, 12
		OX748AA0B4C4431F6	OX6BB3415153E252D74428	9
		OX82641E96DDFE210	OXA045545ADF754FE49440	4, 16, 17
30	7, 15, 20, 21, 22, 26, 29, 30, 32, 33, 34, 41, 42, 49, 52, 54, 55, 56, 57, 59, 60, 63, 64, 65, 66, 72, 75, 76, 78, 79	OX11D3963CFE658	OXE9F618EC66862A0DEB4E	12, 15, 18
		OX3C25D092EFEF9	OXEE0C5AA49BA676F04E05	14, 15, 23

Continued on next page

Table 7 – *Continued from previous page*

n	Key Variables	Key Constant	IV Constant	Monomial Degrees
30	7, 15, 20, 21, 22, 26, 29, 30, 32, 33, 34, 41, 42, 49, 52, 54, 55, 56, 57, 59, 60, 63, 64, 65, 66, 72, 75, 76, 78, 79	0XCDCA70B4903D	0X28094F93A84519B6030	2, 12, 21, 26
		0X613242AFA99E	0X74996C308B57426EC1FF	4, 13, 15, 19, 24, 26, 27
		0X191766116C74F	0X1E8B7D71045E0F56A4EA	4, 18, 24, 25

Table 8. Table showing list of polynomials which are both AU_{α_1} and U_{α_1}. Some of them are also d-AU_{α_1}. The values given in the table are for $n = 10, 20, 30$ and 1152 key initialization rounds of TRIVIUM.

n	Key Variables	Key Constant	IV Constant	Monomial Degrees
10	1, 4, 22, 38, 42, 44, 53, 56, 61, 78	0X37BDD3EAD0BAFABC0	0XDB565D9DB98F4E3389C5	2, 3, 4, 5
		0X47E214EB5727E04C9	0XD34F684B1055DAECE93	2, 4, 7
		0X4547D85442C8D68CF	0XD08829A188F6241E7C2D	4, 5, 8
		0X46F73734324A8C3CF	0XED6F602BFE6161C4B002	5, 7, 8
		0X548E1A39B23F3483B	0X2C2B1447188F2DF15053	6, 7, 8
		0X32C3B8564711127E2	0XC3B65FA580064682A886	2, 5, 6, 7, 8
		0X36700C6F525F4A15E	0X76C0CA72E4037279E52	2, 5, 7
		0X52A20EB6B6861FD2B	0X69EF224FC6FB72AC6C37	2, 3, 6
		0X243E3DFA82D00EE44	0XB4526FDF61F96D7FCAE3	5, 6, 7
		0X36B1281D43A9240B3	0XE58A191A1E6C333C8EFD	2, 3, 5
		0X25964FF8044895C95	0XCFC776D1C4E100F35C85	2, 4, 5
		0X2628BA81850F8F769	0X1FCF571CE4612534B608	4, 8
		0X043DACA1A2026DBDA	0XBDC5DCD77F921AABDF6	4, 7
		0X2126745C279E5A10C	0X1248772E03E133CE0B7B	2, 7
		0X368252990744C0C7	0X74DF32D819F351C27B0E	2, 3, 4
		0X52FFFC0FF6FD88EBD	0XF66572321FFA19728935	3, 7
		0X14B0825030BA0A96B	0X207C5A11622E7FE89689	2, 3, 7
		0X568F9EDC3FA5CFC5	0XCD8D6086AF815B848C24	3, 6, 8
		0X37A8A2D3F4AD45193	0XD49B28D3ABC66F27C37E	3, 6
		0X457B6B0466DE7552E	0XD167CC3093E7E699466	5, 6
		0X2188425AC63CCD33F	0X90C929DD67D3678472EE	2, 4, 5, 6, 8
		0X2454FEF2819CFDFE8	0X9E71576A5F36051743D5	6, 7
		0X37FE4B0255D1D295C	0XD70079FAE0F0308EC206	4, 6, 7, 8
		0X53CD508F74BBC7DBE	0XC37E2A7F2F8164D022BB	5, 7, 8
		0X4708A09334FCAFE4F	0X4A4C60F2FECB3B1FFA4F	2, 3, 5
		0X11CCD131147B71B01	0X82C85493CE4525CC267A	4, 7
		0X073A6C0377AF88B83	0X6351165578DB3B77F014	3, 5
20	0, 1, 9, 10, 14, 19, 27, 29, 41, 42, 52, 55, 62, 64, 68, 69, 71, 75, 78, 79	0XCD8AC4B29BEE0B1	0X1DFF5B9FFE4363C2F1A3	2, 5, 8, 13, 17
		0X6725535534737CA	0XDDAE21B901422A1643A	8, 12, 15, 16, 17
		0XC481FD7BC1F523	0XC37057969DFB005C79DC	5, 6, 8, 9, 14
		0XDF7305B0CFDB228	0XC9C17DF5198908297669	4, 6, 8, 17, 18

Continued on next page

Table 8 – *Continued from previous page*

n	Key Variables	Key Constant	IV Constant	Monomial Degrees
20	0, 1, 9, 10, 14, 19, 27, 29, 41, 42, 52, 55, 62, 64, 68, 69, 71, 75, 78, 79	OX3480FFC0AD084D6	OXF51C70E932C18D17D41	4, 6, 9, 14, 15
		OXF79DC891384AFF0	OXDDAF2C635F1725E5722C	2, 3, 5, 11, 15, 17
		OX80A26F93FFE786E	OX49025F652E977970AAA3	3, 4, 5, 6, 9, 14
		OX1438B4C6E410610	OXEC881E225AE17BE12D06	2, 6, 7, 9, 16
		OX3907E66406C1230	OXCC4F643389D174E09308	9, 11, 12, 17
		OX1C2904C43FF6577	OXE73A4739E4C117D70E8E	7, 11, 12, 13, 16, 17
		OX2E93E577A837AAC	OXF50C2B06C5B100F1D712	2, 3, 5, 13, 14
		OXFDAFFE872B1ECA6	OX63F0791A5BD92EA49167	2, 5, 7, 10, 15
		OX1B3537B58870F55	OXA33A411FC4173976088F	2, 3, 5, 8, 9, 10, 14, 15, 18
		OX1E15EFE0723A1A0	OXAFF45320480C32FE05AD	2, 6, 11, 12, 13, 14, 15, 17
		OX7E51F8E40591536	OXB9C6CEF795453064BE6	9, 10, 14, 15, 17
		OXD241FF6460C6208	OX5C725E6A96F9353ECCE8	2, 5, 12, 14, 18
		OX69219DE1A75C6B5	OX59FB6A44546208BBA473	5, 8, 9, 12, 13, 15
		OX8CA5215750A80AE	OXBBFE302CAEC030A95C66	2, 7, 11, 18
		OX92E4EE44F4AA9B0	OXB2E35370E80D3FA438FE	5, 7, 8, 9, 10, 11, 12, 14
		OXC906517717370E8	OX407C62FEAAD57DE22435	6, 8, 9, 15
		OX5E2587E52504105	OX492770685C260EB94076	3, 4, 5, 7, 9, 11, 14
		OX66BE1B647D74852	OXE2B64E025081086192F3	2, 4, 5, 7, 8, 11, 13
		OXC987FF2679818EA	OXECBC1922F4E82FE0E298	3, 9, 14, 15, 16
		OXA01F4042A39D2AF	OXB42E343741AE2885A4B8	8, 10, 11, 15, 16
		OX6FEDB601C5D0F7	OXACF51C7A59AC427CBA18	2, 4, 13, 14, 16, 17, 18
		OX349068A2D3BE11B	OXF51A7B67A45C5173EDB0	2, 6, 9, 10, 11, 12
		OX9904566610C1359	OX5C921B727602478B4F1F	2, 11, 13, 18
		OX631BFA24A283F98	OX8BEE5BDF986177DEFCB7	2, 4, 7, 8, 14, 15, 17
		OX41B6D6E060B45	OXF4301269A0A373516F83	4, 6, 7, 9, 15
		OX6AE3E77490E6D0B	OXED4B6FCC7E5B1FFAA681	2, 6, 12, 15, 17
		OXF9BB1A903D2B55A	OXBEFF617BF05E74ED8172	6, 9, 11, 18
		OXADB103911781696	OX78001622345E7535AF89	2, 3, 10, 12, 13, 14
		OXD4BAF7074479E09	OX3CB7239F46CD1A18C135	5, 6, 13, 16, 18
		OXBCF4D6769BCEFB	OX6D344C7B4AC745BC07FC	10, 11, 12, 18
		OXD989E1257E60721	OX85F9933760D63491E6D	2, 8, 13, 18
		OXFE4EC2B5DF70C87	OX7E0D7707ABF24E5811D8	4, 7, 8, 10, 11,14, 17
		OXAA07D7C6F262C91	OX4F821468B1891D2AD371	2, 3, 4, 5, 7, 12
		OX82641E96DDFE210	OXA045545ADF754FE49440	4, 12, 13, 16, 17

Continued on next page

Table 8 – *Continued from previous page*

n	Key Variables	Key Constant	IV Constant	Monomial Degrees
		OX2A3B12E5B3AAA	OX9107625D556D1E48A3B5	3, 7, 13, 16, 17, 18, 20, 23, 25
		OX11D3963CFE658	OXE9F618EC66862A0DEB4E	9, 12, 13, 14, 15, 18
		OXF8534CF8A0C4	OXCEDD5CCE04F12DF6FA42	7, 9, 10, 14, 15, 18
		OXE0D05859F75D	OXDE0D17F6F4A032F4345A	2, 4, 5, 8, 13, 15, 16, 18
		OX1767659F97A78	OXDB0E189FAA7523B7F38C	3, 5, 11, 12, 13, 16, 18, 19, 24
		OX3C25D092EFEF9	OXEE0C5AA49BA676F04E05	4, 8, 10, 14, 15, 23, 24
		OX358F63BC9862E	OX2B8A12AF7C7513BFB545	4, 5, 8, 10, 14, 15, 16, 23, 25
		OXCDCA70B4903D	OX28094F93A84519B6030	2, 6, 12, 16, 21, 24, 26
		OX186E1140CAE7A	OXE5893222F3CF2AD91C84	3, 10, 17, 21, 24
		OXF5633C0E0766	OX3A2161ED1A9A6C545C99	6, 8, 14, 16, 17, 18, 23, 25
30	7, 15, 20, 21, 22, 26, 29, 30, 32, 33, 34, 41, 42, 49, 52, 54, 55, 56, 57, 59, 60, 63, 64, 65, 66, 72, 75, 76, 78, 79	OX3EF1C76CC3786	OX91441019D7A5F99C0E2	5, 8, 15, 16, 19, 22, 26, 27
		OX1E3305EE66BF7	OX84052206580263DB7246	3, 9, 12, 14, 23
		OX2BFEF0DB6F4F7	OX21D64C13071A1E0AA4DF	10, 14, 24, 28
		OX22BE07DCB8255	OX14B48826D4E3EE8AA4A	10, 11, 13, 14, 17, 22, 24, 25
		OX2C53E5CA904F8	OX4CF8318FB91A7BD1C2D0	4, 5, 8, 14, 17, 18, 19, 22, 24, 27
		OX93726691E2D0	OX2C4C389C765606937AF4	6, 10, 15, 18, 19, 13, 16
		OX3ED1D244BD2B1	OXBB5B758E8FB029E57666	2, 6, 7, 8, 15, 23, 25
		OX2DF6C79AE5433	OX920D16223BEE4EB5822E	3, 4, 8, 9, 12, 13, 20
		OX378C02C3FDF2B	OX77681A2286592408308D	3, 10, 11, 13, 15, 22, 23, 26, 28
		OX3B97E24D24147	OX694F280DCB2B108F1385	2, 9, 11, 12, 24, 28
		OXC7294829B50A	OXF303799BF930108F4B0F	4, 8, 11, 15, 16
		OX378763FE6C96	OX2FBC5FB87C8125734B6E	2, 3, 6, 7, 8, 12, 16, 18, 23, 25, 28
		OX3BECF5CC75818	OXC3B33304C9FD300B28F3	5, 12, 14, 17, 19, 21, 22, 23, 24
		OX3049A0E2FB512	OX50986952B94273E8F099	9, 13, 16, 24, 26
		OX313C07B28B127	OX30005763E511714B24C0	10, 11, 17, 18, 25, 26
		OX613242AFA99E	OX74996C308B57426EC1FF	4, 5, 8, 11, 12, 13, 15, 17, 19, 21, 22, 24, 25, 26, 27
		OX5AE80FC1F4DB	OXD5776A122F7F7B0049B1	3, 10, 15, 21, 23, 24
		OX191766116C74F	OX1E8B7D71045E0F56A4EA	4, 13, 17, 18, 24, 25

Randomized Batch Verification of Standard ECDSA Signatures

Sabyasachi Karati, Abhijit Das, and Dipanwita Roychoudhury

Department of Computer Science and Engineering
IIT Kharagpur, India
{skarati,abhij,drc}@cse.iitkgp.ernet.in

Abstract. In AfricaCrypt 2012, several algorithms are proposed for the batch verification of ECDSA signatures. In this paper, we propose three randomization methods for these batch-verification algorithms. Our first proposal is based on Montgomery ladders, and the second on computing square-roots in the underlying field. Both these techniques use numeric arithmetic only. Our third proposal exploits symbolic computations leading to a seminumeric algorithm. We theoretically and experimentally establish that for standard ECDSA signatures, our seminumeric randomization algorithm in tandem with the batch-verification algorithm S2′ gives the best speedup over individual verification. If each ECDSA signature contains an extra bit to uniquely identify the correct y-coordinate of the elliptic-curve point appearing in the signature, then the second numeric randomization algorithm followed by the naive batch-verification algorithm N′ yields the best performance gains. We detail our study for NIST prime and Koblitz curves.

Keywords: ECDSA, Elliptic curve, Koblitz curve, Montgomery ladder, Symbolic computation, Batch verification, Randomization.

1 Introduction

An ECDSA signature on a message M is a triple (M, r, s), where r is the x-coordinate of an elliptic-curve point R, and s is an integer that absorbs the hash of M. Both r and s are reduced modulo the size n of the elliptic-curve group. During verification, two scalars u, v are computed using modulo n arithmetic, and the point R is reconstructed as $R = uP + vQ$, where P is the base point in the elliptic-curve group, and Q is the signer's public key. Verification succeeds if and only if $x(R) = r$.

Suppose that we want to verify a batch of t ECDSA signatures (M_i, r_i, s_i). For the i-th signature, the verification equation is $R_i = u_i P + v_i Q_i$. The t signatures can be combined as

$$\sum_{i=1}^{t} R_i = \left(\sum_{i=1}^{t} u_i \right) P + \left(\sum_{i=1}^{t} v_i Q_i \right). \tag{1}$$

Since the y-coordinates of R_i are not available in the signatures, we cannot straightaway compute the sum on the left side. In AfricaCrypt 2012, several batch-verification algorithms are proposed to solve this problem [1]. The naive algorithms are based upon the

R.S. Chakraborty et al. (Eds.): SPACE 2014, LNCS 8804, pp. 237–255, 2014.

determination of the missing y-coordinate of each R_i using a square-root computation (we have $y_i^2 = r_i^3 + ar_i + b$). The symbolic-manipulation algorithms treat the unknown y-coordinates as symbols. Batch verification involves the eventual elimination of all these y-coordinates from Eqn(1) using the elliptic-curve equation. The symbolic algorithm S2′ turns out to be the fastest of the batch-verification algorithms proposed in [1].

In IndoCrypt 2012, Bernstein et al. [2] propose two attacks on these algorithms. They suggest that these attacks can be largely eliminated by randomizing batch verification (a concept introduced by Naccache et al. [3]). For random non-zero multipliers $\xi_1, \xi_2, \ldots, \xi_t$, the verification equations are now combined as

$$\sum_{i=1}^{t} \xi_i R_i = \left(\sum_{i=1}^{t} \xi_i u_i \right) P + \left(\sum_{i=1}^{t} \xi_i v_i Q_i \right). \tag{2}$$

Since the y-coordinates of R_i are not available, Eqn(2) is not directly applicable. In this paper, we propose three efficient ways of randomizing the batch-verification algorithms of [1]. We mostly concentrate on standard ECDSA signatures. If the ECDSA signature contains an extra bit to identify the correct square-root y of $r^3 + ar + b$ [4], we call this an ECDSA# signature. In another variant known as ECDSA* [4,5], the entire point R replaces r in the signature. Neither ECDSA# nor ECDSA* is accepted as a standard. Since ECDSA* results in an unreasonable expansion in the signature size without any increase in the security, we do not consider this variant in this paper. ECDSA#, however, adds only one extra bit to a signature, and so we study the implications of having this extra bit. Our three randomization techniques are based on the following ideas.

- Montgomery ladders: Given only the x-coordinate of an elliptic-curve point R, one can uniquely obtain the x-coordinate of any non-zero multiple ξR [6]. We first compute $x(\xi_i R_i)$ for all signatures in the batch. Then we feed these x-coordinates to the batch-verification algorithms.
- Numeric computation: We explicitly compute y_i from each r_i by taking a square-root of $r_i^3 + ar_i + b$. In ECDSA#, we uniquely obtain R_i from the extra bit. In ECDSA, we have two possibilities $\pm R$. We start with any possibility and numerically compute ξR or $-\xi R$ using standard elliptic-curve doubling and addition formulas.[1]
- Seminumeric computation (Joye's method): We treat each y_i as a symbol, and compute $\xi_i R_i$ as a point in the form $(h_i, k_i y_i)$, where the field elements h_i and k_i are computed from the knowledge of $r_i = x(R_i)$ alone. We precompute the quantity $r_i^3 + ar_i + b$ and follow a slightly modified version of the standard elliptic-curve scalar-multiplication algorithm. Joye in [7] proves that in prime fields the y-coordinate of $\xi_i R_i$ is of the form $(h_i(r_i), k_i(r_i)y_i)$ for functions h_i, k_i of r_i alone. Here, we complement that study by providing explicit computational determination of h_i, k_i, and exploit this procedure to obtain a randomization algorithm that performs better than the above two methods for standard ECDSA signatures. We also derive such explicit formulas for Koblitz curves.

---

[1] A study of this method is inspired by a comment from an anonymous referee of an earlier version of this paper.

Since the only batch-verification algorithms that deal with standard ECDSA signatures are found in [1], randomizing these algorithms is of practical importance in real-time cryptographic applications like the authentication of messages in vehicular ad hoc networks.

We experiment with the NIST prime family of elliptic curves [8]. Montgomery ladders face a few problems. Each iteration in the scalar-multiplication loop involves one addition and one doubling. More importantly, it is not known how to adapt Montgomery ladders to windowed scalar multiplication.Montgomery's paper [9] proposes some ways of generating short Montgomery chains. As pointed out in [10,11], the creations of the addition chains in these improved variants are rather costly. The practical method of [9] is effective only when the scalar multiplier remains constant, so the addition chain can be precomputed. Since this is not the case with randomizers, we have implemented only the binary ladder. The numeric and the seminumeric randomization algorithms can be adapted to any windowed variant. We theoretically and experimentally establish that the binary Montgomery ladder is slower than the best known windowed variants of the numeric and the seminumeric algorithms. Montgomery arithmetic is efficient for prime curves of the particular form $By^2 = x^3 + Ax^2 + x$. However, the NIST prime curves have large prime orders and cannot be converted to a curve in the Montgomery form which contains the point $(0,0)$ of order two. Point multiplication using Montgomery ladders is more resistant to simple side-channel attacks (SCA) than the numeric and seminumeric methods. In this paper, SCA resistance is not of concern, since verification of signatures uses no private keys.

The rest of this paper is organized as follows. In Section 2, we provide a brief introduction to the ECDSA batch-verification algorithms and the attacks against those. Sections 3 elaborates the three randomization methods introduced above. Section 4 makes a theoretical and experimental comparison of the relative performances of the three methods, and discusses the effects of randomization on the performance of the batch verification of ECDSA and ECDSA# signatures. Section 5 deals with NIST Koblitz curves. Section 6 concludes the paper.

2   Background and Notations

Let (M_i, r_i, s_i), $i = 1, 2, \ldots, t$, be a batch of t ECDSA signatures that we want to verify simultaneously. We work over the elliptic curve

$$y^2 = x^3 + ax + b. \tag{3}$$

defined over a large prime field $\mathbb{F}_p$. We assume that the group $E(\mathbb{F}_p)$ is of prime order n with a generator P. For simplicity, we assume that all of the t signatures come from the same signer, that is, $Q_i = Q$ for all i.

2.1   ECDSA Batch Verification

The right side of Eqn(1) can be computed numerically using two scalar multiplications (or one double scalar multiplication). Let this point be (α, β). If R_i are reconstructed as

$u_i P + v_i Q$, the effort is essentially the same as individual verification. The algorithms of [1] solve this problem in many ways.

The naive method N computes y_i by taking the square root of $r_i^3 + a r_i + b$. Since there are two square roots (in general) for each r_i, the ambiguity in the *sign* of y_i can be removed by trying all of the $m = 2^t$ combinations. If Eqn(1) holds for any of these choices, the batch of signatures is accepted. In ECDSA#, the y_i values can be uniquely identified, and we can avoid trying all the $m = 2^t$ combinations. This variant of the naive method is referred to as N'. If the underlying field is large, the square-root computations may have huge overheads.

Algorithms S1 and S2 avoid this overhead by computing the left side of Eqn(1) symbolically. Each y_i is treated as a symbol satisfying $y_i^2 = r_i^3 + a r_i + b$. Symbolic addition gives $(g(y_1, y_2, \ldots, y_t), h(y_1, y_2, \ldots, y_t)) = (\alpha, \beta)$, where g and h are polynomials in y_i with each y_i-degree $\leqslant 1$.

Algorithm S1 makes a linearization by repeatedly squaring $g(y_1, y_2, \ldots, y_t) = \alpha$ (or multiplying by even-degree monomials). At this stage too, the equations $y_i^2 = r_i^3 + a r_i + b$ are used to keep the y_i-degrees $\leqslant 1$ in each generated equation. The linearized system has $2^{t-1} - 1 = \frac{m}{2} - 1$ variables corresponding to the square-free monomials in $y_1, y_2, \ldots, y_t$ of even degrees. The system is solved by Gaussian elimination. The equation $h(y_1, y_2, \ldots, y_t) = \beta$ is then used to solve for each y_i. Finally, it is verified whether $y_i^2 = r_i^3 + a r_i + b$ for all i.

Algorithm S2 uses a faster elimination trick. The equation $g(y_1, y_2, \ldots, y_t) = \alpha$ is written as $\gamma(y_2, y_3, \ldots, y_t) y_1 + \delta(y_2, y_3, \ldots, y_t)$. Multiplying this by $\gamma y_1 - \delta$ and using $y_1^2 = r_1^3 + a r_1 + b$ gives an equation free from y_1. The other variables $y_2, y_3, \ldots, y_t$ are eliminated one by one in the same way. Eventually, the batch is accepted if we obtain the zero polynomial after all y_i are eliminated.

An improved variant of S1 and S2 significantly speeds up the symbolic-addition phase. Let $\tau = \lceil t/2 \rceil$. Eqn(1) is rewritten as $\sum_{i=1}^{\tau} R_i = (\alpha, \beta) - \sum_{i=\tau+1}^{t} R_i$. The two sides are individually computed symbolically. These variants of S1 and S2 are referred to as S1' and S2'.

2.2   Attacks on ECDSA Batch Verification

In the first attack of Bernstein et al. [2], the batch verifier handles $t - 2$ genuine signatures along with the two forged signatures (r, s) and $(r, -s)$ on the same message M. Since the sum of the elliptic-curve points (r, s) and $(r, -s)$ is $\mathcal{O}$, the entire batch of t signatures is verified as genuine.

In the second attack, the forger knows a valid key pair (d_1, Q_1), and can fool the verifier by a forged signature for any message M_2 under any valid public key Q_2 along with a message M_1 under the public key Q_1. The forger selects a random k_2, computes $R_2 = k_2 P$ and $r_2 = x(R_2)$. For another random s_2, the signature on M_2 under Q_2 is presented as (r_2, s_2). For the message M_1, the signature (r_1, s_1) is computed as $R_1 = r_2 s_2^{-1} Q_2$, $r_1 = x(R_1)$, and $s_1 = (e_1 + r_1 d_1)(k_2 - e_2 s_2^{-1})^{-1}$, where $e_1 = H(m_1)$, $e_2 = H(m_2)$, and H is a secure hash function. Now, $R_1 + R_2$ and $(e_1 s_1^{-1} + e_2 s_2^{-1}) P + r_1 s_1^{-1} Q_1 + r_2 s_2^{-1} Q_2$ have the same value as $(k_2 P + r_2 s_2^{-1} Q_2)$. These forged signatures are verified if they are in the same batch.

Both these attacks become infeasible by the use of randomizers. If the verifier chooses l-bit randomizers, the security of the batch-verification procedure increases by 2^l. The randomizers need not be of full lengths (of lengths close to that of the prime order p of the relevant elliptic-curve group). As discussed in [12], much smaller randomizers typically suffice to make most attacks on batch-verification schemes infeasible. If the underlying field is of size d bits, then the best known algorithms (the square-root methods) to solve the ECDLP take $O(2^{d/2})$ times. As a result, $d/2$-bit randomizers do not degrade the security of the ECDSA scheme. Another possibility is to take $l = 128$ to get 128-bit security independent of the security guarantees of ECDSA.

3   Randomization of ECDSA Batch Verification

For randomizing ECDSA batch verification as per Eqn(2), the basic problem is to compute the x-coordinate $x(\xi R)$ from $r = x(R)$ and an l-bit scalar $\xi = 1\xi_{l-2}\xi_{l-3}\ldots\xi_1\xi_0$.

3.1   Montgomery Ladders

Montgomery ladders are discussed in [13,14,6]. For the sake of completeness, we present the relevant formulas for point addition and doubling. Suppose that $x(P_1) = h_1$, $x(P_2) = h_2$ and $x(P_1 - P_2) = h_4$ are known to us. We can compute $h_3 = x(P_1 + P_2)$ and $h_5 = x(2P_1)$ by Eqns (4) and (5), respectively.

$$h_3 h_4 (h_1 - h_2)^2 = (h_1 h_2 - a)^2 - 4b(h_1 + h_2). \tag{4}$$
$$4h_5(h_1^3 + ah_1 + b) = (h_1^2 - a)^2 - 8bh_1. \tag{5}$$

The above formulas [13] are adapted from Montgomery's original derivation [6]. Fischer et al. [15] propose a slightly improved addition formula given by

$$(h_4 + h_3)(h_1 - h_2)^2 = 2(h_1 + h_2)(h_1 h_2 + a) + 4b.$$

The Montgomery ladder described in Algorithm 1 never uses nor computes the y-coordinate of any point in its repeated double-and-add point-multiplication loop. The loop maintains the invariance $T - S = R$. Since $x(T)$, $x(S)$ and $x(T - S) = x(R)$ are known, we can compute $x(T + S), x(2S)$ and $x(2T)$.

Algorithm 1. Montgomery Ladder for Computing $x(\xi R)$ from ξ and $x(R)$

Initialize $x(S) := x(R)$ and $x(T) := x(2R)$.
For $(i = l - 2, l - 3, \ldots, 1, 0)$ {
    If $(\xi_i = 0)$, assign $x(T) := x(T + S)$ and $x(S) := x(2S)$;
    else assign $x(S) := x(T + S)$ and $x(T) := x(2T)$;
}
Return $x(S)$.

In many cases, using projective coordinates can speed up the Montgomery-ladder loop. Both the x- and the z-coordinates can be computed from the knowledge of $x(R)$ alone (we assume $z(R) = 1$). Some explicit formulas can be found at [16,17].

Fischer et al. [15] propose an optimization of the Montgomery loop. Irrespective of the bit value ξ_i, the loop computes the x- and z-coordinates of two points $P + Q$ and $2P$, where P is one of the points S, T, and Q is the other point. These operations can be combined together yielding a reduced count of field operations. The problem with Algorithm 1 is that no effective windowed adaptation of it is known (see [10,11]).

3.2 Numeric Computation

We first compute a square-root y of $r^3 + ar + b$. The point R is either (r, y) or $(r, -y)$. An ECDSA# signature has enough information to identify which of these two points is the correct R. An ECDSA signature cannot resolve this ambiguity. However, that is not a serious problem, since both ξR and $-\xi R$ have the same x-coordinate. Therefore, we start with any of the two points $\pm R$, and compute its ξ-th multiple using any standard elliptic-curve scalar-multiplication algorithm. The y-coordinate of this multiple is also computed as a byproduct.

A square root of $r^3 + ar + b$ modulo the prime p can be computed by well-known algorithms (like Tonelli-Shanks algorithm). If $p \equiv 3 \pmod 4$, then $(r^3 + ar + b)^{(p+1)/4}$ $\pmod p$ is such a square root. Each square-root finding algorithm essentially requires the cost of an exponentiation in the field $\mathbb{F}_p$.

The numeric method has an important bearing on the naive batch-verification methods N and N′ of [1]. These two algorithms start by computing the square roots of $r_i^3 + ar_i + b$. If these are randomized by the numeric method, the y-coordinates of $\xi_i R_i$ are already available (up to sign in ECDSA, and uniquely in ECDSA#), and need not be computed again from the x-coordinates of $\xi_i R_i$. This lets the naive algorithms save significant time. The symbolic batch-verification methods (like S2′) do not use and therefore do not benefit from an explicit knowledge of the y-coordinates.

The numeric method in the context of ECDSA# has another advantage. Since the points R_i are now known uniquely, we can use multiple scalar multiplication. For example, computing $\xi_1 R_1 + \xi_2 R_2$ in a single double-and-add loop needs only l doubling and at most l addition operations, where l is the length of the randomizers. On the contrary, computing $\xi_1 R_1$ and $\xi_2 R_2$ separately by even the best windowed method requires $2l$ doubling operations and some more additions. Thus, the naive batch-verification algorithm N′ derives an additional boost in its performance from multiple scalar multiplication.

3.3 Seminumeric Computation (Joye's Method)

We treat the y-coordinate of $R = (r, y)$ as a symbol satisfying $y^2 = r^3 + ar + b$.

Theorem 1: Any non-zero multiple uR of R can be expressed as (h, ky), where h and k are field elements fully determined by (u and) the x-coordinate r of R.

Proof. R itself can be so expressed with $h = r$ and $k = 1$. Next, suppose that $P_1 = (h_1, k_1 y)$ and $P_2 = (h_2, k_2 y)$ are two distinct non-zero multiples of R with $P_3 = P_1 + P_2 \neq \mathcal{O}$. The addition formula gives $P_3 = (h_3, k_3 y)$, where

$$h_3 = \left(\frac{k_1 - k_2}{h_1 - h_2} \right)^2 (r^3 + ar + b) - h_1 - h_2, \text{ and } k_3 = \left(\frac{k_1 - k_2}{h_1 - h_2} \right) (h_1 - h_3) - k_1.$$

Let $P_4 = 2P_1$. We have $P_4 = (h_4, k_4 y)$, where

$$h_4 = \left(\frac{3h_1^2 + a}{2k_1}\right)^2 \left(\frac{1}{r^3 + ar + b}\right) - 2h_1, \text{ and } k_4 = \left(\frac{3h_1^2 + a}{2k_1}\right)\left(\frac{h_1 - h_4}{r^3 + ar + b}\right) - k_1.$$

Finally, the opposite of (h, ky) is $(h, (-k)y)$. This completes the inductive proof.   ●

We represent the multiple (h, ky) of R by the pair (h, k) of field elements. The *symbol* y need not be explicitly maintained. R itself is represented by the pair $(r, 1)$. Upon $(r, 1)$ as input, we precompute the quantity $r^3 + ar + b$ and its inverse, and run the standard repeated double-and-add loop of Algorithm 2 with these revised addition and doubling formulas. At the end of the loop, the two computed field elements h, k yield the desired multiple $\xi R = (h, ky)$. In short, we do not need to carry out any symbolic computation at all for obtaining ξR.

Algorithm 2. Seminumeric Computation of $\xi R = (h, ky)$ from ξ and $R = (r, y)$

Precompute the field elements $r^3 + ar + b$ and $(r^3 + ar + b)^{-1}$.
Initialize $S := (r, 1)$.
For $(i = l - 2, l - 3, \ldots, 1, 0)$ {
    Assign $S := 2S$ (use seminumeric doubling formula).
    If $(\xi_i = 1)$, assign $S := S + R$ (use seminumeric addition formula).
}
Return S.

The modified addition formula involves only one extra field multiplication (by the precomputed quantity $r^3 + ar + b$) compared to the standard elliptic-curve addition formula. Point doubling requires two extra field multiplications (each by the precomputed inverse $(r^3 + ar + b)^{-1}$). In Jacobian projective coordinates, we can rearrange the doubling formula to absorb those two extra field multiplications. The standard double-and-add algorithm can be adapted to any windowed variant. Some variants require precomputing multiples uR of R for some small values of u. These multiples are precomputed as pairs of field elements.

The knowledge of the entire points R_1, R_2 allows us to compute $\xi_1 R_1 + \xi_2 R_2$ using a single double-and-add loop, yielding noticeable speedup over two point multiplications. If the y-coordinates of R_1 and R_2 are treated as symbols y_1, y_2, then too $\xi_1 R_1 + \xi_2 R_2$ can be computed seminumerically. Any non-zero point of the form $uR_1 + vR_2$ can be expressed as $(h + jy_1 y_2, ky_1 + ly_2)$ for field elements h, j, k, l uniquely determined by the x-coordinates r_1, r_2 (and u, v) alone. Addition and doubling of such points can be rephrased numerically in terms of these field elements. For example, let $P_1 = (h_1 + j_1 y_1 y_2, k_1 y_1 + l_1 y_2)$ and $P_2 = (h_2 + j_2 y_1 y_2, k_2 y_1 + l_2 y_2)$ be two (distinct) points of the form $uR_1 + vR_2$. In order to compute their sum, we first compute the slope $\lambda = \frac{(k_1 - k_2)y_1 + (l_1 - l_2)y_2}{(h_1 - h_2) + (j_1 - j_2)y_1 y_2}$. Using the symbolic-manipulation techniques of [1], we free the denominator of y_1, y_2 (multiply by $(h_1 - h_2) - (j_1 - j_2)y_1 y_2$ and substitute $y_i^2 = r_i^3 + ar_i + b$ for $i = 1, 2$). We simplify the numerator too to express λ as $\alpha y_1 + \beta y_2$. Therefore, λ^2 and $x(P_1 + P_2) = \lambda^2 - x(P_1) - x(P_2)$ are of the form $\gamma + \delta y_1 y_2$. This process of symbolic computation of $x(P_1 + P_2)$ can be replaced by explicit numeric formulas in $h_1, k_1, j_1, l_1, h_2, k_2, j_2, l_2$. The y-coordinate of

$P_1 + P_2$ and point doubling can be analogously handled. The resulting numeric formulas turn out to be clumsy, and are not expected to benefit the computation of $\xi_1 R_1 + \xi_2 R_2$ in a single double-and-add loop. For the weighted sum of three or more points, this idea of seminumeric computation can be extended at least in theory, but chances of getting practical benefits are rather slim.

4   Comparison among the Randomization Algorithms

In this section, we count the field operations in the randomization algorithms. For each of these algorithms, we take the best variant (windowed, if applicable, and with a suitable choice of the coordinate systems) known to us. We then experimentally validate our theoretical observations.

4.1   Comparison of Montgomery Ladders and Seminumeric Method

For the purpose of theoretical comparison, we use standard projective coordinates in the Montgomery-ladder method, and Jacobian projective coordinates in the NAF variant of the seminumeric method. The Montgomery-ladder method in standard projective coordinates produced the best results almost always, whereas the NAF variant of the seminumeric method in Jacobian projective coordinates gave us the best results for curves over large fields. Comparisons among other variants can be analogously carried out.

Let us analyze the Montgomery-ladder implementation first. Let $P_1 = (h_1, k_1, l_1)$, $P_2 = (h_2, k_2, l_2)$, and $P_1 - P_2 = (r, -y, 1) \in E(\mathbb{F}_p)$ be given in projective coordinates. We do not use the y-coordinates k_1, k_2, y. We only compute the x- and z-coordinates of $P_1 + P_2$ and $2P_1$ using the following formulas [15]:

$$x(P_1 + P_2) = 2(h_1 l_2 + h_2 l_1)(h_1 h_2 + a l_1 l_2) + 4b l_1^2 l_2^2 - r(h_1 l_2 - h_2 l_1)^2,$$
$$z(P_1 + P_2) = (h_1 l_2 - h_2 l_1)^2,$$
$$x(2P_1) = (h_1^2 - a l_1^2)^2 - 8b h_1 l_1^3, \text{ and } z(2P_1) = 4h_1 l_1 (h_1^2 + a l_1^2) + 4b l_1^4.$$

If we precompute the field element $-4b$, point addition and point doubling require $M_{Mont} = 14M + 5S + 9A + 5(2*)$ field operations (see Table 1 for the notations, and [15] for the derivation of this count). For an l-bit randomizer, the Montgomery-ladder scalar-multiplication does $l M_{Mont}$ operations.

Next, we analyze the seminumeric method. Any non-zero multiple of $(r, y, 1) \in E(\mathbb{F}_p)$ is of the form $(\beta_x, \beta_y y, \beta_z)$ with $\beta_x, \beta_y, \beta_z \in \mathbb{F}_p$. Let $P_1 = (h_1, k_1 y, l_1)$ and $P_2 = (h_2, k_2 y, l_2)$ be two such multiples, where $P_1 \neq \pm P_2$, and y satisfies the equation $y^2 = r^3 + ar + b$ with r known. We modify the point-addition and doubling formulas of Section 3.3 as given in [18]. These formulas assume that $a = -3$. In particular, the x-, y- and z-coordinates of $P_3 = P_1 + P_2 = (h_3, k_3 y, l_3)$ and $P_4 = 2P_2 = (h_4, k_4 y, l_4)$ are computed as:

$$H = h_2 l_1^2 - h_1 l_2^2, \ R = k_2 l_1^3 - k_1 l_2^3, \ R' = R^2 y^2, \ h_3 = R' - H^3 - 2h_1 l_2^2 H^2,$$
$$k_3 = R(k_1 l_2^2 - h_3) - k_1 l_2^3, \text{ and } l_3 = H l_1 l_2.$$

$$H_1 = 3(h_1 - l_1^2)(h_1 + l_1^2), \ H_2 = H_1^2/y^2, \ R'' = 4h_1 k_1^2, \ h_4 = H_2 - 2R'',$$
$$k_4 = H_1(R'' - h_4)/y^2 - 8k_1^4, \text{ and } l_4 = 2k_1 l_1.$$

Table 1. Descriptions of the Symbols

Symbol	Description
M	Finite field Multiplication
S	Finite field Square
I	Finite field Inverse
A	Finite field Addition or subtraction
$(u*)$	Finite field multiplication by the constant element u
M_{Mont}	Montgomery-ladder merged addition-doubling in projective coordinates
A_{Semi}	Seminumeric point addition in the mentioned coordinates
D_{Semi}	Seminumeric point doubling in the mentioned coordinates

We need to perform $A_{Semi} = 13M + 4S + 6A + 1(2*)$ and $D_{Semi} = 6M + 3S + 5A + 1(3*) + 4(2*) + 1(\frac{1}{2}*)$ field operations for point addition and doubling, respectively (with $\frac{1}{2}$, y^2 and y^{-2} precomputed). Each point addition requires only one extra field multiplication than the best implementations mentioned in [16]. Point doubling has the same multiplication count as these best implementations. If we use the w-NAF representation of l-bit randomizers, then there are on an average $\frac{l}{w+1}$ non-zero digits. For each of these non-zero digits, A_{Semi} operations are required. Point doubling (D_{Semi}) is done for each of the l bits. Furthermore, for precomputing 2^{w-2} multiples of $(r, y, 1)$, we need $2^{w-2} - 1$ point additions and one point doubling. Opposites of these multiples take almost zero computation cost.

The seminumeric algorithm is faster than Montgomery-ladder algorithm if:

$$\left(2^{w-2} - 1 + \frac{l}{w+1}\right) A_{Semi} + (l+1)D_{Semi} \leqslant l M_{Mont} \qquad (6)$$

Following the convention of [17], we ignore the times required to multiply a field element by a constant (such as 2, 3 or $1/2$) and to add two field elements, since these operations take negligible times compared to field multiplication and squaring. Moreover, as suggested in [16], we take the squaring and multiplication times the same (that is, $1S = 1M$). With these simplifications, Eqn(6) can be rewritten as $17\left(2^{w-2} - 1 + \frac{l}{w+1}\right) + 9(l+1) \leqslant 19l$. Rearrangement of this equation gives $\left(10 - \frac{17}{w+1}\right) l \geqslant 9 + 17(2^{w-2} - 1)$. Putting $w = 4$ in the equation, we get $l \geqslant 9.09$. This theoretically establishes that for $l \geqslant 10$, the seminumeric algorithm is faster than the Montgomery ladder.

It is important to highlight that the worst-case overhead ($A_{Semi} + D_{Semi}$) of an iteration of the seminumeric loop is more than the overhead M_{Mont} of each iteration of the Montgomery-ladder loop. However, the windowed variants of the seminumeric iteration are much more efficient than this worst case, on an average. Montgomery ladders, on the other hand, are unable to take this advantage.

4.2 Comparison of Numeric and Seminumeric Methods

The numeric and seminumeric methods use essentially the same formulas of scalar multiplication. A seminumeric point addition uses one extra field multiplication by the precomputed quantity $r^3 + ar + b$. Seminumeric point doubling requires exactly the same number of field multiplications as needed by numeric point doubling. The numeric algorithm, on the other hand, has the extra overhead of a square-root computation. As mentioned in Section 3.2, this overhead is essentially that of an exponentiation in $\mathbb{F}_p$. We use an efficient windowed modular exponentiation algorithm. The effect of this overhead on the computation of ξR depends on the bit length of ξ. If ξ is a full-length scalar (that is, of bit length near that of p), then the extra overhead is slightly less than that associated with the extra multiplication in the seminumeric loop. The cryptographically most meaningful length of ξ is about half of that of p. In this case, the square-root computation overhead per bit of the randomizer ξ is doubled, and we expect the seminumeric to be faster than the numeric method.

More precisely, let d be the bit length of q. Each square-root computation by the w-NAF method needs $(1S + (2^{w-2} - 1)M) + (dS + \frac{d}{w+1}M)$ field operations. If we put $1S = 1M$, this is the same as $2^{w-2} + d\left(1 + \frac{1}{w+1}\right)$ multiplications. The w-NAF scalar-multiplication time with an explicitly known y-coordinate and an l-bit scalar is about the same as that of $16\left(2^{w-2} - 1 + \frac{l}{w+1}\right) + 9(l+1)$ field multiplications [16]. Thus, the total overhead of the numeric method is that of

$$2^{w-2} + d\left(1 + \frac{1}{w+1}\right) + 16\left(2^{w-2} - 1 + \frac{l}{w+1}\right) + 9(l+1)$$

multiplications for each point. On the other hand, the seminumeric method with an l-bit scalar needs an equivalent of $17\left(2^{w-2} - 1 + \frac{l}{w+1}\right) + 9(l+1)$ field multiplications for each point, yielding a saving of $\left(d + \frac{d-l}{w+1} + 1\right)$ field multiplications. For $l = \frac{d}{2}$ and $w = 4$, $\left(\frac{11}{10}\right)d + 1$ multiplications are saved.

4.3   Experimental Comparison

The algorithms are implemented in a 2.33 GHz Xeon server running Ubuntu Linux Server Version 2012 LTS. The algorithms are implemented using the GP/PARI calculator [19] (version 2.5.0 compiled by the GNU C compiler 4.6.2). We have used the symbolic-computation facilities of the calculator in our programs. All other functions (like scalar multiplication and square-root computation) are written as subroutines with minimal function-call overheads. Since the algorithms are evaluated in terms of number of field operations, this gives a fair comparison of experimental data with the theoretical estimates. We have implemented windowed, w-NAF and frac-w-NAF methods. We have used affine and projective (standard or Jacobian) coordinates.

The average times of randomization achieved by the Montgomery-ladder and the seminumeric algorithms are listed in Tables 2 and 3 for two NIST prime curves. Here, w is the window size, and l is the bit length of the scalar multiplier (randomizer in the batch-verification application). As mentioned in Section 2.2, we have chosen l to be 128, $d/2$ and d (where $d = |p|$). The seminumeric algorithm is found to be faster than the Montgomery-ladder algorithm, particularly for large randomizers. For NIST prime curves, the experimental speedup is about 25–30%, which is consistent with the theoretical estimates.

Tables 2 and 4 list the overheads associated with the numeric randomization method. In order to compare the performances of the numeric method and the seminumeric

Table 2. Times of Numeric and Seminumeric Scalar Multiplication

Curve	Length of randomizer (in bits)	Numeric Scalar Multiplication (Jacobian Projective Coordinates)		Semiumeric Scalar Multiplication (Jacobian Projective Coordinates)	
		Time (in ms)	w-Algorithm	Time (in ms)	w-Algorithm
P-256	128	2.04	5-NAF-numeric	2.04	4-NAF-seminumeric
	256	3.92	4-NAF-numeric	4.12	4-NAF-seminumeric
	128	2.69	4-NAF-numeric	2.81	4-NAF-seminumeric
P-521	256	5.48	4-NAF-numeric	5.92	4-NAF-seminumeric
	521	10.60	5-NAF-numeric	11.44	5-NAF-seminumeric

Table 3. Times of Montgomery-Ladder and Multiple-Scalar Multiplication

Curve	Length of randomizer (in bits)	Montgomery Ladder * (Standard Projective Coordinates) Time (in ms)	Multiple Scalar Multiplication (Jacobian Projective Coordinates) Time (in ms)
P-256	128	2.72	2.93
	256	5.29	5.67
	128	3.76	4.37
P-521	256	7.45	7.89
	521	15.09	16.30

* No effective windowed variant of Montgommer ladders is known

Table 4. Times for the computation of square roots

Curve	Time (in ms)	Algorithm	w
P-256	0.28	w-numeric	5
P-521	0.76	w-numeric	5

method, we add the best possible numeric scalar multiplication time to the best possible square-root computation time. For full-length randomizers, the best total overheads of the numeric algorithm are $3.92 + 0.28 = 4.20$ and $10.60 + 0.76 = 11.36$ for the two curves P-256 and P-521. In this case, the best overheads incurred by the seminumeric method are very close: 4.12 and 11.44. For half-length randomizers, the best total overheads of the numeric method are $2.04 + 0.28 = 2.32$ and $5.48 + 0.76 = 6.24$ for the two curves. The same overheads for the seminumeric method are slightly better: 2.04 and 5.92. This is the expected pattern as evident from our theoretical estimates. Both the numeric and the seminumeric methods run significantly faster than Montgomery ladders.

In ECDSA#, there is a possibility of using multiple scalar multiplication. Table 3 lists the times for computing the sum $\xi_1 R_1 + \xi_2 R_2$ using a single double-and-add loop. These times are much less than two separate scalar-multiplication times even by the best windowed method.

In an individual verification, one can compute $u_iP + v_iQ$ by a double scalar multiplication. Since P is a fixed base, we can use fixed-base scalar multiplication to compute u_iP. However, Q is not considered to be fixed across different batches (it is assumed to be the same in each batch). So the benefits of double fixed-base scalar multiplication is not clear during individual verification, particularly if the number of signatures with fixed Q is small.

Table 5. Speedup obtained by randomized batch-verification algorithms

Batch-verification algorithm	Randomization algorithm	t	P-256		P-521		
			None*	$l = 128$	None*	$l = 128$	$l = 256$
N	Numeric	3	2.55	1.33	2.60	1.82	1.39
		4	3.15	1.48	3.25	2.12	1.55
		5	3.50	1.55	3.72	2.30	1.65
		6	3.46	1.54	3.85	2.36	1.68
		7	2.93	1.43	3.53	2.23	1.61
		8	2.10	1.20	2.75	1.89	1.43
N'	Numeric	3	2.61	1.48	2.63	1.91	1.53
		4	3.34	1.79	3.37	2.32	1.86
		5	4.01	1.89	4.05	2.58	1.97
		6	4.63	2.11	4.69	2.88	2.20
		7	5.20	2.15	5.28	3.05	2.25
		8	5.73	2.31	5.83	3.27	2.42
S2'	Seminumeric	3	2.98	1.37	2.99	1.97	1.43
		4	3.91	1.54	3.95	2.35	1.62
		5	4.73	1.65	4.87	2.65	1.76
		6	5.41	1.72	5.70	2.87	1.86
		7	5.61	1.74	6.24	3.01	1.91
		8	4.96	1.68	6.08	2.97	1.90

* Without randomization

4.4 Effects of Randomization on Batch-Verification Algorithms

Table 5 illustrates the performance degradation caused by randomization. The speedup figures are computed over individual verification and pertain to the situation where all the signatures come from the same signer. In the table, t is the batch size and l is the bit length of the randomizer. We have taken two cryptographically meaningful values of l (half-length and 128). For original ECDSA signatures, the seminumeric randomization method gives the best performance. For ECDSA#, the extra square-root identifying bits give the points R_i uniquely, so the numeric randomization method is the preferred choice. In each case, the best possible windowed variant is used to compute the speedup. Whenever possible, the best windowed variants are replaced by the faster multiple scalar multiplication method. Table 5 also lists the speedup figures without randomization. Although the increased security provided by randomization incurs reasonable overhead, we still have sizable speedup over individual verification.

5 Adaptation of Randomization Methods to Ordinary Binary Curves

As an illustrative example, we take the family of Koblitz curves recommended by NIST [8]. These curves are defined over binary fields $\mathbb{F}_{2^d}$ by the equation

$$y^2 + xy = x^3 + ax^2 + 1, \text{ with } a = 0 \text{ or } 1. \tag{7}$$

5.1 Montgomery-Ladder Formulas

We now represent elliptic-curve points in the standard projective coordinates. Let $P_1 = (h_1, k_1, l_1)$ and $P_2 = (h_2, k_2, l_2)$ be two non-zero multiples of R. Suppose that $P_1 \neq \pm P_2$ and $P_1 - P_2 = (h_4, k_4, l_4)$. We assume that only the x- and z-coordinates of these points are available. We can compute these coordinates of $P_1 + P_2 = (h_3, k_3, l_3)$ using the following formulas:

$$l_3 = (h_1 k_2)^2 + (h_2 k_1)^2, \qquad x_3 = l_3 h_4 + (h_1 k_2)(h_2 k_1).$$

Compute point doubling $2P_1 = (h_5, k_5, l_5)$ as:

$$h_5 = (h_1^2 + l_1^2)^2, \qquad l_5 = h_1^2 l_1^2.$$

We can easily modify Algorithm 1 to the case of projective coordinates.

5.2 Numeric-Computation Formulas

Now, the relevant problem is the computation of the two values of y from the equation $y^2 + ry + (r^3 + ar^2 + 1) = 0$. We first replace y by ry to convert the equation to the form $y^2 + y + \alpha = 0$, where $\alpha = \frac{r^3 + ar^2 + 1}{r^2}$. The converted equation is solvable if and only if the absolute trace $\mathrm{Tr}(\alpha)$ is zero. In that case, if d is odd, a solution for y is $\alpha^{2^1} + \alpha^{2^3} + \alpha^{2^5} + \cdots + \alpha^{2^{d-2}}$, and the other solution is 1 plus the first solution. These solutions can be efficiently obtained using a half-trace calculation [18].

5.3 Seminumeric-Computation (Joye-Method) Formulas

Let $R = (r, y)$ with y treated as a symbol satisfying the Koblitz-curve equation $y^2 + ry = r^3 + ar^2 + 1$.

Theorem 2: Any non-zero multiple of R can be expressed as $\left(h, k + \left(\frac{y}{r} \right) h \right)$.

Proof   First, notice that P itself can be so expressed with $h = r$ and $k = 0$. Next, suppose that $P_1 = (h_1, k_1 + \left(\frac{y}{r} \right) h_1)$ and $P_2 = (h_2, k_2 + \left(\frac{y}{r} \right) h_2)$ are two distinct non-zero multiples of R with $P_3 = P_1 + P_2 \neq \mathcal{O}$. The point-addition formula on Koblitz curves implies that $P_3 = (h_3, k_3 + \left(\frac{y}{r} \right) h_3)$, where

$$h_3 = \left(\frac{k_1 + k_2}{h_1 + h_2} \right)^2 + \left(\frac{k_1 + k_2}{h_1 + h_2} \right) + h_1 + h_2 + a + \left(\frac{r^3 + ar^2 + b}{r^2} \right)$$

$$= \frac{h_1(h_2^2 + k_2) + h_2(h_1^2 + k_1)}{h_1^2 + h_2^2},$$

$$k_3 = \left(\frac{k_1 + k_2}{h_1 + h_2} \right)(h_1 + h_3) + h_3 + k_1.$$

The double P_4 of P_1, if non-zero, can be expressed as $\left(h_4, k_4 + \left(\frac{y}{r}\right) h_4\right)$, where:

$$h_4 = h_1^2 + \frac{b}{h_1^2}, \qquad k_4 = h_1^2 + \left(h_1 + \frac{k_1}{h_1} + 1\right) h_3.$$

The opposite of $\left(h, k + \left(\frac{y}{r}\right) h\right)$ is $\left(h, (k+h) + \left(\frac{y}{r}\right) h\right)$.   •

For Koblitz curves, the τ-NAF point-multiplication algorithm is computationally very efficient. This motivates using the following theorem.

Theorem 3:   The second-power Frobenius endomorphism on a point of the form $\left(h, k + \left(\frac{y}{r}\right) h\right)$ gives a point in the same form.

Proof   Let $P_1 = \left(h_1, k_1 + \left(\frac{y}{r}\right) h_1\right)$. Then, $P_5 = \left(h_1^2, \left(k_1 + \left(\frac{y}{r}\right) h_1\right)^2\right)$ can be expressed as $\left(h_5, k_5 + \left(\frac{y}{r}\right) h_5\right)$, where:

$$h_5 = h_1^2, \qquad k_5 = k_1^2 + \left(\frac{r^3 + ar^2 + b}{r^2}\right) h_1^2.$$ •

It follows that for all relevant points of the form $\left(h, k + \left(\frac{y}{r}\right) h\right)$, it suffices to store the values of h and k alone. The second term $\left(\frac{y}{r}\right) h$ in the y-coordinate carries no extra information, and does not hamper the arithmetic operations on the points. Indeed, the point negation, doubling, and the second addition formulas are now exactly the same as the numeric formulas for Koblitz curves, without any extra operation. If $a + \frac{r^3 + ar^2 + b}{r^2} = \frac{r^3 + b}{r^2}$ is precomputed, the first formula for computing h_3 does not lead to an increased operation count. Application of the second-power Frobenius endomorphism (computation of k_5), however, now involves a multiplication of h_5 with the precomputed field element $\frac{r^3 + ar^2 + b}{r^2}$, followed by an addition of this product to k_1^2. After the h and k values of ξR are computed by any addition-chain method, one obtains the point $\xi R = \left(h, k + \left(\frac{h}{r}\right) y\right)$.

5.4   Comparison of Montgomery Ladders and Seminumeric Method

For Koblitz curves, we use standard projective coordinates in the Montgomery-ladder method, and affine coordinates in the τ-*NAF* windowed variant of the seminumeric method. These gave us the best respective running times. In fact, affine coordinates outperformed López-Dahab (LD) coordinates [14] in our implementations.

To analyze the Montgomery-ladder implementation, we take $P_1 = (x_1, y_1, z_1)$, $P_2 = (x_2, y_2, z_2)$, and $P_1 - P_2 = (r, r + y, 1) \in E(\mathbb{F}_{2^d})$ in standard projective coordinates. We only compute the x- and z-coordinates of $P_1 + P_2$ and $2P_1$ according to the formulas given in [14,17]:

$$z(P_1 + P_2) = (x_1 z_2)^2 + (x_2 z_1)^2, \ x(P_1 + P_2) = z(P_1 + P_2) \times r + x_1 x_2 z_1 z_2,$$

$$x(2P_1) = x_1^4 + b z_1^4, \text{ and } z(2P_1) = x_1^2 z_1^2$$

Following the implementation of [18], we need $5M + 5S + 2A$ to compute M_{Mont}.

Now, we analyze the seminumeric algorithm in affine coordinates. All non-zero multiples of $(r,y) \in E(\mathbb{F}_{2^d})$ are of the form $(\beta_x, \beta_y + \frac{\beta_x}{r}y)$ with $\beta_x, \beta_y \in \mathbb{F}_{2^d}$. Let $P_1 = (x_1, y_1 + \frac{x_1}{r}y)$ and $P_2 = (x_2, y_2 + \frac{x_2}{r}y)$ be two such multiples with $P_1 \neq \pm P_2$, and y satisfies the equation $y^2 + ry = r^3 + ar^2 + b$ with r known. The following formulas are derived assuming that $b = 1$ and that $B = (r^3 + ar^2 + b)/r^2$ is precomputed. The x- and y-coordinates of $P_3 = P_1 + P_2 = (x_3, y_3 + \frac{x_3}{r}y)$ and $P_4 = \tau(P_1) = (x_4, y_4 + \frac{x_4}{r}y)$ are computed as follows:

$$\lambda = \frac{y_1 + y_2}{x_1 + x_2}, \quad x_3 = \lambda^2 + \lambda + x_1 + x_2 + B, \quad y_x = \lambda(x_1 + x_3) + x_3 + y_1,$$
$$x_5 = x_1^2, \text{ and } y_5 = y_1^2 + Bx_5.$$

$A_{Semi} = 2M + 1S + 1I + 6A$ and $\tau_{Semi} = 1M + 2S$ field operations are needed for each point addition and application of τ, respectively (with B precomputed). Here, point addition does not need any extra multiplication in affine or LD coordinates compared to the formulas given in [20], but the application of τ needs one extra multiplication (in LD coordinates, two extra multiplications are needed). If the addition chain for the scalar multiplier is computed by the τ-NAF representation with w-bit windows [17,18,21], then the density of non-zero digits is on an average $\frac{1}{w+1}$. For each of these non-zero digits, A_{Semi} is required, and τ_{Semi} is required for each non-zero digit in the addition chain. In case of τ-NAF, we use special τ-chains in the precomputation stage [18,21], where 3-, 4- and 5-bit windows need $\Pi_3 = 1\tau_{Semi} + 1A_{Semi}$, $\Pi_4 = 3\tau_{Semi} + 3A_{Semi}$ and $\Pi_5 = 6\tau_{Semi} + 7A_{Semi}$ curve operations, respectively.

For Koblitz-curve scalar multiplication, we have to pay a special attention to the length of the addition chains. Let c be the co-factor of the Koblitz curve given by Eqn (7). Then, we have $\#E(\mathbb{F}_{2^d}) = cn$. Let $\mu = (-1)^{1-a}$, and $\alpha = (\alpha_1 + \tau\alpha_2) \in \mathbb{Z}[\tau]$. The *norm* of α is given by $N(\alpha) = \alpha_1^2 + \mu\alpha_1\alpha_2 + 2\alpha_2^2$. The length of the τ-NAF representation of α is approximately $\log_2(N(\alpha))$. After the partial modular reduction [21], the length of the addition chain reduces to a maximum of $d + a$. This reduction takes place only if $N(\alpha) \geqslant \frac{4}{7}n$. Therefore, we make our analysis on the basis of whether $N(\alpha) \geqslant \frac{4}{7}n$ or not.

- Case 1: $N(\alpha) < \frac{4}{7}n$

  Let $\alpha = (\alpha_1 + \tau\alpha_2)$ with $\alpha_2 = 0$ be the scalar multiplier, and $l = \log_2 \alpha$ the bit length of the multiplier. The length of the addition chain obtained by the τ-NAF representation is approximately $2l$. In contrast, the binary (and NAF) representations produce addition chains of approximate length l. The Montgomery-ladder scalar multiplication needs $C_{Mont} = lM_{Mont} = l(5M + 5S)$ field operations (ignoring additions and subtractions). For w-bit windowed τ-NAF, the required operation count in the seminumeric method is $C_{\tau NAF} = \Pi_w + 2l\left(\tau_{Semi} + \frac{1}{w+1}A_{Semi}\right) = \Pi_w + 2l\left((1M + 2S) + \frac{2M+1S+1I}{w+1}\right)$. Our experimental environment shows the relations between M, S and I as $1S = 0.88M$ and $1I = 4.75M$. Using these relations and putting $w = 5$, we simplify the above operation counts as $C_{Mont} = (9.40M)l$, $C_{\tau NAF} = (6.79M)l + (69.97M)$. Therefore, the seminumeric method is faster than Montgomery ladders for $l \geqslant 30$.
- Case 2: $N(\alpha) \geqslant \frac{4}{7}n$

In this case, the length of the τ-NAF addition chain remains nearly $d + a$ (irrespective of the length l of the scalar multiplier), whereas the length of the binary addition chain used by Montgomery ladders increases with l. As l increases, the running time of the seminumeric algorithm remains nearly constant, and the running time of the Montgomery ladder increases linearly with l. Similar operation counts as done in Case 1 now shows that the seminumeric algorithm is faster than Montgomery ladders for $l \geqslant 0.36d + 7.44$. On the other hand, the condition $N(\alpha) \geqslant \frac{4}{7}n$ requires $l \geqslant 0.5d$ approximately. Therefore, the inequality $l \geqslant 0.36d + 7.44$ is always satisfied. We have $\frac{C_{\tau NAF}}{C_{Mont}} \approx 0.36\frac{d}{l}$. For $l = d/2$, the seminumeric algorithms takes about 72% of the running time of Montgomery ladders, and for $l = d$, about 36%.

Table 6. Times of Numeric and Seminumeric Scalar Multiplication

Curve	Length of randomizer (in bits)	Numeric Scalar Multiplication (Affine Coordinates)		Semiumeric Scalar Multiplication (Affine Coordinates)	
		Time (in ms)	w-Algorithm	Time (in ms)	w-Algorithm
K-283	128	196.00	5-τNAF-numeric	265.04	5-τNAF-Seminumeric
	283	216.00	5-τNAF-numeric	286.64	5-τNAF-Seminumeric
K-571	128	516.00	4-τNAF-numeric	718.25	5-τNAF-Seminumeric
	256	968.00	5-τNAF-numeric	1375.88	5-τNAF-Seminumeric
	571	1072.00	5-τNAF-numeric	1530.30	5-τNAF-Seminumeric

Table 7. Times of Montgomery-ladder and Multiple-Scalar Multiplication

Curve	Length of randomizer (in bits)	Montgomery Ladder * (Standard Projective Coordinates) Time (in ms)	Multiple-Scalar Multiplication (Affine Coordinates) Time (in ms)
K-283	128	292.70	417.00
	283	651.62	908.62
K-571	128	824.02	1115.32
	256	1659.40	2233.56
	571	3714.01	4968.33

* No effective windowed variant of Montgommer ladders is known

Table 8. Times for Root Finding by Half-Trace Computation

Curve	Time (in ms)	Algorithm
K-283	8.31	Quarter memory *
K-571	30.84	Quarter memory *

* See [18]

5.5 Experimental Comparison

We have used the same experimental setup as described in Section 4.3. The average times of randomization achieved by the seminumeric and the Montgomery-ladder algorithms are listed in Tables 6 and 7 for two NIST Koblitz curves. Here, w is the window size, and l is the bit length of the scalar multiplier (randomizer in the batch-verification application). We have chosen l to be 128, $d/2$ and d. The seminumeric algorithm is found to be faster than the Montgomery-ladder algorithm, particularly for large randomizers.

Tables 6 and 8 list the overheads associated with the numeric randomization method. In order to compare the performances of the numeric method and the seminumeric method, we add the best possible numeric scalar multiplication time to the best possible time of root finding using a half-trace computation. Both the numeric and the seminumeric methods run much faster than Montgomery ladders. The seminumeric algorithm is found to be faster than the Montgomery-ladder algorithm, particularly for large randomizers. For Koblitz curves, the speedup is about 10%, 15% and 60% for 128-bit, half-length and full-length randomizers. This pattern is consistent with the theoretical estimates given above.

In ECDSA#, there is a possibility of using multiple scalar multiplication. Table 7 lists the times for computing $\xi_1 R_1 + \xi_2 R_2$ using a single double-and-add loop. This method is much slower than two separate invocations of the best windowed τ-NAF method. In the windowed τ-NAF method, scalar-multiplication times for half-length and full-length scalars are nearly the same (see Section 5.4). Moreover, the τ operation is much more efficient than point doubling. Nevertheless, the randomization overhead being substantial, we do not obtain much speedup from randomized ECDSA batch verification on Koblitz curves (see Table 9). For individual verification, we do not consider fixed-base double exponentiation for the computation of $u_i P + v_i Q$, since Q is not treated as a fixed base across multiple batches.

Table 9. Speedup for NIST Koblitz Curves

Batch-Verification Algorithm	Randomization Algorithm	Batch Size(t)	K-283		k-571		
			None*	$l = 128$	None*	$l = 128$	$l = 256$
N	Numeric	2	1.85	1.00	1.90	1.30	1.02
		3	2.44	1.16	2.64	1.61	1.20
		4	2.55	1.18	3.01	1.75	1.28
		5	2.09	1.07	2.80	1.67	1.24
		6	1.39	0.85	2.10	1.40	1.08
		7	0.79	0.58	1.31	0.99	0.82
N'	Numeric	2	1.90	1.02	1.93	1.32	1.03
		3	2.78	1.23	2.84	1.69	1.24
		4	3.61	1.37	3.72	1.96	1.39
		5	4.39	1.47	4.57	2.18	1.49
		6	5.14	1.54	5.38	2.35	1.57
		7	5.85	1.60	6.17	2.48	1.63
S2'	Seminumeric	2	1.97	0.89	1.98	1.19	0.87
		3	2.89	1.04	2.94	1.48	1.02
		4	3.66	1.13	3.80	1.67	1.11
		5	3.78	1.14	4.25	1.75	1.14
		6	3.48	1.11	4.28	1.76	1.14
		7	2.09	0.93	3.05	1.51	1.03

*Speedup without randomization

6 Conclusion

In this paper, three methods are studied for randomized batch verification of ECDSA signatures. We theoretically and experimentally establish the superiority of the numeric and seminumeric methods over Montgomery ladders. This study is particularly relevant in the context of standard ECDSA signatures.

References

1. Karati, S., Das, A., Roychowdhury, D., Bellur, B., Bhattacharya, D., Iyer, A.: Batch verification of ECDSA signatures. In: Mitrokotsa, A., Vaudenay, S. (eds.) AFRICACRYPT 2012. LNCS, vol. 7374, pp. 1–18. Springer, Heidelberg (2012)
2. Bernstein, D.J., Doumen, J., Lange, T., Oosterwijk, J.-J.: Faster batch forgery identification. In: Galbraith, S., Nandi, M. (eds.) INDOCRYPT 2012. LNCS, vol. 7668, pp. 454–473. Springer, Heidelberg (2012)
3. Naccache, D., M'Raïhi, D., Vaudenay, S., Raphaeli, D.: Can D.S.A. be improved?: Complexity trade-offs with the digital signature standard. In: De Santis, A. (ed.) EUROCRYPT 1994. LNCS, vol. 950, pp. 77–85. Springer, Heidelberg (1995)
4. Antipa, A., Brown, D., Gallant, R., Lambert, R., Struik, R., Vanstone, S.: Accelerated verification of ECDSA signatures. In: Preneel, B., Tavares, S. (eds.) SAC 2005. LNCS, vol. 3897, pp. 307–318. Springer, Heidelberg (2006)
5. Cheon, J.H., Yi, J.H.: Fast batch verification of multiple signatures. In: Okamoto, T., Wang, X. (eds.) PKC 2007. LNCS, vol. 4450, pp. 442–457. Springer, Heidelberg (2007)
6. Montgomery, P.L.: Speeding up Pollard and elliptic curve methods of factorization. In: Mathematics of Computation, vol. 48(177), pp. 243–264 (1987)
7. Joye, M.: Security analysis of RSA-type cryptosystems. Phd thesis, UCL Crypto Group, Belgium (1997)
8. NIST: Recommended elliptic curves for federal government use (1999),
   http://csrc.nist.gov/encryption
9. Montgomery, P.L.: Evaluating recurrences of form $X_{m+n} = f(X_m, X_n, X_{m-n})$ via Lucas chains. Microsoft research article, 582 (1992)
10. Stam, M.: On Montgomery-like representations for elliptic curves over $GF(2^k)$. In: Desmedt, Y.G. (ed.) PKC 2003. LNCS, vol. 2567, pp. 240–253. Springer, Heidelberg (2002)
11. Stam, M.: Speeding up subgroup cryptosystems. PhD thesis, Technische Universiteit Eindhoven (2003)
12. Bellare, M., Garay, J.A., Rabin, T.: Fast batch verification for modular exponentiation and digital signatures. In: Nyberg, K. (ed.) EUROCRYPT 1998. LNCS, vol. 1403, pp. 236–250. Springer, Heidelberg (1998)
13. Brier, E., Joye, M.: Weierstraß elliptic curves and side-channel attacks. In: Naccache, D., Paillier, P. (eds.) PKC 2002. LNCS, vol. 2274, pp. 335–345. Springer, Heidelberg (2002)
14. López, J., Dahab, R.: Fast multiplication on elliptic curves over $GF(2^m)$ without precomputation. In: Koç, Ç.K., Paar, C. (eds.) CHES 1999. LNCS, vol. 1717, pp. 316–327. Springer, Heidelberg (1999)
15. Fischer, W., Giraud, C., Knudsen, E.W., Seifert, J.P.: Parallel scalar multiplication on general elliptic curves over F_p hedged against non-differential side-channel attacks. IACR Cryptology ePrint Archive 2002/007 (2002)
16. Bernstein, D.J., Lange, T.: Explicit-Formulas Database (2007),
    http://www.hyperelliptic.org/EFD/index.html

17. Cohen, H., Frey, G., Avanzi, R., Doche, C., Lange, T., Nguyen, K., Vercauteren, F.: Handbook of Elliptic and Hyperelliptic Curve Cryptography, 2nd edn. Chapman & Hall/CRC (2012)
18. Hankerson, D., Menezes, A.J., Vanstone, S.: Guide to Elliptic Curve Cryptography. Springer-Verlag New York, Inc., Secaucus (2003)
19. PARI Group: PARI/GP home (2008), http://pari.math.u-bordeaux.fr/
20. Lange, T.: A note on López-Dahab coordinates. IACR Cryptology ePrint Archive 2004/323 (2004)
21. Solinas, J.A.: Improved algorithms for arithmetic on anomalous binary curves. Technical report, Originally presented in Advances in Cryptography, Crypto 1997 (1997)

Batch Verification of EdDSA Signatures

Sabyasachi Karati and Abhijit Das

Department of Computer Science and Engineering
IIT Kharagpur, India
{skarati,abhij}@cse.iitkgp.ernet.in

Abstract. In AfricaCrypt 2012 and ACNS 2014, several algorithms are proposed for the batch verification of ECDSA signatures. In this paper, we make a comparative study of these methods for the Edwards curve digital signature algorithm (EdDSA). We describe the adaptation of Algorithms N, N′, S2′ and SP for EdDSA signatures. The randomization methods are also explained in detail. More precisely, we study seminumeric scalar multiplication and Montgomery ladders during randomization of EdDSA signatures. Each EdDSA signature verification involves a square-root computation. One may instead use an ECDSA-like verification procedure which avoids the expensive square-root computation. We study both these variants of EdDSA verification. Experimental results show that for small batch sizes the Algorithms S2′ and SP yield speedup comparable to what is achieved by Algorithm N′ which is originally proposed as the default EdDSA batch-verification algorithm.

Keywords: Elliptic Curve, Edwards Curve, Montgomery Ladder, Symbolic Computation, Batch Verification, ECDSA, EdDSA, Randomization.

1   Introduction

The concept of digital signatures is proposed in [1] by Diffie and Hellman. The first practically applicable signature scheme RSA is proposed by Rivest, Shamir and Adleman in 1978 [2]. The security of the RSA algorithm is based allegedly on the hardness of the factorization of products of two large primes. In 1985, ElGamal proposes a new type of digital signature scheme based on the discrete logarithm problem in prime fields [3]. The ElGamal signature scheme is the first digital-signature scheme which is probabilistic in nature. The Digital Signature Algorithm (DSA) [4] is a variant of the ElGamal digital signature scheme, proposed as a standard by the National Institute of Standards and Technology (NIST) in 1991. In 2001, the Elliptic Curve Digital Signature Algorithm (ECDSA) is proposed by Johnson et al. [5] and is again accepted as a digital-signature standard. Bernstein et al. in 2011 propose the Edwards curve digital signature algorithm (EdDSA) [6]. ECDSA and EdDSA derive their security from the apparent intractability of the discrete logarithm problem in elliptic and Edwards curves defined over finite fields.

To verify an ElGamal-like signature, one requires two finite-field exponentiations (for DSA) or two scalar multiplications in the underlying curve (for ECDSA and EdDSA). Each such modular exponentiation or scalar multiplication is considerably more time-consuming than the other finite-field operations. EdDSA verification additionally

R.S. Chakraborty et al. (Eds.): SPACE 2014, LNCS 8804, pp. 256–271, 2014.

involves a square-root computation in the finite field. This overhead addresses the need of easy batch verification but incurs significant overhead even during individual verification. We can nevertheless adapt the ECDSA verification algorithm to EdDSA, thereby avoiding the costly square-root computation.

In all these ElGamal-like signature schemes, signature verification is somewhat slower than the signing procedure. Many applications (often real-time) need to verify multiple signatures in batches. In 1994, Naccache et al. introduce a method to handle signature batches [7]. They propose the concept of batch verification, where the verifier simultaneously verifies a batch in time less than the total time associated with the individual verification of the signatures. An interactive batch-verification procedure is proposed for DSA signatures in [7]. In 1997, the concept of batch RSA is introduced by Fiat [8]. Harn, in 1998, proposes an efficient scheme for the batch verification of RSA signatures [9]. In this scheme (also see [10]), multiple signatures signed by the same private key can be verified simultaneously. Harn's scheme uses only one exponentiation for batches of any size t. However, its drawback is that it does not adapt to the case of signatures from multiple signers.

The key sizes of ECDSA signatures are much smaller than the key sizes of RSA and DSA signatures at the same security level. In Table 1 derived from [11], L and N stand for the bit lengths of the public and the private keys for DSA, k is the bit length of the modulus in RSA, and f is the order of the base point of the elliptic-curve/Edwards-curve group. In order to achieve 256-bit security, ECDSA/EdDSA needs only 512-bit keys. At the same security level, the DSA and RSA key sizes should be at least $(15360, 512)$ and 15360 bits. Smaller key sizes make ECDSA/EdDSA attractive to many applications. Moreover, smaller key sizes lead to faster verification for ECDSA/EdDSA compared to RSA/DSA.

Table 1. Key sizes for digital-signature algorithms at different security levels

Bits of Security	DSA minimum (L,N)	RSA minimum k	ECDSA/EdDSA minimum f
80	(1024,160)	1024	160
112	(2048,224)	2048	224
128	(3072,256)	3072	256
192	(7680,384)	7680	384
256	(15360,512)	15360	512

The described batch-verification methods are not directly applicable to ECDSA signatures. ECDSA*, a modification of ECDSA introduced by Antipa et al. [12], permits an easy adaptation of the DSA batch-verification protocol of Naccache et al. Cheon and Yi [13] study batch verification of ECDSA* signatures, and report speedup factors of up to 7 for same signer and 4 for different signers. However, ECDSA* is not accepted as a standard signature scheme like DSA, RSA or ECDSA [4]. Thus the use of ECDSA* is unacceptable, particularly in applications where interoperability is of important concern. Moreover, ECDSA* increases the signature size by approximately a factor of two compared to ECDSA without increasing the security.

Edwards curves, a normal form of elliptic curves, are introduced by Edwards in [14]. Bernstein et al. [6] apply these curves to cryptographic usage. Edwards curves offer faster addition and doubling formulas than elliptic curves. Moreover, the unified addition and doubling formulas make Edwards-curve cryptosystems resistant to simple side-channel attacks. A batch-verification procedure is also proposed by Bernstein et al. for Edwards curve digital signatures (EdDSA).

An application of our batch-verification algorithms is in secure vehicle-to-vehicle (V2V) communications in vehicular ad hoc networks (VANETs) (see [15] for a survey). Since signature generation and verification are time-consuming operations, and since vehicles have to verify signatures repeatedly, any algorithm that speeds up the authentication process is of great help in V2V communications. In a busy street where a vehicle needs to authenticate messages from multiple vehicles in real time, individual verification may result in practical bottlenecks. In this situation, it is also expected that multiple messages from the same vehicle get accumulated for being verified. This is precisely the case when our batch-verification algorithms produce the maximum benefits. Like other batch-verification schemes, this performance gain comes at a cost, namely, we forfeit the ability to identify individual faulty signatures. Our algorithm (like any batch-verification algorithm) turns out to be useful only when most signatures are authentic.

The rest of this paper is organized as follows. In Section 2, we provide a brief introduction to the ECDSA batch-verification algorithms of [16,17] and the attacks against those [18]. Sections 3 elaborates the EdDSA algorithm given in [6]. An ECDSA-like variant of EdDSA verification is also discussed. Section 4 explains the adaptation of ECDSA batch-verification algorithms to EdDSA signatures. Section 5 deals with randomization issues in the context of EdDSA batch verification. Our experimental results are supplied and discussed in Section 6. Section 7 concludes the paper.

2   Background on ECDSA Batch Verification

We work over the elliptic curve

$$y^2 = x^3 + ax + b. \tag{1}$$

defined over a large prime field $\mathbb{F}_p$. We assume that the group $E(\mathbb{F}_p)$ is of prime order n. Let P be a fixed generator of $E(\mathbb{F}_p)$.

An ECDSA signature on a message M is a triple (M, r, s), where r is the x-coordinate of an elliptic-curve point R, and s is an integer that absorbs the hash of M. Both r and s are reduced modulo the size n of the elliptic-curve group. During verification, two scalars u, v are computed using modulo n arithmetic, and the point R is reconstructed as $R = uP + vQ$, where P is the base point in the elliptic-curve group, and Q is the signer's public key. Verification succeeds if and only if $x(R) = r$.

Suppose that we want to verify a batch of t ECDSA signatures (M_i, r_i, s_i). For the i-th signature, the verification equation is $R_i = u_i P + v_i Q_i$. The t signatures can be combined as

$$\sum_{i=1}^{t} R_i = \left(\sum_{i=1}^{t} u_i\right) P + \left(\sum_{i=1}^{t} v_i Q_i\right). \tag{2}$$

For simplicity, we assume that all of the t signatures come from the same signer, that is, $Q_i = Q$ for all i. In this case, Eqn(2) can be simplified as

$$\sum_{i=1}^{t} R_i = \left(\sum_{i=1}^{t} u_i \right) P + \left(\sum_{i=1}^{t} v_i \right) Q. \tag{3}$$

Since the y-coordinates of R_i are not available in the signatures, we cannot straightaway compute the sum on the left side. In AfricaCrypt 2012, several batch-verification algorithms are proposed to solve this problem [16]. The naive algorithms are based upon the determination of the missing y-coordinate of each R_i using a square-root computation (we have $y_i^2 = r_i^3 + ar_i + b$). The symbolic-manipulation algorithms treat the unknown y-coordinates as symbols. Batch verification involves the eventual elimination of all these y-coordinates from Eqn(2) or (3) using the elliptic-curve equation. The symbolic algorithm S2$'$ turns out to be the fastest of the batch-verification algorithms proposed in [16].

In IndoCrypt 2012, Bernstein et al. [18] propose two attacks on these batch-verification algorithms. They also suggest that these attacks can be largely eliminated by randomizing the batch-verification process (a concept introduced by Naccache et al. [7]). For randomly chosen non-zero multipliers $\xi_1, \xi_2, \ldots, \xi_t$, the individual verification equations are now combined as

$$\sum_{i=1}^{t} \xi_i R_i = \left(\sum_{i=1}^{t} \xi_i u_i \right) P + \left(\sum_{i=1}^{t} \xi_i v_i Q_i \right) \tag{4}$$

or as

$$\sum_{i=1}^{t} \xi_i R_i = \left(\sum_{i=1}^{t} \xi_i u_i \right) P + \left(\sum_{i=1}^{t} \xi_i v_i \right) Q \tag{5}$$

for the case of the same signer. Since the y-coordinates of R_i are not available in the ECDSA signatures, Eqn(4) or (5) is not directly applicable. Some efficient ways of randomizing the batch-verification algorithms of [16] are proposed in [19]. We mostly concentrate on standard ECDSA signatures (M, r, s) on M. If the ECDSA signature contains an extra bit to identify the correct square-root y of $r^3 + ar + b$ [20], we call this an ECDSA# signature. In another variant known as ECDSA* [20,21], the entire point R replaces r in the signature. Neither ECDSA# nor ECDSA* is accepted as a standard. Since ECDSA* results in an unreasonable expansion in the signature size without any increase in the security, we do not consider this variant in this paper. ECDSA#, however, adds only one extra bit to a signature, and so we study the implications of having this extra bit.

2.1 ECDSA Batch Verification

The right side of Eqn(3) can be computed numerically using two scalar multiplications (or one double scalar multiplication). Let this point be (α, β). If R_i are reconstructed as $u_i P + v_i Q$, the effort is essentially the same as individual verification. The algorithms of [16] solve this problem in many ways.

The naive method N computes y_i by taking the square root of $r_i^3 + ar_i + b$. Since there are two square roots (in general) for each r_i, the ambiguity in the *sign* of y_i can be removed by trying all of the $m = 2^t$ combinations. If Eqn(2) holds for any of these choices, the batch of signatures is accepted. If we use ECDSA#, then the y_i values can be uniquely identified, and we can avoid trying all the $m = 2^t$ combinations. This variant of the naive method is referred to as N'. If the underlying field is large, the square-root computations may have huge overheads.

The symbolic algorithms S1 and S2 avoid this overhead by computing the left side of Eqn(2) symbolically. Each y_i is treated as a symbol satisfying $y_i^2 = r_i^3 + ar_i + b$. This symbolic addition gives $(g(y_1, y_2, \ldots, y_t), h(y_1, y_2, \ldots, y_t)) = (\alpha, \beta)$, where g and h are polynomials in y_i with each y_i-degree $\leqslant 1$.

Algorithm S1 makes a linearization by repeatedly squaring $g(y_1, y_2, \ldots, y_t) = \alpha$ (or multiplying by even-degree monomials). At this stage too, the equations $y_i^2 = r_i^3 + ar_i + b$ are used in order to keep the y_i-degrees $\leqslant 1$ in each generated equation. The linearized system has $2^{t-1} - 1 = \frac{m}{2} - 1$ variables standing for the square-free monomials in $y_1, y_2, \ldots, y_t$ of even degrees. The linearized system is solved by Gaussian elimination. The equation $h(y_1, y_2, \ldots, y_t) = \beta$ is then used to solve for each y_i. Finally, it is verified whether $y_i^2 = r_i^3 + ar_i + b$ for all i.

Algorithm S2 uses a faster elimination trick. The equation $g(y_1, y_2, \ldots, y_t) = \alpha$ is written as $\gamma(y_2, y_3, \ldots, y_t)y_1 + \delta(y_2, y_3, \ldots, y_t)$. Multiplying this by $\gamma y_1 - \delta$ and using $y_1^2 = r_1^3 + ar_1 + b$ gives an equation free from y_1. The other variables $y_2, y_3, \ldots, y_t$ are eliminated one by one in the same way. Eventually, the batch is accepted if we obtain the zero polynomial after all y_i are eliminated.

An improved variant of S1 and S2 significantly speeds up the symbolic-addition phase. Let $\tau = \lceil t/2 \rceil$. Eqn(2) is rewritten as $\sum_{i=1}^{\tau} R_i = (\alpha, \beta) - \sum_{i=\tau+1}^{t} R_i$. The two sides are individually computed symbolically. These variants of S1 and S2 are referred to as S1' and S2'.

In [17], Karati et al. propose a new ECDSA batch-verification algorithm based on elliptic-curve summation polynomial. This algorithm is known as Algorithm SP and, is theoretically and experimentally faster than S2'. In this algorithm, Eqns(2)–(5) are rewritten as

$$\sum_{i=1}^{t} (r_i, y_i) + (\alpha, -\beta) = \mathcal{O},$$

where (α, β) is the numeric sum on the right-hand side. This equation is satisfied if and only if $f_{t+1}(r_1, r_2, \ldots, r_t, \alpha) = 0$, where $f_k(x_1, x_2, \ldots, x_k)$ is the k-th summation polynomial that can be defined by induction on k [17].

2.2 Attacks on ECDSA Batch Verification

In the first attack of Bernstein et al. [18], the batch verifier handles $t - 2$ genuine signatures along with the two forged signatures (r, s) and $(r, -s)$ on the same message M. Since the sum of the elliptic-curve points (r, s) and $(r, -s)$ is $\mathcal{O}$, the entire batch of t signatures is verified as genuine.

In the second attack, the forger knows a valid key pair (d_1, Q_1), and can fool the verifier by a forged signature for any message M_2 under any valid public key Q_2 along with a message M_1 under the public key Q_1. The forger selects a random k_2, computes $R_2 = k_2P$ and $r_2 = x(R_2)$. For another random s_2, the signature on M_2 under Q_2 is presented as (r_2, s_2). For the message M_1, the signature (r_1, s_1) is computed as $R_1 = r_2 s_2^{-1} Q_2$, $r_1 = x(R_1)$, and $s_1 = (e_1 + r_1 d_1)(k_2 - e_2 s_2^{-1})^{-1}$, where $e_1 = H(m_1)$, $e_2 = H(m_2)$, and H is a secure hash function. Now, $R_1 + R_2$ and $(e_1 s_1^{-1} + e_2 s_2^{-1})P + r_1 s_1^{-1} Q_1 + r_2 s_2^{-1} Q_2$ have the same value as $(k_2 P + r_2 s_2^{-1} Q_2)$. These forged signatures are verified if they are in the same batch.

Both these attacks become infeasible by the use of randomizers. If the verifier chooses l-bit randomizers, the security of the batch-verification procedure increases by 2^l. The randomizers need not be of full lengths (of lengths close to that of the prime order n of the relevant elliptic-curve group). As discussed in [22], much smaller randomizers typically suffice to make most attacks on batch-verification schemes infeasible. If the underlying field is of size d bits, then the best known algorithms (the square-root methods) to solve the ECDLP take $O(2^{d/2})$ times. As a result, $d/2$-bit randomizers do not degrade the security of the ECDSA scheme. Another possibility is to take $l = 128$ to get 128-bit security independent of the security guarantees of ECDSA.

3 Edwards Curve Digital Signature Algorithm (EdDSA)

Bernstein et al. in [6] propose the Edwards Curve Digital Signature Algorithm (EdDSA). This signature scheme is based on the group structure of the twisted Edwards curve over a prime field $\mathbb{F}_p$ defined as

$$E : -x^2 + y^2 = 1 + dx^2 y^2, \tag{6}$$

where d is not a square element in $\mathbb{F}_p$ and $d \notin \{0, -1\}$. To set up EdDSA signatures, one fixes the following domain parameters:

$b = $ an integer $\geqslant 10$,

$H = $ a cryptographic hash function whose output is $2b$ bits long,

$p = $ a prime congruent to 1 modulo 4,

$d = $ a non-square element in $\mathbb{F}_p$, $d \neq 0, -1$,

$l = $ a prime in the range $\left[2^{b-4}, 2^{b-3}\right]$,

$B = $ a point of the curve that acts as the base point, $B \neq (0, 1)$.

These domain parameters are same for all the entities participating in a network. The Edwards-curve group is an additive group, where the sum of two points $P_1 = (x_1, y_1)$ and $P_2 = (x_2, y_2)$ on the curve is the point $P_3 = P_1 + P_2 = (x_3, y_3)$ that can be computed using the twisted Edwards-curve addition formula as given in [23]:

$$(x_3, y_3) = (x_1, y_1) + (x_2, y_2) = \left(\frac{x_1 y_2 + x_2 y_1}{1 + dx_1 x_2 y_1 y_2}, \frac{y_1 y_2 + x_1 x_2}{1 - dx_1 x_2 y_1 y_2} \right) \tag{7}$$

Now, we describe the three parts of the EdDSA signature scheme. The signer creates his/her key pair using Algorithm 1. Let M be a message, and the EdDSA signature of

Algorithm 1. EdDSA Key Generation

INPUT: Domain Parameters.
OUTPUT: Public key A, private key k.

- Choose a random b-bit string as k.
- Compute $H(k) = (h_0, h_1, \ldots, h_{2b-1})$.
- Compute $a = 2^{b-2} + \sum_{3 \leq i \leq b-3} 2^i h_i$.
- Compute $A = aB$.

Algorithm 2. EdDSA Signature Generation

INPUT: Domain Parameters, message M, private key k, and $H(k) = (h_0, h_1, \ldots, h_{2b-1})$.
OUTPUT: The EdDSA signature (R', S) on M.

- Compute $r = H(h_b, \ldots, h_{2b-1}, M)$.
- Compute $R = rB \in E$.
- R' = (the sign bit of the x-coordinate of R) $\|$ (the y-coordinate of R).
- Compute $S = r + H(R', A, M)a \pmod{l}$.

the message be (R, S). Algorithm 2 generates the signature of the message. The validity of the signature is checked by Algorithm 3.

In the verification Algorithm 3, we have to compute R from R' which contains the sign bit of the x-coordinate and the y-coordinate of the point R. From the known y-coordinate, we first compute two x-coordinates by $x \equiv \pm\sqrt{\frac{y^2-1}{dy^2+1}} \pmod{p}$, and then solve the sign problem using the sign bit present in R'. We can avoid the square-root computation in the verification method. We propose an alternative signature-verification Algorithm 4 which is a straightforward adaptation of the ECDSA signature-verification

Algorithm 3. EdDSA Signature Verification

INPUT: Domain Parameters, message M, public key A, and signature (R', S).
OUTPUT: Accept or reject.

- Compute $H(R', A, M)$.
- Compute R from R' (using a square-root computation as described in the text).
- Accept the signature if and only if the equation $SB = R + H(R', A, M)A$ holds.

Algorithm 4. Alternative EdDSA Signature Verification

INPUT: Domain Parameters, message M, public key A, and signature (R', S).
OUTPUT: Accept or reject.

- Compute $H(R', A, M)$.
- Extract the y-coordinate R_y of R from R'.
- Accept the signature if and only if the equation $R_y = y(SB - H(R', A, M)A)$ holds.

algorithm. The correctness of Algorithm 4 can be easily proved as follows. We have $S = (r + H(R',A,M)a) \pmod{l}$, that is, $r = S - H(R',A,M)a$. Multiplying both sides by B, we get $rB = SB - H(R',A,M)aB$, that is $R = SB - H(R',A,M)A$. Therefore $y(R) = y(SB - H(R',A,M)A)$.

4   Batch Verification of EdDSA

Like ECDSA, only the y-coordinate of an Edwards-curve point is sent in an EdDSA signature. An extra bit to identify the correct x-coordinate is included in the signature. All the batch-verification algorithms studied in connection with ECDSA apply equally well to EdDSA signatures. Suppose that we want to verify a batch $(M_1,R'_1,S_1), (M_2,R'_2,S_2)$, $\ldots, (M_t,R'_t,S_t)$ of t EdDSA signatures. Let R_i be the corresponding point of R'_i. We combine the individual verification equations for the t signatures as:

$$\left(\sum_{i=1}^{t} S_i\right) B - \sum_{i=1}^{t} H(R'_i,A_i,M_i)A_i = \sum_{i=1}^{t} R_i. \tag{8}$$

If all the signatures are from the same signer, that is, $A_1 = A_2 = \cdots = A_t = A$, then Eqn(8) simplifies to:

$$\left(\sum_{i=1}^{t} S_i\right) B - \left(\sum_{i=1}^{t} H(R'_i,A_i,M_i)\right) A = \sum_{i=1}^{t} R_i. \tag{9}$$

Eqn(9) requires only two scalar multiplications. Unlike ECDSA, an EdDSA signature contains an extra bit of information to identify the x-coordinate of R uniquely (after solving a quadratic equation). We can compute the full Edwards-curve point R_i from R'_i for all i. This calls for t square-root computations modulo p. This algorithm is similar to Algorithm N' of [16] and is called Algorithm EdN' here. If the extra bit is not available in the EdDSA signature (or is ignored) to uniquely distinguish the x-coordinate, we have to try all the 2^t combinations of points to verify the batch. We call this naive method Algorithm EdN. The original EdDSA paper [6] recommends Algorithm EdN' as the default batch-verification algorithm.

4.1   Adaptation of Algorithm S2'

We can remove the overhead of square-root computations altogether. The adaptation of Algorithm S2' can solve this problem. Let us call this adapted version Algorithm EdS2'. We first divide the t Edwards-curve points $R_1, R_2, \ldots, R_t$ in two groups. Then, we rewrite Eqn (8) as:

$$\left(\sum_{i=1}^{\lfloor \frac{t}{2} \rfloor} R_i\right) = \left(\sum_{i=1}^{t} S_i\right) B - \left(\sum_{i=1}^{t} H(R'_i,A_i,M_i)\right) A - \left(\sum_{i=\lfloor \frac{t}{2} \rfloor + 1}^{t} R_i\right). \tag{10}$$

We treat the x-coordinates of the points R_i as symbols and compute the symbolic sum of the two sides of Eqn(10). Let the symbolic sum on the left-hand side of Eqn(10) be Q_1, and that on the right-hand side be Q_2. For a valid batch, Q_1 and Q_2 are two symbolic representations of the same point. We have $y(Q_1) \in \mathbb{F}_p \left[x_1, x_2, \ldots, x_{\lfloor \frac{t}{2} \rfloor} \right]$ and $y(Q_2) \in \mathbb{F}_p \left[x_{\lfloor \frac{t}{2} \rfloor+1}, x_{\lfloor \frac{t}{2} \rfloor+2}, \ldots, x_t \right]$. Let $\phi = y(Q_1) - y(Q_2)$, so ϕ is a polynomial in $\mathbb{F}_p[x_1, x_2, \ldots, x_t]$. In ϕ, the maximum degree of any x_i is 1. We write ϕ as $ux_1 + v$, where $u, v \in \mathbb{F}_p[x_2, \ldots, x_t]$. Multiplying ϕ with $ux_1 - v$, we get

$$(ux_1 - v)\phi = (ux_1 - v)(ux_1 + v) = u^2 x_1^2 - v^2.$$

Substituting x_1^2 by $\frac{y_1^2-1}{dy_1^2+1}$, we get $\phi' = (ux_1 - v)\phi = u^2 \left(\frac{y_1^2-1}{dy_1^2+1} \right) - v^2$. To keep the degrees of all remaining x_i to $\leqslant 1$, a substitution phase follows this elimination, in which we replace x_i^2 by $\frac{y_i^2-1}{dy_i^2+1}$ for all $i = 2, 3, \ldots, t$. Using the same procedure, we eliminate all the symbolic x-coordinates $x_2, x_3, \ldots, x_t$ one by one. At the end, if we obtain the zero polynomial, we accept the batch of signatures, else we reject it.

4.2   Edwards-Curve Summation Polynomials and Adaptation of Algorithm SP

Here, we mention the adaptation necessary to make Algorithm SP of [17] work for EdDSA batch verification. The two base cases f_2 and f_3 of Edwards-curve summation polynomials, and the recurrence relation to compute the summation polynomial f_t for $t \geq 4$ are:

$$f_2(y_1, y_2) = y_1 - y_2,$$
$$f_3(y_1, y_2, y_3) = c^2(V - d^2 U y_1^2 y_2^2)y_3^2 - 2y_1 y_2(V - dU)y_3 + (Vy_1^2 y_2^2 - U),$$
$$\text{where } U = (c^2 - y_1^2)(c^2 - y_2^2) \text{ and } V = (1 - c^2 dy_1^2)(1 - c^2 dy_2^2),$$
$$f_t(y_1, y_2, \ldots, y_t) = \text{Res}_Y (f_{t-k}(y_1, \ldots, y_{t-k-1}, Y), f_{k+2}(y_{t-k}, \ldots, y_t, Y))$$
$$\text{for } t \geqslant 4 \text{ and for any } k \text{ in the range } 1 \leqslant k \leqslant t - 3.$$

The summation polynomial f_t evaluated at the t arguments $y_1, y_2, \ldots, y_t$ is zero if and only if there exists an x_i in $\overline{\mathbb{F}}_p$ for each y_i, where $1 \leqslant i \leqslant t$, such that $-x_i^2 + y_i^2 = 1 + dx_i^2 y_i^2$. If the batch-verification condition of Eqn(8) or (9) is expressed as $\sum_{i=1}^t (x_i, y_i) + (-\alpha, \beta) = \mathcal{O}$, it therefore suffices to check whether $f_{t+1}(y_1, y_2, \ldots, y_t, \beta) = 0$. To restrict our attention to curve points defined over $\mathbb{F}_p$ only, we need to carry out the sanity check introduced in [17]. The sanity check for Edwards curves follows the same procedure as for elliptic curves (check whether the Legendre symbol $\left(\frac{(y_i^2-1)/(dy_i^2+1)}{p} \right) = 1$).

5   Randomization of EdDSA Batch-Verification Algorithms

EdDSA signatures can be randomized easily by methods similar to the randomization methods for ECDSA. For randomly chosen multipliers $\xi_1, \xi_2, \ldots, \xi_t$, we now verify whether the following equality holds:

$$\left(\sum_{i=1}^t \xi_i S_i \right) B - \sum_{i=1}^t \xi_i H(R_i', A_i, M_i) A_i = \sum_{i=1}^t \xi_i R_i. \tag{11}$$

For the case of the same signer, that is, $A_1 = A_2 = \cdots = A_t = A$, Eqn(11) simplifies to:

$$\left(\sum_{i=1}^{t} \xi_i s_i\right) B - \left(\sum_{i=1}^{t} \xi_i H(R_i', A_i, M_i)\right) A = \sum_{i=1}^{t} \xi_i R_i. \tag{12}$$

The default batch-verification algorithm for EdDSA is EdN', in which we explicitly and uniquely compute the points R_i by square-root computations modulo p. Subsequently, their multiples $\xi_i R_i$ can be computed *numerically*. We finally check whether the condition of Eqn(11) or (12) holds. The process does not involve any symbolic or summation-polynomial computation. In a variant denoted by EdN, we assume that R_i cannot be uniquely determined, so we need to try all possible combinations of the signs of x_i. For each combination, randomization proceeds numerically as in the case of EdN'.

We may, however, ignore the presence of the extra bit in R_i' identifying the correct value of x_i. By doing so, we can adapt the randomized Algorithms EdS2' and EdSP to work for EdDSA. This is motivated by a need to avoid costly square-root computations of Algorithm EdN'.

In order to apply Algorithm EdS2' to the batch-verification Eqn(11) or (12), it suffices to compute the y-coordinates of all $\xi_i R_i$. As in the case of ECDSA, we can uniquely compute $y(\xi_i R_i)$ from the knowledge of ξ_i and $y(R_i)$ alone. More precisely, let $R = (x, y)$ be a point on the Edwards curve. Any multiple uR of R can be expressed as (hx, k), where $h, k \in \mathbb{F}_p$ are fully determined by (u and) the y-coordinate of R. R itself is so expressed with $h = 1$ and $k = y$. The sum of two multiples $P_1 = (h_1 x, k_1)$ and $P_2 = (h_2 x, y_2)$ of R is $P_1 + P_2 = (h_3 x, k_3)$, where

$$h_3 = (h_1 k_2 + h_2 k_1)/(1 + d h_1 h_2 k_1 k_2 f),$$
$$k_3 = (k_1 k_2 + h_1 h_2 f)/(1 - d h_1 h_2 k_1 k_2 f),$$

with f precomputed as $f = x^2 = (y^2 - 1)/(dy^2 + 1) \in \mathbb{F}_p$. For Edwards curves, the doubling formula is the same as the addition formula. That is, the double of $P_1 = (h_1 x, k_1)$ is $2P_1 = (h_4 x, k_4)$, where

$$h_4 = 2 h_1 k_1/(1 + d h_1^2 k_1^2 f),$$
$$k_4 = (k_1^2 + h_1^2 f)/(1 - d h_1^2 k_1^2 f).$$

We henceforth refer to this computation of $y(\xi_i R_i)$ as the *seminumeric* randomization method.

We can also use *Montgomery ladders* [24] to compute $y(\xi_i R_i)$. For deriving the Montgomery-ladder formulas, let $P_1 = (h_1, k_1)$ and $P_2 = (h_2, k_2)$ be two points on the curve. For point addition, we need the y-coordinate of the point $P_1 - P_2$ as follows.

$$y(P_1 + P_2) = \frac{2 k_1 k_2 (1 + d h_1^2 h_2^2)}{1 - d h_1^2 h_2^2 (k_1 k_2)^2} - y(P_1 - P_2).$$

Here, $h_i^2 = (k_i^2 - 1)/(d k_i^2 + 1)$ for $i = 1, 2$. Finally, point doubling uses the formula

$$y(2P_1) = \frac{k_1^2 + h_1^2}{1 - d h_1^2 k_1^2},$$

where $h_1^2 = (k_1^2 - 1)/(dk_1^2 + 1)$. These formulas can be easily converted to projective coordinates.

Let us now theoretically compare the performance of the seminumeric method with that of the Montgomery-ladder method. Let $P_1 = (\alpha_1 x, \beta_1, \gamma_1)$ and $P_2 = (\alpha_2 x, \beta_2, \gamma_2)$ be two points on the curve in standard projective coordinates. The seminumeric method computes the sum $P_3 = P_1 + P_2 = (\alpha_3 x, \beta_3, \gamma_3)$ and the double $P_4 = 2P_1 = (\alpha_4 x, \beta_4, \gamma_4)$ as given below:

Point Addition

$A = \gamma_1 \cdot \gamma_2$, $B = A^2$, $C = \alpha_1 \cdot \alpha_2$, $C_1 = C \cdot f_x$, $D = \beta_1 \cdot \beta_2$, $E = d \cdot C_1 \cdot D$, $F = B - E$,
$G = B + E$, $\alpha_3 = A \cdot F \cdot ((\alpha_1 + \beta_1) \cdot (\alpha_2 + \beta_2) - C - D)$, $\beta_3 = A \cdot G \cdot (D + C_1)$,
$\gamma_3 = F \cdot G$.

Point Doubling

$B = (\alpha_1 + \beta_1)^2$, $C = \alpha_1^2$, $C_1 = C \cdot f_x$, $D = \beta_1^2$, $E_1 = C_1 + D$, $E_2 = C + D$, $H = \gamma_1^2$,
$J = E_1 - 2 \cdot H$, $\alpha_4 = (B - E_2) \cdot J$, $\beta_4 = E_1 \cdot (C_1 + D)$, $\gamma_4 = E_1 \cdot J$.

Each of seminumeric point addition and point doubling requires one extra field multiplication than the optimized implementation given in [25]. More precisely, seminumeric point addition and doubling take $(11M + 1S)$ and $(4M + 4S)$ field operations respectively (ignoring the negligible time consumed by multiplication by d and field addition).

The Montgomery-ladder method requires $(14M + 6S)$ field operations for each addition and doubling combined in each iteration.

We can use any windowed variant of point multiplication in the seminumeric point multiplication method. On the contrary, no effective windowed variant is known for Montgomery ladders. Moreover, the practical ladder described in [26] is efficient only for constant multipliers, which is not the case with randomized batch verification. We therefore use only the binary ladder.

Let us use l-bit randomizers. If we use the w-NAF method in the seminumeric computation, the precomputation stage needs $(4M + 4S) + (2^{w-1} - 1)(11M + 1S)$ field operations, and $\left(\frac{l}{w+1}\right)(11M + 1S)$ field operations are required to perform the scalar multiplication. The seminumeric scalar multiplication is faster than the Montgomery-ladder method if

$$(4M + 4S) + (2^{w-1} - 1)(11M + 1S) + (4M + 4S)l + \left(\frac{l(11M + 1S)}{w + 1}\right) \leqslant l(14M + 6S).$$

Putting $w = 4$ and assuming $1M \approx 1S$, we deduce that for $l \geqslant 10$ the seminumeric method is faster than the Montgomery-ladder method.

6   Experimental Results

The algorithms are implemented in a 2.33 GHz Xeon server running Ubuntu Linux Version 2012 LTS. The algorithms are implemented using the GP/PARI calculator [27] (version 2.5.0 compiled by the GNU C compiler 4.6.2). We have used the symbolic-computation facilities of the calculator in our programs. All other functions (like scalar multiplication and square-root computation) are written as subroutines with minimal function-call overheads. Since the algorithms are evaluated in terms of the numbers of field operations, this gives a fair comparison of experimental data with the theoretical estimates. We have implemented windowed, w-NAF and frac-w-NAF methods for square-root computations and for numeric and seminumeric randomization methods. We have used affine and standard projective coordinates. We have performed all the experiments on the Edwards curve Ed25519 [6].

Table 2 lists the overheads associated with all the batch-verification algorithms. We present the times required for the numeric and seminumeric scalar multiplications in Table 4. The best results obtained are highlighted and used in speedup computations. In the randomization of the batch-verification algorithms, the scalars are not constant, so we have to compute the addition chain for each scalar multiplication. The timing figures

Table 2. Overhead (in ms) of different batch-verification algorithms for EdDSA

Batch Size	Algorithm			
t	EdN	EdN$'$	EdS2$'$	EdSP
2	0.08	0.03	0.06	0.06
3	0.24	0.04	0.12	0.10
4	0.63	0.06	0.24	0.12
5	1.54	0.07	0.52	0.28
6	3.71	0.08	0.96	1.36
7	8.74	0.10	2.02	2.72

Table 3. Times (in ms) of square-root computations in the underlying field

↓ Algorithm			Times (in ms)
w-numeric (affine)	$w=3$		0.36
	$w=4$		**0.28**
	$w=5$		**0.28**
w-NAF-numeric (affine)	$w=3$		**0.28**
	$w=4$		**0.28**
	$w=5$		0.32
Frac-w-NAF-numeric (affine)	$w=3$	$m=1$	0.33
	$w=4$	$m=1$	**0.28**
		$m=3$	0.32
		$m=5$	0.32
	$w=5$	$m=1$	0.32
		$m=3$	0.32
		$m=5$	0.32
		$m=7$	0.36
		$m=9$	0.32
		$m=11$	0.32
		$m=13$	0.36

presented in Table 4 include the addition-chain computation times. Table 3 shows the square-root computation times obtained by various windowed algorithms. The times needed to carry out the Montgomery-ladder scalar multiplication are supplied in Table 5. Finally, the overall speedup figures obtained by the four batch-verification algorithms EdN, EdN′, EdS2′ and EdSP are listed in Table 6. In the speedup table, we include the results using both the default signature-verification Algorithm 3 and the ECDSA-like signature-verification Algorithm 4.

For batch sizes in the range $2 \leqslant t \leqslant 7$, the speedup obtained by Algorithms EdS2′ and EdSP is competitive with that obtained by the default batch-verification Algorithm EdN′. Algorithms EdS2′ and EdSP outperform Algorithm EdN′ if we use the default Algorithm 3 for individual verification. On the other hand, if we use the ECDSA-like verification Algorithm 4 for individual verification, Algorithm EdS2′

Table 4. Times (in ms) of the numeric and seminumeric randomization methods

↓ Algorithm			Numeric Methods		SemiNumeric Methods	
			$l = 128$	$l = 255$	$l = 128$	$l = 255$
w-numeric (affine)	$w = 3$		2.28	4.40	2.40	4.68
	$w = 4$		2.28	4.41	2.44	4.61
	$w = 5$		2.45	4.40	2.60	4.69
w-NAF-numeric (affine)	$w = 3$		2.28	4.53	2.44	4.81
	$w = 4$		2.20	4.40	2.33	4.64
	$w = 5$		2.28	4.25	2.36	4.48
Frac-w-NAF-numeric (affine)	$w = 3$	$m = 1$	2.44	4.77	2.61	5.01
	$w = 4$	$m = 1$	2.45	4.76	2.52	4.96
		$m = 3$	2.44	4.73	2.53	4.97
		$m = 5$	2.44	4.73	2.56	4.89
	$w = 5$	$m = 1$	2.40	4.61	2.53	4.80
		$m = 3$	2.48	4.60	2.52	4.85
		$m = 5$	2.44	4.64	2.57	4.85
		$m = 7$	2.49	4.69	2.56	4.88
		$m = 9$	2.48	4.73	2.60	4.88
		$m = 11$	2.48	4.68	2.60	4.89
		$m = 13$	2.52	4.72	2.64	4.89
w-numeric (Jacobian projective)	$w = 3$		1.28	2.48	**1.40**	2.76
	$w = 4$		1.28	2.36	1.44	**2.68**
	$w = 5$		1.36	**2.44**	1.52	**2.68**
w-NAF-numeric (Jacobian projective)	$w = 3$		1.32	2.60	1.48	2.88
	$w = 4$		**1.24**	2.49	1.44	2.81
	$w = 5$		1.28	**2.44**	1.44	2.73
Frac-w-NAF-numeric (Jacobian projective)	$w = 3$	$m = 1$	1.53	2.92	1.60	3.12
	$w = 4$	$m = 1$	1.48	2.88	1.64	3.12
		$m = 3$	1.48	2.84	1.60	3.12
		$m = 5$	1.48	2.84	1.64	3.12
	$w = 5$	$m = 1$	1.49	2.80	1.60	3.04
		$m = 3$	1.48	2.85	1.64	3.04
		$m = 5$	1.48	2.80	1.60	3.04
		$m = 7$	1.48	2.84	1.60	3.09
		$m = 9$	1.52	2.84	1.65	3.08
		$m = 11$	1.53	2.81	1.64	3.04
		$m = 13$	1.52	2.84	1.64	3.08

Table 5. Times (in ms) of the Montgomery-ladder randomization method

Coordinate system	$l = 128$	$l = 255$
Affine	2.96	5.85
Standard projective	1.96	3.88

outperforms Algorithm EdN′ for batch sizes $t \leqslant 7$, and Algorithm EdSP is faster than Algorithm EdN′ for batch sizes $\leqslant 5$.

In short, replacing square-root computations by symbolic or resultant computations does not degrade the batch-verification process, so long as we restrict only to small batches of signatures. However, the overhead of the default batch-verification algorithm EdN′ increases linearly with the batch size, whereas that of EdS2′ or EdSP increases exponentially. Consequently, EdN′ must eventually take over the exponential algorithms (not demonstrated in the experimental results though).

Table 6. Speedup (over individual verification) obtained by different randomized and non-randomized batch-verification methods in the case of the same signer for two verification algorithms

Batch Verification Algorithm	Randomization Algorithm	Batch Size	Algorithm 3		Algorithm 4	
			None*	$l = 128$	None*	$l = 128$
EdN	Numeric	2	1.87	1.29	1.77	1.22
		3	2.60	1.60	2.46	1.51
		4	3.11	1.78	2.94	1.68
		5	3.30	1.84	3.12	1.74
		6	3.01	1.75	2.85	1.65
		7	2.32	1.49	2.19	1.41
EdN′	Numeric	2	1.89	1.30	1.78	1.23
		3	2.69	1.63	2.54	1.54
		4	3.41	1.87	3.22	1.77
		5	4.06	2.06	3.84	1.94
		6	4.66	2.20	4.41	2.08
		7	5.20	2.31	4.92	2.19
EdS2′	Seminumeric	2	2.09	1.33	1.98	1.26
		3	3.10	1.68	2.93	1.59
		4	4.03	1.93	3.81	1.82
		5	4.78	2.08	4.52	1.97
		6	5.30	2.17	5.01	2.06
		7	5.23	2.16	4.95	2.05
EdSP	Seminumeric	2	2.09	1.33	1.98	1.26
		3	3.11	1.69	2.94	1.59
		4	4.13	1.95	3.90	1.84
		5	5.00	2.12	4.73	2.01
		6	4.96	2.11	4.69	2.00
		7	4.75	2.08	4.49	1.96

* without randomization

7   Conclusion

In this paper, we port several batch-verification algorithms proposed for ECDSA to EdDSA signatures. We also address the issues of randomizing the batch-verification process. Our experimental results demonstrate that the default batch-verification algorithm proposed for EdDSA can be slightly improved by using the new developments based on symbolic and resultant computations, at least for small batch sizes. Further advances in this new area of research can substantially enhance the applicability of the new proposals for EdDSA signatures. It is a challenging open problem whether the time complexities of the new algorithms can be brought down from exponential to polynomial. Prospects of achieving breakthroughs are expected to keep research in this area alive in near future.

References

1. Diffie, W., Hellman, M.E.: New directions in cryptography. IEEE Transactions on Information Theory 22, 644–654 (1976)
2. Rivest, R., Shamir, A., Adleman, L.: A method for obtaining digital signatures and public-key cryptosystems. Communications of the ACM 21, 120–126 (1978)
3. ElGamal, T.: A public key cryptosystem and a signature scheme based on discrete logarithms. IEEE Transactions on Information Theory 31, 469–472 (1985)
4. NIST: The digital signature standard. Communications of the ACM 35(7), 36–40 (1992)
5. Johnson, D., Menezes, A., Vanstone, S.A.: The elliptic curve digital signature algorithm (ECDSA). Int. J. Inf. Sec. 1(1), 36–63 (2001)
6. Bernstein, D.J., Duif, N., Lange, T., Schwabe, P., Yang, B.Y.: High-speed high-security signatures. Journal of Cryptographic Engineering 2(2), 77–89 (2012)
7. Naccache, D., M'Raïhi, D., Vaudenay, S., Raphaeli, D.: Can D.S.A. Be Improved?: Complexity trade-offs with the Digital Signature Standard. In: De Santis, A. (ed.) EUROCRYPT 1994. LNCS, vol. 950, pp. 77–85. Springer, Heidelberg (1995)
8. Fiat, A.: Batch RSA. Journal of Cryptology 10, 75–88 (1997)
9. Harn, L.: Batch verifying multiple RSA digital signatures. Electronics Letters 34(12), 1219–1220 (1998)
10. Hwang, M.S., Lin, I.C., Hwang, K.F.: Cryptanalysis of the batch verifying multiple RSA digital signatures. Informatica 11(1), 15–19 (2000)
11. NIST: SP 800-52 Rev. 1. NIST Special publication (2013)
12. Antipa, A., Brown, D., Gallant, R., Lambert, R., Struik, R., Vanstone, S.: Accelerated verification of ECDSA signatures. In: Preneel, B., Tavares, S. (eds.) SAC 2005. LNCS, vol. 3897, pp. 307–318. Springer, Heidelberg (2006)
13. Cheon, J.H., Yi, J.H.: Fast batch verification of multiple signatures. In: Okamoto, T., Wang, X. (eds.) PKC 2007. LNCS, vol. 4450, pp. 442–457. Springer, Heidelberg (2007)
14. Edwards, H.M.: A normal form for elliptic curves. Bulletin of American Mathematical Society 44(3), 393–422 (2007)
15. Das, A., Choudhury, D.R., Bhattacharya, D., Rajavelu, S., Shorey, R., Thomas, T.: Authentication schemes for VANETs: A survey. International Journal of Vehicle Information and Communication Systems 3(1), 1–27 (2013)
16. Karati, S., Das, A., Roychowdhury, D., Bellur, B., Bhattacharya, D., Iyer, A.: Batch verification of ECDSA signatures. In: Mitrokotsa, A., Vaudenay, S. (eds.) AFRICACRYPT 2012. LNCS, vol. 7374, pp. 1–18. Springer, Heidelberg (2012)
17. Karati, S., Das, A.: Faster batch verification of standard ECDSA signatures using summation polynomials. In: Boureanu, I., Owesarski, P., Vaudenay, S. (eds.) ACNS 2014. LNCS, vol. 8479, pp. 438–456. Springer, Heidelberg (2014)
18. Bernstein, D.J., Doumen, J., Lange, T., Oosterwijk, J.-J.: Faster batch forgery identification. In: Galbraith, S., Nandi, M. (eds.) INDOCRYPT 2012. LNCS, vol. 7668, pp. 454–473. Springer, Heidelberg (2012)

19. Karati, S., Das, A., Chowdhury, D.R.: Using randomizers for batch verification of ecdsa signatures. IACR Cryptology ePrint Archive 2012, 582 (2012)
20. Antipa, A., Brown, D., Gallant, R., Lambert, R., Struik, R., Vanstone, S.: Accelerated verification of ECDSA signatures. In: Preneel, B., Tavares, S. (eds.) SAC 2005. LNCS, vol. 3897, pp. 307–318. Springer, Heidelberg (2006)
21. Cheon, J.H., Yi, J.H.: Fast batch verification of multiple signatures. In: Okamoto, T., Wang, X. (eds.) PKC 2007. LNCS, vol. 4450, pp. 442–457. Springer, Heidelberg (2007)
22. Bellare, M., Garay, J.A., Rabin, T.: Fast batch verification for modular exponentiation and digital signatures. In: Nyberg, K. (ed.) EUROCRYPT 1998. LNCS, vol. 1403, pp. 236–250. Springer, Heidelberg (1998)
23. Bernstein, D.J., Birkner, P., Joye, M., Lange, T., Peters, C.: Twisted Edwards curves. In: Vaudenay, S. (ed.) AFRICACRYPT 2008. LNCS, vol. 5023, pp. 389–405. Springer, Heidelberg (2008)
24. Montgomery, P.L.: Speeding up pollard and elliptic curve methods of factorization. Mathematics of Computation 48(177), 243–264 (1987)
25. Bernstein, D.J., Lange, T.: Explicit-formulas database (2007), http://www.hyperelliptic.org/EFD/index.html
26. Montgomery, P.L.: Evaluating recurrences of form $X_{m+n} = f(X_m, X_n, X_{m-n})$ via Lucas chains. Microsoft research article, 582 (1992)
27. PARI Group: PARI/GP home (2008), http://pari.math.u-bordeaux.fr/

Faster Randomness Testing with the NIST Statistical Test Suite

Marek Sýs and Zdeněk Říha

Masaryk University, Brno, Czech Republic
{syso,zriha}@fi.muni.cz

Abstract. Randomness testing plays an important role in cryptography. Randomness is typically examined by batteries of statistical tests. One of the most frequently used test batteries is the NIST Statistical Test Suite. The tests of randomness should be rather fast since they usually process large volumes of data. Unfortunately, this is not the case for the NIST STS, where a complete test can take hours. Alternative implementations do exist, but are not very efficient either or they do not focus on the most time-consuming tests. We reimplemented all NIST STS tests and achieved interesting speedups in most of the tests, including the tests with the highest time complexity. Overall, our implementation runs 30 times faster than the original code.

Keywords: Berlekamp-Massey algorithm, NIST STS, randomness statistical testing.

1 Introduction

Randomness is connected with many areas of computer science, in particular with cryptography. Well designed cryptographic primitives like hash functions, stream ciphers, etc., should produce pseudorandom data. Randomness testing therefore plays an important and fundamental role in cryptography. Randomness is typically examined by empirical tests of randomness. Each test examines data by looking at a specific feature (number of ones, m-bit blocks, etc.). Tests are usually grouped into test batteries (also called test suites) to provide more complex randomness analysis. When testing any new source of (pseudo)randomness, the statistical test suites are of crucial importance. New sources of (pseudo)randomness include pseudorandom generators and entropy collectors for various kinds of environments (including smartcard, wireless sensor nodes, mobile devices, servers, desktops, etc.) and quite many new ideas and/or environments are emerging, so the tests are run very frequently in practice. Passing statistical tests of randomness is an important step for a (pseudo)random data generator being recognized or approved by certification bodies or other authorities.

All tests measure how the observed statistics of the analysed feature fit the expected statistics. Empirical tests of randomness compare the expected and obtained characteristics by standard statistical methods. Thus randomness is

R.S. Chakraborty et al. (Eds.): SPACE 2014, LNCS 8804, pp. 272–284, 2014.
© Springer International Publishing Switzerland 2014

characterized and described in the terms of probability. The result of each test is a P-value that represents the probability that the chosen test statistic will assume values that are equal to or worse than the observed test statistics. This concept allows one to evaluate randomness according to several examined features at once. Combination of several P-values increases the confidence about the randomness/non-randomness of given data. Confidence about the data randomness can be also increased by increasing the analysed data volume. In practice, the analysed data volume is usually in the order of GBs and therefore the speed of these tests should be high. Unfortunately, most batteries are not implemented efficiently.

There are five well-known batteries – NIST STS [3], Diehard [4], TestU01 [6], ENT [7] and CryptX [8]. Only the first three batteries are commonly used for the randomness analysis, since CryptX is a commercial software and ENT provides only a very basic randomness testing. Position of the NIST STS is special as it has been published as an official NIST document. Therefore NIST STS is often used in preparation of formal certifications or approvals. Diehard and its novel implementation Dieharder were proposed for testing randomness of numbers rather than bitstreams. The newest and most powerful battery TestU01 was introduced in 2007 by Lecleuyer and Simard. TestU01 [6] incorporates new tests and implements the current state of the art of randomness testing. Diehard/Dieharder and TestU01 also implement some of the NIST tests, but they do not implement all NIST tests (Diehard) or the tests are not efficient (TestU01).

From time to time, there appear news about optimised versions of NIST STS. However, no such optimisation with either full description of the changes or NIST 'approval' exists, at least to our best knowledge. The goal of our work is to rewrite the NIST STS battery into a new version, with the same tests, with much better time- and space-efficient implementation of empirical tests of randomness and to provide a full description of the optimisations in an open publication, together with the source code openly available.

This paper is organised as follows: Section 2 provides an overview of the NIST tests, alternative implementations and the performance of the original code. Section 3 briefly describes our improvements. Section 4 discusses how we evaluated our algorithms and Section 5 summarizes the results of the performance testing.

2 Statistical Test Suites

The NIST tests are defined in [3]. The NIST Statistical Test Suite (NIST STS) package implements all the NIST tests. Although some particular NIST tests are also implemented in other test batteries (Diehard, TestU01), we further focus on the reimplementation of the whole NIST STS package.

2.1 NIST Statistical Tests

The original NIST document [1] defined 16 empirical test of randomness. These tests were developed to test the hardware or software based cryptographic random or pseudorandom number generators. During the next two revisions [2,3], the Lempel-Ziv test was removed due to implementation problems identified by the NIST. The current set of the NIST tests consists of 15 tests. All tests are parameterised by a parameter n that denotes the length (in bits) of the processed bitstream. Although all the tests are proposed to detect deviations from randomness for the whole bitstream, only several tests can detect local non-randomness. These tests are also parameterised by a second parameter denoted by m or M [3]. Tests parameterised by m are developed to detect the presence of too many m-bit patterns in a sequence. Tests with the second parameter M examine distribution of the specific feature across n/M parts (of equal size M bits) of a given bitstream. All tests in NIST STS compute P-values using asymptotic reference distributions (χ^2 or normal) and therefore reasonable results are obtained only for appropriate settings of the parameters n, m and M. Overview of all the tests and meaningful settings of their parameters are summarized in Table 1.

Table 1. The recommended size n of the bitstream for the particular tests. Some tests are parameterised by a second parameter m, M, respectively. The table shows meaningful settings of the second parameter depending on n.

Test #	Test name	n	m or M
1.	Frequency (Monobit)	$n > 100$	-
2.	Frequency within a Block		$20 \leq M \leq n/100$
3.	Runs	$n \geq 100$	-
4.	Longest run of ones in a block		
5.	Binary Matrix Rank	$n > 38912$	-
6.	Discrete Fourier Transform (Spectral)	$n \geq 1000$	-
7.	Non-overlapping Template Matching		$2 \leq m \leq 21$
8.	Overlapping Template Matching		$1 \leq m \leq n$
9.	Maurer's Universal		$1 \leq m \leq n$
10.	Linear complexity	$n > 10^6$	$500 \leq M \leq 5000$
11.	Serial		$3 \leq m \leq \lfloor \log_2 n \rfloor - 3$
12.	Approximate Entropy		$m \leq \lfloor \log_2 n \rfloor - 6$
13.	Cumulative sums	$n > 100$	
14.	Random Excursions	$n \geq 10^6$	
15.	Random Excursions Variant	$n \geq 10^6$	

2.2   NIST STS

The NIST test suite implements various random number generators and the 15 empirical tests developed to test randomness of binary sequences. The whole package is written in ANSI C in order to obtain a platform independent code. The source code of NIST STS was ported to Windows XP and Ubuntu Linux, and with minor modifications it also may be ported to different platforms. The NIST STS transforms an input file (stored as ASCII characters '0' and '1' or as binary data) to a byte array, where each byte (value 0 or 1) represents a single bit of the analysed bitstream. Byte representation of data allows one to use the same implementation of tests on little- and big-endian systems. The code universality comes at the expense of memory and time inefficiency of tests. Some of the tests have a preprocessing phase, but it is negligible for large volumes of data. The time complexity of each test is linear according to data volume n. The performance of the Rank test described in Figure 2 illustrates the linearity of tests. Performance of the tests with the second parameter (m, M) depends on its particular value. Table 2 shows run times of tests (implemented in the NIST STS) obtained after processing 20 MB of pseudorandom data ($n = 167,772,160$) with minimum and maximum recommended values of m or M. Table also shows the percentage to identify the time critical tests.

Table 2. Run times of particular tests obtained for minimum and maximum values of their second parameters m or M

Test	m, M	Time(ms)	%	m, M	Time (ms)	%
Frequency (Monobit)	-	203	0.12	-	203	0.01
Frequency within a Block	$n/100$	46	0.03	20	63	0.00
Runs	-	1140	0.67	-	1140	0.08
Longest run of ones in a block	-	656	0.39	-	656	0.04
Binary Matrix Rank	-	3781	2.23	-	3781	0.25
Spectral	-	24625	14.50	-	24625	1.63
Non-overlapping Template	2	1750	1.03	21	140015	9.28
Overlapping Template	2	672	0.40	24	3343	0.22
Maurer's Universal	-	2843	1.67	-	2843	0.19
Linear complexity	500	122390	72.04	5000	1187453	78.69
Serial	2	3687	2.17	24	85297	5.65
Approximate Entropy	2	4422	2.60	24	55860	3.70
Cumulative sums	-	984	0.58	-	984	0.07
Random Excursions	-	562	0.33	-	562	0.04
Random Excursions Variant	-	2125	1.25	-	2125	0.14
Total		*169886*	*100*		*1508950*	*100*

2.3 NIST Reimplementations

There were some attempts to reimplement the NIST STS efficiently. In [9] authors rewrite the NIST STS package to a byte-oriented implementation. Byte-oriented code allows one to speed up most tests, since some precomputation (lookup tables) can be used. Authors also made other improvements to the source code and finally obtained 13.45 average speedup of tests. However, this average speedup says nothing about the overall time, since it does not reflects the fact that *durations of particular tests are quite different*. The most time-consuming test (Linear complexity) is only 3 times faster in the reimplemented version [9]. Thus the overall speedup is significantly smaller and the whole testing process is at most 4 times faster. In [10] authors also tried to reimplement the NIST STS, but they obtained mostly worse results than in [9]. Unfortunately, both implementations are not publicly available and therefore we use only the published textual results to compare the perfomance. We contacted the authors of both papers, and we got some response with authors not sharing the source codes.

3   Improvements

Although we probably use ideas and principles similar to those in [9] to speed up some of the tests, our optimizations have been proposed and implemented independently. Moreover, we were able to apply these ideas to speed up the most time-consuming tests, which are Linear complexity, Non-overlapping template matching and the Serial tests.

All our optimizations are based on three basic ideas. We use lookup tables (LUTs), fast extraction of an integer from the byte array and word-word operations instead of bit-bit operations. Each optimization is used for a different type of tests determined by its complexity. Although the run time of each NIST test is linear to the number of bits n, the run times of particular tests vary significantly as we can see in Table 2. Run times of fast (simple) tests are usually influenced by the second parameter m. Poor performance of the most time-consuming tests is caused by subroutines for complex algorithms like Berlekamp-Massey, Gauss elimination or Fast Fourier Transformation.

3.1   Classes of Tests

NIST STS tests can be divided (according to their complexity and used optimizations) into three classes as follows:

1. Fastest tests that process each bit of bitstream once – *Frequency, Block Frequency, Runs, Longest run, Cumulative sums, Random Excursion* and *Random Excursion Variant.*
2. Fast tests that process m-bit blocks – *Non-overlapping template matching, Overlapping template matching, Universal, Serial* and *Approximate entropy.* Run times of these tests are dependent on m since each bit of the m-bit block is compared with some pattern in the NIST STS implementation.
3. Slow and complicated tests – *Linear complexity, Spectral, Rank* – tests that use quadratic algorithms (Linear complexity, Rank) or sub-quadratic algorithm (Spectral).

3.2   Optimizations of Simple Tests

Tests from the class 1 are optimized by the LUTs since these tests compute single value characteristics of bits like proportion of '0' and '1' bits, frequency of bit change (runs), length of runs and cumulative sum of bits. Tests use LUTs that consist of precomputed values for all k-bit blocks indexed by a block interpreted as an integer value. In our implementations, we use $k = 8$ as an appropriate value since the LUTs have a reasonable number of entries ($2^k = 256$). To run the tests we need to divide the bitstream into 8-bit blocks and continuously compute bit characteristics using corresponding table values. Choosing $k = 8$ we have 8-bit blocks since the bitstream is stored as a byte array. The use of LUTs can be illustrated on the Frequency test that computes the number of ones in the bitstream. The frequency test uses a LUT with entries $LUT[i] = v_i$, where v_i represents the number of ones (Hamming weight) in the index i (8-bit block). To compute the number of ones in a bitstream, it is sufficient to sum the corresponding LUT values for all bytes in a byte array. It should be noted that for other tests we use several LUTs that describe the input, output and internal characteristics of 8-bit blocks. For a more detailed description of tests from the first class, look into the source code available at [11].

Tests from the class 2 process m-bit blocks of the bitstream. To speed up these tests, we implemented a fast function *get_nth_block* that can extract arbitrary m-bit block ($m \leq 25$) from a given bitstream (byte array). Upper bound 25 of the block size is sufficient for all the tests from this class since m is upper-bounded by $\log_2 n - 3$ (Serial test). For 20 MB of data this upper bound has the value $m = 24$ and therefore function *get_nth_block* can be used. Function *get_nth_block* is fast and it is able to return all m-bit blocks from a 100 MB bitstream within a second on a standard modern computer. More effective optimization is based on the observation that all these tests (except Universal) can be evaluated from a single histogram of m-bit blocks.

In these tests, we use the histogram represented by the array H of frequencies (integers) of m-bit blocks indexed by blocks themselves. The histogram is computed using the function *get_nth_block* that is used to extract overlapping m-bit blocks b_i for $i \in \{0, 1, \cdots, n - m\}$ from the bitstream. These blocks are used as indexes to H for incrementing the corresponding frequencies $H[b_i]$. Since access to the array H and the increment are very fast operations, the histogram can be obtained also within a second (on the standard modern computer for 100 MB of data). Figure 1 illustrates the typical dependency between parameter m and the performance of the test.

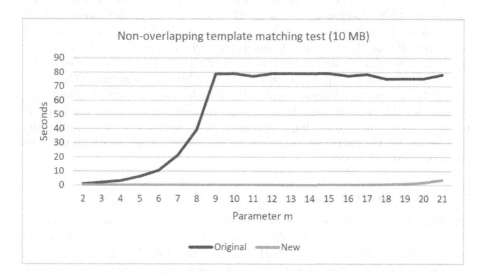

Fig. 1. Run times of the Non-overlapping test

The time complexity of the test depends on the number of searched templates (predefined k-bit patterns), which rise exponentially with the parameter m. Due to exponential nature of the number of templates, the original implementation imposes a practical limit on the maximum number of templates being tested (148). This limit is in effect for all $m > 9$ as we can see in the Figure 1, where the time complexity becomes constant.

Our implementation computes a histogram H for an arbitrary $m < 25$ in the same way and in a single pass. Therefore the complexity of our implementation is constant – independent on m (the real execution is influenced by processor cache management as you can see in Figure 1). Moreover, we compute H for all m-bit patterns and could easily provide complete statistics, yet for the reason of compatibility with the original version we stick to the limit of the maximum number of templates.

3.3 Spectral Test

The Spectral test is the only test that is not reimplemented in our battery. The Spectral test uses the Fast Fourier Transformation and therefore its run time is determined by the prime factors of n rather than by the value n itself. To speed up this test, it suffices to use n with small factors. The best choice is to take n of the form $n = 2^k$, for which the Spectral test run time is comparable to fast tests in the class 1.

3.4 Binary Matrix Rank Test

The Rank test uses the Gaussian elimination subroutine to examine whether the rank of the 32x32 boolean matrix is 32, 31 or less. Our implementation is based on the same idea as the Rank test in [9]. We use word-word operations instead of bit-bit operations. Since the square boolean matrix has the size 32, we represent it as an array of 32 unsigned integers, each of them representing a row of the matrix. Rank of the matrix is computed using fast bitwise operations XOR, AND and shift. The XOR operation realizes the row addition. Bitwise AND and shift are used for the pivot finding. Although our implementation of the Rank test is probably very similar to the implementation in [9], we improve it by adding the stop condition. We stop the computation if there are two columns with no pivot (thus the rank is less than 31).

3.5 Linear Complexity Test

The Linear complexity test is focused on determining the linear complexity L of a finite binary sequence. The linear complexity of a sequence equals to the length of the smallest linear feedback shift register (LFSR) that generates the given sequence. The Linear complexity test uses an efficient Berlekamp-Massey algorithm to compute this smallest LFSR. The Berlekamp-Massey (BM) algorithm for a binary sequence can be described by the following pseudocode:

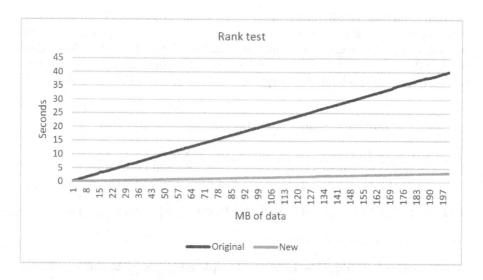

Fig. 2. Run time of the Rank test

Data: binary sequence $S = \{s_0, s_1, \cdots, s_{n-1}\}$ of the length n
Result: shortest LFSR generating S
Set arrays b, c to 1;
Set length L of c to 0;
$m \leftarrow -1$;
for $N \leftarrow 0$ *to n-1* **do**
$\quad$ Compute $d \leftarrow \sum_{i=0}^{L} c_i s_{N-i}$;
$\quad$ **if** $d = 1 \pmod{} 2$ **then**
$\quad\quad$ update c by c $\leftarrow$ c XOR (b >> N-m) ;
$\quad\quad$ t $\leftarrow$ c;
$\quad\quad$ **if** $L \leq n/2$ **then**
$\quad\quad\quad$ t $\leftarrow$ b;
$\quad\quad\quad$ L $\leftarrow$ N + 1 - L;
$\quad\quad\quad$ m $\leftarrow$ N ;
$\quad\quad$ **end**
$\quad$ **end**
end
return c;
$\quad\quad$ **Algorithm 1.** Pseudocode of the Berlekamp-Massey algorithm

The BM algorithm is an iterative method that constructs the smallest LFSR c_N generating the subsequence $S_N = \{s_0, s_1, \cdots, s_N\}$ of $S_n = \{s_0, s_1, \cdots, s_{n-1}\}$, $s_j \in \{0, 1\}$ in the N-th iteration. The BM tests whether the LFSR c_{N-1} that generates the subsequence S_{N-1} also generates the S_N sequence. The BM algorithm computes the discrepancy d that denotes the Hamming weight of the sequence S_N masked with the shifted LFSR c_{N-1} (stored as binary array). The BM algorithm uses another LFSR b_{N-1} (t is used to copy c to b) that represents the last LFSR (different to c_{N-1}) computed up to $N - 1$ iteration. If the discrepancy d is even then $c_N = c_{N-1}$ and $b_N = b_{N-1}$. Table 3 illustrates how the discrepancy is computed from the LFSR. The table shows that the LFSR $b = x_2 + 1$ stored as a bit-array $b = 101$ forms a LFSR for S_4, i.e., $b_4 = 101$ since all discrepancies (sequence masked by shifted b) are even.

Table 3. Principles of the Berlekamp-Massey algorithm

```
   index   |0 1 2 3 4 5 6 7                      index =|0 1 2 3 4 5 6 7 8
   S10 =   |0 1 0 1 1 0 1 1 1                      S10 =|0 1 0 1 1 0 1 1 1
     b =   |1 0 1              d = 0      b' = b >> 2 =|    1 0 1          d = 1
 b >> 1 =  |  1 0 1            d = 2      c' = c >> 6 =|        1 1 1 d = 3
 b >> 2 =  |    1 0 1          d = 1  c'' = b' XOR c' =|    1 0 1 1 1 1 d = 4
```

In the case of an odd d the LFSR c_N is replaced by the right shifted c XORed with $b_{N-1} >> (N - m)$ and b_N is set to c_{N-1}. The idea of combining of c_{N-1}, b_{N-1} to c_N is to get even discrepancy for the application of a new c_N. Table 3 shows the principle of the combination of LFSRs b_7, c_7 (represented by b', c') obtaining the new c_8 (represented by c'').

LFSR $b = 101$ forms the smallest LFSR for S_3, but not for the sequence S_4 and therefore the discrepancy for LFSR b and the subsequence S_4 is odd $(d = 1)$. LFSR $c = 111$ forms the smallest LFSR for S_7, but not for the sequence S_8 $(d = 3)$. The new smallest LFSR c for S_8 is constructed in the way that the discrepancy for a new $c = 1010111$ (represented by the bit array c'') is combined as XOR (in this case $d = 1+3 = 4$) of two odd discrepancies computed earlier for b', c'. It suffices to work with the shifted bit arrays b', c' instead of the original LFSRs b, c. Bit-arrays b', c' represent b, c shifted appropriately for the computation of d.

All improvements to the BM algorithm are based on the following observations:

1. the discrepancy d in the N-th iteration can be computed as the Hamming weight of the masked sequence S_n by bit array c',
2. the next discrepancy in $N + 1$-th iteration is computed using $c' = c' >> 1$ that is shifted one bit to the right.

Our speedup of the BM algorithm is based on word (integer, long) representation of bit arrays S_n, c' and b'. This representation allows one to use fast bitwise operations. AND is used for masking of the word array S_N by the word array c'. The discrepancy d is computed from the masked S_n using a LUT storing the Hamming weights of bytes. XOR is used for the combination of b' and c' into a new $c'' = c'\ XOR\ b'$. In each iteration c' is shifted one bit to the right $c' = c' >> 1$. We made other improvements concerning elimination of processing zero words. For more details about the improvements look at the source code [11].

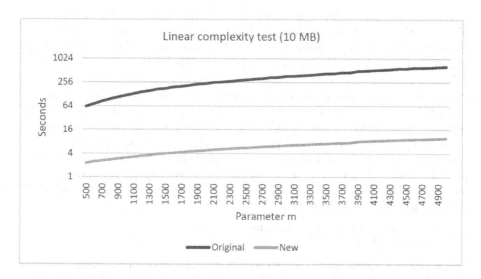

Fig. 3. Run time of the Linear complexity test (note the logarithmic scale of the y axis).

4   Implementation Testing

After the implementation of the faster variants of the algorithms we ran series of tests. The first tests were aimed at verification of the correctness. We verified the correctness of all values that are outputs from the tests (we ran both the original and new implementation and compared the results).

Many of the results are floating point numbers stored in the *double* type. Comparing floating point numbers can be tricky. We compiled the program with the improved consistency of floating-point operations. In majority of tests all the results stored as doubles matched perfectly in all the bits. In exceptional cases (Runs test) the results differed in a single (least significant) bit due to compiler computational optimizations. In these cases we had to allow for the differences in the least significant bit of the mantissa of the double type. Moreover we allow for the negligible difference of *FLT_EPSILON* for the same reasons in the Approximate entropy tests. We also had to consider special values of floating point numbers (e.g., the variable a storing the INDefinite value does not fullfil the $a == a$ condition) during comparison of the results.

We performed series of tests of all the algorithms with many different lengths of the bitsteams and with different parameters. We used pseudorandom bit sequences and also special values such as zeros, ones and alternating ones and zeros.

We followed the NIST parameter recommendations and typically performed the tests for all the bitstream lengths between 1 and 1,000,000 bits. We also performed the tests for randomly chosen bitstream lengths between 1 bit and 800,000,000 bits such that the length $n_{i+1} = n_i * 10 + rand()\%8$ was computed to catch possible errors caused by bitstream lengths not being a multiple of 8.

We were not able to perform all the above mentioned tests due to time complexity of the tests (Spectral, Non-overlapping template matching, Approximate entropy, Serial, Linear complexity) or high number of possible configurations (Block Frequency) for the time-consuming tests. Therefore we only performed a subset of the tests.

In a few configurations our implementation does provide a result while the original implementation is not able to compute a result (e.g., the Random Excursion test is limited in the number of cycles), in some situations our implementation does not support unusual parameters while the original implementation does (e.g., the Serial test with $m > 25$). In such situations, we could not compare the results. In all other situations the results do match. The limitations of our implementation with respect to the original implementation and the NIST recommendations (see Table 1) are:

– Overlapping template matching test: $m \leq 25$,
– Serial: $m \leq 25$.

The above mentioned limitation of the m above 25 can be easily shifted towards 32 as described in the Readme.txt file at [11]. The verification tests are time-consuming, but if you are interested you can run them on your own system as described in the source codes.

5   Performance Testing

We measured both the number of CPU cycles and the time consumed in milliseconds. As the results of both measurements are consistent, we present only the results in milliseconds (for very short tests the duration in milliseconds is recomputed from the number of CPU cycles). We performed all the tests ten times and we used the minimum value to avoid the noise introduced by the OS scheduling.

The source code, including the verification of the results and the speed measurement, can be compiled on Linux systems (tested with gcc 4.4.7 on RHEL 6.5), but we primarily used MS Windows for testing. The speed improvement was measured on a Windows 8.1 Fujitsu S792 notebook equipped with Intel Core i7 having 2 cores[1] running at 3 GHz and 8 GB of memory. The code was compiled using MS Visual Studio 2013. We produced a x64 binary in the Release mode with the default parameters.

Although the speed measurements were performed with a 64-bit binary on a 64-bit operating system, our implementation compiles also on a 32-bit system with a similar performance. The source code relies on the fact that the size of *int* is at least 32 bits and the processor works in the little-endian architecture.

The speed improvements are summarized in the Table 4. As you can see, the Linear complexity test significantly influences the overall numbers. We present the final results with the Linear complexity test configured to $m = 5000$. For the other extreme value of $m = 500$ the speedup factor of the test is 37x, which decreases the overall speedup to 10x.

---

[1] No multithreading is used in the application.

Table 4. Run times (for 20 MB of data) of the original implementation NIST STS, the implementation from [9] and our new implementation. Parameters m or M were chosen to be able to compare all three implementations.

Test	m, M	Original (ms)	New (ms)	Speedup Our vs. NIST	Speedup [9] vs. NIST
Frequency (Monobit)		203	15	13.5	9.82
Frequency within a Block	128	94	31	3.0	9.63
Runs		1140	31	36.8	5.84
Longest run of ones in a block		656	31	21.2	6.51
Binary Matrix Rank		3781	297	12.7	7.91
Spectral		24625	25062	0.98	-
Non-overlapping Template	9	139641	343	407.1	3.13
Overlapping Template	9	1359	406	3.3	15.15
Maurer's Universal		2843	156	18.2	12.8
Linear complexity	5000	1187453	18421	64.5	3.92
Serial	9	24078	313	76.9	48.73
Approximate Entropy	8	16484	312	52.8	54.16
Cumulative sums		984	31	31.7	3.31
Random Excursions		562	515	1.1	1.26
Random Excursions Variant		2125	515	4.3	6.09
Total		*1406028*	*46464*	*30.3*	-

6   Conclusion

We reimplemented the NIST STS with the focus on tests with the non-linear time complexity. Significant improvements were accomplished thanks to the byte oriented data storage, word-oriented data processing, the use of look up tables and other smart optimisations.

With the exception of the Spectral test, where the optimisations will be aimed at the parameter n, we achieved excellent speedup results for the three most time-consuming tests. The optimized Linear complexity test is 27.5x faster than original implementation for $m = 500$ and the speedup improves towards 64.5x for $m = 5000$. The speedup of the Non-overlapping template matching test is in the interval between 5.3x and 483x, where for the most usual parameters $m = 9$ and $m = 10$ the speedup of 407x is outstanding. Improvements of the Serial test relate to the use of a single pass calculation of block frequencies (instead of three independent calculations) and bring the speedup improvements in the range between 12x and 155x, in the dependence on m. The speedup is 155x for the default value of $m = 16$. Due to above mentioned improvements, we were able to achieve the overall speedup of about 30 times (compared to the NIST STS implementation). This means that the typical test setups that require hours to run can be executed within dozens of minutes now.

Acknowledgement. Credits go to Vashek Matyas for his crucial involvement in organizing the research and editing this paper. The first author was supported by the Ministry of Education, Youth, and Sport project CZ.1.07/2.3.00/30.0037 – Employment of Best Young Scientists for International Cooperation Empowerment. The second author was supported by the Czech Science Foundation, project GAP202/11/0422.

References

1. Rukhin, A., Soto, J., Nechvatal, J., Smid, M., Barker, E., Leigh, S., Levenson, M., Vangel, M., Banks, D., Heckert, A., Dray, J., Vo, S.: A Statistical Test Suite for Random and Pseudorandom Number Generators for Cryptographic Applications. NIST Special Publication 800-22 (May 2001),
   http://csrc.nist.gov/groups/ST/toolkit/rng/documents/SP800-22b.pdf
2. Rukhin, A., Soto, J., Nechvatal, J., Smid, M., Barker, E., Leigh, S., Levenson, M., Vangel, M., Banks, D., Heckert, A., Dray, J., Vo, S.: A Statistical Test Suite for Random and Pseudorandom Number Generators for Cryptographic Applications. NIST Special Publication 800-22rev1 (August 2008),
   http://csrc.nist.gov/groups/ST/toolkit/rng/documents/SP800-22rev1.pdf
3. Rukhin, A., Soto, J., Nechvatal, J., Smid, M., Barker, E., Leigh, S., Levenson, M., Vangel, M., Banks, D., Heckert, A., Dray, J., Vo, S.: A Statistical Test Suite for the Validation of Random Number Generators and Pseudo Random Number Generators for Cryptographic Applications, Version STS-2.1, NIST Special Publication 800-22rev1a (April 2010),
   http://csrc.nist.gov/publications/nistpubs/800-22-rev1a/SP800-22rev1a.pdf
4. Marsaglia, G.: The Marsaglia random number CDROM including the DIEHARD battery of tests of randomness (1996), http://stat.fsu.edu/pub/diehard
5. Brown, R.G.: Dieharder: A Random Number Test Suite, Version 3.31.1 (2004)
6. L'Ecuyer, P., Simard, R.: TestU01: A C library for empirical testing of random number generators. ACM Trans. Math. Softw. 33 (2007)
7. Walker, J.: ENT – A pseudorandom number sequence test program (1993), http://www.fourmilab.ch/random/
8. Caelli, W., et al.: Crypt X Package Documentation, Information Security Research Centre and School of Mathematics, Queensland University of Technology (1992), Crypt-X: http://www.isrc.qut.edu.au/resource/cryptx/
9. Suciu, A., Marton, K., Nagy, I., Pinca, I.: Byte-oriented efficient implementation of the NIST statistical test suite. In: Proceedings of the 2010 IEEE International Conference on Automation, Quality and Testing, Robotics (AQTR 2010), vol. 2, pp. 1–6. IEEE Computer Society, Washington, DC (2010)
10. Sadique Uz Zaman, J.K.M., Ghosh, R.: Review on fifteen Statistical Tests proposed by NIST. Journal of Theoretical Physics and Cryptography 1 (November 2012)
11. Sýs, M., Říha, Z.: Optimised implementation of NIST STS (2014), https://github.com/sysox/NIST-STS-optimised

t-Private Systems: Unified Private Memories and Computation

Jungmin Park and Akhilesh Tyagi

Dept. of Electrical & Computer Engineering
Iowa State University
Ames, Iowa, 50010, USA
{jmpark00,tyagi}@iastate.edu

Abstract. A t-private system consists of computing logic along with ROMs to store the persistent private keys. Ishai *et al.* [4] have developed a t-private logic schema with zero information loss against a probing adversary with up to t probes per cycle. Valamehr *et al.* [12] describe memory coding schemes to protect against a physical access adversary who observes transistor level fatigue through destructive slicing of the silicon chip. The two schemes cannot be combined to build a unified t-private system consisting of both memory and computing logic. For instance, Valamehr coding schemes do not have an associated computing logic schema. The keys after being read from ROM first have to be decoded and then re-encoded for t-private logic, opening them to probing attacks. In this paper, we propose a new unified *computable* t-private model to support both memory coding and logic coding. We develop the computing schema, logic preserving implementations of logic gates such as AND, OR and NOT, for the new computable t-private memories. Our computable t-private model takes fewer gates, less storage, fewer random bits than the existing schemes, and yet limits the adversary success probability. The memory is analyzed in the physical adversary framework of Valamehr, and computing logic is analyzed in the zero information loss framework of Ishai *et al.* [4].

Keywords: memory attacks, t-private circuit, secure storage, side channel attack.

1 Introduction

Side channel leakage in computational systems is a long acknowledged problem. Even though cryptographic systems have theoretically perfect secrecy, it can be broken by an adversary using side channel leakage information which is correlated to intermediate results or state of the algorithm. Side channel attacks include power attacks (SPA, DPA)[5] [7], electromagnetic radiation attacks [1] [10], timing attacks [6] or probing attacks. The goal of countermeasures against side channel attacks is to significantly reduce or remove the correlation between side channel leakage and the data or state processed by the computational system.

R.S. Chakraborty et al. (Eds.): SPACE 2014, LNCS 8804, pp. 285–302, 2014.

A representative approach to counteract side channel attacks is to mask intermediate values with randomized bits at the gate level. Ishai *et al.* [4] proposed *t*-private circuit using such a masking method. They assume that an adversary can probe or observe up to *t* nodes in the circuit. Their assumption is that the adversary is perfect, and hence able to probe the circuit state of the logic with 100% certainty. The Ishai's *t*-private circuits need at least *t* random bits to ensure zero correlation between *t* probed nodes each clock cycle. This makes information loss to the adversary equal to 0.

t-private logic only targets the privacy of computation. However, cryptographic systems also include some memory, particularly, memories that hold private keys which are typically Read Only Memory (ROM). Many secret keys associated with a cryptographic system are stored in ROMs. For instance, hundreds of 1024-bit RSA private keys are not uncommon for a Trusted Platform Module (TPM) [2]. ROMs are especially vulnerable to *t*-probing adversary of Ishai since their state does not change over time unlike computation. Moreover, these keys in memory can be targeted directly by physical attacks [11]. The adversary with physical access to the secret key part of the chip can succeed even if power has been turned off. The physical access based attacks slice the silicon until individual transistors are exposed by a Focused Ion Beam (FIB). An electron microscope is used to examine the silicon. Halderman *et al.* [3] proposed "cold-boot attack" which is a method to extract a significant fraction of data stored in a powered-off memory (e. g. DRAM) by cooling the chip to around $-50°C$. Valamehr *et al.* [12] developed several masking methods to prevent such memory attacks. The simplest of them is Ishai's [4] *t*-private coding applied to memory resident data. The key idea is that the secret key (x_i) does not need to be stored in the memory in its original form. Instead, a $t + 1$-tuple $[r_1, r_2, \ldots, r_t, x_i \oplus r_1 \oplus \cdots \oplus r_t]$ is stored. We call this memory masking with *t* random bits a *t-private memory*. An adversary must learn all the *t* random bits and the encoded bit in order to reveal even a single bit of the secret key. The adversary attack model for ROM is based on the persistent physical access attack - not the transient probing attack for computational logic. The memory attack has statistical observation limitations. Therefore, Valamehr *et al.* [12] assume that it succeeds only with probability *p* for each bit. Unlike Ishai's perfect secrecy analysis model, they define the success probability P_{succ} of this memory attack as a new figure of merit. It captures the event that at least one bit of the secret key has been learned. Even though a successful outcome of P_{succ} event does not break a cryptographic system, the possible key space can be reduced considerably when other side channel attacks are combined.

Practical computing systems consist of both memory and computational logic components. In order to build a *t*-private system, we need both a *t*-private memory and *t*-private logic that integrate seamlessly. Ishai's *t*-private scheme is not the most efficient one when applied to memory protection. Most of Valamehr's memory protection schemes [12] are not *computable* in the sense that a computational logic schema does not exist within the coded domain (unlike Ishai scheme). These stored coded keys have to be decoded first before being used for computation, hence exposing them to probing attacks. This is a big weakness. In this paper, we develop a unified computable coding scheme applicable to both memory and computation logic. This scheme is more efficient than Valamehr's schemes in their memory analysis framework. It also shows zero information loss in the Ishai's analysis framework. We believe that our proposed coding scheme is an ideal candidate to build t-private systems unifying the memory and computing logic. In summary, this paper makes the following contributions:

1) We analyze the storage overhead and the success probability (P_{succ}) of various t-private memory schemas within a unified framework that is easier to understand than Valamehr's. However, it may overestimate P_{succ}. We also quantify and describe a trade-off between these two attributes – storage overhead and P_{succ}.

2) We introduce a new notion of *computable* encoding method for t-private memories to capture the schemes which can compute with the encoded keys using a complementary t-private logic. We also propose a new, computable, t-private, inspection resistant memory with a corresponding computable encoding method. This new approach requires new t-private logic combinational gates which are more efficient than Ishai's [4] t-private circuits in their use of random bits without any loss of privacy.

3) We propose new combinational logic circuits suitable for our new memory scheme.

We define our adversary model and the notation (variables/parameters used) in Section 2. Our new more general analysis of t-private memories is presented in Section 3. Section 4 develops our proposed t-private memory scheme. Logic schema for our proposed memory is presented in Section 5. Hardware implementation results are presented in Section 6. Finally, Section 7 concludes the paper.

2   Assumptions and Notation

We assume that the memory leaks information in contrast to Micali's paper [8] in which they assume that only computation leaks information. An adversary conducts experiments to reveal the bits stored in the memory with a measurement apparatus. Let $\mathcal{L}$ be the leakage function selected by an adversary. The value of leakage of any bit x_i in the memory $\mathcal{M}$ is converted to the finite field $GF(2)$ based on the ability of an adversary: $f : \mathcal{L}(x_i) \rightarrow \{0, 1\}$ for $x_i \in \mathcal{M}$.

We assume that an adversary has limited capability to learn any memory resident bit exactly due to noisy measurement apparatus. Hence, we define the limited leakage probability of a bit as $\mathbf{Pr}[f(\mathcal{L}(x_i)) = x_i] = p$ $\forall x_i \in \mathcal{M}$.

This p is the characteristic of the memory (encoding) schema. If adversary's target is computational circuit $\mathcal{C}$, our assumption is the same as Ishai's adversary model [4]. In other words, an adversary can probe t_p nodes every cycle: $\mathbf{Pr}[f(\mathcal{L}(y_i)) = y_i] = 1$ $\forall y_i \in Y$, $Y \subset \mathcal{C}$, $|Y| = t_p$.

A *memory attack* is a set of such experiments that are possibly adaptively controlled. We assume that the goal of a memory attack is to reveal at least one bit in the memory with probability 1. Success probability of a memory attack captures this goal.

Definition 1 (Success Probability). *We define the success probability P_{succ} of a memory attack as the probability that at least one bit of the original secret key has been revealed.*

Memory may store multiple keys with the same key length k. The parameters/variables of the memory schema, adversary experiments, and memory attacks are defined in Table 1. If not otherwise stated, these variables hold for the rest of the paper.

3 t-Private Memory: Schemas, Architecture, and Analysis

Table 1. Variables used in this paper

k	key length
p	leakage probability for 1 bit
P_{succ}	probability of successful attack
r_i	random bit
x_i	one-bit secret key
t	the number of random bits
t_p	the number of probing nodes per clock cycle
n	the number of keys
c	the number of bits to be stored per key
$\mathbf{T}$	random bit matrix
T_{ij}	the ith row and jth column element of $\mathbf{T}$
$\vec{a} = [a_1, \ldots, a_t]$	a binary vector
$\bar{x}$	complement of x
$\wedge$	bit-wise AND operation

The k raw bits of a key $[x_k, x_{k-1}, \ldots, x_1]$ can be stored in memory in many ways. The t-privacy schemes could conceivably be transistor level schemes. However, encoding schemes applied at the write-port of a memory are more obvious and effective. A memory schema is a pair of encoding & decoding functions for memory. The base case is to do nothing - just store and retrieve the raw bits - with a schema of the identity function. All the following memory schemas except for t-private system are from Valamehr *et al.* [12]. The unified analysis is ours.

A bit x_i of the secret key can be hidden by creating $t + 1$ random shares using t random bits $[r_1, r_2, \ldots, r_t, x_i \oplus r_1 \oplus r_2 \oplus \cdots \oplus r_t]$ where r_i's are random bits. The t random bits constitute t shares. The $(t+1)st$ share is derived by an XOR of the t random bits and the original bit x_i.

The easiest memory architecture for the secrecy is to store all the $t + 1$ share bits of a raw bit of the secret key. Therefore the total number of stored bits for a secret key of length k is $k(t + 1)$. In this schema, each key bit uses a different set of t random bits. The set of random bits can be re-used or shared between various key bits. Depending on this reuse and sharing of random bits, the storage overhead and the success probability of the memory attack can vary. There are four memory schemes in [12] which will be analyzed in this section (all except the dynamic matrix scheme using hash function). Fig. 1 shows these architectural memory schemes.

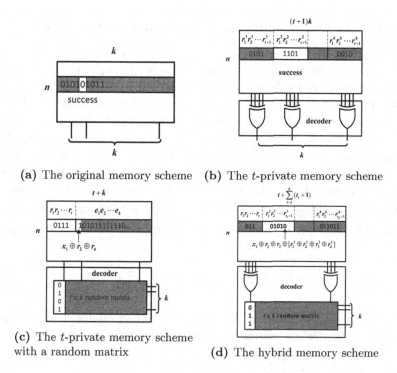

(a) The original memory scheme   (b) The *t*-private memory scheme

(c) The *t*-private memory scheme with a random matrix

(d) The hybrid memory scheme

Fig. 1. 4 architectural memory schemes

3.1 Original Memory Scheme without Secrecy

Original memory refers to raw memory without any protection against memory attacks. The total number of bits stored for the n secret keys with key length k is nk. This value is the storage reference/baseline. We define the storage overhead as the ratio of the number of bits used for the secret keys storage to the storage reference. The success probability P_{succ} of memory attacks is $1 - (1 - p)^k$, where $(1 - p)^k$ is the probability of the adversary experiments failing on all of the k key bits.

3.2 *t*-Private Memory Scheme

Each bit x_i of the secret key is represented by t random bits and the encoded bit $e_i = x_i \oplus r_1 \oplus \ldots \oplus r_t$ which are stored in the memory. Each key bit uses its own set of t random bits. Total number of bits stored for n secret keys is $cn = (t+1)k \cdot n$ and therefore the storage overhead is $t + 1$. The success probability is

$$P_{succ} = 1 - (1 - p')^k \tag{1}$$

where $p' = p^{t+1}$, which is the probability that an adversary learns t random bits and the encoded bit to reveal x_i. p' is less than p since $0 \le p \le 1$. As noted earlier, this scheme mirrors the t-private circuits introduced in Ishai *et al.* [4].

3.3 t-Private Memory Scheme Using a Random Matrix T

The straightforward t-private memory requires t random bits per key bit. This may be an unreasonably large random bit overhead. This scheme attempts to reduce the number of random bits needed for the entire schema. Randomly selected t_i random bits $R_i = \{r_j | r_j \in R, |R_i| = t_i\}$ from a set of t random bits $R = \{r_1, r_2, \ldots, r_t\}$ per key bit are used to encode each bit x_i of the secret key. The encoded bit e_i of x_i is $x_i \oplus \left[\bigoplus_{r_j \in R_i} r_j \right]$. The position/index j of randomly selected t_i random bits are stored in a fixed $t \times k$ random matrix $\mathbf{T}$. For example, if r_1, r_2, r_5 are randomly selected for encoding x_1, the first column T_1 of the random matrix $\mathbf{T}$ is $[1, 1, 0, 0, 1, 0, \ldots]^T$. The random matrix $\mathbf{T}$ is used for decoding $x_i = e_i \oplus \left[\bigoplus_{j=1}^{t} r_j \cdot T_{ji} \right]$. In this case, c is $t + k$ and total number of bits stored for n secret keys including a $t \times k$ random matrix table is equal to $(t + k)n + tk$. The storage overhead is

$$\frac{(t+k)n + tk}{nk} = 1 + t\left(\frac{1}{n} + \frac{1}{k}\right).$$

In order to reveal a single secret key-bit x_i, all of the t random bits and the ith column T_i of the random matrix $\mathbf{T}$ should be required:

$$x_i = e_i \oplus \left[\bigoplus_{j=1}^{t} r_j \cdot T_{ji} \right], \quad \text{where } r_j \in R, T_{ji} \in T_i.$$

The failing cases of our memory attack scenario are divided into two cases. The first case is that an adversary does not know all the random bits. The second case corresponds to the case that an adversary does not know the ith column of the random matrix $\mathbf{T}$ even though all the random bits are known. Note that we assume that the leakage probability of the matrix $\mathbf{T}$'s random bit is also p, which is independently distributed. Thus, the failure probability P_{fail} of this attack is equal to the sum of the probabilities of two cases . The success probability P_{succ} is given by the following equations:

$$P_{succ} = 1 - P_{fail} = 1 - \{ \quad \underbrace{1 - p^t}_{\text{the first case's probability}} \quad + \quad \underbrace{p^t(1 - p^{t+1})^k}_{\text{the second case's probability}} \quad \}$$

$$= p^t\{1 - (1 - p^{t+1})^k\}. \tag{2}$$

Compared with Eq (1), the success probability of the t-private memory scheme using a random matrix is p^t factor less than the success probability of the t-private scheme for the same t.

3.4 Hybrid Memory Scheme

The hybrid scheme is a combination of t-private memory scheme and t-private memory scheme using a fixed random matrix. This scheme is devised in [12] in order to minimize p_{succ} per random bit. Intuitively, it uses a few of the t bits to reduce p with the classical t-private scheme. The rest of the t private bits are used in a random matrix schema. The details of the hybrid schema and analysis in [12] are ambiguous. In the following, we have chosen a version of many possible designs for the hybrid schema.

The number of random bits t_i to encode each secret key bit x_i with the t-private scheme is a parameter individualized to each x_i. We let the set of the random bits be $R'_i = \{r^i_1, r^i_2, \ldots, r^i_{t_i}\}$. Another set of random bits per secret key $R = \{r_1, r_2, \ldots, r_t\}$ is required for the encoding method with a $t \times k$ random matrix **T**. Each secret key bit x_i can be encoded by the following equation:

$$e_i = x_i \oplus \{r^i_1 \oplus \cdots \oplus r^i_{t_i}\} \oplus \left[\bigoplus_{r_j \in R_i} r_j\right] \quad \text{for } 1 \leq i \leq k$$

where R_i is a randomly selected subset of $R = \{r'_1, \ldots, r'_t\}$.
The storage overhead is

$$\frac{n\left[t + \sum_{i=1}^{k}(t_i + 1)\right] + tk}{nk} = 1 + t\left(\frac{1}{n} + \frac{1}{k}\right) + \frac{1}{k}\sum_{i=1}^{k} t_i.$$

The failing cases for an adversary are also divided into two cases as in the t-private scheme using a random matrix. The first case is that an adversary does not know all of the t random bits $\{r_1, r_2, \ldots, r_t\}$ to encode with the random matrix. The second case is that an adversary does not know the ith column of the random matrix **T** and all t_i random bits for the t-private encoding even though (conditioned on) all the random bits $\{r_1, r_2, \ldots, r_t\}$ are known. The success probability P_{succ} is

$$P_{succ} = 1 - P_{fail} = 1 - \{ \underbrace{1 - p^t}_{\text{the first case's probability}} + \underbrace{p^t \prod_{i=1}^{k}(1 - p^{t_i + t + 1})}_{\text{the second case's probability}} \}$$

$$= p^t \left[1 - \prod_{i=1}^{k}(1 - p^{t_i + t + 1})\right]. \tag{3}$$

The t-private memory scheme with a random matrix is the special case of this hybrid memory scheme when all t_i for $1 \leq i \leq k$ is zero. Compared to the t-private memory scheme with a random matrix when both t is equal and all t_i's are the same, the success probability of the hybrid scheme decreases slightly since p^{t+1} in Eq. (2) is larger than $p^{t_i + t + 1}$ Eq. (3). But the storage overhead increases by t_i.

3.5   Comparison

Table 2 shows the storage overhead and the success probability of the 4 architectural schemes. We assume that the key length k is 128 bits and the number of secret keys n is 10 and the leakage probability of each bit p is 0.9. Fig. 2 shows the storage overhead and the success probability of the t-private scheme, the t-private scheme with a random matrix and the hybrid memory scheme with $t_i = 10$ parametrized by the number of random bits t. Compared to the t-private memory scheme with a random matrix, the hybrid memory scheme does not have any advantage since the storage overhead is larger without a significant reduction in the success probability. In the following sections, our proposed memory scheme will be compared to the t-private memory scheme with a random matrix.

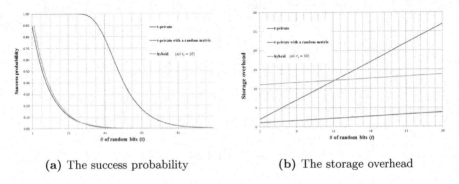

(a) The success probability   **(b)** The storage overhead

Fig. 2. Comparison between t-private scheme, t-private scheme with a random matrix and the hybrid scheme when $p = 0.9, k = 128, n = 10, t_i = 10$

4   New Approach

$X\ r_t r_{t-1} \dots r_1$

$+\ c_{t+1} c_t c_{t-1} \dots c_1$

$\overline{}$

$e_{t+1} e_t e_{t-1} \dots e_1$

$e_{t+1} e_t e_{t-1} \dots e_1$

$-\ c_{t+1} c_t c_{t-1} \dots c_1$

$\overline{}$

$d_{t+1} d_t d_{t-1} \dots d_1 =$
$X\ r_t r_{t-1} \dots r_1$

Fig. 3. t-Private: (Left) Encoding; (Right) Decoding

Note that all the encoding schemes in Section 3 except for the classical t-private memory scheme require the stored keys to be decoded before they can be used in a cryptographic computation (such as AES encryption). A more secure and private system can be designed if the computation with the key is also implemented as private logic (along the lines of Ishai scheme [4]). A memory encoding scheme that does not require the key to be decoded so that the key can participate in a computation implemented with private logic is called a *computable* encoding or schema. In such cases, a private logic family consistent with the memory encoding must exist. In a memory schema that is not computable, the decoded key can be attacked dynamically in flight. The only attacks that a non-computable memory schema prevents against are static memory attacks such as chip slicing based observation of transistor fatigue.

t-private encoding is obviously a computable schema. The t-private storage can be used directly in the t-private encryption/decryption implementation without additional decoding. Hence, the t-private memory scheme should be selected in order to prevent the adversary from attacking the raw key at the decoding step even though it does not have the best success probability and storage overhead tradeoff.

Basic Encoding Scheme: t-private implementations require many random bits - they do not share/reuse random bits (unlike the random matrix schema). They pose a t^2 factor area overhead and a factor t delay overhead. Our goal was to come up with a computable version of random matrix method. Alternately, we need a scheme that reuses random bits in a t-private logic implementation. We propose the computable and t-private encoding with these properties. We could use addition like invertible function with the t-private masking method to reduce the success probability. Note that such a function is not commutative in the bits of its operand. In other words, unlike the t random bits in Ishai's t-privacy schema, the order of these bits within the coding operand matters. Each ordering of t random bits gives a different seed and hence a different encoding. This allows any permutation of t random bits to give a different random seed from the encoding perspective. This results in a possibility of $t!/(a!b!) \approx t!/((t/2)! * (t/2)!)$ reuses of t random bits, where a is the number of 1's and b is the number of 0's of the t random bits.

Table 2. The storage overhead and the success probability of the 4 architectural schemes

	Original scheme	t-private scheme	t-private scheme with **T**	Hybrid scheme
Storage overhead	1	$1+t$	$1+t\left(\frac{1}{n}+\frac{1}{k}\right)$	$1+t\left(\frac{1}{n}+\frac{1}{k}\right)+\frac{1}{k}\sum_{i=1}^{k}t_i$
P_{succ}	$1-(1-p)^k$	$1-(1-p^{t+1})^k$	$p^t\{1-(1-p^{t+1})^k\}$	$p^t\left[1-\prod_{i=1}^{k}(1-p^{t_i+t+1})\right]$

Fig. 3 shows the basic idea. We add two $t+1$-bit words for encoding. One operand is derived by concatenating the bit to be encoded x with t random bits $r_t, r_{t-1}, \ldots r_1$. This word is added to another random constant c (either one c per chip or one c per x). Note that different permutations of the t random bits $r_{i_t}, r_{i_{t-1}}, \ldots r_{i_1}$ lead to different encoded result when added to c. Decoding consists of simply subtracting c from the encoded word $e_{t+1}e_t \ldots e_1$. The most significant bit of the decoded word is x.

Refined Encoding Schema: The basic encoding schema has some flaws that expose the bit x when forming complex entangling gates such as AND and OR as discussed in Section 5. In order to fix that, instead of x at the MSB of arithmetic word with random bits, we use the Ishai code $x \oplus r_t \oplus \cdots \oplus r_1$.

We define the computable and t-private encoding for x_i (bit to be coded) as follows:

$$\vec{e}_i = Encode(x_i) = [x_i \oplus r^i_t \oplus r^i_{t-1} \oplus \cdots \oplus r^i_1, \vec{r}_i] + \vec{c}_i$$

where $\vec{r}_i$ and $\vec{c}_i$ are vectors/words of t random bits $[r^i_t, r^i_{t-1}, \ldots, r^i_1]$ and constant bits $[c^i_{t+1}, c^i_t, \ldots, c^i_1]$ respectively. Note that this schema uses a constant word per x_i. We form an arithmetic word comprising of t random bits and x_i. By placing x_i at the most significant end we allow all the t random bits to effect its encoding. A simpler encoding would have added $[x_i, r_t, \ldots, r_1]$ to a constant vector per chip or per computation session. Note that since the constant vector $\vec{c}$ is constant over longer periods - entire computation session, entire boot-up phase, to be conservative, it may not contribute to the entropy of encoding. We must assume that the adversary knows such a persistent $\vec{c}$.

The decoding can then be done as follows:

$$\vec{d}_i = Decode(\vec{e}_i) = \vec{e}_i - \vec{c}_i = [x_i \oplus r^i_t \oplus \cdots \oplus r^i_1, r^i_t, \ldots, r^i_1].$$

Most significant bit of $\vec{d}_i$ is $x_i \oplus r^i_t \oplus \cdots \oplus r^i_1$. The decoded vector $\vec{d}_i$ can be directly connected to t-private encryption/decryption logic. This computable and t-private encoding method does not reveal the original key bit after this decoding process. Algorithm 1 represents our computable t-private encoding/decoding method. Note that this algorithm creates all m reuses of each bit within the encoding of the same key. Such a localized reuse may not be optimal in practice. It is presented in the algorithm for its simplicity. In practice, for CAD, we will likely incorporate global randomized reuse. Also note that we have used a random instance of a permutation of t bits π_r picked uniformly from $t!$ space. $\pi_r(i) = j$ maps the ith bit position to jth bit position. Fig. 4 shows our proposed computable and t-private memory scheme.

Since $t + 1$ encoded bits per key bit are stored in the memory in this scheme, the storage overhead is

$$\frac{nk(t + 1)}{nk} = t + 1.$$

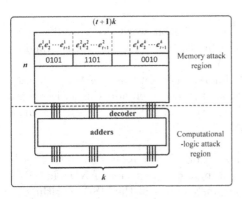

Fig. 4. The proposed memory scheme

Constant Vector $\vec{c}$ Storage/ Routing: The constant vector $\vec{c}_i$ need not to be stored in memory. Its lifetime is only from the producer gate to the consumer gate. It can be hardwired in the routing of wires from the producer gate to the consumer gate. For a per chip or per session constant $\vec{c}$, similar hardwiring will work with a bootup or session-startup initialization step. For a random choice of $\vec{c}_i$ per x_i, we assume that the adversary learns each bit

---

Algorithm 1 Computable *t*-private memory encoding/decoding scheme

---

Encoding

Input : A k-bit secret key $\vec{x} = [x_k, x_{k-1}, \ldots, x_i, \ldots, x_1]$; $g = \lceil k/m \rceil$ distinct t-bit random vectors $\vec{r^0} = [r_t^0, r_{t-1}^0, \ldots, r_1^0]$, $\vec{r^1} = [r_t^1, r_{t-1}^1, \ldots, r_1^1]$, $\ldots$, $\vec{r^{g-1}} = [r_t^{g-1}, r_{t-1}^{g-1}, \ldots, r_1^{g-1}]$; constant vector (per chip or per computation session) $\vec{c} = [c_{t+1}, c_t, \ldots, c_1]$

Output : Encoded secret key bit vectors, $\vec{e_i}$ for $i = 1, 2, \ldots, k$ such that $e(\vec{x}) = \vec{e_k}\vec{e_{k-1}} \ldots \vec{e_1}$

for $i = 1 \rightarrow k$ **do**

$\quad j \leftarrow k \% g$

$\quad$ Key bit x_i is XORed with the t random bits in jth random vector : $y_i = x_i \oplus r_t^j \oplus r_{t-1}^j \oplus \cdots \oplus r_1^j$

$\quad$ Concatenate XORed bit y_i with a randomly picked permutation of t bits π_r :
$$y_i \| \pi_r(\vec{r^j}) = \left[y_i, r_{\pi_r^{-1}(t)}^j, r_{\pi_r^{-1}(t-1)}^j, \ldots, r_{\pi_r^{-1}(1)}^j \right]$$

$\quad$ Add constant vector $\vec{c}$: $\vec{e_i} = \left[y_i, r_{\pi_r^{-1}(t)}^j, r_{\pi_r^{-1}(t-1)}^j, \ldots, r_{\pi_r^{-1}(1)}^j \right] + \vec{c}$

end for

Decoding

Input : Encoded secret key vectors, $\vec{e_i}$ for $i = 1, 2, \ldots, k$; constant vector $\vec{c}$

Output : Decoded secret key vectors, $\vec{d_i} = [y_i, r_t, \ldots, r_1]$ for $i = 1, 2, \ldots, k$

for $i = 1 \rightarrow k$ **do**

$\quad$ Subtract constant vector $\vec{c}$: $\vec{d_i} = [e_{t+1}^i, e_t^i, \ldots, e_1^i] - \vec{c} = [x_i \oplus r_t^j \oplus r_{t-1}^j \oplus \cdots \oplus r_1^j, r_t^j, r_{t-1}^j, \ldots, r_1^j]$ for $j = k \% g$

end for

---

with probability 0.5 randomly. This requires the adversary to conduct all possible 2^{t+1} $\vec{c_i}$ experiments to reveal a key bit. The success probability P_{succ} then is

$$\frac{1}{2^{t+1}}(1 - (1 - p^{t+1})^k). \tag{4}$$

However, since the goal of this paper is to save on random bits, henceforth in this paper, we assume that $\vec{c}$ is a constant per chip or per computation session. Furthermore, the adversary knows $\vec{c}$. Hence we cannot use the entropy of $\vec{c}$ in our security analysis.

$$(1 - (1 - p^{t+1})^k). \tag{5}$$

If we assume instead the memory attack model with probability p to reveal each bit of $\vec{c_i}$ then the success probability is $P_{succ} = p^{t+1} \times (1 - (1 - p^{t+1})^k)$. Similarly, if we assume that the constant vector is fixed for the chip design or for each boot-up session, we give the benefit of doubt to the adversary leading to $P_{succ} = (1 - (1 - p^{t+1})^k)$. Effectively, this gives us two types of t-private systems: **(1)** ones with constant $\vec{c}$ with higher success probability but with lower number of random bits requirement (which is the one analyzed in the following), **(2)** constant $\vec{c_i}$ per x_i with lower success probability at the cost of higher number of random bits.

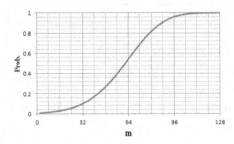

Fig. 5. The success probability according to m reused random bits when $p = 0.9, t = 91$

When a permutation of a vector of t random bits is reused upto m times for encoding other information/key bits, we need to consider two cases for revealing the coded bits. In the earlier analysis, we have assumed probability p for slicing attack to succeed at revealing a specific coded bit b_i. The other possibility due to reuse is that another bit a_l might be revealed through slicing attack with probability p, and it is reused at the bit position of b_i. Eq. (5) should be changed into the following equation to account for such reuse:

$$P_{succ\_reuse} = \left(1 - (1 - (p + (1 - p)q)^{t+1})^k\right) \qquad (6)$$

where q is the probability that a reused bit a_l is revealed through slicing attack and is routed to the bit under consideration b_i.

$$q = 1 - \left(1 - \frac{p}{t}\right)^m . \qquad (7)$$

In Eq. (7), $\frac{p}{t}$ is the probability that a reused bit b_i is revealed by slicing attack of another bit a_l. It results from the leakage/slicing attack success probability p of another bit a_l and the probability that the reused bit a_l is routed to b_i's position. Note that a random permutation π_r maps a bit position i to another bit position j with probability $1/t$ over all $t!$ permutations. When slicing memory inspection of a bit fails with probability $(1 - p)$, the event that a reuse might reveal needs to be considered resulting in the success probability P_{succ_reuse} to increase by the factor of $(1 - p)q$.

Fig. 5 shows the success probability parametrized by reuse factor m when p is 0.9 and t is 91. The success probability is 0.1 when the reuse factor m is 30. For $m = 86$, the success probability goes up to 0.9. Fig. 6 shows the success probability of our proposed memory scheme and t-private schemes. Our proposed schema requires only 5 random bits for $P_{succ} = 0.0078$ as in Fig. 6.(b).

Now let us consider the complexity of the $t + 1$-bit ripple carry adders used for encoding and decoding in terms of number of logic gates. Since one of the adder operands is a constant, a full adder bit-slice design can be made simpler than the typical full adder. If a constant bit b_0 is 0, the carry-out bit c_1 is $a_0 c_0$ where a_0 and c_0 is an input and a carry-in bit, respectively. The sum bit s_0 is $a_0 \oplus c_0$. If a constant bit b_0 is 1, the carry-out bit c_1 is $a_0 + c_0$ and the sum bit s_0 is $(a_0 \oplus c_0)'$. Only 2 logic gates are needed for a specialized full adder leading to total number of logic gates for the $t + 1$-bit adder as $2(t + 1)$.

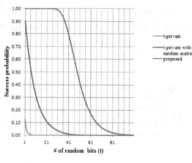

(a) The success probability

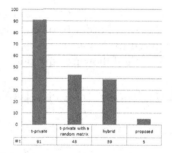

(b) The number of random bits(t) when $P_{succ} = 0.0078$

Fig. 6. Performance comparison between proposed scheme and t-private schemes

5   New Computable and t-Private Logic Schema and Gates

Consider an inverter $y = \bar{x}$. If x is encoded with our schema, the incoming $(t + 1)$-tuple represents the encoding $(x, \vec{r_x}, \vec{c_x})$. The inverter needs to recode the output, however, with respect to the vector $(y, \vec{r_y}, \vec{c_y})$. This will require first decoding the incoming $(t + 1)$-tuple and then recoding it. Had we used the basic encoding schema, this would have revealed x in the open temporarily, open to a probing attack. No bit x_i should be in-flight in the raw form even momentarily creating a weak link. We overcome this by using $x_i \oplus r_1^i \oplus r_2^i \oplus \cdots \oplus r_t^i$ as MSB in addition.

With this scheme, the MSB of the decoded vector $\vec{d_i} = [x_i \oplus r_t^i \oplus \cdots \oplus r_1^i, r_t^i, \ldots, r_1^i]$ is identical to Ishai encoding of private circuits [4], and hence can be connected to Ishai's t-private combinational logic gates. The classical t-private scheme has t^2 area and t time overhead. We only save on the random bits by adopting this approach. We however propose a more efficient combinational logic using the decoded vectors which have the same functionality as the traditional logic operation with lower overhead.

5.1   AND Operation

Let two encoded bit vectors be $\vec{e_1} = [x_1 \oplus r_t^1 \oplus \cdots \oplus r_1^1, \vec{r_1}] + \vec{c_1}$ and $\vec{e_2} = [x_2 \oplus r_t^2 \oplus \cdots \oplus r_1^2, \vec{r_2}] + \vec{c_2}$ from the memory. They are decoded by the decoder, which are denoted by $\vec{d_1}$ and $\vec{d_2}$. First, consider the simple case in which t is 1. Two decoded bit vectors are $\vec{d_1} = [x_1 \oplus r_1, r_1]$ and $\vec{d_2} = [x_2 \oplus r_1', r_1']$. The result of the AND operation should be $[x_1 \cdot x_2 \oplus r_1'', r_1'']$. How can we obtain the result and r_1'' ? Let us perform the following computation:

$$\vec{d_1} \wedge \vec{d_2} = [(x_1 \oplus r_1) \cdot (x_2 \oplus r_1'), r_1 \cdot r_1']$$
$$= [x_1 \cdot x_2 \oplus r_1 \cdot x_2 \oplus x_1 \cdot r_1' \oplus r_1 \cdot r_1', r_1 \cdot r_1']$$

$x_1 \cdot x_2 \oplus r_1 \cdot x_2 \oplus x_1 \cdot r_1' \oplus r_1 \cdot r_1'$ in the above equation should be changed into $x_1 \cdot x_2 \oplus r_1 \cdot r_1'$ in order to obtain desired result and thus additional computations are required to remove $r_1 \cdot x_2 \oplus x_1 \cdot r_1'$. We define the AND operation in this case ($t = 1$) as the following equations:

$$
\begin{aligned}
AND(\vec{d_1}, \vec{d_2}) &= [x_1 \oplus r_1, r_1] \; AND \; [x_2 \oplus r_1', r_1'] \\
&= [(x_1 \oplus r_1) \cdot (x_2 \oplus r_1') \underbrace{\oplus (x_1 \oplus r_1) \cdot r_1' \oplus (x_2 \oplus r_1') \cdot r_1}_{\text{additional computations}}, r_1 \cdot r_1'] \\
&= [x_1 \cdot x_2 \oplus r_1'', r_1'']
\end{aligned}
$$

where r_1'' is equal to $r_1 \cdot r_1'$.

Let us now increase the value of t to develop our intuition. Two decoded vectors are $\vec{d_1} = [x_1 \oplus \bigoplus r_j, \vec{r}]$ and $\vec{d_2} = [x_2 \oplus \bigoplus r_j', \vec{r'}]$. In this case, the AND operation is equal to the following equation:

$$
\begin{aligned}
AND(\vec{d_1}, \vec{d_2}) &= [x_1 \oplus \bigoplus r_j, \vec{r}] \; AND \; [x_2 \oplus \bigoplus r_j', \vec{r'}] \\
&= [(x_1 \oplus \bigoplus r_j) \cdot (x_2 \oplus \bigoplus r_j') \oplus \underbrace{\left\{ (x_1 \oplus \bigoplus r_j) \cdot (\bigoplus r_j') \right\} \oplus \left\{ (x_2 \oplus \bigoplus r_j') \cdot (\bigoplus r_j) \right\}}_{\text{additional computations (6 operations)}}, \\
&\qquad (\bigoplus r_j') \cdot \vec{r}] \hspace{4cm} (8) \\
&= [x_1 \cdot x_2 \oplus \left\{ (\bigoplus r_j) \cdot (\bigoplus r_j') \right\}, (\bigoplus r_j') \cdot \vec{r}]
\end{aligned}
$$

where $\bigoplus r_j = r_1 \oplus r_2 \oplus \cdots \oplus r_t$ and $(\bigoplus r_j') \cdot \vec{r} = [(r_1' \oplus \cdots \oplus r_t') r_1, \ldots, (r_1' \oplus \cdots \oplus r_t') r_t]$. The number of gates required is $t + 7$ for $t + 1$ AND gates and 6 additional operations. Thus, the area/gate complexity of this AND operation is $O(t)$. This is more efficient than Ishai's t-private model which has the area complexity of $O(t^2)$ [4]. Moreover, this computation can be performed in $O(\log t)$ time as opposed to $O(t)$ in the original private circuits.

5.2 OR Operation

We define the OR operation as follows:

$$
\begin{aligned}
OR(\vec{d_1}, \vec{d_2}) &= [x_1 \oplus \bigoplus r_j, \vec{r}] \; OR \; [x_2 \oplus \bigoplus r_j', \vec{r'}] \\
&= [\underbrace{(\overline{(x_1 \oplus \bigoplus r_j)} \cdot \overline{(x_2 \oplus \bigoplus r_j')})}_{} \oplus \underbrace{\left\{ \overline{(x_1 \oplus \bigoplus r_j)} \cdot (\bigoplus r_j') \right\} \oplus \left\{ \overline{(x_2 \oplus \bigoplus r_j')} \cdot (\bigoplus r_j) \right\}}_{\text{additional computations (6 operations)}}, \\
&\qquad (\bigoplus r_j') \cdot \vec{r}] \hspace{4cm} (9) \\
&= [(x_1 + x_2) \oplus \left\{ (\bigoplus r_j) \cdot (\bigoplus r_j') \right\}, (\bigoplus r_j') \cdot \vec{r}]
\end{aligned}
$$

An OR gate is a logic dual of an AND gate. Hence, OR operation logic also has the same area complexity of $O(t)$. It has the same structure as the AND operation logic except for the additional NOT gates.

5.3   NOT Operation

The NOT operation is modeled by the following equations:

$$NOT(\vec{d_i}) = [(x_i \oplus r_1 \oplus \cdots \oplus r_t)', \vec{r}]$$
$$= [x_i' \oplus \bigoplus r_j, \vec{r}]$$

5.4   The Perfect Secrecy

The original secret bit x_i must not be revealed when the adversary probes $t_p \leq t$ nodes in a t-private logic circuit. The t-privacy parameter determines the bounds of probing experiments for perfect secrecy. In Ishai's privacy model, there is no grey zone analysis - you either have perfect secrecy ($p = 0$) or you are unacceptably compromised. We develop a t-private circuit privacy analysis consistent with our memory attack analysis. If the adversary can probe two nodes ($x_1 \oplus \bigoplus r_j^1$) and $\bigoplus r_j^1$ in the proposed AND or OR logic circuit exactly, x_1 is leaked easily. Assuming that the adversary can access any circuit node equally likely with 100% certainty, the probability that x_1 is learned is given by the following equation:

$$P_{succ} = \frac{\binom{t}{2}}{\binom{n}{t}}$$
$$= \frac{t(t-1)t!(n-t)!}{2n!}$$

where n is the number of total nodes. Since n is much larger than t generally, P_{succ} is very low. For example, when n and t are 100 and 10, respectively, P_{succ} is 2.6×10^{-12}. In order to make P_{succ} close to zero, $(x_i \oplus \bigoplus r_j) \cdot (\bigoplus r_j')$ which consists of two terms in Eq. (8) or Eq. (9) can be resolved into $\bigoplus \{(x_i \oplus \bigoplus r_j) \cdot r_j'\}$ which consists of t terms.

The perfect secret circuit is defined as a circuit that appears like a pseudorandom number generator. There is no appreciable (poly adversary limited or whatever other restrictions are placed on the adversary) correlation between inputs and outputs. Given any input, the probability of any output vector should be the same. It does not depend on the input :

$$\mathbf{Pr}[y|x_i] = \mathbf{Pr}[y] \quad \forall x_i.$$

where x_i is the input and y is the output. This is the same property required of encryption functions. For example, the traditional AND gate does not have perfect secrecy since the output depends on inputs. AND-XOR network with a random bit has the perfect secrecy for inputs of AND gates [9]. Fig. 7 shows the schematic of the first bit of the vector term in Eq. (8) which needs the perfect

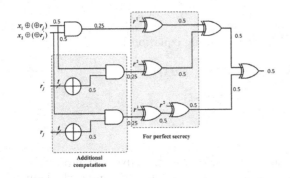

Fig. 7. An output of AND operation for the perfect secrecy

secrecy. For the perfect secrecy, additional XOR gates and new random bits are inserted. Numbers in the logic circuit represents the probability that the node is one. The probability that the output is one is always equal to 0.5, does not depend on inputs. Also, the vector $(\bigoplus r'_j) \cdot \vec{r}$ in Eq. (8) should be changed into $[(\bigoplus r'_j)r_t \oplus r''_1, (\bigoplus r'_j)r_{t-1} \oplus r''_1, \ldots, (\bigoplus r'_j)r_2 \oplus r''_{\lceil t/2 \rceil},$ $(\bigoplus r'_j)r_1 \oplus r''_{\lceil t/2 \rceil}]$ for the perfect secrecy. This technique can also be applied to OR logic circuit for the perfect secrecy in a similar manner. We compare the number of intermediate random bits for the perfect secrecy of three t-private AND circuits which are Ishai's t-private model, our earlier modified t-private model [9] and computable t-private model. Table 3 shows the comparison of the number of intermediate random bits per AND/OR gate for our HOST scheme, Ishai's t-private scheme, proposed computable t-private without perfect secrecy, and proposed computable t-private with perfect secrecy. The last two rows show the total number of random bits used among these private schemes for a circuit with N gates.

Table 3. Number of Random Bits Used for an AND Gate and for an N-gate Circuit

AND Gate	Modified t-private (HOST)	Ishai's t-private	Computable t-private	Computable t-private - perfect secrecy
# of random bits	$\lceil \frac{t+1}{2} \rceil = O(t)$	$\frac{t(t+1)}{2} = O(t^2)$	2	$\lceil \frac{t}{2} \rceil$
N-gate circuit	Modified t-private (HOST)	Ishai's t-private	Computable t-private	Computable t-private - perfect secrecy
# of random bits	Nt	Nt^2	$N * ((t/m) + 2)$	$N * ((t/m) + \lceil \frac{t}{2} \rceil + 2)$

6   Hardware Implementation

We implemented t-private memories including the random matrix method and our proposed computable and t-private memory. We used Xilinx ISE tools for the synthesis and the target device is Xilinx Virtex-5 FPGA (XC5VFX70T-3FF1136). Table 4 shows the parameters and the number of used Block RAMs, LUTs and delay for each decoder. In case of t-private memory, 63 random bits are required for $P_{succ} = 0.14$. The stored bits of encoded keys in memory total $nk(t+1) = 10 * 128 * (63 + 1)$. Since the width of Block RAM in FPGA is limited to 1152 bits, we set the width of the Block RAM to be 1024. Thus, 16 decoded bits (1024 / 64) per 1 clock can be generated and 8 clock cycles are needed for decoding 1 key, which is the reference clock to compare used LUTs and delays for decoders of t-private memories. Since we set the total clock cycles for decoding a key to be 8, 35 bits which include 19 bits for random bits and 16 encoded bits

Table 4. Hardware Implementation on FPGA

	t-private	t-private with R.M	proposed computable and t-private
# keys	10	10	10
# bits of a key	128	128	128
t	63	19	4
P_{succ}	0.14	0.135	0.016
Block RAM	1024 * 80	(35*80) + (304*8)	80*80
# decoded bits per 1 clock	16	16	16
Input bits of decoder	64*16 = 1024	19+16+(19*16) = 339	80
# LUTs	208	25	16
Delay(ns)	1.926	1.998	0.931

of 16 secret-key bits are released from a block RAM and 304 bits (16×19) also are output from another block RAM for a random matrix simultaneously.

Our proposed memory scheme has lower storage needs (only 7% of t-private memory) even though the success probability is almost 10% lower than the t-private memory. Also, the decoder of our proposed memory has lower area and time overhead – specifically it requires 92% lower area, 51% less delay and 36% less area, 53% less delay compared to t-private memory and t-private memory with a random matrix, respectively.

7   Conclusions

Side channel attacks and static inspection attacks on silicon chips have necessitated techniques to make circuit implementations resistant (private) to these probes and inspections. t-private circuits protect the privacy of the data in flight during computation. Memories (on-chip or off-chip) however are not protected by t-private circuits.

Valamehr et al. [12] introduced a few memory protection schemes. We introduce a unified analysis framework to compare these schemes. Effectiveness metrics for these schemes include area/gate count overhead, time overhead, number of random bits needed, and adversary success probability per random bit. In this paper, we specifically analyzed the storage overhead and the success probability of t-private memories, t-private memories with random matrix (for random bits reuse), and a hybrid private memory.

Ideally, we would like to design a private computing circuit with unified private memory. In such a computing system, data and keys never appear in their raw form, thereby protecting privacy of data and keys. We consider a memory scheme to be computable if the encoded stored keys can be directly used in t-private computations.

Most of the memory schemes presented in Valamehr et al. [12] are not computable. The main new interesting technique they develop is to judiciously reuse random bits while still limiting the adversary to low success probability. We develop a new memory schema that is computable, and yet reuses many random bits by bringing in an arithmetic function into encoding. We present the computable and t-private encoding method and corresponding logic operations (AND, OR and NOT) suitable for our memory scheme. The new private circuits are more efficient than Ishai's t-private model (only t area overhead compared to t^2 area overhead of Ishai). We verified that our memory model has advantages in performance (the success probability and delay) and area cost by implementing it on FPGA.

Acknowledgements. This work was supported in part by NSF Grant IIP - 0968939, NSF Grant STARSS - 1441640 and DHS Science & Technology Directorate.

References

1. Gandolfi, K., Mourtel, C., Olivier, F.: Electromagnetic analysis: Concrete results. In: Koç, Ç.K., Naccache, D., Paar, C. (eds.) CHES 2001. LNCS, vol. 2162, pp. 251–261. Springer, Heidelberg (2001)
2. T. C. Group. Trusted Platform Module Specification and Architecture (2013), http://www.trustedcomputinggroup.org/resources/tpm_main_specification/
3. Halderman, J.A., Schoen, S.D., Heninger, N., Clarkson, W., Paul, W., Cal, J.A., Feldman, A.J., Felten, E.W.: Least we remember: Cold boot attacks on encryption keys. In: USENIX Security Symposium (2008)
4. Ishai, Y., Sahai, A., Wagner, D.: Private circuits: Securing hardware against probing attacks. In: Boneh, D. (ed.) CRYPTO 2003. LNCS, vol. 2729, pp. 463–481. Springer, Heidelberg (2003)
5. Kocher, P., Jaffe, J., Jun, B.: Differential power analysis. In: Wiener, M. (ed.) CRYPTO 1999. LNCS, vol. 1666, pp. 388–397. Springer, Heidelberg (1999)
6. Kocher, P.C.: Timing attacks on implementations of diffie-hellman, RSA, DSS, and other systems. In: Koblitz, N. (ed.) CRYPTO 1996. LNCS, vol. 1109, pp. 104–113. Springer, Heidelberg (1996)
7. Messerges, T.S., Dabbish, E.A., Sloan, R.H., Member, S.: Examining smart-card security under the threat of power analysis attacks. IEEE Transactions on Computers 51, 541–552 (2002)
8. Micali, S., Reyzin, L.: Physically observable cryptography. In: Naor, M. (ed.) TCC 2004. LNCS, vol. 2951, pp. 278–296. Springer, Heidelberg (2004)
9. Park, J., Tyagi, A.: t-private logic synthesis on fpgas. In: 2012 IEEE International Symposium on Hardware-Oriented Security and Trust (HOST), pp. 63–68 (June 2012)
10. Quisquater, J.-J., Samyde, D.: ElectroMagnetic Analysis (EMA): Measures and counter-measures for smart cards. In: Attali, S., Jensen, T. (eds.) E-smart 2001. LNCS, vol. 2140, pp. 200–210. Springer, Heidelberg (2001)
11. Samyde, D., Skorobogatov, S., Anderson, R., Quisquater, J.-J.: On a new way to read data from memory. In: Proceedings of the First International IEEE Security in Storage Workshop, SISW 2002, pp. 65–69. IEEE Computer Society, Washington, DC (2002)
12. Valamehr, J., Chase, M., Kamara, S., Putnam, A., Shumow, D., Vaikuntanathan, V., Sherwood, T.: Inspection resistant memory: architectural support for security from physical examination. In: Proceedings of the 39th Annual International Symposium on Computer Architecture, ISCA 2012, pp. 130–141. IEEE Computer Society, Washington, DC (2012)

Android Malware Analysis Using Ensemble Features

A. M. Aswini and P. Vinod

Department of Computer Science & Engineering,
SCMS School of Engineering & Technology, Ernakulam, Kerala, India 683 582
{aswinimohan95,pvinod21}@gmail.com

Abstract. This paper presents a static feature extraction framework for Android malware analysis. The techniques are implemented by extracting prominent features from the components of Android application package i.e. `AndroidManifest.XML` files. Five different types of features likely permissions, count of permission, hardware features, software features as well as API calls from 1175 .apk files are mined for performing the investigation. The objective of this work is to evaluate if independent features are effective in comparison to ensemble features. Feature reduction is performed to investigate the impact of varied feature length on classification accuracy. Feature selection techniques such as *Bi–Normal Separation*, *Mutual Information*, *Relevancy score*, *Kolmogorov dependence* and *Kullback Leibler* are administered to choose the significant attributes. The proposed method introduced here using dimensionality reduction and machine learning algorithms produces an overall classification accuracy of 93.02% with ensemble features. Comparing the empirical results of ensemble features with individual features, the former improved the classification accuracy with Bi–Normal Separation.

Keywords: Android malware, Ensemble features, Feature selection, Static Analysis.

1 Introduction

Smartphones with complete functionalities of a basic phone are equipped with the additional capabilities like web browsing, Wi–fi, digital media access etc. These gadgets have the ability to incorporate small computer programs called apps that can be used for entertainment as well as to perform many other useful tasks.

Android is an OS based on the Linux kernel primarily designed for touchscreen devices. It is the fastest growing mobile operating system that contributes a world–class platform for the development of applications and games for its users and provide an open marketplace for the distribution of these apps [5].

According to the Symantec Corporation Internet Security Threat Report 2014 [6], popular legitimate applications from the Google Play are downloaded by the attackers and are repackaged with additional code thereby generating

R.S. Chakraborty et al. (Eds.): SPACE 2014, LNCS 8804, pp. 303–318, 2014.
© Springer International Publishing Switzerland 2014

third party apps. Trojans mostly disguised as legitimate applications are a part of these malicious codes injected to mobile apps. Such programs uploaded to the mobile marketplaces are downloaded and installed by the users unaware of its maliciousness.

The compromised smartphones are vulnerable to threats like stealing user credentials, stack based buffer overflow resulting in arbitrary code execution, activating unknown services in the device without user's knowledge, denial of service attacks etc. Some forms of attacks exercised by the malware authors are execution of code using Android debugger bridge (adb), cross site scripting for redirecting to vulnerable domains and memory corruption for gaining root privileges. The desktop security solutions in Antivirus based on signature generation cannot detect zero–day malware attacks. These techniques are not completely scalable for smartphones as it require more memory and processing power [13].

Due to these above mentioned drawbacks of the existing detection system, we perform static analysis implementing dimensionality reduction and machine learning algorithms for Android malware analysis. We extract permissions, software/hardware features and Application Programming Interface (API) calls that are significant for mobile malware identification. The contributions of this work are the following:

- Employed attribute ranking methods like *Bi–Normal Separation, Mutual Information, Relevancy score, Kolmogorov dependence* and *Kullback Leibler* to mine precise attributes for classification.
- The most prominent attributes that contribute to the characterization of mobile malware can be determined.
- Optimal feature length, best classifier as well as attribute selection method are found out using this detection mechanism.
- An accuracy of 93.02% is achieved using ensemble features with Bi–Normal Separation feature selection.

The remaining sections are organized as follows: Section 2 includes the related works. Section 3 explains the proposed methodology. Section 4 contains the experiment carried out followed by the results and findings. Section 5 discusses about the inference and finally the conclusion and future work is presented in Section 6.

2   Related Works

The authors [20] used permissions to detect malicious apps in Android OS. A total of 124,769 benign and 480 malicious files were used in their work. The requested and required permissions, number of required permissions, normal, signature, dangerous permissions, number of files with .so extension, number of elf files, count of executable, shared objects were considered as the features. Results showed that a permission–based detector can detect more than 81% of malicious samples.

The authors [21] proposed a machine learning based malware detector to discriminate normal and malware applications. The features used were permissions mined from 200 .apk samples. The generated models were trained and evaluated using the Area Under ROC Curve (AUC). They obtained an accuracy of 91.58% using Random Forest classifier.

PUMA [22] detects malicious Android apps by extracting permissions. They collected 239 Android malware samples, and obtained a 0.92 of AUC using the Random forest classifier. Except the Bayesian–based classifiers, the methods achieved accuracy rates higher than 80%. The best classifier was Random Forest trained with 50 trees with an accuracy of 86.41%.

This [23] approach used the <uses–permission> and the <uses–feature> tags present in the manifest file. Manhattan, Euclidean and Cosine distance were applied and obtained AUC of 0.88 using Manhattan distance with average as the combination rule (85% accuracy). Using Euclidean distance, they obtained more than 0.90 of AUC with 87.57% of accuracy. The best results of 0.91 of AUC and nearly 90% of accuracy was obtained using Cosine similarity.

MAMA [24] used permissions and feature tags within the manifest file. The best results are obtained with Random Forest, using 100 trees, achieving an accuracy of 87% and an AUC of 0.95 for malware detection.

DREBIN [26] performs static analysis by extracting maximum possible number of features of an app's code from manifest file. The features are grouped in sets of strings (such as permissions, API calls and network addresses) and are embedded in a joint vector space. About 123,453 applications and 5,560 malware samples are used for the investigation and it detects 94% of the malware with relatively less false alarms.

Authors in [16], [17], [19] devised a supervised anomaly detector named Andromaly to extract 88 prominent features. Detection rates were better for the database with benign games than benign tools when used in combination with the 4 malicious apps. The NB and Logistic Regression were found to be the better classifiers.

DroidAPIMiner in [25] was used to extract API calls using a modified Androguard tool and different classifiers were evaluated using the set of features. They achieved an accuracy of 99% and false positive rate of 2.2% using k–NN classifier.

In [27] the authors presented a static analyzer, Droid Permission Miner, that mines prominent permissions present in the .apk files. Feature selection techniques like *Bi–Normal Separation (BNS)* and *Mutual Information (MI)* were used in their work and obtained an accuracy of 81.56% with 15 features proving *MI* to be better method.

3   Proposed Methodology

This section deals with our static framework for Android malware detection that implements machine learning techniques. Different features that belong to distinct feature categories are extracted and dimensionality reduction is employed to prune the feature space. Androguard [1] is used for mining permissions, count of permissions, software/hardware features and API calls for identifying malicious apps. The permissions, software/hardware features and permission count are mined from the Android Manifest File. However, the API calls from each .apk files are also extracted using the Androguard tool. The individual features are used for classification in the first phase followed by the experimentation with ensemble features. The architecture for our proposed model is shown in Figure 1 for individual features and Figure 2 for ensemble model. These models are briefly described in the following subsections.

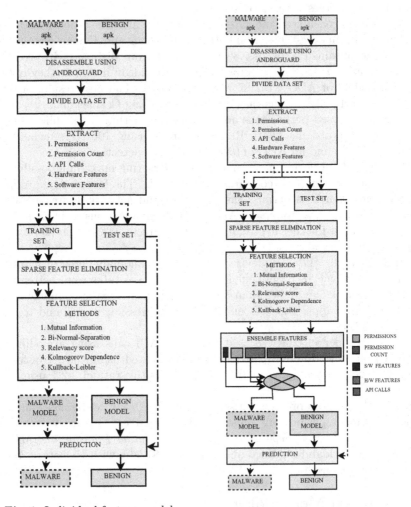

Fig. 1. Individual feature model

Fig. 2. Ensemble model

3.1   Dataset Preparation

Dataset is prepared using 1175 .apk files comprising of 575 malicious samples collected from Contagiodump [2] and from different user agencies. Also, 600 benign applications were downloaded from various publicly available Internet sources. The benign samples are divided such that 300 files are included in the test set and the other 300 samples are allocated to train set. From the 575 illegitimate samples, 287 .apk files are included in the test set and the remaining 288 files are added to the train set.

3.2 Feature Categories

The individual feature model as well as ensemble model generation requires features that are extracted from five distinct categories. Different categories of features are listed below.

- *Permissions:* The activities of an application depends upon the permissions requested by it. It is declared statically and there is no provision to declare it dynamically. Android architecture provides a well framed permission mechanism to provide security.
- *Permission count:* This feature set is generated by computing the number of permissions requested by an application.
- *Hardware features:* These are the features required by the app for its execution. It provides information about the set of hardware features on which the application depends.
- *Software features:* These are the software features required by the application for its execution.
- *API calls:* The application programming interface calls are invoked at the execution time to perform some specific tasks.

3.3 Feature Extraction

The Android .apk files [18] are provided as input to the disassembler tool Androguard. These files are initially in the binary format. The .xml files are human readable Manifest files generated from the input .apk files using python script androaxml.py. The permissions (within <uses-permission> tag) as well as s/w and h/w features (within <uses-feature> tag) are extracted from these xml files. Similarly, the python script androapkinfo.py is used to mine the API calls of the samples. After extracting permissions from each .apk file, the number of permissions requested by each file is determined. The count of permissions existing in a file is considered as another feature for generating the classification model.

3.4 Pre–processing Phase

In this phase, feature pruning is carried out to eliminate the attributes that results in misclassification. After removing the irrelevant attributes, features common to both the classes $(M \cap B)$ are considered. Common features are given high precedence over other category of attributes such as union of malware and benign features $(M \cup B)$, discriminant benign and discriminant malware features as they are reported to be insignificant for the detection of malicious samples [27].

3.5   Feature Selection Techniques

Feature selection is exercised to synthesize the input data into convenient size so as to extract a subset of k prominent features from a set of n features (large feature space). The techniques discussed below implements dimensionality reduction to exclude redundant features. The selected attributes are used to fabricate the classification model to predict unknown samples. Equations of the five feature selection techniques used in this work are discussed in Table 1.

Table 1. Feature selection techniques

Method	Equation	Description
BNS [10] [11] [12]	$BNS = \|F^{-1}(tpr) - F^{-1}(fpr)\|$ $$TruePositiveRate = \frac{(TP)}{(TP + FN)}$$ $$FalsePositiveRate = \frac{(FP)}{(TN + FP)}$$	Selects positive and negative features and is not biased to any class. Its value is determined from the statistical table for Z–Score [4].F^{-1} is the inverse cumulative probability function of standard normal distribution
MI [8]	$MI(f,C) =$ $$\sum_{C \in \{M,B\}} \sum_{f} P(f,C) log \left(\frac{P(f,C)}{P(f)P(C)} \right)$$	It gives the extent to which an attribute f reduces the uncertainty in determining the appropriate class C. $P(f,C)$ is the joint probability distribution, $P(f)$ and $P(C)$ are the marginal probability distributions of variables f and C.
RS [7]	$$RS(t_k, C_i) = log \left(\frac{(P(t_k\|C_i) + d)}{(P(\bar{t}_k\|\bar{C}_i) + d)} \right)$$	It is based on the conditional probabilities of a feature in the training set. $P(t_k\|C_i)$ is the presence of feature t_k in class C_i ,$P(\bar{t}_k\|\bar{C}_i)$ is the absence of feature t_k in class C_i and d is the number of samples with feature t_k in class C_i.
KO [14]	$$KO(f) = \sum_{j=1}^{\|C\|} p(f) \left(p(f\|C_j) - p(f\|\bar{C}_j) \right)$$	This method scores each feature f depending on its relation with the classes C_j, $\bar{C}_j$. $P(f\|C_j)$ is the presence of feature f in class C_j, $P(f\|\bar{C}_j)$ is the presence of feature f in class $\bar{C}_j$, $\|C\|$ is the total number of classes and $P(f)$ is the probability of feature f.
KL [14]	$$KL(f) = -P(f\|M)log \left(\frac{P(f)}{P(f\|M)} \right) -$$ $$P(f\|B)log \left(\frac{P(f)}{P(f\|B)} \right)$$	$P(f\|M)$ is the presence of feature f in class M (malware), $P(f\|B)$ is the presence of feature f in class B(benign) and $P(f)$ is the probability of an attribute f.

These techniques are applied to the top 78 common permissions and prominent 2166 APIs common to both malware and benign train set to reduce the feature space. The common features $(M \cap B)$ are arranged in the decreasing order of their BNS, MI, RS, KO and KL scores respectively. The top BNS scored attributes are not used as it does not provide better accuracy according to the previous work [27]. Hence, we considered bottom BNS and top MI, RS, KO and KL attributes with diverse feature lengths.

3.6 Ensemble Features

This feature space is generated by combining the optimal feature sets of five individual categories of feature (Permissions, count of permissions, s/w and h/w features and API calls). The top ranked features are combined to create ensemble feature space to improve the classification accuracy. The ensemble features are constructed by discarding all extraneous attributes (refer Fig.2).

3.7 Classification

The malware and benign models are developed using classifiers (AdaBoostM1 with J48 as base classifier (ADA) [28], Random Forest (RF)[9] [No: of Trees= 40, seed=3] and J48) implemented in WEKA [15]. Unknown samples are predicted using these learned models.

3.8 Evaluation Parameters

Accuracy [30] gives the degree of correctness of a model in classifying the test samples. Here, FP gives the misclassification of benign samples, TP indicate correctly classified malware instances, FN represents wrongly classified malware samples and TP denotes correctly classified malware files.

$$Accuracy = (TP + TN)/(TP + TN + FP + FN) \tag{1}$$

The investigations carried out in this work are listed below:

1. *Determination of robust feature selection method.*
2. *Evaluate the optimal feature vector length.*
3. *Estimation of best feature category (permissions, permission count, software/ hardware features or API calls).*
4. *Determination of the best classifier that reduced misclassification.*
5. *Comparative study of ensemble and individual features.*

4 Experiments and Findings

The experiments are performed on a computer with Ubuntu 12.04 OS, Intel core i3 CPU and 4GB RAM. The two phases involve (1) considering independent attributes and (2) use of ensemble features. The experiments are carried out in two ways; using test/train set and cross validation.

4.1   Evaluation Based on Train and Test Set

Performance Evaluation with Independent Features. The models for classification are created by considering the frequencies of attributes in each file, and individually recording the presence/absence of an attribute (known as Boolean features). In each sample, the permissions and software/hardware features are declared only once so their presence/absence (0 or 1) are considered in the feature vector. In case of API call, the investigation is carried out in two ways (presence/absence and frequency).

Boolean Feature Vector Table (FVT): From the training samples, a total of 195 and 109 unique permissions are obtained respectively from benign and malware files and 78 common permissions are obtained from these unique lists. These 78 permissions are arranged based on their BNS, MI, RS, KO and KL scores in descending order. BNS features are selected from the bottom and top MI, RS, KO and KL scored attributes are considered. For KO, 34 benign as well as 44 malware prominent features are obtained from the 78 common permissions. Classification models are generated using top 10, 20 ⋯ 70 ranked permissions based on the five selection methods. The same activity is carried out with the permission count for the training samples. A total of 7,174 and 29,765 unique API calls are obtained for malware and benign apps. During the pre–processing phase, 50% of infrequent APIs are eliminated thus reducing the feature space to 14,882 benign and 3587 malware APIs respectively. From this pruned feature set, 2166 common APIs are determined. After implementing Kolmogorov dependence (KO), out of 2166 api calls, 786 malware and 1378 benign prominent features are obtained. Classification models are generated using significant API calls (scored on the basis of five feature selection methods), specifying their presence/absence in a sample for variable feature length (i.e. 50, 100, 200 ⋯ 1000). The 40 h/w and 7 s/w attributes obtained are used without reducing their feature space.

Table 2. Accuracies for BNS, MI, RS and KL scored permissions

Feature selection Method	BNS			MI			RS			KL		
Classifier / Feature Length	J48	ADA	RF	J48	ADA	RF	J48	ADA	RF	J48	ADA	RF
10	82.14	82.31	84.69	84.69	85.03	85.03	83.84	82.31	83.33	85.20	85.71	85.20
20	85.03	85.37	89.62	86.05	87.24	87.58	85.37	86.90	88.77	82.14	86.56	87.07
30	87.92	89.79	**92.51**	84.69	87.24	87.58	88.77	86.56	89.96	83.50	86.73	88.09
40	86.90	88.26	92.00	84.35	88.09	91.49	87.92	88.94	90.98	84.86	88.09	90.98
50	87.24	89.11	92.17	86.56	89.62	91.66	87.07	90.47	91.32	86.56	88.94	92.51
60	87.41	89.28	91.15	87.58	88.94	92	87.41	88.60	91.66	87.58	88.94	92
70	87.41	89.11	91.83	87.41	89.29	92.51	87.41	89.11	91.83	87.41	89.28	92.51

The results of the above experiments are reviewed here. The 30 BNS permission feature resulted in higher accuracy using Random Forest (i.e. 92.51%). It is observed that the classification model generated using MI, RS, KO and KL features does not identify malicious apps effectively as it uses more number of permissions than BNS for improved performance (refer Table 2). Similar experiment is performed for the count of permissions. The optimal feature length is observed to be 71 with an accuracy of 92.34% using BNS/MI/KL with Random Forest (refer Table 3). For API calls, the Boolean features (with feature length of 50) provided improved accuracy of 90.81% using BNS (refer Table 4). The results obtained using the software and hardware features without implementing feature selection technique are shown in Table 6. The 40 h/w and 7 s/w features depicted less accuracy (56.12 and 52.04% respectively).

Due to lack of space, the accuracies for Kolmogorov dependence (KO) with feature lengths that are found to be optimal are only projected in Table 6.

Table 3. Accuracies for BNS, MI, RS and KL scored permission count

Feature selection Method / Feature Length	BNS			MI			RS			KL		
	J48	ADA	RF	J48	ADA	RF	J48	ADA	RF	J48	ADA	RF
11	84.69	86.90	87.07	86.22	87.41	88.09	85.54	84.01	86.05	86.22	87.07	86.90
21	85.20	87.92	90.81	86.05	87.75	89.62	86.39	87.75	90.13	84.35	87.07	89.96
31	87.41	88.26	91.15	84.69	88.77	89.96	88.26	89.28	90.81	84.35	87.41	90.30
41	86.90	89.11	91.83	84.35	88.77	91.83	87.92	88.94	91.32	84.86	87.41	91.66
51	87.24	89.11	91.83	86.56	87.92	91.83	87.07	89.28	91.83	86.56	89.62	91.34
61	87.41	88.43	92.17	87.58	87.58	92.17	87.41	88.77	90.98	87.58	87.58	92.17
71	87.41	88.43	**92.34**	87.41	88.43	**92.34**	87.41	88.43	92.17	87.41	88.43	**92.34**

Table 4. Accuracies for BNS, MI, RS and KL scored API calls (Boolean features)

Feature selection Method / Feature Length	BNS			MI			RS			KL		
	J48	ADA	RF	J48	ADA	RF	J48	ADA	RF	J48	ADA	RF
50	84.01	86.22	**90.81**	83.50	82.99	82.48	83.84	85.54	88.94	83.50	82.82	82.99
100	87.24	88.77	90.81	85.54	86.73	88.60	86.39	89.28	91.49	85.30	85.54	87.41
200	87.75	89.45	89.79	85.71	89.79	88.26	87.58	89.28	91.32	85.71	87.24	88.43
300	86.05	89.79	90.81	85.71	90.64	89.79	87.07	90.47	90.47	85.71	88.09	88.09
400	86.05	90.81	89.79	85.54	87.58	90.47	86.73	88.94	91.32	86.05	88.43	88.77
500	86.90	89.79	90.47	87.41	90.30	90.81	86.73	89.79	89.79	86.22	88.77	89.79
600	87.75	90.81	90.13	87.41	90.47	91.15	87.07	90.13	91.15	86.22	88.60	89.45
700	89.11	88.77	90.98	86.22	89.11	90.47	87.07	88.09	91.32	86.22	89.45	89.62
800	88.94	90.13	91.15	87.75	90.81	90.47	87.07	88.77	90.98	87.41	89.11	89.28
900	88.77	90.64	91.15	87.75	90.47	90.81	88.09	91.15	91.49	87.41	89.11	90.47
1000	88.77	90.64	90.64	87.75	90.30	90.47	88.09	91.15	90.47	87.41	89.28	90.30

Frequency FVT: For API calls, the classification model is generated using the frequencies of API in the samples. BNS gives an accuracy of 91.83% with 100 features using Random forest. A minor increase in accuracy is attained using Relevancy Score (Acc. 92.51% with 400 features) but MI, KO and KL shows less performance (refer Table 5 and Table 6). Summarizing the results for independent features, BNS is better for every feature categories as it uses less attributes for classification. Permissions give 92.51% accuracy compared to API calls and permission count (refer Tables 2-6). For all the cases, Random Forest gives better results.

Table 5. Accuracies for BNS, MI, RS and KL scored API calls (Frequency features)

Feature selection Method / Feature Length	BNS			MI			RS			KL		
	J48	ADA	RF	J48	ADA	RF	J48	ADA	RF	J48	ADA	RF
50	84.69	85.20	90.13	83.50	81.46	82.48	87.58	88.60	90.64	83.50	83.50	82.65
100	87.07	89.62	**91.83**	83.84	86.56	88.94	86.22	89.45	90.47	85.03	86.05	86.90
200	87.24	89.45	91.35	85.37	88.94	90.47	87.58	88.60	90.81	85.54	88.43	88.77
300	86.22	89.28	89.96	85.54	89.62	90.13	88.60	91.49	91.49	85.54	88.09	88.09
400	86.22	88.77	90.98	86.05	90.30	89.79	88.09	91.15	92.51	84.69	85.71	88.77
500	86.39	89.28	91.81	84.86	89.79	90.81	88.09	89.79	92	86.05	89.11	90.30
600	86.73	89.79	91.32	84.86	90.13	90.47	88.09	90.64	90.98	86.05	88.60	90.13
700	86.73	90.81	91.32	87.92	89.45	90.98	88.26	91.15	90.98	86.05	87.92	90.13
800	87.75	90.64	91.66	88.43	90.13	90.81	88.26	91.66	91.32	87.24	88.94	89.28
900	87.41	90.81	91.68	88.26	90.64	90.30	87.41	89.96	91.32	87.24	88.43	90.13
1000	87.41	90.30	91.32	88.26	90.13	91.49	87.41	89.96	91.66	87.24	89.62	90.47

Table 6. Accuracies for software/hardware features and KO features (API calls, permissions and permission count) for benign and malware feature lists (projected the accuracies only for optimal feature lengths of corresponding feature categories due to lack of space)

Features	s/w	h/w	API calls				Permissions & count			
			Boolean		Frequency		Permissions		Permission count	
			Benign	Malware	Benign	Malware	Benign	Malware	Benign	Malware
Classifier ⟍ Feature Length	7	40	1000	200	200	600	30	30	35	45
J48	51.19	53.23	83.50	88.26	84.35	85.03	67.68	84.69	82.82	85.88
Adaboost MI (J48)	51.19	54.08	86.90	89.45	87.24	87.58	68.53	84.18	85.37	87.24
Random Forest	51.04	56.12	89.11	90.13	90.64	90.13	70.40	88.09	86.90	89.79

Performance Evaluation with Ensemble Features

Two ensemble models are generated for the five feature selection techniques using (1) the frequencies of prominent API in each file and (2) considering the Boolean value of APIs with the presence/absence of other four categories of features. From Table 7, ensemble model fabricated using frequency with BNS gives an accuracy of 93.87% (for 218 features) with RF classifier. MI (Acc. 94.04%), RS (Acc. 93.87%), KO (93.36% with Benign prominent feature set) and KL(93.53%) depict similar accuracy but employs 1118, 518, 292 and 598 features respectively. The ensemble model designed by Boolean values in FVT of API calls, permissions, count of permissions and software/hardware features is found to be 93.02% with BNS (for 168 features). MI(Acc. 93.53%), RS(Acc. 93.84%), KO(92.85% with malware prominent feature set) and KL(94.21%) have improved accuracies using 718, 618, 292 and 998 features respectively. These two observations indicates that that the ensemble model constructed by employing the Boolean features with BNS provide higher accuracy with 168 features.

Permissions and API calls that are rarely and widely used by malicious and legitimate samples with their descriptions are given in the Appendix A (Tables 10-13).

4.2   Cross–Validation

Cross–validation [29] is implemented to predict the accuracy of a learning model. This approach is significant in the cases where the size of the learning data is very small or when the model is generated with large number of attributes. For a dataset of N specimens, k-fold cross–validation (also known as rotation-estimation) splits the dataset into k mutually exclusive subsets and testing/training are performed k times. In order to estimate the accuracy of a classifier, we performed 10-fold cross–validation (refer Table 8 for the results). In case of KO, 'M' represents malware features and 'B' represents benign attributes .

Table 7. Accuracies for Ensemble features (Boolean and Frequency of features)

Model	Ensemble features (Frequency)					Ensemble features (Boolean)				
Feature selection method	BNS	MI	RS	KO	KL	BNS	MI	RS	KO	KL
Classifier ⟍ Feature Length	218	1118	518	292	598	**168**	718	618	292	998
J48	87.92	87.41	87.92	87.75	88.94	88.26	89.28	89.64	88.77	87.92
Adaboost M1(J48)	90.64	91.83	91.49	93.19	90.30	91.15	90.64	91	91.32	93.02
RF (40) Seed 3	93.87	94.04	93.87	93.36	93.53	**93.02**	93.53	93.84	92.85	94.21

Table 8. Accuracies attained by Random forest classifier after cross validation with prominent features of individual feature categories and ensemble features for five feature selection methods; Represented in the form $\alpha/(\beta)$; where, (α) represents accuracy and (β) represents feature space

Selection techniques	Permissions	Permission count	API Calls (Frequency)	API Calls (Boolean)	Ensemble (Frequency)	Ensemble (Boolean)
			Features			
BNS	91.14/(30)	91.23/(71)	90.97/(100)	89.53/(50)	93.53/(218)	92.51/(168)
MI	91.40/(70)	91.65/(71)	91.74/(1000)	90.80/(600)	94.04/(1118)	94.12/(718)
RS	91.23/(70)	91.57/(71)	91.82/(400)	92.08/(500)	93.95/(518)	93.36/(618)
KL	91.57/(50)	91.65/(71)	90.72/(500)	91.40/(900)	93.95/(598)	93.61/(998)
KO	86.72/(30,M)	87.82/(45,M)	90.97/(200,B)	89.02/(200,M)	91.23/(292)	92.51/(292)

4.3 Processing Time

The time consumed by prominent BNS features for processing are computed in seconds (secs). This is compared with the time taken by the prominent attribute sets of other feature selection techniques that give improved accuracies with increased feature space (refer Table 9).

Table 9. Processing time (in secs) of prominent BNS features compared with the attribute sets of other feature selection techniques (that exhibit improved accuracy with more features); represented in the form $\delta(\beta, \gamma)$; where, (δ) represents processing time for Random forest, (β) depicts feature space and (γ) gives attribute selection technique

Classification approach	Permissions	API Calls (Frequency)	API Calls (Boolean)	Ensemble (Frequency)	Ensemble (Boolean)
			Attributes		
Test/train set	1.21×10^{-9}[30,BNS]/ 1.45×10^{-9}[50,KL]	1.46×10^{-9}[100,BNS]/ 2.3×10^{-9}[400,RS]	1.28×10^{-9}[50,BNS]/ 2.15×10^{-9}[500,RS]	1.43×10^{-9}[218,BNS]/ 1.77×10^{-9}[1118,MI]	1.33×10^{-9}[168,BNS]/ 1.68×10^{-9}[718,MI]
Cross validation	0.33[30,BNS]/ 0.46[50,KL]	0.52[100,BNS]/ 1.07[400,RS]	0.39[50,BNS]/ 1.38[500,RS]	0.61[218,BNS]/ 2.23[1118,MI]	0.57[168,BNS]/ 1.63[718,MI]

5 Inference

The following are the inferences made from this work:

- For independent features, permissions are found to be the desired attributes as the accuracy attained with BNS is 92.51% (with a small feature length of 30). The functioning of an app is based on the permissions requested by it and all malicious apps need some permissions that are different from the benign .apk files.
- Ensemble models combine the optimal feature space of individual features and gains the strength of this combination. So these models are better than the models built using individual features.
- BNS assigns higher rank to an attribute in comparison with MI, RS, KO and KL (refer Appendix B, Figure.3 and Figure.4).
- Random Forest being an ensemble based learning method aggregated the results from multiple classifiers and performed better in all cases.

- Increase in feature length included the features that are not apt for model generation and reduced the classification accuracy.
- In *PUMA* [22], permissions and count of permissions are used as features to attain 86.41% accuracy. *MAMA* [24] extracted permissions as well as features present in the uses–feature tags and obtained best results with Random Forest (accuracy of 87%). *Droid Permission Miner* [27], extracted permissions and implemented Bi–Normal Separation (BNS) and Mutual Information (MI) to obtain an accuracy of 81.56% (with MI using 15 features). Our work with five feature categories and ensemble features show reasonable performance when compared with [22], [24] and [27]. Here, the accuracy attained is 92.51% with 30 permissions. Using the count of permissions, the accuracy is 92.34%. With 100 API calls, the accuracy is 91.83% for BNS with Random forest classifier. The accuracies of the proposed ensemble model using BNS is 93.02% (with Boolean features using 168 features) and 93.87% (with frequency attributes using 218 features) with Random Forest classifier.

6   Conclusion and Future Scope

We presented a static malware analysis framework using permissions, count of permissions, software/hardware features and API calls by implementing machine learning algorithms. The ensemble model performed better compared to the individual model. In this work, BNS synthesized precise features that improved the classification accuracy. The accuracy for ensemble model with Boolean features is 93.02% with 168 features and individual model with 30 permissions are 92.51% using BNS. Thus, our proposed method can be used for the initial classification of .apk samples with reduced false alarms. In future, features like Dalvik opcode, Java reflection and Android Manifest attributes can also be used individually and as ensemble features. Also, data flow and analysis on API call with and without parameters can be used as in [25] to improve the applicability of our implemented scheme.

Acknowledgements: We would like to thank all the anonymous reviewers for their valuable suggestions that assisted us to enhance the quality of our work.

References

1. Androguard, http://code.google.com/p/androguard/ (accessed September 12, 2013)
2. Malware apk, http://contagiominidump.blogspot.in/2011/07/take-sample-leave-sample-mobile-malware.html
   (accessed September 22, 2013)
3. Apk file format, http://www.file-extensions.org/article/android-apk-file-format-description (accessed October 5, 2013)
4. Z-score Table,
   http://www.stat.tamu.edu/lzhou/stat302/standardnormaltable.pdf
   (accessed October 13, 2013)
5. Android Developers, http://developer.android.com/about/index.html (accessed March 10, 2014)
6. Symantec Corporation, Internet Security Threat Report 2014, vol. 19 (2014)

7. Feature selection, Ling, Fei Xia, `http://courses.washington.edu/ling572/winter2013/slides/class7_feature_selection.pdf` (accessed April 9, 2014)

8. Battiti, R.: Using Mutual Information for Selecting Features in Supervised Neural Net Learning. IEEE Transactions oN Neural Networks 5(4) (1994)

9. Liaw, A., Wiener, M.: Classification and Regression by Random Forest, 18–22 (December 2002)

10. Forman, G.: An Extensive Empirical Study of Feature Selection Metrics for Text Classification, Special Issue on Variable and Feature Selection. Journal of Machine Learning Research, 1289–1305 (2003)

11. Tang, L., Liu, H.: Bias Analysis in Text Classification for Highly Skewed Data. In: ICDM, pp. 781–784. IEEE Computer Society (2005)

12. Forman, G.: BNS Scaling: A Complement to Feature Selection for SVM Text Classification In Hewlett-Packard Labs Tech Report HPL-2006-19 (2006)

13. Filiol, E., Jacob, G., Le Liard, M.: Evaluation Methodology and Theoretical Model for Antiviral Behavioural Detection Strategies. Journal in Computer Virology (2006); WTCV 2006 Special Issue, Bonfante, G., Marion, J.-Y. (eds.)

14. Bonev, B.I.: Feature Selection based on Information Theory, `http://www.dccia.ua.es/~boyan/papers/TesisBoyan.pdf` (accessed May 10, 2014)

15. Frank, E., Hall, M.A., Holmes, G., Kirkby, R., Pfahringer, B.: WEKA - A Machine Learning Workbench for Data Mining. In: The Data Mining and Knowledge Discovery Handbook, pp. 1305–1314 (2005)

16. Shabtai, A., Elovici, Y.: Applying Behavioral Detection on Android-Based Devices. In: Cai, Y., Magedanz, T., Li, M., Xia, J., Giannelli, C. (eds.) Mobilware 2010. LNICST, vol. 48, pp. 235–249. Springer, Heidelberg (2010)

17. Shabtai, A.: Malware Detection on Mobile Devices. In: 11th International Conference on Mobile Data Management (2010)

18. Heger, D.A.: Mobile Devices - An Introduction to the Android Operating Environment Design, Architecture, and Performance Implications (2011)

19. Shabtai, A., Kanonov, U., Elovici, Y., Glezer, C., Weiss, Y.: Andromaly: A Behavioral Malware Detection Framework for Android Devices. J. Intell. Inf. Syst. (2012)

20. Huang, C.-Y., Tsai, Y.-T., Hsu, C.-H.: Performance Evaluation on Permission-Based Detection for Android Malware. In: Pan, J.-S., Yang, C.-N., Lin, C.-C. (eds.) Advances in Intelligent Systems & Applications. SIST, vol. 21, pp. 111–120. Springer, Heidelberg (2012)

21. Aung, Z., Zaw, W.: Permission-Based Android Malware Detection. International Journal of Scientific & Technology Research 2, 228–234 (2013)

22. Sanz, B., Santos, I., Laorden, C., Ugarte-Pedrero, X., Bringas, P.G., Álvarez, G.: PUMA: Permission Usage to Detect Malware in Android. In: Herrero, Á., et al. (eds.) Int. Joint Conf. CISIS'12-ICEUTE'12-SOCO'12. AISC, vol. 189, pp. 289–298. Springer, Heidelberg (2013)

23. Sanz, B., Santos, I., Ugarte-Pedrero, X., Laorden, C., Nieves, J., Bringas, P.G.: Instance-based Anomaly Method for Android Malware Detection. In: SECRYPT 2013, pp. 387–394 (2013)

24. Sanz, B., Santos, I., Laorden, C., Ugarte-Pedrero, X., Nieves, J., Bringas, P.G., Álvarez, G.: Mama: manifest Analysis for Malware Detection in Android. In: Cybernetics and Systems, pp. 469–488 (2013)

25. Aafer, Y., Du, W., Yin, H.: DroidAPIMiner: Mining API-Level Features for Robust Malware Detection in Android. In: Zia, T., Zomaya, A., Varadharajan, V., Mao, M. (eds.) SecureComm 2013. LNICST, vol. 127, pp. 86–103. Springer, Heidelberg (2013)

26. Arp, D., Spreitzenbarth, M., Hubner, M., Gascon, H., Rieck, K.: Drebin: Efficient and Explainable Detection of Android Malware in Your Pocket. In: 17th Network and Distributed System Security Symposium (NDSS) (February 2014)

27. Aswini, A.M., Vinod, P.: Droid Permission Miner: Mining Prominent Permissions for Android Malware Analysis. In: 5th International Conference on the Applications of the Digital Information and Web Technologies (ICADIWT 2014), pp. 81–86 (2014)

28. Freund, Y., Schapire, R.E.: Experiments with a new boosting algorithm. In: Thirteenth International Conference on Machine Learning, pp. 148–156 (1996)

29. Kohavi, R.: A Study of Cross-Validation and Bootstrap for Accuracy Estimation and Model Selection. In: 14th International Joint Conference on Artificial Intelligence, IJCAI 1995, Canada, August 20-25, pp. 1137–1145 (1995)

30. Tan, P.-N., Steinbach, M., Kumar, V.: Introduction to Data Mining. Addison-Wesley (2005) ISBN 0-321-32136-7

Appendix A

Table 10. Prominent permissions and their description

Permissions	Description
WRITE_EXTERNAL_STORAGE	Permission for an application to write to the external storage
READ_PHONE_STATE	Permission read only access to phone state
CHANGE_WIFI_STATES	Allows changing wi-fi connectivity state
WAKE_LOCK	Allows using PowerManager WakeLocks to keep processor from sleeping or screen from dimming
SEND_SMS	Allows an app to send SMS Permission for the app to access network information
ACCESS_WIFI_STATE	Permission for the app to access network information
ACCESS_COARSE_LOCATION	Permission for the app to access approximate location by means o towers and wi-fi
ACCESS_FINE_LOCATION	Permission for the app to access precise location by means of towers and wi-fi
READ_CONTACTS	To read contact list of the device's user

Table 11. Trivial permissions and their description

Permissions	Description
RECEIVE_WAP_PUSH	Permission to monitor incoming wap push
WRITE_CALL_LOG	Permission for an application only to write user's contact data
READ_CALL_LOG	Permission for an application to read call log
CLEAR_APP_CACHE	Permission for an application to clear the caches of all apps that are installed
UPDATE_DEVICE_STATUS	Permission for an application to update device statistics
DEVICE_POWER	Permission for an application for low-level access to power management
CALL_PREVILEGED	Permission for an application to call any phone number without using dialer user interface to confirm the call
BATTERY_STATS	Permission for an app to collect battery statistics

Table 12. Significant API calls and their description

API calls	Description
onCreateOptionsMenu()	It is called only one time, i.e, the first time when the options menu is shown. It is used to initialize the contents of the activity's standard options menu. Menu items are placed in menu
onDraw()	Override these calls to implement custom view. Used when the contents of the view has to be changed
onActivityResult()	Gives the results back from an Activity when it ends
onCreateDialog()	To implement dialog designs present in the dialog design guide
onTouchEvent()	Called when an event like a touch screen motion event occurs
onOptionItemSelected()	Called when an item in the options menu is selected
onAttachedToWindow()	It is called when the view is window attached
onKeyUp()	Called at the time of an event like a key up event

Table 13. Trivial API calls and their description

API Calls	Description
setLanguage()	Sets the text to speech language
setMarginEnd()	Provides additional space on the end side of this view. It sets the end margin
setWebViewClient()	Sets the webViewClient that is capable of receiving requests
shouldOverrideKeyEvent()	Provides chance to the host application to handle the key events simultaneously
setPitch()	Sets the speech pitch
addSpeech()	Adds mapping between text and a sound file
setSpeechRate()	API calls to set speech rate
setName()	API calls to set name of the suit

Appendix B

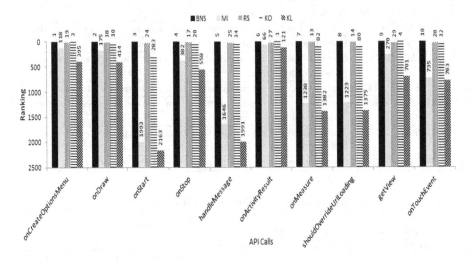

Fig. 3. Comparing the ranks of bottom BNS scored API calls with their MI, RS, KO and KL ranks (Lower ranks indicate high significance)

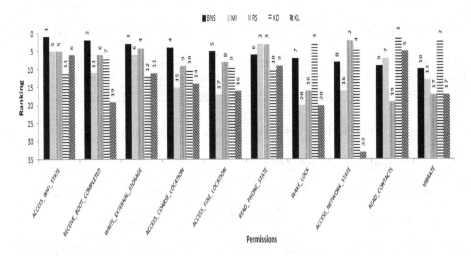

Fig. 4. Comparing the ranks of bottom BNS scored permissions with their MI, RS, KO and KL ranks (Lower ranks indicate high significance)

Linux Malware Detection Using eXtended–Symmetric Uncertainty

K.A. Asmitha and P. Vinod

Department of Computer Science & Engineering,
SCMS School of Engineering & Technology, Ernakulam, Kerala, India 683 582
{asmitha030,pvinod21}@gmail.com

Abstract. We propose a novel two step dimensionality reduction approach based on correlation using machine learning techniques for identifying unseen malicious Executable Linkable Files (ELF). System calls used as features are dynamically extracted in a sandbox environment. The extended version of symmetric uncertainty (X-SU) proposed by us, ranks feature by determining Feature–Class correlation using entropy, information gain and further eliminate the redundant features by estimating Feature–Feature correlation using weighted probabilistic information gain. Three learning algorithms (J48, Adaboost and Random Forest) are employed to generate prediction models, from the system call traces. Optimal feature vector constructed using minimum feature length (27 no.) resulted in over all classification accuracy of 99.40% with very less false alarm to identify unknown malicious specimens.

Keywords: Dynamic analysis, Symmetric uncertainty, Linux malware, Correlation, Feature selection.

1 Introduction

With the widespread use of computer system and network, the number of malware has increased to an unprecedented rate. The increased use of vulnerable on–line systems, with heterogeneous operating systems are exposed to ever–growing number of threats. Thus, the challenge is to track down and identify threats which can be generalized to circumvent new attacks for preventing computer systems. Linux is an operating system which seems to have a world-wide acceptance. The primary reason for its high popularity is the open source nature and acceptance in large number of desktop and server systems. The penetration of Linux malware is exponentially increasing due to the lack of awareness associated with the Linux operating system. We cite two reports to highlight the disquieting rate at which new malware is proliferating. The 2013 Server Security Survey [19] reveal that organizations are facing increasing difficulty in identifying and mitigating advanced attacks aimed at network servers. Also, most of the companies rely on technologies that are ineffective and obsolete. According to the global threat intelligence report [20] by the Security Engineering Research Team, it is very expensive in terms of money to overcome the aftershock of an attack, more than $3000 per day expense is incurred to mitigate and recover from

R.S. Chakraborty et al. (Eds.): SPACE 2014, LNCS 8804, pp. 319–332, 2014.
© Springer International Publishing Switzerland 2014

malware attacks. Thus, there is an urgent need to undermine unseen threats exposed to systems.

Zero day malware can easily bypass the existing commercial antivirus softwares as the signature database comprises known patterns of malicious programs. If the malware signature relies on the syntactic features of the suspicious code, it can be easily evaded by obfuscation techniques by modifying the code structure without altering the program semantics. Moreover, the antivirus softwares have to maintain a large signatures database to mitigate the threats. Also, the signature generation and distribution is a time consuming process, as the former requires strict code analysis and later involve a trigger from user. Finally, pattern–based detection demand human intervention which might not prove to be an ineffective solution.

In order to resolve the above mentioned problems of the existing malware detection system, we introduced a new approach employing non–signature technique based on mining system calls, which are extracted by executing each specimens in a sandbox environment. Here, our approach is to obtain reduced feature length that is highly correlated to class also have minimum feature to feature redundancy. This improves classification rate and prediction of new samples at reduced time.

Since system calls can capture the interactions of a program with its environment, the unintended communication which cause security violations can be captured. The major contribution of this paper is a novel approach which can effectively classify unknown malware and benign executables with high accuracy and minimum feature length. The effectiveness of the proposed scheme is evaluated on a collection of Linux malware samples obtained from VX–heavens [17]. Following are the key contributions of this article: (a) A novel method to identify Linux malware, (b) Extraction and evaluation of significant features(i.e. system calls) by extermination of redundant features dynamically, (c) Automatic generation of efficient and generalised prediction models that capture the behavior of a program as a whole and (d) Generation of optimal feature vector with minimum feature length ensuring higher detection accuracy.

The rest of the paper is organized as follows: the related works are explained in Section 2. The proposed method is discussed in Section 3. In section 4 we present experiments, results and discussions. Finally, we conclude the work with pointers to open research issues.

2   Related Works

Authors in [4] proposed an approach to discriminating worms from benign programs by mining feature set that examine the sequence of features present in a process trace. Support vector machine (SVM) and Naïve Bayes (NB) are used for classification and prediction. Also, the authors designed a "black-box" classifier to avoid the user interpretation.

The authors in [1] proposed a detection scheme based on system call sequences. In this, they analyzed the processes executing at high privileges, and compared the normal system call trace with the sequence of the system call obtained post malware attack.

In [6] the author proposed a novel method to identify zero-day malware by extracting features from Portable Executables. The methodology is a three–fold approach comprising of (a) features selection (b) elimination of redundant features and (c) classification using data mining techniques. The author in [10] proposed a new approach for Linux malware detection by mining feature set collected from ELF headers of Linux executables. Also, a number of well–known classifiers implemented in WEKA [7][13] to evaluate the method.

In [5], author proposed a system called IMAD to identify zero–day malware without any apriori knowledge. The proposed scheme detect malware programs during its execution. Also, they developed a classifier to classify samples with variable length feature vector (i.e. n-$grams$). Genetic algorithm was used to optimize the learning process and detection accuracy was observed to increase by tuning parameters. Also, authors performed comparative analysis of the obtained results with well–known classification techniques namely SVM, RIPPER, C4.5, Naïve Bayes.

The authors in [8] proposed a new approach known as hypergrams to represent variable length system call sequences for in–execution malware analysis and detection. A k-dimensional hyperspace was used to visualize the n-$grams$ where, k represents the number of unique system call sequences of a program in execution. The programs mark their impact in this space and explore the matching paths in the hyperspace for classification. The results were compared with traditional n-$gram$ method.

In [9], [11] a new approach to detect run–time behavior of a process known as genetic footprint was proposed. Information maintained in the process control block (PCB) of an executing process was used as features. The author also performed a comparison with other existing solutions.

3   Architecture

The proposed method operate by extracting the system call sequences (i.e. dynamic behavior) by executing the program, followed by elimination of redundant features for the preparation of effective prediction models. Here, the architecture of the proposed method and main components are discussed (refer, Figure 1).

3.1   Dataset Preparation

A total of 226 Linux malware samples of different families is collected from VX-Heavens (http://vx.netlux.org) repository. Benign files comprising of 442 executables is gathered from different directories of Linux such as /bin, /sbin and /usr/bin. Malware samples used in the dataset are (a) backdoor (13 no.) (b) exploit (43 no.) (c) floodor (37 no.) (d) hacktool (22 no.) (e) virus (54 no.) (f) rootkit (23 no.) and (g) net-worm (16 no.).

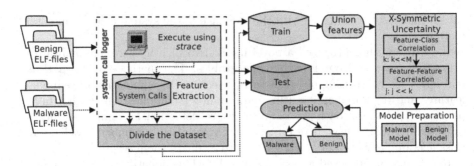

Fig. 1. The Architecture of Proposed Method

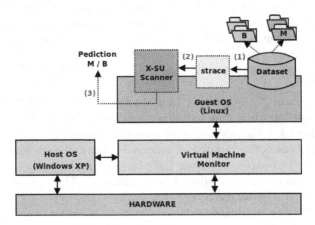

Fig. 2. The steps for gathering system calls (1) take each sample from dataset (2) execute using strace and fed logfile to X-SU (3) preprocess, prepare models and predict unknown samples as benign or malware

3.2   System Call Logger

As our approach is based on dynamic analysis we intended to capture the dynamic properties of a process in the system. Thus, system call trace of executables are extracted. As execution of malware specimens may harm the host system, executable is monitored in virtual machine. A Linux application called strace [18] is used to execute each process for a minute to capture system calls interaction during its the execution. The collected trace file consists of arguments and return values are preprocessed to extract system call name without parameters and return values. An example of *strace* (with arguments and return values) as well as preprocessed output file is depicted in Figure 2.

3.3   Divide the Dataset

A total of 668 files are considered in the dataset, out of which 442 are benign 226 are malware specimens. Dataset is splitted into two partitions (1) training

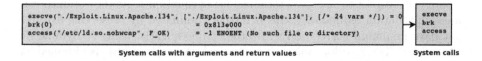

Fig. 3. Extraction of system call from output of *strace*

set: which is used for feature extraction and preparation of learning models and (2) test set: used to evaluate the appropriateness of the developed models. Out of 226 malware samples 113 samples were used for both training and test set. Likewise, 221 samples of total 442 benign files are used as training and test set.

3.4 Feature Selection

Noisy features can exaggerate the minor discrepancies in the dataset thereby it can reduce the predictive performance of classification models. Thus, feature selection is considered as a crucial approach to eliminate irrelevant attributes. It reduces the training time involved, as few features are used to develop model and for predictability of samples in future.

High–ranked system calls are determined that have greater ability to identify malware from benign executable. In [12], it is already verified that the union and intersection features demonstrates discriminating ability of target classes (malware or benign). Thus, we have utilized union features (149 system calls from malware and benign samples). Through our study, we also figure out the impact of varying feature length on detection accuracy.

Representative features (system calls) are identified using a feature selection method called X–Symmetric Uncertainty (X-SU) and used to frame a powerful classification model. The details of X–Symmetric Uncertainty and ranking of system calls using the designated score for preparing models are discussed below.

(A) X–Symmetric Uncertainty(X–SU): Here, a two–step dimensionality reduction is employed and the features are ranked based on estimating (a) first, the feature to class correlation (i.e. the ability of a feature to predict a target class) and (b) second, the feature to feature inter–correlation (i.e. the ability to predict one feature using another feature). The above correlation is determined in terms of information theoretic feature technique known as *entropy* and *information gain*. The representative feature space thus obtained contribute to classification accuracy as it is less likely to have insignificant attributes.

There are mainly two broad methods to compute the inter–correlation among two variables they are (1) determine the linear correlation coefficient which measure the degree of proximity between two variables and (2) using information theory[3]. The former is not used as it assumes all correlations as linear in nature. Thus, information theoretic methods like entropy and information gain is used in our approach. Entropy is the measure of uncertainty of a feature, equation (1) is used for computing entropy of a feature. We adopt a two step approach, initially, extract features that can identify malware or benign population. Score of a feature with respect to class is determined using equation 1. As the obtained features may contain redundancy, this is further eliminated by preserving features that have minimum correlation with other. Subsequently, using X–Symmetric uncertainty (X–SU) values for each system call in range of [0-1] is obtained. A value 1 indicate that feature can predict another feature and zero value depict the features are least correlated and can considered relevant features.

$$H(A) = -\sum_i p(a_i) * log_2(p(a_i)) \tag{1}$$

where, $H(A)$ is the entropy of feature A alone and $p(a_i)$ is the probability of this feature. The two steps of dimensionality reduction adopted is briefly discussed below.

Step 1. **Feature–Class Correlation:**
The features are ranked based on the feature to class correlation which is computed using the entropy of each feature and information gain of each feature with respect to the class. Entropy of feature can be calculated using the equation (1) and information gain is determined with equation (2) respectively.

$$IG(f,C) = -\sum_{i=1}^{|C|} P(C_i) * log_2(P(C_i)) + \sum_{i=1}^{|C|} P(f|C_i) * log_2(P(f|C_i))$$
$$+ \sum_{i=1}^{|C|} P(\bar{f}|C_i) * log_2(P(\bar{f}|C_i)) \tag{2}$$

where, $P(C_i)$ is the probability of class and $P(f|C_i)$ is the conditional probability of a feature given the probability of class C_i. For feature–class correlation, a high correlation to class indicate the feature identifies the classes precisely. The biasing of information gain towards the higher valued attributes is avoided by normalizing the correlations using symmetric uncertainty and it can be computed by using equation (3)

$$SU_f = 2 * (IG(f,C)/(H(f) + H(C))) \tag{3}$$

Step 2. **Feature-Feature Correlation:**
The top 50 ranked features obtained previous step is used to determine all possible bigrams of the system call. The process of extracting the bigram features is depicted in the Figure 3. These bigrams are later used for estimating the feature to feature inter–correlations. A high correlation between the features indicate redundancy thus, a system call is discarded considering it insignificant for classification. At the same time, the zero or less inter–correlation among features indicate that features can independently considered as the representative features for

identification. The feature–feature inter–correlation is computed by using equations (1) and (4).

$$Prob_{IG(f_a,f_b)} = - \sum_{i=1}^{|C|} P(C_i) * log_2(P(C_i)) + \sum_{i=1}^{|C|} P(f_a) * P(f_a|f_b) * log_2(P(f_a|f_b))$$

$$+ \sum_{i=1}^{|C|} P(\bar{f_a}) * P(\bar{f_a}|f_b) * log_2(P(\bar{f_a}|f_b))$$

$$(4)$$

where, the $Prob_{IG(f_a,f_b)}$ is the weighted probabilistic information gain, $P(f_a)$ is the probability of feature f_a in all unigrams and $P(f_a|f_b)$ is the probability of feature f_a after observing another feature f_b. Finally, the symmetric uncertainty can be estimated using the equation (5).

$$SU_{f_a,f_b} = 2 * ((Prob_{IG(f_a,f_b)})/(H(f_a) + H(f_b)))$$

$$(5)$$

The top ranked features are determined and is further processed to obtain prominent system calls from a pair (bigram) of system call sequence used for the classification/prediction. The extraction of system calls from the significant bigrams after determining SU between pair of system calls is represented in Figure 3.

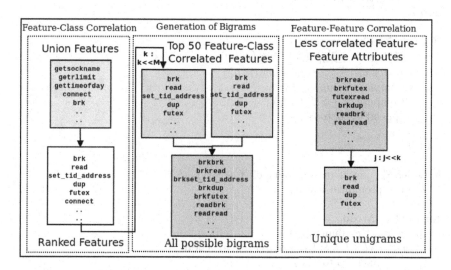

Fig. 4. The schematic diagram depict extraction of significant system calls using X–SU

Algorithm 1 shows the extraction of prominent system call with X–Symmetric Uncertainty.

Algorithm 1. Extraction of prominent features using X-SU

Input: X-SU $((f_a, f_b, ...f_n), C)$
f_i : feature/system call
C : Class Malware/Benign
δ : Feature Length
Output: F_best $= ((f_a, f_b, ...f_j))$ where $j \ll n$

1. Begin
2. //Compute $SU_{f_i,C}$ for feature f_i

for $i = 1 \leftarrow N$ **do**
    $H(f_i) = -\sum_{i=1}^{|C|} p(f_i) * log_2(p(f_i))$
    $H(C) = -\sum_{i=1}^{|C|} p(c_i) * log_2(p(c_i))$
    Compute $IG(F, C)$
    append (f_i) to S_{List}
end for

4. Sort S_{List} in descending order of $SU_{(f_i,C)}$
5. $f_a = $ getFirstElement(S_{List})

if $f_a <>$ NULL **then**
    f_b=getNextElement(S_{List})
end if

if $f_b <>$ NULL **then** then
    $H(f_a) = -\sum_{i=1}^{|C|} p(f_a) * log_2(p(f_a))$
    $H(f_b) = -\sum_{i=1}^{|C|} p(f_b) * log_2(p(f_b))$
    Compute $Prob_{IG(f_a,f_b)}$
    Compute $X - SU(f_a, f_b)$
    append f_a, f_b to S'_{List}

end if

6. Order S'_{List} in increasing value of $X - SU(f_a, f_b)$
7. //prune prominent features

for $i = 1 \leftarrow N$ **do**
    p=extractUnigram(S'_{List})
    if $p <> NULL$ && $! Present(F_{best}, p)$ **then**
        append p to F_{best}
    end if
end for

9. Return F_{best}

3.5   Learning and Classification

In this section, the details of classification phase is described and it particularly consists of two steps (1) learning and (2) prediction. In first step, the selected classifiers are used to develop learning models using the training set and later its performance is evaluated using test set. Here, the AdaboostM1 with J–48 as base classifier, J–48 and Random forest is utilized, motivated by prior work [12]. In this study, we used the standard implementations of classifiers in Waikato Environment for Knowledge Acquisition (WEKA) with default settings.

4   Experiments and Results

In this section, we discuss the experimental setup and the results obtained from our study. Following investigations are carried out:

- *What is the effect of feature length on classification accuracy?*
- *Which classifier is suitable for identifying unseen malware & benign samples?*
- *Whether proposed method is effective in synthesizing robust attributes?*
- *A comparative study of the detection accuracies of the proposed system with existing solutions.*

4.1   Experimental Setup

The experiment is performed with 442 benign samples and 226 Malware samples. 50% of dataset is used for training and remaining is reserved for prediction phase.

A Linux OS installed virtual machine is used to extract the system calls from the collected samples using "`strace`". Each time a clean virtual machine state was used to accurately collect the system call trace. The training models are generated with optimal features (i.e. the top ranked features with minimum feature length) using AdaboostM1(J48), J48 and Random forest.

J48: It is a decision tree based classification algorithm, in which a tree is constructed with a set of input–output samples. It adopt a top–down learning approach and resultant tree traversal produces rules that is used to identify the samples as benign or malware.

Boosted Classifiers: The Boosted classifiers are ensemble based and it often improve performance over single classifiers. Boosting employ a group of weighted models by repetitive learning a model from a weighted data set, evaluating it, and re–weighting the data set based on the performance. To predict the class with the highest weight it uses the group of models and their weights.

Random Forest: Random forest [2] is ensemble–based classification approach. It gives a degree of improvement over bagging by minimizing correlation between classifiers in the ensemble. In this, multiple versions of a classifiers with random subset of the features instead of all features.

4.2   Evaluation Measures

Through our experimentation we are mainly focused on the over–all Detection Accuracy (DA). The effectiveness of any malware scanner is based on high detection rate with minimum false detection. The performance of classifiers are estimated using certain matrices. Detection accuracy which measures the number of correctly classified instances (DA) can be calculated using equation (5):

$$Acc = (TP + TN)/(TP + TN + FP + FN) \tag{6}$$

$$TruePositiveRate\ (TPR) = TP/(TP + FN) \tag{7}$$

$$FalsePositiveRate\ (FPR) = FP/(TN + FP) \tag{8}$$

where, TP–True Positives which represent the number of correctly identified malware instances, TN–True Negatives which denote correctly classified benign samples whereas FP–False Positives designate misclassified benign files and FN– False Negatives represents misclassified malware instances.

4.3   Results and Discussions

The classification accuracies for top ranked features with high feature–class correlation and low feature–feature correlation with varying feature length is reported in Table 1 and 2 respectively. The experiment is performed with variable *feature length* (5, 10, 15...55). The *feature length* (FL) characterizes the number of features considered at the time of preparing the prediction model.

Table 1. Accuracy (%) for *Feature–Class* correlation

Classifiers \ Feature Length	5	10	15	20	25	30	35	40	45	50	55
J48	96.10	96.10	96.10	96.10	96.70	97.00	97.40	97.60	97.60	97.6	97.60
AdaboostM1[J48]	98.80	98.80	98.80	98.80	98.80	99.40	97.6	99.40	99.40	99.40	99.40
Random Forest	98.10	99.10	99.10	99.10	99.10	**99.40**	99.40	99.40	99.40	99.40	99.40

In a realistic–scenario the classification model should be constructed using optimal features with minimum length. From Table 1 and 2 it is seen that the reduced feature length can represent the features of higher dimensions with similar strength. Also, from Table 1 it can be observed that *30* prominent features can predict the class with 99.4 % accuracy, and it is further reduced to a significant *27* features reported in Table 2. If we further reduce the feature length, the accuracy declines due to lack of significant features that can represent the nature of whole dataset.

Subsequently, *feature–feature* inter–correlation can be used to eliminate the highly correlated features which may lead to miss–classifications. Moreover, the

Table 2. Accuracy (%) for *Feature–Feature* correlation were β indicate the number of unique unigrams generated from the corresponding pair of system calls (α)

FL $\alpha(\beta)$ / Classifiers	5(6)	10(11)	15(16)	20(21)	25(24)	30(27)	35(29)	40(30)	45(30)	50(30)	55(35)
J48	88.32	95.80	97.60	97.60	96.40	97.60	97.40	97.60	97.60	97.6	97.60
AdaboostM1[J48]	90.41	98.50	98.80	98.80	98.80	99.40	97.6	99.40	99.40	99.40	99.40
Random Forest	92.21	98.50	98.80	98.80	99.10	**99.40**	99.40	99.40	99.40	99.40	99.40

model preparation time can be reduced by using minimum feature length and thereby reduces prediction time. The details about the analysis of time is given in Table 3. The optimum features and its descriptions are depicted in Table 5.

From Table 1–Table 3 we can conclude that the Adaboost and Random Forest outperformed J48 in terms of detection accuracy as well as in terms of TPR and FPR.

Accuracy alone can never be considered as an appropriate parameter. This is due to the fact that an ideal malware scanner should report higher TPR with low FPR. However, a real time antivirus does not attempt to achieve higher accuracy but maintain minimum false alarm rate at reasonable TPR [14]. This is to assure that the scanner does not flag a benign system file as malignant and subsequently remove such erroneously reported files from system. This would ultimately result in system/network break-down. The TPR and FPR is depicted in Table 3 and it is observed that the feature length with 27 system calls produce a TPR of 100% and FPR of .90%.

Table 3. Performance analysis of detector (TPR, FPR, prediction time) with X-SU were α indicates the pair of system calls considered and β is the significant system calls from a pair of calls

FL ($\alpha(\beta)$)	Classifier	TPR	FPR	Time(μs)	FL ($\alpha(\beta)$)	Classifier	TPR	FPR	Time(μs)
10(11)	J48	91.15	1.80	.00036	35(29)	J48	95.50	1.35	.00037
	AdaboostM1[J48]	98.50	1.35	.00047		AdaboostM1[J48]	100	0.90	.00057
	Random Forest	99.11	1.80	.00048		Random Forest	100	0.90	.00057
15(16)	J48	95.57	1.35	.00034	40(30)	J48	95.57	1.35	.00039
	AdaboostM1[J48]	98.23	0.90	.00047		AdaboostM1[J48]	91.15	1.80	.00053
	Random Forest	99.11	1.35	.00054		Random Forest	91.15	1.80	.00067
20(21)	J48	93.80	1.35	.00039	45(30)	J48	91.15	1.80	.00039
	AdaboostM1[J48]	98.23	0.90	.00048		AdaboostM1[J48]	100	0.90	.00053
	Random Forest	99.11	1.35	.00066		Random Forest	100	0.90	.00067
25(24)	J48	93.80	1.35	.00042	50(30)	J48	91.15	1.80	.00039
	AdaboostM1[J48]	98.23	0.90	.00053		AdaboostM1[J48]	100	0.90	.00053
	Random Forest	99.11	1.35	.00062		Random Forest	100	0.90	.00067
30(27)	J48	95.50	1.35	.00034	55(35)	J48	91.15	1.80	.00041
	AdaboostM1[J48]	**100**	**0.90**	**.00052**		AdaboostM1[J48]	100	0.90	.00057
	Random Forest	*100*	*0.90*	*0.00055*		Random Forest	100	0.90	.00059

The main focus of our study is to compare the proposed scheme with the effectiveness of other feature selection methods such as Class Discrimination Measure (CDM), Odds Ratio (OR) and Elimination of Sparse Features (ESF)

reported in [12]. Table 4 exhibit that the detection accuracies of each feature selection methods. Also, the information theoretic feature selection methods like CDM and OR have a detection accuracy of 95.5% and 97.3% respectively. Our new method (X–SU) achieves more than 99% detection rate. Also the minimum feature length was 30 for the previous methods [12] and with the proposed scheme it is further reduced to 27.

Table 4. Comparison of Percentage Accuracy of proposed scheme with other solutions

feature selection method	Ex-SU	OR	CDM	ESF
Feature Length / Classifiers	27	30	30	117
J48	97.60	94.91	76.64	96.40
AdaboostM1[J48]	99.40	96.70	78.14	96.10
Random Forest	99.40	97.30	79.94	96.10

5 Conclusion

In this paper we present a novel approach towards the detection of unseen Linux malware samples based on dynamic analysis. The dynamic behavior of programs like system calls of Linux malware and benign samples are collected. A two step dimensionality reduction technique to accurately detect seen and unseen malware specimens which is referred to us by extended Symmetric uncertainty (X–SU) was developed. A total of 149 union features are used for the investigation, out of which 27 optimum features are selected using X–SU. Top 50 Feature–class correlated features further reduced using feature–feature correlations to prune significant 27 system calls. The results of our investigation demonstrate that proposed method achieves a detection accuracy of 99.4% with 100% TPR and very less false alarms.

Our proposed method has the following advantages. The low overhead during both prediction model preparation and detection makes it real–time deployable. It examines the common system calls of complete dataset instead of relying on one executable i.e. a generalized solution for detection. Therefore, it can automatically identify new malware samples and could be used to assist malware scanners.

Security analyst make use of automatic analysis tool for understanding the behaviour of any suspicious program. Intelligent malware authors or black hat hackers are already aware of such tool, and they develop sophisticated malware which remain dormant after detecting the presence of sandbox/analysis environment. In order to address this issue coarse grained analysis of malware specimens could be performed using hypervisors such as Ether[15], Cobra[16] or Cuckoo sandbox [21] and our main focus will be to deal with stealthy malware to improve our system.

Acknowledgements. We would like to thank all the anonymous reviewers who have helped us to improve the quality of our work.

References

1. Forrest, S., Hofmeyr, S., Somayaji, A., Longstaff, T., et al.: A sense of self for Unix processes. In: IEEE Symposium on Security and Privacy, pp. 120–128 (1996)
2. Breiman, L.: Random forests. Machine Learning 45(1), 5–32 (2001)
3. Yu, L., Liu, H.: Feature Selection for High-Dimensional Data: A Fast Correlation-Based Filter Solution. In: ICML, pp. 856–863 (2003)
4. Wang, X., Yu, W., Champion, A., Fu, X., Xuan, D.: Detecting Worms via Mining Dynamic Program Execution. In: Proceedings of Third International Conference on Security and Privacy in Communication Networks and the Workshops, SecureComm, pp. 412–421 (2007)
5. Mehdi, B., Tanwani, A.K., Farooq, M.: IMAD: In-execution Malware Analysis And Detection. In: Proceedings of the Generic and Evolutionary Conference, pp. 1553–1560 (2009)
6. Shafiq, M.Z., Tabish, S.M., Mirza, F., Farooq, M.: PE-Miner: Mining Structural Information to Detect Malicious Executables in Realtime. In: Kirda, E., Jha, S., Balzarotti, D. (eds.) RAID 2009. LNCS, vol. 5758, pp. 121–141. Springer, Heidelberg (2009)
7. Hall, M., Frank, E., Holmes, G., Pfahringer, B., Reutemann, P., Witten, I.H.: The WEKA Data Mining Software: An Update. SIGKDD Explorations 11(1) (2009)
8. Mehdi, B., Ahmed, F., Khayyam, S.A., Farooq, M.: Towards a Theory of Generalizing System Call Representation For In–Execution malware Detection. In: Proceedings of the IEEE International Conference on Communication, pp. 1553–1560 (2010)
9. Shahzad, F., Bhatti, S., Shahzad, M., Farooq, M.: In-Execution Malware Detection using Task Structures of Linux Process. In: IEEE International Conference on Communication, pp. 1–6 (2011)
10. Shahzad, F., Farooq, M.: Elf-miner: Using structural knowledge and data mining methods to detect new (linux) malicious executables. Knowledge and Information Systems, 1–24 (2011)
11. Shahzad, F., Shahzad, M., Farooq, M.: In-execution dynamic malware analysis and detection by mining information in process control blocks of Linux OS. Inf. Sci. 231, 45–63 (2013)
12. Asmitha, K.A., Vinod, P.: A machine learning approach for linux malware detection. In: 2014 International Conference on Issues and Challenges in Intelligent Computing Techniques (ICICT), pp. 830–835. IEEE (2014)
13. Hall, E.F.M.A., Holmes, G., Kirkby, R., Pfahringer, B.: WEKA - A Machine Learning Workbench for Data Mining. In: The Data Mining and Knowledge Discovery Handbook, pp. 1305–1314 (2005)
14. Moskovitch, R., Stopel, D., Feher, C., Nissim, N., Japkowicz, N., Elovici, Y.: Unknown malcode detection and the imbalance problem. Journal in Computer Virology 5(4), 295–308 (2009)
15. Dinaburg, A., Royal, P., Sharif, M., Lee, W.: Ether: Malware Analysis via Hardware Virtualization Extensions. In: Proceedings of the ACM Conference on Computer and Communications Security, CCS (2008)
16. Vasudevan, A., Yerraballi, R.: Cobra: Finegrained Malware Analysis using Stealth Localized Executions. In: Proceedings of the IEEE Symposium on Security and Privacy (2006)
17. VX Heavens Virus Collection, http://vx.netlux.org (last accessed on January 20, 2014)

18. Strace tool, http://sourceforge.net/projects/strace/ (last accessed on February 17, 2014)
19. Server Security Survey Report (2013),
    https://www.bit9.com/research/2013-server-security-survey-report/
    (last accessed on January 4, 2014)
20. Global Threat Intelligence Report (2013),
    http://www.solutionary.com/research/threat-reports/
    annual-threat-report/ (last accessed on January 3, 2014)
21. Open source automated malware analysis system,
    http://www.cuckoosandbox.org/ (last accessed on January 18, 2014)

Appendix A

Table 5. Optimal features and its descriptions

Sl.No	System calls	Descriptions	Sl.No	System calls	Descriptions
1	uname	print system information	14	ioctl	control device
2	socket	create an endpoint for communication	15	gettimeofday	get time
3	set_tid_address	set pointer to thread ID	16	getsockname	get socket name
4	rt_sigprocmask	examine and change blocked signals	17	getresuid32	get real, effective and saved user IDs
5	rt_sigaction	examine and change a signal action	18	getdents64	get directory entries
6	read	read from a file descriptor	19	getcwd	get current working directory
7	poll	wait for some event on a file descriptor	20	futex	fast userspace locking system call
8	openat	open a file relative to a directory file descriptor	21	fcntl64	manipulate file descriptor
9	open	start a program on a new virtual terminal (VT)	22	eventfd2	create a file descriptor for event notification
10	munmap	unmap files or devices into memory	23	dup	duplicate a file descriptor
11	mprotect	set protection on a region of memory	24	close	close a file descriptor
12	mmap2	map files or devices into memory	25	brk	change data segment size
13	lseek	reposition read/write file offset	26	access	check real user's permissions for a file

Author Index